THE IRAQ WAR

THE IRAQ WAR

A Documentary and Reference Guide

Thomas R. Mockaitis

Documentary and Reference Guides

 GREENWOOD

AN IMPRINT OF ABC-CLIO, LLC
Santa Barbara, California • Denver, Colorado • Oxford, England

Copyright 2012 by Thomas R. Mockaitis

All rights reserved. No part of this publication may be reproduced, stored in a retrieval
system, or transmitted, in any form or by any means, electronic, mechanical,
photocopying, recording, or otherwise, except for the inclusion of brief quotations in a
review, without prior permission in writing from the publisher.

Library of Congress Cataloging-in-Publication Data

Mockaitis, Thomas R., 1955–
   The Iraq War : a documentary and reference guide / Thomas R. Mockaitis.
     p. cm. — (Documentary and reference guides)
   Includes bibliographical references and index.
   ISBN 978–0–313–34387–2 (hard copy : acid-free paper) — ISBN 978–0–313–34388–9 (ebook)
1. Iraq War, 2003– —Sources. I. Title.
DS79.76.M625 2012
956.7044′3—dc23   2012009296

ISBN: 978–0–313–34387–2
EISBN: 978–0–313–34388–9

16 15 14 13 12   1 2 3 4 5

This book is also available on the World Wide Web as an eBook.
Visit www.abc-clio.com for details.

Greenwood
An Imprint of ABC-CLIO, LLC

ABC-CLIO, LLC
130 Cremona Drive, P.O. Box 1911
Santa Barbara, California 93116-1911

This book is printed on acid-free paper ∞

Manufactured in the United States of America

CONTENTS

Contents

READER'S GUIDE TO RELATED DOCUMENTS

Weapons of Mass Destruction

INTRODUCTION

THE NATURE OF HISTORICAL INQUIRY

Historians reconstruct and interpret the past using primary sources. Primary sources are documents written at the time of the events under study. While most people think of official documents as the most important primary sources, any contemporary source sheds light on the past. Until the twentieth century, primary sources were entirely written. However, historians of the recent past must also consider photographs, sound recordings, radio, film, television, e-mails, and other sources. While some documents were historically conscious (the author was writing for a future audience), most were written to deal with matters in their own day and age. The author of a diary, for example, knows that someone in the future will read his or her words. A receipt or bill of sale serves only to record a business transaction for the near term. It survives longer largely by chance.

Depending on the period they study, historians face two broad challenges: a shortage of sources and an abundance of them. The farther back in time one goes, the thinner the historical record becomes. Historians of the ancient, medieval, and early modern periods face a problem akin to assembling a jigsaw puzzle with a number of pieces missing. Modern historians confront the opposite problem. They frequently have access to thousands of documents and must weigh the value of each on its own merits and relative to those of the other sources. Even then they will always find gaps in the evidence, which must be filled in with deduction and sometimes mere speculation.

Reconstructing the past is a daunting enough task; interpreting it is even harder. Primary sources were created within a context. Writer and reader shared a complex set of conscious beliefs, ideas, and unconscious assumptions, a worldview separating them from the historian who studies their era. What the writer *meant* may be difficult to determine even when the historian can read what the writer wrote.

THE CHALLENGE OF INTERPRETING IRAQ

In addition to the usual problems of evidence, studying a conflict that began in 2003 and ended (at least for the U.S.) in 2011 poses further challenges. A purist would say that such an event is too contemporary to be suitable for historical inquiry. An American historian of war, especially one who has taught and written about the conflict as it unfolded, shares a context and worldview with those involved in it, but he or she lacks the detachment time and distance will provide future analysts. Secrecy also compounds the already vexing problem of sources. Thousands upon thousands of documents dealing with the Iraq War have been written, but many of them, including the most important, will remain classified for years to come. This situation provides a new spin on an old problem, a shortage of evidence, or at least of the right kind of evidence—the puzzle with its missing pieces once more.

These challenges might be enough to convince any sane historian to leave the topic to his or her successors in some distant future. Studying the recent past, however, is not only interesting but important, especially to the policy maker and to the educated, nonacademic reader. The former needs information upon which to base decisions; the latter wants to understand the world better. This historian thus does the best job he can with the available material. One valuable task he can perform is to assemble available sources into a readable anthology. This volume seeks to do just that.

DOCUMENTS AND ORGANIZATION

This anthology contains 97 documents organized topically into five chapters. Chapter 1 focuses on the case for war made by the administration of George W. Bush and the challenges to it. Chapter 2 deals with the invasion of Iraq. It examines the invasion plans and the decision to adopt the "shock and awe" strategy. Chapter 3 examines the challenges of postwar reconstruction. It also considers the controversial question of why the United States was so poorly prepared for the task. Chapter 4 covers the insurgency and how the U.S. strategy for responding to it evolved. Chapter 5 traces the evolution of post–Saddam Hussein democracy in Iraq through the 2010 elections.

All documents excerpted in this anthology are in the public domain. Most come from U.S. government sources (Congress, the White House, U.S. agencies, etc.). The critic will rightly point out that such evidence presents but one side of events. With the exception of some captured Iraqi documents translated into English, few open sources present the conflict from the insurgents' perspective. Perhaps this will change with time. I have selected, excerpted, and arranged the documents to make it easier to understand events as they unfolded. A brief analysis accompanying each source should also help the reader comprehend the conflict. In the final analysis, however, this book is no more than a starting place for those seeking to learn more about the conflict.

1

THE CASE FOR WAR

The Gulf War

On August 2, 1990, Saddam Hussein invaded Kuwait, which he accused of slant-drilling into Iraqi oilfields. Perceiving an immediate threat to its close ally Saudi Arabia, the United States decided to intervene. President George H. W. Bush assembled a coalition of over 30 nations and deployed a force of half a million military personnel to the Persian Gulf. A month-long air campaign beginning on January 17, 1991, degraded Iraqi forces in preparation for a ground offensive that began on February 24 and lasted four days. Coalition forces expelled the Iraqis from Kuwait and surrounded the Republican Guards. In a controversial decision, President Bush allowed these forces to withdraw rather than have General Schwarzkopf destroy them. The allies also failed to prevent a massacre of southern Iraqi Shi'a, who had risen against Hussein in expectation that the coalition would liberate them. These perceived failures and the decision not to invade Iraq led many in the administration of George W. Bush to view the Gulf War as unfinished business that they needed to bring to a satisfactory conclusion by removing Saddam Hussein from power.

The decision to invade Iraq generated enormous controversy at the time the administration made it. Controversy increased significantly following the occupation when U.S. forces found virtually none of the chemical, biological, or nuclear weapons that had been offered as the main reason for going to Baghdad in the first place. A search of Iraqi archives produced no evidence of an al-Qaeda link prior to the invasion. Absence of evidence after the fact does not, however, invalidate the decision. The key consideration is not what has come to light since the occupation but what the administration knew and believed prior to launching the attack.

The documents in this section relate to the decision to invade Iraq. They address several key questions: When did the president decide upon war? Did the 9/11 attacks make the threat posed by Saddam unacceptably high, or did they provide a pretext for war? What evidence that Iraq possessed weapons of mass destruction (WMD) had been uncovered? Viewed in chronological order from before 9/11, the president's remarks suggest a determination to invade Iraq in search of a pretext for doing so.

THE PRESIDENT'S INTENTIONS

Republican candidate Governor George H. W. Bush raised the issue of Iraq during his campaign for president. He accused the Clinton administration of failing to enforce sanctions and allowing the 1990–1991 Gulf War coalition to break down. Governor Bush's remarks during a debate with democratic candidate Vice President Al Gore and throughout the campaign have led many observers to ask whether he intended to invade Iraq and remove Hussein even before 9/11 created the opportunity to do so. Iraq figured prominently in both his 2002 and 2003 State of the Union Addresses and in his September 2002 speech to the UN General Assembly.

- **Document 1: Excerpt of Transcript of 2000 Presidential Candidate Debate**
- **When:** October 11, 2000
- **Where:** Wake Forest University, Winston-Salem, North Carolina
- **Significance:** Then-governor George W. Bush met Vice President Al Gore for their second debate. In response to a question on how to resolve the Middle East conflict (Israel-Palestine), the governor introduced the issue of Saddam Hussein.

The coalition against Saddam has fallen apart or it's unraveling, let's put it that way. The sanctions are being violated. We don't know whether he's developing weapons of mass destruction. He better not be or there's going to be a consequence should I be the president. . . .

[In a follow-up question, the moderator asked Governor Bush if he wished to remove Saddam. Bush responded:]

I would like to, of course, and I presume this administration would as well. We don't know—there are no inspectors now in Iraq, the coalition that was in place isn't as strong as it used to be. He is a danger. We don't want him fishing in troubled waters in the Middle East. And it's going to be hard, it's going to be important to rebuild that coalition to keep the pressure on him [*sic*].

- **Source:** Debate between presidential candidates Vice President Al Gore and Governor George W. Bush, October 11, 2000, *Commission on Presidential Debate*, http://www.debates.org/index.php?page=october-11-2000-debate-transcript, accessed March 19, 2012.

- **Analysis:** The 9/11 attacks provided a powerful justification for attacking any state that appeared to harbor terrorists or to support terrorism. Because the Bush administration made its case for war in the aftermath of the worst terrorist incident in U.S. history, most people forgot that for some people in the administration the desire to deal with Iraq long preceded the al-Qaeda attacks. The president himself may have considered Iraq unfinished business from the administration of his father, George H. W. Bush. In this debate he specifically complained that Hussein was still in power and indicated that he wished to see him removed. Read in conjunction with **Document 2**, Governor Bush's remarks suggest that 9/11 provided a pretext for a war his administration already wished to fight. Despite his assertions to the contrary, there is no evidence that the Gulf War coalition had "fallen apart."

- **Document 2: Letter from Project for a New American Century to President William J. Clinton**
- **When:** January 26, 1998
- **Where:** Washington, DC
- **Significance:** The letter reveals the desire of neocons to remove Saddam Hussein from power.

The Honorable William J. Clinton
President of the United States
Washington, DC

Dear Mr. President:

We are writing you because we are convinced that current American policy toward Iraq is not succeeding, and that we may soon face a threat in the Middle East more serious than any we have known since the end of the Cold War. In your upcoming State of the Union Address, you have an opportunity to chart a clear and determined course for meeting this threat. We urge you to seize that opportunity, and to enunciate a new strategy that would secure the interests of the U.S. and our friends and allies around the world. That strategy should aim, above all, at the removal of Saddam Hussein's regime from power. We stand ready to offer our full support in this difficult but necessary endeavor.

The policy of "containment" of Saddam Hussein has been steadily eroding over the past several months. As recent events have demonstrated, we can no longer depend on our partners in the Gulf War coalition to continue to uphold the sanctions or to punish Saddam when he blocks or evades UN inspections. Our ability to ensure that Saddam Hussein is not producing weapons of mass destruction, therefore, has substantially diminished. Even if full inspections were eventually to resume, which now seems highly unlikely, experience has shown that it is difficult if not impossible to monitor Iraq's chemical and biological weapons production. The lengthy period during which the inspectors will have been unable to enter many Iraqi facilities has made it even less likely that they will be able to uncover all of Saddam's secrets. As a result, in the not-too-distant future we will be unable to determine with any reasonable level of confidence whether Iraq does or does not possess such weapons.

Such uncertainty will, by itself, have a seriously destabilizing effect on the entire Middle East. It hardly needs to be added that if Saddam does acquire the capability to deliver weapons of mass destruction, as he is almost certain to do if we continue along the present course, the safety of American troops in the region, of our friends and allies like Israel and the moderate Arab states, and a significant portion of the world's supply of oil will all be put at hazard. As you have rightly declared, Mr. President, the security of the world in the first part of the 21st century will be determined largely by how we handle this threat.

Given the magnitude of the threat, the current policy, which depends for its success upon the steadfastness of our coalition partners and upon the cooperation of Saddam Hussein, is dangerously inadequate. The only acceptable strategy is one that eliminates the possibility that Iraq will be able to use or threaten to use weapons of mass destruction. In the near term, this means a willingness to undertake military action as diplomacy is clearly failing. In the long term, it means removing Saddam Hussein and his regime from power. That now needs to become the aim of American foreign policy.

We urge you to articulate this aim, and to turn your Administration's attention to implementing a strategy for removing Saddam's regime from power. This will require a full complement of diplomatic, political and military efforts. Although we are fully aware of the dangers and difficulties in implementing this policy, we believe the dangers of failing to do so are far greater. We believe the U.S. has the authority under existing UN resolutions to take the necessary steps, including military steps, to protect our vital interests in the Gulf. In any case, American policy cannot continue to be crippled by a misguided insistence on unanimity in the UN Security Council.

We urge you to act decisively. If you act now to end the threat of weapons of mass destruction against the U.S. or its allies, you will be acting in the most fundamental national security interests of the country. If we accept a course of weakness and drift, we put our interests and our future at risk.

Sincerely,

Elliott Abrams   Richard L. Armitage   William J. Bennett
Jeffrey Bergner   John Bolton   Paula Dobriansky
Francis Fukuyama   Robert Kagan   Zalmay Khalilzad
William Kristol   Richard Perle   Peter W. Rodman
Donald Rumsfeld   William Schneider, Jr.   Vin Weber
Paul Wolfowitz   R. James Woolsey   Robert B. Zoellick

- **Source:** Letter to President Clinton, Project for a New American Century, January 28, 1998, available at http://www.newamericancentury .org/iraqclintonletter.htm, accessed April 24, 2008.

- **Analysis:** Written five years before the invasion of Iraq, this letter takes on greater significance for what it reveals about the attitudes of key Bush appointees. Three signatories of the letter filled key positions in his first administration. Donald Rumsfeld became secretary of defense, Paul Wolfowitz became his assistant, and Richard Perle served as chairman of the Defense Policy Board Advisory Committee. All advocated war with Iraq. The president's own remarks in the debate with Al Gore (**Document 1**) make clear his strong preference for removing Hussein from power.

  For its eight years in office the Clinton administration had pursued a policy of containment akin to that which had proven successful during the Cold War. Contrary to the assertion of the letter, the policy had not failed. The United States maintained a no-fly zone over the Shi'a region of southern Iraq and the Kurdish north. An embargo hampered Iraqi efforts to rearm. While Saddam Hussein faced no danger from an internal challenge to his authority, he posed no immediate threat to the United States or its allies.

- **Document 3: Excerpt of State of the Union Address**
- **When:** January 29, 2002
- **Where:** Washington, DC
- **Significance:** This speech contains the famous reference to North Korea, Iran, and Iraq as an "axis of evil."

My hope is that all nations will heed our call, and eliminate the terrorist parasites who threaten their countries and our own. Many nations are acting forcefully. Pakistan is now cracking down on terror, and I admire the strong leadership of President Musharraf.

But some governments will be timid in the face of terror. And make no mistake about it: If they do not act, America will.

Our second goal is to prevent regimes that sponsor terror from threatening America or our friends and allies with weapons of mass destruction. Some of these regimes have been pretty quiet since September the 11th. But we know their true nature. North Korea is a regime arming with missiles and weapons of mass destruction, while starving its citizens.

Iran aggressively pursues these weapons and exports terror, while an unelected few repress the Iranian people's hope for freedom.

Iraq continues to flaunt its hostility toward America and to support terror. The Iraqi regime has plotted to develop anthrax, and nerve gas, and nuclear weapons for over a decade. This is a regime that has already used poison gas to murder thousands of its own citizens—leaving the bodies of mothers huddled over their dead children. This is a regime that agreed to international inspections—then kicked out the inspectors. This is a regime that has something to hide from the civilized world.

States like these, and their terrorist allies, constitute an axis of evil, arming to threaten the peace of the world. By seeking weapons of mass destruction, these regimes pose a grave and growing danger. They could provide these arms to terrorists, giving them the means to match their hatred. They could attack our allies or attempt to blackmail the United States. In any of these cases, the price of indifference would be catastrophic.

We will work closely with our coalition to deny terrorists and their state sponsors the materials, technology, and expertise to make and deliver weapons of mass destruction. We will develop and deploy effective missile defenses to protect America and our allies from sudden attack. And all nations should know: America will do what is necessary to ensure our nation's security.

We'll be deliberate, yet time is not on our side. I will not wait on events, while dangers gather. I will not stand by, as peril draws closer and closer. The United States of America will not permit the world's most dangerous regimes to threaten us with the world's most destructive weapons.

Our war on terror is well begun, but it is only begun. This campaign may not be finished on our watch—yet it must be and it will be waged on our watch.

We can't stop short. If we stop now—leaving terror camps intact and terror states unchecked—our sense of security would be false and temporary. History has called

America and our allies to action, and it is both our responsibility and our privilege to fight freedom's fight.

- **Source:** George W. Bush, "State of the Union 2002," transcript available at http://georgewbush-whitehouse.archives.gov/news/releases/2002/01/20020129-11.html, accessed April 4, 2008.

- **Analysis:** Whatever plans the newly elected President Bush had for dealing with Saddam Hussein were interrupted by the 9/11 attacks and the subsequent invasion of Afghanistan. In his second State of the Union message, delivered on January 29, 2002, however, President Bush returned to the subject of Iraq. He highlighted the defeat of the Taliban as a major victory in the global war on terrorism. He also identified North Korea, Iran, and Iraq as members of an "axis of evil," state sponsors of terrorism who threatened the United States' security. Significantly, he singled out Iraq as the most immediate concern. He referred directly to the possibility of a "state sponsor of terrorism" providing a terrorist organization with a weapon of mass destruction. The president concluded that time was not on America's side, implying the need to act quickly and decisively.

  Set within the context of the other documents discussed here, the 2002 State of the Union Address must be seen as part of an extended public relations campaign. Persuaded that Saddam Hussein had to be removed from power, the administration needed to make a compelling case to the American people for invading Iraq. While 9/11 made their task much easier, the connection between al-Qaeda and Iraq was by no means clear, nor could anyone say with confidence that Saddam had WMD which he could pass to a terrorist organization. In the post-9/11 world, however, the White House had only to create sufficient anxiety and doubt in the popular imagination to persuade people of the necessity of invading Iraq.

- **Document 4: Excerpt of President Saddam Hussein of Iraq, Address to Arab Leaders**
- **When:** April 22, 2002
- **Where:** Beirut, Lebanon
- **Significance:** Saddam Hussein called for solidarity among Arab states to resist Western aggression.

In the name of God, Most Gracious, Most Merciful, Dear Arab brothers, Kings, Presidents, Emirs and officials, and through you, to our dear Arab people everywhere, Assalamu Alaykum—peace be upon you.

Once again, I bring to you my viewpoints and suggestions. I may be exasperating but my only excuse to you, after God, is that I am seeking what might please God and what might give us glory before our people and history. And make us gain the true respect of the nations and peoples of the world. At a time when our Palestinian brothers are being killed, our sacred places violated, our wealth being ransacked, or about to be, on a large scale, we must agree upon a plan of action with the help of God, to summon our will and faith....

Zionism, the American administrations, and any who has or will become their allies, have prepared themselves to confront the Arab nation, including Palestine as one nation. So it is our duty, by the rule of our doctrine (to avoid saying by the rule of the Sharia and of integrity), to prepare ourselves on this basis: we are guided by the rule of history and destiny. We are bound by duty to stand together with the guidance of God the merciful. Zionism has the upper hand over the American administrations to use them against us, and it becomes one and the same with us, against our nation, as we have repeatedly said, to facilitate the realization of the Zionists' covetous schemes in our Arab nation. Therefore, it is our duty to stand together, to mobilize our utmost forces in all fields, and not to hope for anything good for our nation and Arab security from the US. For the American administration will walk as they walk now up to their knees in Arab and Muslim blood. We must all believe that no one can defeat our nation by injustice since it is justly on its own land. Our nation would only be defeated if it abandons its distinctive attributes, and duties, and if its guides go to sleep. Our people are awake, dear brothers, so it is our patriotic, national, moral, Arab, faithful, and constitutional duty that is calling us in our capacity of rulers not to go to sleep, nor to be inadvertent or weaken. Anyone who does not follow this in his attitude with his nation, will lose himself and lose his way. Even when the people find that they have to change any one of us if they get angry, it would be a loss had he taken the right path. And I do not think that any one of us, including the writer of this letter, would choose this fate or accept it for himself.

The strength of the nation is a living part of its capability to defend its national security from any threats. The wealth of the nation is part of its strength and effective means.... You may also know that the US with the support of the UK has hindered medicine contracts for the Iraqi people despite the fact that their prices had already been paid long before August 1990. They have stopped all the other means of life for the Iraqi people in order to kill them and decrease the number of the population. The US and UK do all these things although their national security is not threatened by our countries. If it is security for themselves and for the world that they want, they will get it by respecting other peoples, their land, national and Arab choices, their choice of doctrine, beliefs and values.

I am not ignoring the comments made by some of my brothers in oil producing countries, that oil is not a weapon, it is not a cannon, a tank, or a jet fighter. I say: Yes, oil is not a tank, a jet fighter or a cannon, but it can be used as a weapon, when the muzzles of the cannons, tanks and jet fighters are not working, or are not meant to be used. As for saying: we cannot, or we are not ready to use the weapon for those who have no weapons, and that oil is not a cannon, a tank or a jet fighter for those who have oil, then what would, and by what can we confront those who want to exploit us, the aggressors, and the usurpers?

On this occasion, I would like remind my brothers of some of their fathers' and grandfathers' values when they confronted any aggression. Every man would go out to face the enemy even if the battle was at its fiercest stage, or if the aggressor had launched the attack with rifles, cannons, and jet fighters. It would be disgraceful for any man not to go out to the battlefield even if he had nothing but an axe, a dagger, or club, otherwise the law (of who does not have a weapon equal to the weapon of the aggressor or the usurper, must surrender to those who have better weapons) would be applied.

If anyone was late or stayed behind, he would be called names that I do not think that any one of us would accept for himself. He would even be forbidden to sit on the chairs of men in gatherings and meetings and no one would serve him coffee. The history of our nation is full of such examples, whether in the wars and struggles for independence or in the annals of conflicts between fighting tribes.

Now, haven't the Palestinians faced the bombs, jet fighters, cannons, missiles and rifles? What would be said of the attitude of Palestinians had they not confronted the aggressors in this way?! Haven't the Zionists used even water and food when they besieged the Palestinians, especially in heroic Jenin? Did they use water and food as a weapon in the battle against those heroes?

. . . Therefore, oil should be used as a weapon that will come in succession in the battle, and not as an absolute alternative weapon. As for the question: what weapon do we begin with? Well, let's begin brothers . . . we did not suggest the weapon of oil until we were aware that our Arab brothers were not ready to use the other weapons, and so that no one could say that we have a weapon, the use of which does not require any bloodshed, or that we have not used the oil weapon, so let's try it, before resorting to other weapons. . . .

In this case, don't the Arabs have the right to use the elements of their strength to defend their lives, sovereignty, honor, and beliefs? Neutralizing the elements of our strength leaves our weakness breaches without protection. Therefore, neutralizing our oil, which is one of the elements of our economic strength, means that we are strengthening our enemy over ourselves and enabling him to overcome us.

For these reasons, I see that:

1. Arabs should express their solidarity with their brothers' security and safety, and the oil exporters, including Iraq, immediately decrease the production of their oil for exportation by 50 percent and directly deprive the US and the Zionist entity from the other exported half and to threaten any country or company with the same measure if they export the oil they import from Arab countries. We should thus be strongly ringing the bells of protest and solidarity, so that those who harm and kill our people can see and hear. We will thus embarrass the American Administration before its people, and make them hear the voice of Arabs with a respect that is equal to their obedient or humiliating submission to the Zionist Lobby and its evil aims. This measure should be immediately effective, once agreed upon, until further notice, and until the nation's demands in solidarity with the rights of the heroic people of Palestine are met, without any bargaining or procrastination. The Arabs should take a collective attitude, and if any one of them deviated, God forbid, he would be described and treated by the Arab nation as if he had abandoned his duties regarding his nation and its national security. This attitude should be publicly unveiled before the people of the concerned country. In this way, we can save the

Arab nation, and provide the Palestinian people with the support by other measures funded by the increase in the prices of oil after stopping its exportation.

2. To allocate a quota of the exported oil proportional to the stand taken by the countries that express understanding of or support for Arab rights. By contrast, the quota will be decreased according to the stands of the countries, which condemn us. In this respect, special attention should be given to the members of the Security Council, especially the permanent members.

3. The Arab countries should work in solidarity with Islamic oil producing countries to take the same measures as Arabs as mentioned in paragraphs 1 and 2, above.

4. The Arab countries should work together, represented by oil producing countries that are members of OPEC, with the support of Muslim members, to have the OPEC adopt a resolution of full solidarity with this and the measures afore mentioned.

5. A council of a number, that will be agreed upon, of Arab ministers of Oil and Foreign Affairs, or of the ministers of Oil and Foreign Affairs of oil producing countries, should be appointed to follow up the details of paragraphs 2, 3, 4. The Arab Summit should be in a position that enables it to convene urgent meetings, whenever necessary, according to a number of Presidents and Kings who will be nominated by the Summit.

6. The Arab nation should be prepared from every side to confront any reaction or aggression, in solidarity and as one nation, with the faith that the foreigner cannot force us to do anything we collectively refuse, and that if the foreigner tries anything against the weakest country among us, this country will be stronger than all the force of the foreigner, when it is in [the] bosom of its Nation, under its banner and the protection of its sword, and the solidarity of its people.

Saying this, I pray to God to guide us together in implementing it, or in any other opinion you deem is a better one, if it is capable of stopping the wrong doers' aggression on our nation, at the forefront of which are the people of Palestine, and to restore the usurped rights of our nation, at the forefront of which is Palestine.

- **Source:** Turi Munthe, ed., *The Saddam Hussein Reader* (New York: Thunder's Mouth, 2002), 369–78.
- **Analysis:** In this speech Saddam Hussein called for Arab solidarity to resist Western aggression. He implicitly linked the American threat to Iraq with the plight of Palestinians and referred to the inseparable link between the United States and Zionism. He called upon the league to use oil as a weapon against the West.

  Saddam's choice of words reveals another of his ploys. Although widely regarded as a secular Arab, even one who persecuted clerics, he adopted the language of a pious Muslim. Osama bin Laden had argued that the United States was making war not against al-Qaeda but against Islam. Saddam no doubt wished to make the same connection. His pleas fell on ostensibly sympathetic but unhelpful ears. While the Arab League would condemn the invasion of Iraq, it offered no material support, and it did not leverage its oil production to influence the U.S.-led coalition.

- **Document 5: Brent Scowcroft, "Don't Attack Saddam"**
- **When:** August 15, 2002
- **Where:** New York City
- **Significance:** The first President Bush's national security advisor argues against war with Iraq.

Our nation is presently engaged in a debate about whether to launch a war against Iraq. Leaks of various strategies for an attack on Iraq appear with regularity. The Bush administration vows regime change, but states that no decision has been made whether, much less when, to launch an invasion.

It is beyond dispute that Saddam Hussein is a menace. He terrorizes and brutalizes his own people. He has launched war on two of his neighbors. He devotes enormous effort to rebuilding his military forces and equipping them with weapons of mass destruction. We will all be better off when he is gone.

That said, we need to think through this issue very carefully. We need to analyze the relationship between Iraq and our other pressing priorities—notably the war on terrorism—as well as the best strategy and tactics available were we to move to change the regime in Baghdad.

Saddam's strategic objective appears to be to dominate the Persian Gulf, to control oil from the region, or both. That clearly poses a real threat to key U.S. interests. But there is scant evidence to tie Saddam to terrorist organizations, and even less to the September 11 attacks. Indeed Saddam's goals have little in common with the terrorists who threaten us, and there is little incentive for him to make common cause with them.

He is unlikely to risk his investment in weapons of mass destruction, much less his country, by handing such weapons to terrorists who would use them for their own purposes and leave Baghdad as the return address. Threatening to use these weapons for blackmail—much less their actual use—would open him and his entire regime to a devastating response by the U.S. While Saddam is thoroughly evil, he is above all a power-hungry survivor.

Saddam is a familiar dictatorial aggressor, with traditional goals for his aggression. There is little evidence to indicate that the United States itself is an object of his aggression. Rather, Saddam's problem with the U.S. appears to be that we stand in the way of his ambitions. He seeks weapons of mass destruction not to arm terrorists, but to deter us from intervening to block his aggressive designs.

Given Saddam's aggressive regional ambitions, as well as his ruthlessness and unpredictability, it may at some point be wise to remove him from power. Whether and when that point should come ought to depend on overall U.S. national security priorities. Our pre-eminent security priority—underscored repeatedly by the president—is the war on terrorism. An attack on Iraq at this time would seriously jeopardize, if not destroy, the global counterterrorist campaign we have undertaken.

The United States could certainly defeat the Iraqi military and destroy Saddam's regime. But it would not be a cakewalk. On the contrary, it undoubtedly would be very expensive—with serious consequences for the U.S. and global economy—and could as well be bloody. In fact, Saddam would be likely to conclude he had nothing left to lose, leading him to unleash whatever weapons of mass destruction he possesses.

Israel would have to expect to be the first casualty, as in 1991 when Saddam sought to bring Israel into the Gulf conflict. This time, using weapons of mass destruction, he might succeed, provoking Israel to respond, perhaps with nuclear weapons, unleashing an Armageddon in the Middle East. Finally, if we are to achieve our strategic objectives in Iraq, a military campaign very likely would have to be followed by a large-scale, long-term military occupation.

But the central point is that any campaign against Iraq, whatever the strategy, cost and risks, is certain to divert us for some indefinite period from our war on terrorism. Worse, there is a virtual consensus in the world against an attack on Iraq at this time. So long as that sentiment persists, it would require the U.S. to pursue a virtual go-it-alone strategy against Iraq, making any military operations correspondingly more difficult and expensive. The most serious cost, however, would be to the war on terrorism. Ignoring that clear sentiment would result in a serious degradation in international cooperation with us against terrorism. And make no mistake, we simply cannot win that war without enthusiastic international cooperation, especially on intelligence.

Possibly the most dire consequences would be the effect in the region. The shared view in the region is that Iraq is principally an obsession of the U.S. The obsession of the region, however, is the Israeli-Palestinian conflict. If we were seen to be turning our backs on that bitter conflict—which the region, rightly or wrongly, perceives to be clearly within our power to resolve—in order to go after Iraq, there would be an explosion of outrage against us. We would be seen as ignoring a key interest of the Muslim world in order to satisfy what is seen to be a narrow American interest.

Even without Israeli involvement, the results could well destabilize Arab regimes in the region, ironically facilitating one of Saddam's strategic objectives. At a minimum, it would stifle any cooperation on terrorism, and could even swell the ranks of the terrorists. Conversely, the more progress we make in the war on terrorism, and the more we are seen to be committed to resolving the Israel-Palestinian issue, the greater will be the international support for going after Saddam.

If we are truly serious about the war on terrorism, it must remain our top priority. However, should Saddam Hussein be found to be clearly implicated in the events of September 11, that could make him a key counterterrorist target, rather than a competing priority, and significantly shift world opinion toward support for regime change.

In any event, we should be pressing the United Nations Security Council to insist on an effective no-notice inspection regime for Iraq—anytime, anywhere, no permission required. On this point, senior administration officials have opined that Saddam Hussein would never agree to such an inspection regime. But if he did, inspections would serve to keep him off balance and under close observation, even if all his weapons of mass destruction capabilities were not uncovered. And if he refused, his rejection could provide the persuasive casus belli which many claim we do not now have. Compelling evidence that Saddam had acquired nuclear-weapons capability could have a similar effect.

In sum, if we will act in full awareness of the intimate interrelationship of the key issues in the region, keeping counterterrorism as our foremost priority, there is much potential for success across the entire range of our security interests—including Iraq. If we reject a comprehensive perspective, however, we put at risk our campaign against terrorism as well as stability and security in a vital region of the world.

- **Source:** U.S. Congress, Congressional Record, 107th Cong., 2nd sess., 2002, 7763–64. Accessed July 13, 2011.
- **Analysis:** Former security advisor Brent Scowcroft, who had served in the White House during the 1991 Gulf War, argued against invading Iraq. He acknowledged that Saddam wished to dominate the Gulf but questioned the evidence linking the dictator to al-Qaeda or any other terrorist group. Although brutal, Saddam was also pragmatic. He would not risk a confrontation with the West by providing any nefarious group with WMD if he had them to spare. Finally, Scowcroft reasoned, while removing Saddam at some future date might be necessary, nothing dictated urgency in doing so.

  Above all, the former security advisor insisted, invading Iraq would hurt rather than help the war on terror. It would cost the United States international support and credibility. It would also be a long, drawn-out, and costly affair that would divert resources from the struggle with al-Qaeda and its affiliates. Although the administration ignored Scowcroft's warning, his conclusions proved to be quite prophetic.

- **Document 6: Excerpt of Vice President Richard Cheney, "The Risks of Inaction Are Far Greater Than the Risk of Action," Speech to the 103rd National Convention of the Veterans of Foreign Wars**
- **When:** August 26, 2002
- **Where:** Nashville, Tennessee
- **Significance:** The vice president argued that delaying military action against Saddam Hussein would only embolden him and make him more dangerous.

[T]he President and I never for a moment forget our number one responsibility: to protect the American people against further attack, and to win the war that began last September 11th.

The danger to America requires action on many fronts all at once. We are reorganizing the federal government to protect the nation against further attack. The new Department of Homeland Security will gather under one roof the capability to identify threats, to check them against our vulnerabilities, and to move swiftly to protect the nation.

At the same time, we realize that wars are never won on the defensive. We must take the battle to the enemy. We will take every step necessary to make sure our country is secure, and we will prevail.

Much has happened since the attacks of 9/11. But as Secretary Rumsfeld has put it, we are still closer to the beginning of this war than we are to its end. The United States has entered a struggle of years—a new kind of war against a new kind of enemy. The terrorists who struck America are ruthless, they are resourceful, and they hide in many countries. They came into our country to murder thousands of innocent men, women, and children. There is no doubt they wish to strike again, and that they are working to acquire the deadliest of all weapons.

Against such enemies, America and the civilized world have only one option: wherever terrorists operate, we must find them where they dwell, stop them in their planning, and one by one bring them to justice.

In Afghanistan, the Taliban regime and al Qaeda terrorists have met the fate they chose for themselves. And they saw, up-close and personal, the new methods and capabilities of America's armed services. . . .

The combination of advantages already seen in this conflict—precision power from the air, real-time intelligence, special forces, the long reach of Naval task forces, and close coordination with local forces represents a dramatic advance in our ability to engage and defeat the enemy. These advantages will only become more vital in future campaigns. President Bush has often spoken of how America can keep the peace by redefining war on our terms. That means that our armed services must have every tool to answer any threat that forms against us. It means that any enemy conspiring to harm America or our friends must face a swift, a certain and a devastating response. [Applause.]

As always in America's armed forces, the single most important asset we have is the man or woman who steps forward and puts on the uniform of this great nation. Much has been asked of our military this past year, and more will be asked in the months and the years ahead. Those who serve are entitled to expect many things from us in return. They deserve the very best weapons, the best equipment, the best support, and the best training we can possibly provide them. And under President Bush they will have them all. [Applause.]

The President has asked Congress for a one-year increase of more than $48 billion for national defense, the largest since Ronald Reagan lived in the White House. And for the good of the nation's military families, he has also asked Congress to provide every person in uniform a raise in pay. We think they've earned it. [Applause.]

In this war we've assembled a broad coalition of civilized nations that recognize the danger and are working with us on all fronts. The President has made very clear that there is no neutral ground in the fight against terror. Those who harbor terrorists share guilt for the acts they commit. Under the Bush Doctrine, a regime that harbors or supports terrorists will be regarded as hostile to the United States.

The Taliban has already learned that lesson, but Afghanistan was only the beginning of a lengthy campaign. Were we to stop now, any sense of security we might have would be false and temporary. There is a terrorist underworld out there, spread among more than 60 countries. The job we have will require every tool at our means of diplomacy, of finance, of intelligence, of law enforcement, and of military power.

But we will, over time, find and defeat the enemies of the United States. In the case of Osama bin Laden—as President Bush said recently—"If he's alive, we'll get him. If he's not alive—we already got him." [Applause.]

But the challenges to our country involve more than just tracking down a single person or one small group. Nine-eleven and its aftermath awakened this nation to danger, to the true ambitions of the global terror network, and to the reality that weapons of mass destruction are being sought by determined enemies who would not hesitate to use them against us.

It is a certainty that the al Qaeda network is pursuing such weapons, and has succeeded in acquiring at least a crude capability to use them. We found evidence of their efforts in the ruins of al Qaeda hideouts in Afghanistan. And we've seen in recent days additional confirmation in videos recently shown on CNN—pictures of al Qaeda members training to commit acts of terror, and testing chemical weapons on dogs. Those terrorists who remain at large are determined to use these capabilities against the United States and our friends and allies around the world.

As we face this prospect, old doctrines of security do not apply. In the days of the Cold War, we were able to manage the threat with strategies of deterrence and containment. But it's a lot tougher to deter enemies who have no country to defend. And containment is not possible when dictators obtain weapons of mass destruction, and are prepared to share them with terrorists who intend to inflict catastrophic casualties on the United States.

The case of Saddam Hussein, a sworn enemy of our country, requires a candid appraisal of the facts. After his defeat in the Gulf War in 1991, Saddam agreed under U.N. Security Council Resolution 687 to cease all development of weapons of mass destruction. He agreed to end his nuclear weapons program. He agreed to destroy his chemical and his biological weapons. He further agreed to admit U.N. inspection teams into his country to ensure that he was in fact complying with these terms.

In the past decade, Saddam has systematically broken each of these agreements. The Iraqi regime has in fact been very busy enhancing its capabilities in the field of chemical and biological agents. And they continue to pursue the nuclear program they began so many years ago. These are not weapons for the purpose of defending Iraq; these are offensive weapons for the purpose of inflicting death on a massive scale, developed so that Saddam can hold the threat over the head of anyone he chooses, in his own region or beyond.

On the nuclear question, many of you will recall that Saddam's nuclear ambitions suffered a severe setback in 1981 when the Israelis bombed the Osirak reactor. They suffered another major blow in Desert Storm and its aftermath.

But we now know that Saddam has resumed his efforts to acquire nuclear weapons. Among other sources, we've gotten this from the firsthand testimony of defectors—including Saddam's own son-in-law, who was subsequently murdered at Saddam's direction. Many of us are convinced that Saddam will acquire nuclear weapons fairly soon.

Just how soon, we cannot really gauge. Intelligence is an uncertain business, even in the best of circumstances. This is especially the case when you are dealing with a totalitarian regime that has made a science out of deceiving the international community. Let me give you just one example of what I mean. Prior to the Gulf War,

America's top intelligence analysts would come to my office in the Defense Department and tell me that Saddam Hussein was at least five or perhaps even 10 years away from having a nuclear weapon. After the war we learned that he had been much closer than that, perhaps within a year of acquiring such a weapon.

Saddam also devised an elaborate program to conceal his active efforts to build chemical and biological weapons. And one must keep in mind the history of U.N. inspection teams in Iraq. Even as they were conducting the most intrusive system of arms control in history, the inspectors missed a great deal. Before being barred from the country, the inspectors found and destroyed thousands of chemical weapons, and hundreds of tons of mustard gas and other nerve agents.

Yet Saddam Hussein had sought to frustrate and deceive them at every turn, and was often successful in doing so. I'll cite one instance. During the spring of 1995, the inspectors were actually on the verge of declaring that Saddam's programs to develop chemical weapons and longer-range ballistic missiles had been fully accounted for and shut down. Then Saddam's son-in-law suddenly defected and began sharing information. Within days the inspectors were led to an Iraqi chicken farm. Hidden there were boxes of documents and lots of evidence regarding Iraq's most secret weapons programs. That should serve as a reminder to all that we often learned more as the result of defections than we learned from the inspection regime itself.

To the dismay of the inspectors, they in time discovered that Saddam had kept them largely in the dark about the extent of his program to mass produce VX, one of the deadliest chemicals known to man. And far from having shut down Iraq's prohibited missile programs, the inspectors found that Saddam had continued to test such missiles, almost literally under the noses of the U.N. inspectors.

Against that background, a person would be right to question any suggestion that we should just get inspectors back into Iraq, and then our worries will be over. Saddam has perfected the game of cheat and retreat, and is very skilled in the art of denial and deception. A return of inspectors would provide no assurance whatsoever of his compliance with U.N. resolutions. On the contrary, there is a great danger that it would provide false comfort that Saddam was somehow "back in his box."

Meanwhile, he would continue to plot. Nothing in the last dozen years has stopped him—not his agreements; not the discoveries of the inspectors; not the revelations by defectors; not criticism or ostracism by the international community; and not four days of bombings by the U.S. in 1998. What he wants is time and more time to husband his resources, to invest in his ongoing chemical and biological weapons programs, and to gain possession of nuclear arms.

Should all his ambitions be realized, the implications would be enormous for the Middle East, for the United States, and for the peace of the world. The whole range of weapons of mass destruction then would rest in the hands of a dictator who has already shown his willingness to use such weapons, and has done so, both in his war with Iran and against his own people. Armed with an arsenal of these weapons of terror, and seated atop ten percent of the world's oil reserves, Saddam Hussein could then be expected to seek domination of the entire Middle East, take control of a great portion of the world's energy supplies, directly threaten America's friends throughout the region, and subject the United States or any other nation to nuclear blackmail.

Simply stated, there is no doubt that Saddam Hussein now has weapons of mass destruction. There is no doubt he is amassing them to use against our friends, against our allies, and against us. And there is no doubt that his aggressive regional ambitions will lead him into future confrontations with his neighbors—confrontations that will involve both the weapons he has today, and the ones he will continue to develop with his oil wealth.

Ladies and gentlemen, there is no basis in Saddam Hussein's conduct or history to discount any of the concerns that I am raising this morning. We are, after all, dealing with the same dictator who shoots at American and British pilots in the no-fly zone, on a regular basis, the same dictator who dispatched a team of assassins to murder former President Bush as he traveled abroad, the same dictator who invaded Iran and Kuwait, and has fired ballistic missiles at Iran, Saudi Arabia, and Israel, the same dictator who has been on the State Department's list of state sponsors of terrorism for the better part of two decades.

In the face of such a threat, we must proceed with care, deliberation, and consultation with our allies. I know our president very well. I've worked beside him as he directed our response to the events of 9/11. I know that he will proceed cautiously and deliberately to consider all possible options to deal with the threat that an Iraq ruled by Saddam Hussein represents. And I am confident that he will, as he has said he would, consult widely with the Congress and with our friends and allies before deciding upon a course of action. He welcomes the debate that has now been joined here at home, and he has made it clear to his national security team that he wants us to participate fully in the hearings that will be held in Congress next month on this vitally important issue.

We will profit as well from a review of our own history. There are a lot of World War II veterans in the hall today. For the United States, that war began on December 7, 1941, with the attack on Pearl Harbor and the near-total destruction of our Pacific Fleet. Only then did we recognize the magnitude of the danger to our country. Only then did the Axis powers fully declare their intentions against us. By that point, many countries had fallen. Many millions had died. And our nation was plunged into a two-front war resulting in more than a million American casualties. To this day, historians continue to analyze that war, speculating on how we might have prevented Pearl Harbor, and asking what actions might have averted the tragedies that rate among the worst in human history.

America in the year 2002 must ask careful questions, not merely about our past, but also about our future. The elected leaders of this country have a responsibility to consider all of the available options. And we are doing so. What we must not do in the face of a mortal threat is give in to wishful thinking or willful blindness. We will not simply look away, hope for the best, and leave the matter for some future administration to resolve. As President Bush has said, time is not on our side. Deliverable weapons of mass destruction in the hands of a terror network, or a murderous dictator, or the two working together, constitutes as grave a threat as can be imagined. The risks of inaction are far greater than the risk of action.

Now and in the future, the United States will work closely with the global coalition to deny terrorists and their state sponsors the materials, technology, and expertise to make and deliver weapons of mass destruction. We will develop and deploy effective missile defenses to protect America and our allies from sudden attack. And the entire world must know that we will take whatever action is necessary to defend our freedom and our security.

> . . .

I am familiar with the arguments against taking action in the case of Saddam Hussein. Some concede that Saddam is evil, power-hungry, and a menace—but that, until he crosses the threshold of actually possessing nuclear weapons, we should rule out any preemptive action. That logic seems to me to be deeply flawed. The argument comes down to this: yes, Saddam is as dangerous as we say he is; we just need to let him get stronger before we do anything about it.

Yet if we did wait until that moment, Saddam would simply be emboldened, and it would become even harder for us to gather friends and allies to oppose him. As one of those who worked to assemble the Gulf War coalition, I can tell you that our job then would have been infinitely more difficult in the face of a nuclear-armed Saddam Hussein. And many of those who now argue that we should act only if he gets a nuclear weapon, would then turn around and say that we cannot act because he has a nuclear weapon. At bottom, that argument counsels a course of inaction that itself could have devastating consequences for many countries, including our own.

Another argument holds that opposing Saddam Hussein would cause even greater troubles in that part of the world, and interfere with the larger war against terror. I believe the opposite is true. Regime change in Iraq would bring about a number of benefits to the region. When the gravest of threats are eliminated, the freedom-loving peoples of the region will have a chance to promote the values that can bring lasting peace. As for the reaction of the Arab "street," the Middle East expert Professor Fouad Ajami predicts that after liberation, the streets in Basra and Baghdad are "sure to erupt in joy in the same way the throngs in Kabul greeted the Americans." Extremists in the region would have to rethink their strategy of Jihad. Moderates throughout the region would take heart. And our ability to advance the Israeli-Palestinian peace process would be enhanced, just as it was following the liberation of Kuwait in 1991.

The reality is that these times bring not only dangers but also opportunities. In the Middle East, where so many have known only poverty and oppression, terror and tyranny, we look to the day when people can live in freedom and dignity and the young can grow up free of the conditions that breed despair, hatred, and violence.

In other times the world saw how the United States defeated fierce enemies, then helped rebuild their countries, forming strong bonds between our peoples and our governments. Today in Afghanistan, the world is seeing that America acts not to conquer but to liberate, and remains in friendship to help the people build a future of stability, self-determination, and peace.

We would act in that same spirit after a regime change in Iraq. With our help, a liberated Iraq can be a great nation once again. Iraq is rich in natural resources and human talent, and has unlimited potential for a peaceful, prosperous future. Our goal would be an Iraq that has territorial integrity, a government that is democratic and pluralistic, a nation where the human rights of every ethnic and religious group are recognized and protected. In that troubled land all who seek justice, and dignity, and the chance to live their own lives, can know they have a friend and ally in the United States of America.

- **Source:** Dick Cheney, "Vice President Speaks at VFW 103rd National Convention," http://georgewbush-whitehouse.archives.gov/news/releases/2002/08/20020826.html, accessed July 13, 2011.
- **Analysis:** Vice President Cheney used the same reasoning employed by President Bush to justify war with Iraq. He began by placing the coming conflict in the context of the global war on terrorism, comparing Iraq to Afghanistan as a state sponsor of terrorism. He then rebutted arguments that the West could afford to contain Saddam Hussein while allowing the weapons inspectors to do their work. He noted that since Hussein had thwarted previous inspections by limiting access to Iraqi facilities, further inspections might be of limited value. Drawing dubious parallels with the appeasement policy toward Nazi Germany, Cheney insisted that Hussein would interpret delay as weakness.

  The vice president's most persuasive argument was, however, emotional. In the climate of fear following 9/11, he could easily argue that the risks of inaction, no matter how small, were unacceptable. Even the slightest possibility that Hussein had or would acquire WMD that he might pass on to al-Qaeda raised the spectator of another catastrophic attack on the United States, a chance that few Americans were willing to take.

- **Document 7: Excerpt of President Bush's Speech to the United Nations General Assembly**
- **When:** September 12, 2002
- **Where:** New York City
- **Significance:** Having made his case for war to the American people, the president tried to persuade the international community to back the U.S.-led effort to remove Saddam Hussein.

Above all, our principles and our security are challenged today by outlaw groups and regimes that accept no law of morality and have no limit to their violent ambitions. In the attacks on America a year ago, we saw the destructive intentions of our enemies. This threat hides within many nations, including my own. In cells and camps, terrorists are plotting further destruction, and building new bases for their war against civilization. And our greatest fear is that terrorists will find a shortcut to their mad ambitions when an outlaw regime supplies them with the technologies to kill on a massive scale.

In one place—in one regime—we find all these dangers, in their most lethal and aggressive forms, exactly the kind of aggressive threat the United Nations was born to confront.

Twelve years ago, Iraq invaded Kuwait without provocation. And the regime's forces were poised to continue their march to seize other countries and their resources. Had Saddam Hussein been appeased instead of stopped, he would have endangered the peace and stability of the world. Yet this aggression was stopped—by the might of coalition forces and the will of the United Nations.

To suspend hostilities, to spare himself, Iraq's dictator accepted a series of commitments. The terms were clear, to him and to all. And he agreed to prove he is complying with every one of those obligations.

He has proven instead only his contempt for the United Nations, and for all his pledges. By breaking every pledge—by his deceptions, and by his cruelties—Saddam Hussein has made the case against himself.

In 1991, Security Council Resolution 688 demanded that the Iraqi regime cease at once the repression of its own people, including the systematic repression of minorities—which the Council said, threatened international peace and security in the region. This demand goes ignored.

Last year, the U.N. Commission on Human Rights found that Iraq continues to commit extremely grave violations of human rights, and that the regime's repression is all pervasive. Tens of thousands of political opponents and ordinary citizens have been subjected to arbitrary arrest and imprisonment, summary execution, and torture by beating and burning, electric shock, starvation, mutilation, and rape. Wives are tortured in front of their husbands, children in the presence of their parents—and all of these horrors concealed from the world by the apparatus of a totalitarian state.

In 1991, the U.N. Security Council, through Resolutions 686 and 687, demanded that Iraq return all prisoners from Kuwait and other lands. Iraq's regime agreed. It broke its promise. Last year the Secretary General's high-level coordinator for this issue reported that Kuwait, Saudi, Indian, Syrian, Lebanese, Iranian, Egyptian, Bahraini, and Omani nationals remain unaccounted for—more than 600 people. One American pilot is among them.

In 1991, the U.N. Security Council, through Resolution 687, demanded that Iraq renounce all involvement with terrorism, and permit no terrorist organizations to operate in Iraq. Iraq's regime agreed. It broke this promise. In violation of Security Council Resolution 1373, Iraq continues to shelter and support terrorist organizations that direct violence against Iran, Israel, and Western governments. Iraqi dissidents abroad are targeted for murder. In 1993, Iraq attempted to assassinate the Emir of Kuwait and a former American President. Iraq's government openly praised the attacks of September the 11th. And al Qaeda terrorists escaped from Afghanistan and are known to be in Iraq.

In 1991, the Iraqi regime agreed to destroy and stop developing all weapons of mass destruction and long-range missiles, and to prove to the world it has done so by complying with rigorous inspections. Iraq has broken every aspect of this fundamental pledge.

From 1991 to 1995, the Iraqi regime said it had no biological weapons. After a senior official in its weapons program defected and exposed this lie, the regime admitted to producing tens of thousands of liters of anthrax and other deadly biological agents for use with Scud warheads, aerial bombs, and aircraft spray tanks. U.N. inspectors believe Iraq has produced two to four times the amount of biological agents it declared, and has failed to account for more than three metric tons of material that could be used to produce biological weapons. Right now, Iraq is expanding and improving facilities that were used for the production of biological weapons.

United Nations' inspections also revealed that Iraq likely maintains stockpiles of VX, mustard and other chemical agents, and that the regime is rebuilding and expanding facilities capable of producing chemical weapons.

And in 1995, after four years of deception, Iraq finally admitted it had a crash nuclear weapons program prior to the Gulf War. We know now, were it not for that war, the regime in Iraq would likely have possessed a nuclear weapon no later than 1993.

> ## DID YOU KNOW?
>
> ### Saddam Hussein
>
> Saddam Hussein Abd al-Majid al-Tikrit was born in 1937 in the town of Tikrit, north of Baghdad. Despite his modest origins and limited education, he rose to power in Iraq through his work for the Ba'ath Party, which seized control of Iraq in 1967. He became the chief deputy of President Hassan al-Bakr, whom he forced into retirement in 1979. From then until the U.S.-led invasion of 2003, Saddam Hussein ruled Iraq with an iron hand. During the 1980s he engaged in a protracted, wasteful struggle with Iran, using weapons supplied by the United States. Following the Gulf War, he remained a major security concern of the West. He went into hiding after the coalition occupied Iraq but was captured in December 2003. He was tried by an Iraqi court for various crimes committed as dictator and executed on December 30, 2006.

Today, Iraq continues to withhold important information about its nuclear program—weapons design, procurement logs, experiment data, an accounting of nuclear materials and documentation of foreign assistance. Iraq employs capable nuclear scientists and technicians. It retains physical infrastructure needed to build a nuclear weapon. Iraq has made several attempts to buy high-strength aluminum tubes used to enrich uranium for a nuclear weapon. Should Iraq acquire fissile material, it would be able to build a nuclear weapon within a year. And Iraq's state-controlled media has reported numerous meetings between Saddam Hussein and his nuclear scientists, leaving little doubt about his continued appetite for these weapons.

Iraq also possesses a force of Scud-type missiles with ranges beyond the 150 kilometers permitted by the U.N. Work at testing and production facilities shows that Iraq is building more long-range missiles that it can inflict mass death throughout the region.

In 1990, after Iraq's invasion of Kuwait, the world imposed economic sanctions on Iraq. Those sanctions were maintained after the war to compel the regime's compliance with Security Council resolutions. In time, Iraq was allowed to use oil revenues to buy food. Saddam Hussein has subverted this program, working around the sanctions to buy missile technology and military materials. He blames the suffering of Iraq's people on the United Nations, even as he uses his oil wealth to build lavish palaces for himself, and to buy arms for his country. By refusing to comply with his own agreements, he bears full guilt for the hunger and misery of innocent Iraqi citizens.

In 1991, Iraq promised U.N. inspectors immediate and unrestricted access to verify Iraq's commitment to rid itself of weapons of mass destruction and long-range missiles. Iraq broke this promise, spending seven years deceiving, evading, and harassing U.N. inspectors before ceasing cooperation entirely. Just months after the 1991 cease-fire, the Security Council twice renewed its demand that the Iraqi regime cooperate fully with inspectors, condemning Iraq's serious violations of its obligations. The Security Council again renewed that demand in 1994, and twice more in 1996, deploring Iraq's clear violations of its obligations. The Security Council renewed its demand three more times in 1997, citing flagrant violations; and three more times in 1998, calling Iraq's behavior totally unacceptable. And in 1999, the demand was renewed yet again.

As we meet today, it's been almost four years since the last U.N. inspectors set foot in Iraq, four years for the Iraqi regime to plan, and to build, and to test behind the cloak of secrecy.

We know that Saddam Hussein pursued weapons of mass murder even when inspectors were in his country. Are we to assume that he stopped when they left? The history, the logic, and the facts lead to one conclusion: Saddam Hussein's regime is a grave and gathering danger. To suggest otherwise is to hope against the evidence. To assume this regime's good faith is to bet the lives of millions and the peace of the world in a reckless gamble. And this is a risk we must not take.

Delegates to the General Assembly, we have been more than patient. We've tried sanctions. We've tried the carrot of oil for food, and the stick of coalition military strikes. But Saddam Hussein has defied all these efforts and continues to develop weapons of mass destruction. The first time we may be completely certain he has a— nuclear weapons is when, God forbids, he uses one. We owe it to all our citizens to do everything in our power to prevent that day from coming.

The conduct of the Iraqi regime is a threat to the authority of the United Nations, and a threat to peace. Iraq has answered a decade of U.N. demands with a decade of defiance. All the world now faces a test, and the United Nations a difficult and defining moment. Are Security Council resolutions to be honored and enforced, or cast aside without consequence? Will the United Nations serve the purpose of its founding, or will it be irrelevant? . . .

My nation will work with the U.N. Security Council to meet our common challenge. If Iraq's regime defies us again, the world must move deliberately, decisively to hold Iraq to account. We will work with the U.N. Security Council for the necessary resolutions. But the purposes of the United States should not be doubted. The Security Council resolutions will be enforced—the just demands of peace and security will be met—or action will be unavoidable. And a regime that has lost its legitimacy will also lose its power.

Events can turn in one of two ways: If we fail to act in the face of danger, the people of Iraq will continue to live in brutal submission. The regime will have new power to bully and dominate and conquer its neighbors, condemning the Middle East to more years of bloodshed and fear. The regime will remain unstable—the region will remain unstable, with little hope of freedom, and isolated from the progress of our times. With every step the Iraqi regime takes toward gaining and deploying the most terrible weapons, our own options to confront that regime will narrow. And if an emboldened regime were to supply these weapons to terrorist allies, then the attacks of September the 11th would be a prelude to far greater horrors.

If we meet our responsibilities, if we overcome this danger, we can arrive at a very different future. The people of Iraq can shake off their captivity. They can one day join a democratic Afghanistan and a democratic Palestine, inspiring reforms throughout the Muslim world. These nations can show by their example that honest government, and respect for women, and the great Islamic tradition of learning can triumph in the Middle East and beyond. And we will show that the promise of the United Nations can be fulfilled in our time.

Neither of these outcomes is certain. Both have been set before us. We must choose between a world of fear and a world of progress. We cannot stand by and do nothing while dangers gather. We must stand up for our security, and for the permanent rights and the hopes of mankind. By heritage and by choice, the United States of America will make that stand. And, delegates to the United Nations, you have the power to make that stand, as well.

DID YOU KNOW?

WMD

A weapon of mass destruction (WMD) causes mass casualties and/or extensive destruction. "WMD" usually refers to three categories of weapons: nuclear, chemical, and biological. Nuclear weapons include traditional nuclear devices that produce a devastating explosion and spread radiation as well as radiological bombs, in which conventional explosives disperse radioactive material over a wide area. Chemical weapons are generally caustic or poisonous substances dispersed as aerosols. Saddam Hussein used poisonous gas (both nerve agents and mustard gases) against the Kurds in northern Iraq in 1988. Biological weapons are pathogens distributed among a target population to cause mass casualties. While any germ or virus may be used in this capacity, certain pathogens such as anthrax have proven most effective as biological weapons.

- **Source:** George W. Bush, "Address to the United Nations General Assembly," available at http://georgewbush-whitehouse.archives.gov/news/releases/2002/09/print/20020912-1.html, accessed April 4, 2008.

- **Analysis:** President Bush made the case for stronger action against Iraq. He began with a litany of Saddam Hussein's misdeeds, beginning with the 1990 invasion of Iraq and continuing through his refusal to comply with UN demands. The president went on to catalog Hussein's human-rights abuses and the suffering he imposed on his own people. Most importantly, however, Bush stressed Iraq's alleged links to terrorist organizations and his quest for WMD, highlighting the danger that Hussein would supply terrorists with such weapons. Finally, the president challenged the United Nations either to confront Iraq or become irrelevant.

- **Document 8: Excerpt of Remarks by the President on Iraq**
- **When:** October 7, 2002
- **Where:** Cincinnati Museum Center, Cincinnati Union Terminal, Cincinnati, Ohio
- **Significance:** The president associated Iraq with the 9/11 attacks.

Thank you all. Thank you for that very gracious and warm Cincinnati welcome. I'm honored to be here tonight; I appreciate you all coming.

Tonight I want to take a few minutes to discuss a grave threat to peace, and America's determination to lead the world in confronting that threat.

The threat comes from Iraq. It arises directly from the Iraqi regime's own actions—its history of aggression, and its drive toward an arsenal of terror. Eleven years ago, as a condition for ending the Persian Gulf War, the Iraqi regime was required to destroy its weapons of mass destruction, to cease all development of such weapons, and to stop all support for terrorist groups. The Iraqi regime has violated all of those obligations. It possesses and produces chemical and biological weapons. It is seeking nuclear weapons. It has given shelter and support to terrorism, and practices terror against its own people. The entire world has witnessed Iraq's eleven-year history of defiance, deception and bad faith.

We also must never forget the most vivid events of recent history. On September the 11th, 2001, America felt its vulnerability—even to threats that gather on the other side of the earth. We resolved then, and we are resolved today, to confront every threat, from any source, that could bring sudden terror and suffering to America.

Members of the Congress of both political parties, and members of the United Nations Security Council, agree that Saddam Hussein is a threat to peace and must disarm. We agree that the Iraqi dictator must not be permitted to threaten America and the world with horrible poisons and diseases and gases and atomic weapons. Since we all agree on this goal, the issues is: how can we best achieve it?

Many Americans have raised legitimate questions: about the nature of the threat; about the urgency of action—why be concerned now; about the link between Iraq developing weapons of terror, and the wider war on terror. These are all issues we've discussed broadly and fully within my administration. And tonight, I want to share those discussions with you.

First, some ask why Iraq is different from other countries or regimes that also have terrible weapons. While there are many dangers in the world, the threat from Iraq stands alone—because it gathers the most serious dangers of our age in one place. Iraq's weapons of mass destruction are controlled by a murderous tyrant who has already used chemical weapons to kill thousands of people. This same tyrant has tried to dominate the Middle East, has invaded and brutally occupied a small neighbor, has struck other nations without warning, and holds an unrelenting hostility toward the United States.

By its past and present actions, by its technological capabilities, by the merciless nature of its regime, Iraq is unique. As a former chief weapons inspector of the U.N. has said, "The fundamental problem with Iraq remains the nature of the regime, itself. Saddam Hussein is a homicidal dictator who is addicted to weapons of mass destruction."

Some ask how urgent this danger is to America and the world. The danger is already significant, and it only grows worse with time. If we know Saddam Hussein has dangerous weapons today—and we do—does it make any sense for the world to wait to confront him as he grows even stronger and develops even more dangerous weapons?

In 1995, after several years of deceit by the Iraqi regime, the head of Iraq's military industries defected. It was then that the regime was forced to admit that it had produced more than 30,000 liters of anthrax and other deadly biological agents. The inspectors, however, concluded that Iraq had likely produced two to four times that amount. This is a massive stockpile of biological weapons that has never been accounted for, and capable of killing millions.

We know that the regime has produced thousands of tons of chemical agents, including mustard gas, sarin nerve gas, VX nerve gas. Saddam Hussein also has experience in using chemical weapons. He has ordered chemical attacks on Iran, and on more than forty villages in his own country. These actions killed or injured at least 20,000 people, more than six times the number of people who died in the attacks of September the 11th.

And surveillance photos reveal that the regime is rebuilding facilities that it had used to produce chemical and biological weapons. Every chemical and biological weapon that Iraq has or makes is a direct violation of the truce that ended the Persian Gulf War in 1991. Yet, Saddam Hussein has chosen to build and keep these weapons despite international sanctions, U.N. demands, and isolation from the civilized world.

Iraq possesses ballistic missiles with a likely range of hundreds of miles—far enough to strike Saudi Arabia, Israel, Turkey, and other nations—in a region where more than 135,000 American civilians and service members live and work. We've also discovered through intelligence that Iraq has a growing fleet of manned and unmanned aerial vehicles that could be used to disperse chemical or biological weapons across broad areas. We're concerned that Iraq is exploring ways of using these UAVS for missions targeting the United States. And, of course, sophisticated delivery systems aren't required for a chemical or biological attack; all that might be required are a small container and one terrorist or Iraqi intelligence operative to deliver it.

And that is the source of our urgent concern about Saddam Hussein's links to international terrorist groups. Over the years, Iraq has provided safe haven to terrorists such as Abu Nidal, whose terror organization carried out more than 90 terrorist attacks in 20 countries that killed or injured nearly 900 people, including 12 Americans. Iraq has also provided safe haven to Abu Abbas, who was responsible for seizing the Achille Lauro and killing an American passenger. And we know that Iraq is continuing to finance terror and gives assistance to groups that use terrorism to undermine Middle East peace.

We know that Iraq and the al Qaeda terrorist network share a common enemy— the United States of America. We know that Iraq and al Qaeda have had high-level contacts that go back a decade. Some al Qaeda leaders who fled Afghanistan went to Iraq. These include one very senior al Qaeda leader who received medical treatment in Baghdad this year, and who has been associated with planning for chemical and biological attacks. We've learned that Iraq has trained al Qaeda members in bomb-making and poisons and deadly gases. And we know that after September the 11th, Saddam Hussein's regime gleefully celebrated the terrorist attacks on America.

Iraq could decide on any given day to provide a biological or chemical weapon to a terrorist group or individual terrorists. Alliance with terrorists could allow the Iraqi regime to attack America without leaving any fingerprints.

Some have argued that confronting the threat from Iraq could detract from the war against terror. To the contrary; confronting the threat posed by Iraq is crucial to winning the war on terror. When I spoke to Congress more than a year ago, I said that those who harbor terrorists are as guilty as the terrorists themselves. Saddam Hussein is harboring terrorists and the instruments of terror, the instruments of mass death and destruction. And he cannot be trusted. The risk is simply too great that he will use them, or provide them to a terror network.

Terror cells and outlaw regimes building weapons of mass destruction are different faces of the same evil. Our security requires that we confront both. And the United States military is capable of confronting both.

Many people have asked how close Saddam Hussein is to developing a nuclear weapon. Well, we don't know exactly, and that's the problem. Before the Gulf War, the best intelligence indicated that Iraq was eight to ten years away from developing a nuclear weapon. After the war, international inspectors learned that the regime has been much closer—the regime in Iraq would likely have possessed a nuclear weapon no later than 1993. The inspectors discovered that Iraq had an advanced nuclear weapons development program, had a design for a workable nuclear weapon, and was pursuing several different methods of enriching uranium for a bomb.

Before being barred from Iraq in 1998, the International Atomic Energy Agency dismantled extensive nuclear weapons-related facilities, including three uranium enrichment sites. That same year, information from a high-ranking Iraqi nuclear engineer who had defected revealed that despite his public promises, Saddam Hussein had ordered his nuclear program to continue.

The evidence indicates that Iraq is reconstituting its nuclear weapons program. Saddam Hussein has held numerous meetings with Iraqi nuclear scientists, a group he calls his "nuclear mujahideen"—his nuclear holy warriors. Satellite photographs reveal that Iraq is rebuilding facilities at sites that have been part of its nuclear program in the past. Iraq has attempted to purchase high-strength aluminum tubes and other equipment needed for gas centrifuges, which are used to enrich uranium for nuclear weapons.

If the Iraqi regime is able to produce, buy, or steal an amount of highly enriched uranium a little larger than a single softball, it could have a nuclear weapon in less than a year. And if we allow that to happen, a terrible line would be crossed. Saddam Hussein would be in a position to blackmail anyone who opposes his aggression. He would be in a position to dominate the Middle East. He would be in a position to threaten America. And Saddam Hussein would be in a position to pass nuclear technology to terrorists.

Some citizens wonder, after 11 years of living with this problem, why do we need to confront it now? And there's a reason. We've experienced the horror of September the 11th. We have seen that those who hate America are willing to crash airplanes into buildings full of innocent people. Our enemies would be no less willing, in fact, they would be eager, to use biological or chemical, or a nuclear weapon.

Knowing these realities, America must not ignore the threat gathering against us. Facing clear evidence of peril, we cannot wait for the final proof—the smoking gun—that could come in the form of a mushroom cloud. As President Kennedy said in October of 1962, "Neither the United States of America, nor the world community of nations can tolerate deliberate deception and offensive threats on the part of any nation, large or small. We no longer live in a world," he said, "where only the actual firing of weapons represents a sufficient challenge to a nations security to constitute maximum peril."

Understanding the threats of our time, knowing the designs and deceptions of the Iraqi regime, we have every reason to assume the worst, and we have an urgent duty to prevent the worst from occurring.

Some believe we can address this danger by simply resuming the old approach to inspections, and applying diplomatic and economic pressure. Yet this is precisely what the world has tried to do since 1991. The U.N. inspections program was met with systematic deception. The Iraqi regime bugged hotel rooms and offices of inspectors to find where they were going next; they forged documents, destroyed evidence, and developed mobile weapons facilities to keep a step ahead of inspectors. Eight so-called presidential palaces were declared off-limits to unfettered inspections. These sites actually encompass twelve square miles, with hundreds of structures, both above and below the ground, where sensitive materials could be hidden.

The world has also tried economic sanctions—and watched Iraq use billions of dollars in illegal oil revenues to fund more weapons purchases, rather than providing for the needs of the Iraqi people.

The world has tried limited military strikes to destroy Iraq's weapons of mass destruction capabilities—only to see them openly rebuilt, while the regime again denies they even exist.

The world has tried no-fly zones to keep Saddam from terrorizing his own people—and in the last year alone, the Iraqi military has fired upon American and British pilots more than 750 times.

After eleven years during which we have tried containment, sanctions, inspections, even selected military action, the end result is that Saddam Hussein still has chemical and biological weapons and is increasing his capabilities to make more. And he is moving ever closer to developing a nuclear weapon.

Clearly, to actually work, any new inspections, sanctions or enforcement mechanisms will have to be very different. America wants the U.N. to be an effective organization that helps keep the peace. And that is why we are urging the Security Council to adopt a new resolution setting out tough, immediate requirements. Among those requirements: the Iraqi regime must reveal and destroy, under U.N. supervision, all existing weapons of mass destruction. To ensure that we learn the truth, the regime must allow witnesses to its illegal activities to be interviewed outside the country—and these witnesses must be free to bring their families with them so they all beyond the reach of Saddam Hussein's terror and murder. And inspectors must have access to any site, at any time, without pre-clearance, without delay, without exceptions.

The time for denying, deceiving, and delaying has come to an end. Saddam Hussein must disarm himself—or, for the sake of peace, we will lead a coalition to disarm him.

Many nations are joining us in insisting that Saddam Hussein's regime be held accountable. They are committed to defending the international security that protects the lives of both our citizens and theirs. And that's why America is challenging all nations to take the resolutions of the U.N. Security Council seriously.

And these resolutions are clear. In addition to declaring and destroying all of its weapons of mass destruction, Iraq must end its support for terrorism. It must cease the persecution of its civilian population. It must stop all illicit trade outside the Oil For Food program. It must release or account for all Gulf War personnel, including an American pilot, whose fate is still unknown.

By taking these steps, and by only taking these steps, the Iraqi regime has an opportunity to avoid conflict. Taking these steps would also change the nature of the Iraqi regime itself. America hopes the regime will make that choice. Unfortunately, at least so far, we have little reason to expect it. And that's why two administrations—mine and President Clinton's—have stated that regime change in Iraq is the only certain means of removing a great danger to our nation.

I hope this will not require military action, but it may. And military conflict could be difficult. An Iraqi regime faced with its own demise may attempt cruel and desperate measures. If Saddam Hussein orders such measures, his generals would be well advised to refuse those orders. If they do not refuse, they must understand that all war criminals will be pursued and punished. If we have to act, we will take every precaution that is possible. We will plan carefully; we will act with the full power of the United States military; we will act with allies at our side, and we will prevail.

There is no easy or risk-free course of action. Some have argued we should wait—and that's an option. In my view, it's the riskiest of all options, because the longer we wait, the stronger and bolder Saddam Hussein will become. We could wait and hope that Saddam does not give weapons to terrorists, or develop a nuclear weapon to blackmail the world. But I'm convinced that is a hope against all evidence. As Americans, we want peace—we work and sacrifice for peace. But there can be no peace if our security depends on the will and whims of a ruthless and aggressive dictator. I'm not willing to stake one American life on trusting Saddam Hussein.

Failure to act would embolden other tyrants, allow terrorists access to new weapons and new resources, and make blackmail a permanent feature of world events. The United Nations would betray the purpose of its founding, and prove irrelevant to the problems of our time. And through its inaction, the United States would resign itself to a future of fear.

That is not the America I know. That is not the America I serve. We refuse to live in fear. This nation, in world war and in Cold War, has never permitted the brutal and lawless to set history's course. Now, as before, we will secure our nation, protect our freedom, and help others to find freedom of their own.

Some worry that a change of leadership in Iraq could create instability and make the situation worse. The situation could hardly get worse, for world security and for the people of Iraq. The lives of Iraqi citizens would improve dramatically if Saddam Hussein were no longer in power, just as the lives of Afghanistan's citizens improved after the Taliban. The dictator of Iraq is a student of Stalin, using murder as a tool of terror and control, within his own cabinet, within his own army, and even within his own family.

On Saddam Hussein's orders, opponents have been decapitated, wives and mothers of political opponents have been systematically raped as a method of intimidation, and political prisoners have been forced to watch their own children being tortured.

America believes that all people are entitled to hope and human rights, to the non-negotiable demands of human dignity. People everywhere prefer freedom to slavery; prosperity to squalor; self-government to the rule of terror and torture. America is a friend to the people of Iraq. Our demands are directed only at the regime that enslaves them and threatens us. When these demands are met, the first and greatest benefit will come to Iraqi men, women and children. The oppression of Kurds, Assyrians, Turkomans, Shi'a, Sunnis and others will be lifted. The long captivity of Iraq will end, and an era of new hope will begin.

Iraq is a land rich in culture, resources, and talent. Freed from the weight of oppression, Iraq's people will be able to share in the progress and prosperity of our time. If military action is necessary, the United States and our allies will help the Iraqi people rebuild their economy, and create the institutions of liberty in a unified Iraq at peace with its neighbors.

Later this week, the United States Congress will vote on this matter. I have asked Congress to authorize the use of America's military, if it proves necessary, to enforce U.N. Security Council demands. Approving this resolution does not mean that military action is imminent or unavoidable. The resolution will tell the United Nations, and all nations, that America speaks with one voice and is determined to make the demands of the civilized world mean something. Congress will also be sending a message to the dictator in Iraq: that his only chance—his only choice is full compliance, and the time remaining for that choice is limited.

Members of Congress are nearing an historic vote. I'm confident they will fully consider the facts, and their duties.

The attacks of September the 11th showed our country that vast oceans no longer protect us from danger. Before that tragic date, we had only hints of al Qaeda's plans and designs. Today in Iraq, we see a threat whose outlines are far more clearly defined, and whose consequences could be far more deadly. Saddam Hussein's actions have put us on notice, and there is no refuge from our responsibilities.

We did not ask for this present challenge, but we accept it. Like other generations of Americans, we will meet the responsibility of defending human liberty against violence and aggression. By our resolve, we will give strength to others. By our courage, we will give hope to others. And by our actions, we will secure the peace, and lead the world to a better day.

May God bless America.

- **Source:** George Bush, "Remarks by the President on Iraq, Cincinnati Museum Center—Cincinnati Union Terminal, Cincinnati, Ohio," October 7, 2002, available at http://georgewbush-whitehouse .archives.gov/news/releases/2002/10/20021007-8.html, accessed December 1, 2011.

- **Analysis:** On the eve of the congressional vote authorizing him to use force against Iraq, the president reiterated arguments made in his UN speech. He also addressed the objections raised to the idea of invading

Iraq. He exaggerated the extent and nature of Iraq's weapons program and insisted the regime had direct ties to al-Qaeda, a claim that has since been shown to be false. He accused Saddam of training a "nuclear mujahedeen," a reference to the Arab fighters (some of whom later formed al-Qaeda) who had gone to Afghanistan to fight the Soviets. As he had done on previous occasions, the president stressed the urgency of acting to remove Saddam Hussein before another devastating attack on the United States occurred.

- **Document 9: Excerpt of the State of the Union Address**
- **When:** January 28, 2003
- **Where:** Washington, DC
- **Significance:** The president continued to focus on the threat posed by Iraq, focusing on a false claim that Saddam Hussein had attempted to get uranium from Niger.

Our nation and the world must learn the lessons of the Korean Peninsula and not allow an even greater threat to rise up in Iraq. A brutal dictator, with a history of reckless aggression, with ties to terrorism, with great potential wealth, will not be permitted to dominate a vital region and threaten the United States.

Twelve years ago, Saddam Hussein faced the prospect of being the last casualty in a war he had started and lost. To spare himself, he agreed to disarm of all weapons of mass destruction. For the next 12 years, he systematically violated that agreement. He pursued chemical, biological, and nuclear weapons, even while inspectors were in his country. Nothing to date has restrained him from his pursuit of these weapons—not economic sanctions, not isolation from the civilized world, not even cruise missile strikes on his military facilities.

Almost three months ago, the United Nations Security Council gave Saddam Hussein his final chance to disarm. He has shown instead utter contempt for the United Nations, and for the opinion of the world. The 108 U.N. inspectors were sent to conduct—were not sent to conduct a scavenger hunt for hidden materials across a country the size of California. The job of the inspectors is to verify that Iraq's regime is disarming. It is up to Iraq to show exactly where it is hiding its banned weapons, lay those weapons out for the world to see, and destroy them as directed. Nothing like this has happened.

The United Nations concluded in 1999 that Saddam Hussein had biological weapons sufficient to produce over 25,000 liters of anthrax—enough doses to kill several million people. He hasn't accounted for that material. He's given no evidence that he has destroyed it.

The United Nations concluded that Saddam Hussein had materials sufficient to produce more than 38,000 liters of botulinum toxin—enough to subject millions of people to death by respiratory failure. He hadn't accounted for that material. He's given no evidence that he has destroyed it.

Our intelligence officials estimate that Saddam Hussein had the materials to produce as much as 500 tons of sarin, mustard and VX nerve agent. In such quantities, these chemical agents could also kill untold thousands. He's not accounted for these materials. He has given no evidence that he has destroyed them.

U.S. intelligence indicates that Saddam Hussein had upwards of 30,000 munitions capable of delivering chemical agents. Inspectors recently turned up 16 of them—despite Iraq's recent declaration denying their existence. Saddam Hussein has not accounted for the remaining 29,984 of these prohibited munitions. He's given no evidence that he has destroyed them.

From three Iraqi defectors we know that Iraq, in the late 1990s, had several mobile biological weapons labs. These are designed to produce germ warfare agents, and can be moved from place to a place to evade inspectors. Saddam Hussein has not disclosed these facilities. He's given no evidence that he has destroyed them.

The International Atomic Energy Agency confirmed in the 1990s that Saddam Hussein had an advanced nuclear weapons development program, had a design for a nuclear weapon and was working on five different methods of enriching uranium for a bomb. The British government has learned that Saddam Hussein recently sought significant quantities of uranium from Africa. Our intelligence sources tell us that he has attempted to purchase high-strength aluminum tubes suitable for nuclear weapons production. Saddam Hussein has not credibly explained these activities. He clearly has much to hide.

The dictator of Iraq is not disarming. To the contrary; he is deceiving. From intelligence sources we know, for instance, that thousands of Iraqi security personnel are at work hiding documents and materials from the U.N. inspectors, sanitizing inspection sites and monitoring the inspectors themselves. Iraqi officials accompany the inspectors in order to intimidate witnesses.

Iraq is blocking U-2 surveillance flights requested by the United Nations. Iraqi intelligence officers are posing as the scientists inspectors are supposed to interview. Real scientists have been coached by Iraqi officials on what to say. Intelligence sources indicate that Saddam Hussein has ordered that scientists who cooperate with U.N. inspectors in disarming Iraq will be killed, along with their families.

Year after year, Saddam Hussein has gone to elaborate lengths, spent enormous sums, taken great risks to build and keep weapons of mass destruction. But why? The only possible explanation, the only possible use he could have for those weapons, is to dominate, intimidate, or attack.

With nuclear arms or a full arsenal of chemical and biological weapons, Saddam Hussein could resume his ambitions of conquest in the Middle East and create deadly havoc in that region. And this Congress and the America people must recognize another threat. Evidence from intelligence sources, secret communications, and statements by people now in custody reveal that Saddam Hussein aids and protects terrorists, including members of al Qaeda. Secretly, and without fingerprints, he could provide one of his hidden weapons to terrorists, or help them develop their own.

Before September the 11th, many in the world believed that Saddam Hussein could be contained. But chemical agents, lethal viruses and shadowy terrorist networks are not easily contained. Imagine those 19 hijackers with other weapons and other plans—this time armed by Saddam Hussein. It would take one vial, one canister, one crate slipped into this country to bring a day of horror like none we have ever known. We will do everything in our power to make sure that that day never comes.

Some have said we must not act until the threat is imminent. Since when have terrorists and tyrants announced their intentions, politely putting us on notice before they strike? If this threat is permitted to fully and suddenly emerge, all actions, all words, and all recriminations would come too late. Trusting in the sanity and restraint of Saddam Hussein is not a strategy, and it is not an option.

The dictator who is assembling the world's most dangerous weapons has already used them on whole villages—leaving thousands of his own citizens dead, blind, or disfigured. Iraqi refugees tell us how forced confessions are obtained—by torturing children while their parents are made to watch. International human rights groups have catalogued other methods used in the torture chambers of Iraq: electric shock, burning with hot irons, dripping acid on the skin, mutilation with electric drills, cutting out tongues, and rape. If this is not evil, then evil has no meaning.

And tonight I have a message for the brave and oppressed people of Iraq: Your enemy is not surrounding your country—your enemy is ruling your country. And the day he and his regime are removed from power will be the day of your liberation.

The world has waited 12 years for Iraq to disarm. America will not accept a serious and mounting threat to our country, and our friends and our allies. The United States will ask the U.N. Security Council to convene on February the 5th to consider the facts of Iraq's ongoing defiance of the world. Secretary of State Powell will present information and intelligence about Iraqi's legal—Iraq's illegal weapons programs, its attempt to hide those weapons from inspectors, and its links to terrorist groups.

We will consult. But let there be no misunderstanding: If Saddam Hussein does not fully disarm, for the safety of our people and for the peace of the world, we will lead a coalition to disarm him.

- **Source:** George W. Bush, "State of the Union," January 28, 2003, available at http://georgewbush-whitehouse.archives.gov/news/releases/2003/01/20030128-19.html, accessed April 23, 2008.
- **Analysis:** President Bush reiterated his case for strong measures against Iraq, linking Saddam's regime to international terrorism and asserting the dictator's intention to gain WMD. While he had made these charges before, he provided concrete detail, including intelligence on alleged Iraqi efforts to purchase Nigerian uranium. Suspect at the time of the speech, this information later proved to be false. He also detailed certain chemical warfare capabilities that Saddam Hussein did in fact have (and had possessed since the Iran-Iraq War) but exaggerated the threat that they posed.

- **Document 10: President Saddam Hussein of Iraq, Interview with Tony Benn**
- **When:** February 4, 2003
- **Where:** Baghdad
- **Significance:** Saddam Hussein denied Iraq had WMD or ties to al-Qaeda.

Saddam: Welcome to Baghdad. You are conscious of the role that Iraqis have set out for themselves, inspired by their own culture, their civilisation and their role in human history.

This role requires peace in order to prosper and progress. Having said that, the Iraqis are committed to their rights as much as they are committed to the rights of others.

Without peace they will be faced with many obstacles that would stop them from fulfilling their human role.

Benn: Mr President, may I ask you some questions. The first is, does Iraq have any weapons of mass destruction?

Saddam: Most Iraqi officials have been in power for over 34 years and have experience of dealing with the outside world.

Every fair-minded person knows that when Iraqi officials say something, they are trustworthy.

A few minutes ago when you asked me if I wanted to look at the questions beforehand I told you I didn't feel the need so that we don't waste time, and I gave you the freedom to ask me any question directly so that my reply would be direct.

This is an opportunity to reach the British people and the forces of peace in the world.

There is only one truth and therefore I tell you as I have said on many occasions before that Iraq has no weapons of mass destruction whatsoever. We challenge anyone who claims that we have to bring forward any evidence and present it to public opinion.

Benn: I have another which has been raised: Do you have links with al-Qaeda?

Saddam: If we had a relationship with al-Qaeda and we believed in that relationship we wouldn't be ashamed to admit it. Therefore I would like to tell you directly and also through you to anyone who is interested to know that we have no relationship with al-Qaeda.

Benn: In relation to the inspectors, there appear to be difficulties with inspectors, and I wonder whether there's anything you can tell me about these difficulties and whether you believe they will be cleared up before Mr. Hans Blix and Mr. ElBaradei come back to Baghdad?

Saddam: You are aware that every major event must encounter some difficulty.

On the subject of the inspectors and the resolutions that deal with Iraq you must have been following it and you must have a view and a vision as to whether these resolutions have any basis in international law.

Nevertheless the Security Council produced them. These resolutions—implemented or not—or the motivation behind these resolutions could lead the current situation to the path of peace or war. Therefore it's a critical situation.

Let us also remember the unjust suffering of the Iraqi people. For the last 13 years since the blockade was imposed, you must be aware of the amount of harm that it has caused the Iraqi people, particularly the children and the elderly, as a result of the shortage of food and medicine and other aspects of their life.

Therefore we are facing a critical situation.

On that basis, it is not surprising that there might be complaints relating to the small details of the inspection which may be essential issues as far as we are concerned and the way we see the whole thing. It is possible that those Iraqis who are involved with the inspection might complain about the conduct of the inspectors and they complain indeed.

It is also possible that some inspectors either for reasons of practical and detailed procedure, or for some other motives, may complain about the Iraqi conduct.

Every fair-minded person knows that as far as resolution 1441 is concerned, the Iraqis have been fulfilling their obligations under the resolution.

When Iraq objects to the conduct of those implementing the Security Council resolutions, that doesn't mean that Iraq wishes to push things to confrontation.

Iraq has no interest in war. No Iraqi official or ordinary citizen has expressed a wish to go to war.

The question should be directed at the other side. Are they looking for a pretext so they could justify war against Iraq?

If the purpose was to make sure that Iraq is free of nuclear, chemical and biological weapons then they can do that. These weapons do not come in small pills that you can hide in your pocket.

These are weapons of mass destruction and it is easy to work out if Iraq has them or not. We have said many times before and we say it again today that Iraq is free of such weapons.

So when Iraq objects to the conduct of the inspection teams or others, that doesn't mean that Iraq is interested in putting obstacles before them which could hinder the efforts to get to the truth.

It is in our interest to facilitate their mission to find the truth.

The question is does the other side want to get to the same conclusion or are they looking for a pretext for aggression? If those concerned prefer aggression then it's within their reach.

The super powers can create a pretext any day to claim that Iraq is not implementing resolution 1441.

They have claimed before that Iraq did not implement the previous resolutions.

However, after many years it became clear that Iraq had complied with these resolutions. Otherwise, why are they focusing now on the latest resolution and not the previous ones?

Benn: May I broaden the question out, Mr. President, to the relations between Iraq and the UN, and the prospects for peace more broadly, and I wonder whether with all its weaknesses and all the difficulties, whether you see a way in which the UN can reach that objective for the benefit of humanity?

Saddam: The point you raised can be found in the United Nations charter. As you know Iraq is one of the founders and first signatories of the charter.

If we look at the representatives of two super powers—America and Britain—and look at their conduct and their language, we would notice that they are more motivated by war than their responsibility for peace.

And when they talk about peace all they do is accuse others they wish to destroy in the name of peace.

They claim they are looking after the interests of their people. You know as well as I do that this is not the truth.

Yes the world would respect this principle if it was genuinely applied.

It's not about power but it is about right and wrong, about when we base our human relations on good, and respect this principle.

So it becomes simple to adhere to this principle because anyone who violates it will be exposed to public opinion.

Benn: There are people who believe this present conflict is about oil, and I wonder if you would say something about how you see the enormous oil reserves of Iraq being developed, first for the benefit of the people of Iraq and secondly for the needs of mankind.

Saddam: When we speak about oil in this part of the world—we are an integral part of the world—we have to deal with others in all aspects of life, economic as well as social, technical, scientific and other areas.

It seems that the authorities in the US are motivated by aggression that has been evident for more than a decade against the region.

The first factor is the role of those influential people in the decision taken by the president of the US based on sympathy with the Zionist entity that was created at the expense of Palestine and its people and their humanity.

These people force the hand of the American administration by claiming that the Arabs pose a danger to Israel, without remembering their obligation to God and how the Palestinian people were driven out of their homeland.

The consecutive American administrations were led down a path of hostility against the people of this region, including our own nation and we are part of it.

Those people and others have been telling the various US administrations, especially the current one, that if you want to control the world you need to control the oil.

Therefore the destruction of Iraq is a pre-requisite to controlling oil. That means the destruction of the Iraqi national identity, since the Iraqis are committed to their principles and rights according to international law and the UN charter.

It seems that this argument has appealed to some US administrations especially the current one that if they control the oil in the Middle East, they would be able to control the world. They could dictate to China the size of its economic growth and interfere in its education system and could do the same to Germany and France and perhaps to Russia and Japan.

They might even tell the same to Britain if its oil doesn't satisfy its domestic consumption.

It seems to me that this hostility is a trademark of the current US administration and is based on its wish to control the world and spread its hegemony.

People have the right to say that if this aggression by the American administration continues, it would lead to widespread enmity and resistance.

We won't be able to develop the oil fields or the oil industry and therefore create worldwide co-operation as members of the human family when there is war, destruction and death.

Isn't it reasonable to question this approach and conclude that this road will not benefit anyone, including America or its people?

It may serve some short-term interests or the interests of some influential powers in the US but we can't claim that it serves the interest of the American people in the long run or other nations.

Benn: There are tens of millions, maybe hundreds of millions of people in Britain and America, in Europe and worldwide, who want to see a peaceful outcome to this problem, and they are the real Americans in my opinion, the real British, the real French, the real Germans, because they think of the world in terms of their children.

I have 10 grandchildren and in my family there is English, Scottish, American, French, Irish, Jewish, Indian, Muslim blood, and for me politics is about their future, their survival.

And I wonder whether you could say something yourself directly through this interview to the peace movement of the world that might help to advance the cause they have in mind?

Saddam: First of all we admire the development of the peace movement around the world in the last few years.

We pray to God to empower all those working against war and for the cause of peace and security based on just peace for all.

And through you we say to the British people that Iraqis do not hate the British people.

Before 1991 Iraq and Britain had a normal relationship as well as normal relations with America.

At that time the British government had no reason to criticise Iraq as we hear some voices doing these days.

We hope the British people would tell those who hate the Iraqis and wish them harm that there is no reason to justify this war and please tell them that I say to you because the British people are brave—tell them that the Iraqis are brave too.

Tell the British people if the Iraqis are subjected to aggression or humiliation they would fight bravely.

Just as the British people did in the Second World War and we will defend our country as they defended their country each in its own way.

The Iraqis don't wish war but if war is imposed upon them—if they are attacked and insulted—they will defend themselves. They will defend their country, their sovereignty and their security.

We will not disappoint those who believe in the principles of justice.

And we will uphold the principles of justice and right that we strongly believe in.

- **Source:** Tony Benn, interview with Saddam Hussein, BBC News, February 4, 2003, http://news.bbc.co.uk/2/hi/2726831.stm, accessed July 13, 2011.

- **Analysis:** In an interview with a British journalist a month before the invasion, Saddam Hussein denied charges that he possessed WMD and had close ties with al-Qaeda. Aware that public support in Britain was weak, he appealed to the British people over the heads of their leaders in hopes of getting them to demand that their country pull out of Operation Iraqi Freedom (OIF). Ironically, though his assertions were largely true, few who heard them believed the ruthless and deceptive dictator. Britain joined the United States and took responsibility for capturing and overseeing Basra.

- **Document 11: Excerpt of British Prime Minister Tony Blair, Speech on Iraq, British House of Commons**
- **When:** March 18, 2003
- **Where:** London, UK
- **Significance:** Blair made an emphatic argument that Parliament approve sending British forces to Iraq.

At the outset I say: it is right that this House debate this issue and pass judgement. That is the democracy that is our right but that others struggle for in vain.

And again I say: I do not disrespect the views of those in opposition to mine.

This is a tough choice. But it is also a stark one: to stand British troops down and turn back; or to hold firm to the course we have set.

I believe we must hold firm.

The question most often posed is not why does it matter? But: why does it matter so much? Here we are: the Government with its most serious test, its majority at risk, the first Cabinet resignation over an issue of policy. The main parties divided.

People who agree on everything else, disagree on this and likewise, those who never agree on anything, finding common cause.

The country and Parliament reflect each other: a debate that, as time has gone on has become less bitter but not less grave.

So: why does it matter so much?

Because the outcome of this issue will now determine more than the fate of the Iraqi regime and more than the future of the Iraqi people, for so long brutalised by Saddam. It will determine the way Britain and the world confront the central security threat of the 21st Century; the development of the UN; the relationship between Europe and the US; the relations within the EU and the way the US engages with the rest of the world.

It will determine the pattern of international politics for the next generation.

But first, Iraq and its WMD.

In April 1991, after the Gulf War Iraq was given 15 days to provide a full and final declaration of all its WMD.

Saddam had used the weapons against Iran, against his own people, causing thousands of deaths. He had had plans to use them against allied forces. It became clear after the Gulf War that the WMD ambitions of Iraq were far more extensive than hitherto thought. This issue was identified by the UN as one for urgent remedy. UNSCOM, the weapons inspection team, was set up. They were expected to complete their task following the declaration at the end of April 1991.

The declaration when it came was false—a blanket denial of the programme, other than in a very tentative form. So the 12 year game began.

The inspectors probed. Finally in March 1992, Iraq admitted it had previously undeclared WMD but said it had destroyed them.

It gave another full and final declaration.

Again the inspectors probed but found little.

In October 1994, Iraq stopped co-operating with UNSCOM altogether. Military action was threatened. Inspections resumed.

In March 1995, in an effort to rid Iraq of the inspectors, a further full and final declaration of WMD was made. By July 1995, Iraq was forced to admit that too was false.

In August they provided yet another full and final declaration.

Then, a week later, Saddam's son-in-law, Hussein Kamal defected to Jordan. He disclosed a far more extensive BW programme and for the first time said Iraq had weaponised the programme; something Saddam had always strenuously denied. All this had been happening whilst the inspectors were in Iraq. Kamal also revealed Iraq's crash programme to produce a nuclear weapon in 1990.

Iraq was forced then to release documents which showed just how extensive those programmes were.

In November 1995, Jordan intercepted prohibited components for missiles that could be used for WMD.

In June 1996, a further full and final declaration was made.

That too turned out to be false.

In June 1997, inspectors were barred from specific sites.

In September 1997, another full and final declaration was made. Also false. Meanwhile the inspectors discovered VX nerve agent production equipment, something always denied by the Iraqis.

In October 1997, the US and the UK threatened military action if Iraq refused to comply with the inspectors. But obstruction continued.

Finally, under threat of action, in February 1998, Kofi Annan went to Baghdad and negotiated a memorandum with Saddam to allow inspections to continue.

They did.

For a few months.

In August, co-operation was suspended.

In December the inspectors left. Their final report is a withering indictment of Saddam's lies, deception and obstruction, with large quantities of WMD remained unaccounted for.

The US and the UK then, in December 1998, undertook Desert Fox, a targeted bombing campaign to degrade as much of the Iraqi WMD facilities as we could.

In 1999, a new inspections team, UNMOVIC, was set up. But Saddam refused to allow them to enter Iraq.

So there they stayed, in limbo, until after Resolution 1441 when last November they were allowed to return.

What is the claim of Saddam today?

Why exactly the same claim as before: that he has no WMD.

Indeed we are asked to believe that after seven years of obstruction and non-compliance finally resulting in the inspectors leaving in 1998, seven years in which he hid his programme, built it up even whilst inspection teams were in Iraq, that after they left he then voluntarily decided to do what he had consistently refused to do under coercion.

When the inspectors left in 1998, they left unaccounted for:

- 10 thousand litres of anthrax
- a far reaching VX nerve agent programme
- up to 6,500 chemical munitions
- at least 80 tonnes of mustard gas, possibly more than ten times that amount
- unquantifiable amounts of sarin, botulinum toxin and a host of other biological poisons
- an entire Scud missile programme

We are now seriously asked to accept that in the last few years, contrary to all history, contrary to all intelligence, he decided unilaterally to destroy the weapons. Such a claim is palpably absurd.

1441 is a very clear Resolution. It lays down a final opportunity for Saddam to disarm. It rehearses the fact that he has been, for years in material breach of 17 separate UN Resolutions.

It says that this time compliance must be full, unconditional and immediate. The first step is a full and final declaration of all WMD to be given on 8 December.

I won't to go through all the events since then—the House is familiar with them—but this much is accepted by all members of the UNSC.

The 8 December declaration is false. That in itself is a material breach.

Iraq has made some concessions to co-operation but no-one disputes it is not fully co-operating.

Iraq continues to deny it has any WMD, though no serious intelligence service anywhere in the world believes them.

On 7 March, the inspectors published a remarkable document. It is 173 pages long, detailing all the unanswered questions about Iraq's WMD. It lists 29 different areas where they have been unable to obtain information. . . .

On this basis, had we meant what we said in Resolution 1441, the Security Council should have convened and condemned Iraq as in material breach.

What is perfectly clear is that Saddam is playing the same old games in the same old way. Yes there are concessions. But no fundamental change of heart or mind.

But the inspectors indicated there was at least some co-operation; and the world rightly hesitated over war. We therefore approached a second Resolution in this way.

We laid down an ultimatum calling upon Saddam to come into line with Resolution 1441 or be in material breach.

Not an unreasonable proposition, given the history.

But still countries hesitated: how do we know how to judge full co-operation?

We then worked on a further compromise. We consulted the inspectors and drew up five tests based on the document they published on 7 March. Tests like interviews with 30 scientists outside of Iraq, production of the anthrax or documentation showing its destruction.

The inspectors added another test: that Saddam should publicly call on Iraqis to co-operate with them.

So we constructed this framework: that Saddam should be given a specified time to fulfil all six tests to show full co-operation; that if he did so the inspectors could then set out a forward work programme and that if he failed to do so, action would follow.

So clear benchmarks; plus a clear ultimatum.

I defy anyone to describe that as an unreasonable position.

Last Monday, we were getting somewhere with it. We very nearly had majority agreement and I thank the Chilean President particularly for the constructive way he approached the issue.

There were debates about the length of the ultimatum. But the basic construct was gathering support.

Then, on Monday night, France said it would veto a second Resolution whatever the circumstances.

Then France denounced the six tests. Later that day, Iraq rejected them.

Still, we continued to negotiate.

Last Friday, France said they could not accept any ultimatum. On Monday, we made final efforts to secure agreement. But they remain utterly opposed to anything which lays down an ultimatum authorising action in the event of non-compliance by Saddam.

Just consider the position we are asked to adopt. Those on the Security Council opposed to us say they want Saddam to disarm but will not countenance any new Resolution that authorises force in the event of non-compliance.

That is their position. No to any ultimatum; no to any Resolution that stipulates that failure to comply will lead to military action.

So we must demand he disarm but relinquish any concept of a threat if he doesn't. From December 1998 to December 2002, no UN inspector was allowed to inspect anything in Iraq. For four years, not a thing. What changed his mind? The threat of force. From December to January and then from January through to February, concessions were made. What changed his mind?

The threat of force.

And what makes him now issue invitations to the inspectors, discover documents he said he never had, produce evidence of weapons supposed to be non-existent, destroy missiles he said he would keep? The imminence of force.

The only persuasive power to which he responds is 250,000 allied troops on his doorstep.

And yet when that fact is so obvious that it is staring us in the face, we are told that any Resolution that authorises force will be vetoed.

Not just opposed. Vetoed. Blocked.

The way ahead was so clear. It was for the UN to pass a second Resolution setting out benchmarks for compliance; with an ultimatum that if they were ignored, action would follow.

The tragedy is that had such a Resolution been issued, he might just have complied. Because the only route to peace with someone like Saddam Hussein is diplomacy backed by force.

Yet the moment we proposed the benchmarks, canvassed support for an ultimatum, there was an immediate recourse to the language of the veto.

And now the world has to learn the lesson all over again that weakness in the face of a threat from a tyrant, is the surest way not to peace but to war.

Looking back over 12 years, we have been victims of our own desire to placate the implacable, to persuade towards reason the utterly unreasonable, to hope that there was some genuine intent to do good in a regime whose mind is in fact evil. Now the very length of time counts against us. You've waited 12 years. Why not wait a little longer?

And indeed we have.

1441 gave a final opportunity. The first test was the 8th of December. He failed it.

But still we waited. Until the 27th of January, the first inspection report that showed the absence of full co-operation. Another breach. And still we waited.

Until the 14th of February and then the 28th of February with concessions, according to the old familiar routine, tossed to us to whet our appetite for hope and further waiting. But still no-one, not the inspectors nor any member of the Security Council, not any half-way rational observer, believes Saddam is co-operating fully or unconditionally or immediately.

Our fault has not been impatience.

The truth is our patience should have been exhausted weeks and months and years ago. Even now, when if the world united and gave him an ultimatum: comply or face forcible disarmament, he might just do it, the world hesitates and in that hesitation he senses the weakness and therefore continues to defy.

What would any tyrannical regime possessing WMD think viewing the history of the world's diplomatic dance with Saddam? That our capacity to pass firm resolutions is only matched by our feebleness in implementing them.

That is why this indulgence has to stop. Because it is dangerous. It is dangerous if such regimes disbelieve us. Dangerous if they think they can use our weakness, our hesitation, even the natural urges of our democracy towards peace, against us. Dangerous because one day they will mistake our innate revulsion against war for permanent incapacity; when in fact, pushed to the limit, we will act. But then when we act, after years of pretence, the action will have to be harder, bigger, more total in its impact. Iraq is not the only regime with WMD. But back away now from this confrontation and future conflicts will be infinitely worse and more devastating.

But, of course, in a sense, any fair observer does not really dispute that Iraq is in breach and that 1441 implies action in such circumstances. The real problem is that, underneath, people dispute that Iraq is a threat; dispute the link between terrorism and WMD; dispute the whole basis of our assertion that the two together constitute a fundamental assault on our way of life.

There are glib and sometimes foolish comparisons with the 1930s. No-one here is an appeaser. But the only relevant point of analogy is that with history, we know what happened. We can look back and say: there's the time; that was the moment; for example, when Czechoslovakia was swallowed up by the Nazis—that's when we should have acted.

But it wasn't clear at the time. In fact at the time, many people thought such a fear fanciful. Worse, put forward in bad faith by warmongers. Listen to this editorial—from a paper I'm pleased to say with a different position today—but written in late 1938 after Munich when by now, you would have thought the world was tumultuous in its desire to act.

"Be glad in your hearts. Give thanks to your God. People of Britain, your children are safe. Your husbands and your sons will not march to war. Peace is a victory for all mankind. And now let us go back to our own affairs. We have had enough of those menaces, conjured up from the Continent to confuse us."

Naturally should Hitler appear again in the same form, we would know what to do. But the point is that history doesn't declare the future to us so plainly. Each time is different and the present must be judged without the benefit of hindsight.

So let me explain the nature of this threat as I see it.

The threat today is not that of the 1930s. It's not big powers going to war with each other.

The ravages which fundamentalist political ideology inflicted on the 20th century are memories.

The Cold War is over.

Europe is at peace, if not always diplomatically.

But the world is ever more interdependent. Stock markets and economies rise and fall together.

Confidence is the key to prosperity.

Insecurity spreads like contagion.

So people crave stability and order.

The threat is chaos.

And there are two begetters of chaos.

Tyrannical regimes with WMD and extreme terrorist groups who profess a perverted and false view of Islam.

Let me tell the House what I know.

I know that there are some countries or groups within countries that are proliferating and trading in WMD, especially nuclear weapons technology.

I know there are companies, individuals, some former scientists on nuclear weapons programmes, selling their equipment or expertise.

I know there are several countries—mostly dictatorships with highly repressive regimes—desperately trying to acquire chemical weapons, biological weapons or, in particular, nuclear weapons capability. Some of these countries are now a short time away from having a serviceable nuclear weapon. This activity is not diminishing. It is increasing.

We all know that there are terrorist cells now operating in most major countries. Just as in the last two years, around 20 different nations have suffered serious terrorist outrages. Thousands have died in them.

The purpose of terrorism lies not just in the violent act itself. It is in producing terror. It sets out to inflame, to divide, to produce consequences which they then use to justify further terror.

Round the world it now poisons the chances of political progress: in the Middle East; in Kashmir; in Chechnya; in Africa.

The removal of the Taliban in Afghanistan dealt it a blow. But it has not gone away.

And these two threats have different motives and different origins but they share one basic common view: they detest the freedom, democracy and tolerance that are the hallmarks of our way of life.

At the moment, I accept that association between them is loose. But it is hardening.

And the possibility of the two coming together—of terrorist groups in possession of WMD, even of a so-called dirty radiological bomb is now, in my judgement, a real and present danger.

And let us recall: what was shocking about 11 September was not just the slaughter of the innocent; but the knowledge that had the terrorists been able to, there would have been not 3,000 innocent dead, but 30,000 or 300,000 and the more the suffering, the greater the terrorists' rejoicing.

3 kilograms of VX from a rocket launcher would contaminate a quarter of a square kilometre of a city.

Millions of lethal doses are contained in one litre of Anthrax. 10,000 litres are unaccounted for.

11 September has changed the psychology of America. It should have changed the psychology of the world.

Of course Iraq is not the only part of this threat. But it is the test of whether we treat the threat seriously.

Faced with it, the world should unite. The UN should be the focus, both of diplomacy and of action. That is what 1441 said. That was the deal. And I say to you to break it now, to will the ends but not the means that would do more damage in the long term to the UN than any other course.

To fall back into the lassitude of the last 12 years, to talk, to discuss, to debate but never act; to declare our will but not enforce it; to combine strong language with weak intentions, a worse outcome than never speaking at all.

And then, when the threat returns from Iraq or elsewhere, who will believe us? What price our credibility with the next tyrant? No wonder Japan and South Korea, next to North Korea, has issued such strong statements of support.

I have come to the conclusion after much reluctance that the greater danger to the UN is inaction: that to pass Resolution 1441 and then refuse to enforce it would do the most deadly damage to the UN's future strength, confirming it as an instrument of diplomacy but not of action, forcing nations down the very unilateralist path we wish to avoid.

But there will be, in any event, no sound future for the UN, no guarantee against the repetition of these events, unless we recognise the urgent need for a political agenda we can unite upon.

What we have witnessed is indeed the consequence of Europe and the United States dividing from each other. Not all of Europe—Spain, Italy, Holland,

Denmark, Portugal—have all strongly supported us. And not a majority of Europe if we include, as we should, Europe's new members who will accede next year, all 10 of whom have been in our support.

But the paralysis of the UN has been born out of the division there is. And at the heart of it has been the concept of a world in which there are rival poles of power. The US and its allies in one corner. France, Germany, Russia and its allies in the other. I do not believe that all of these nations intend such an outcome. But that is what now faces us.

I believe such a vision to be misguided and profoundly dangerous. I know why it arises. There is resentment of US predominance. There is fear of US unilateralism. People ask: do the US listen to us and our preoccupations? And there is perhaps a lack of full understanding of US preoccupations after 11th September. I know all of this.

But the way to deal with it is not rivalry but partnership. Partners are not servants but neither are they rivals. I tell you what Europe should have said last September to the US. With one voice it should have said: we understand your strategic anxiety over terrorism and WMD and we will help you meet it. We will mean what we say in any UN Resolution we pass and will back it with action if Saddam fails to disarm voluntarily; but in return we ask two things of you: that the US should choose the UN path and you should recognise the fundamental overriding importance of re-starting the MEPP, which we will hold you to.

I do not believe there is any other issue with the same power to re-unite the world community than progress on the issues of Israel and Palestine. Of course there is cynicism about recent announcements. But the US is now committed, and, I believe genuinely, to the Roadmap for peace, designed in consultation with the UN. It will now be presented to the parties as Abu Mazen is confirmed in office, hopefully today.

All of us are now signed up to its vision: a state of Israel, recognised and accepted by all the world, and a viable Palestinian state.

And that should be part of a larger global agenda. On poverty and sustainable development. On democracy and human rights. On the good governance of nations.

That is why what happens after any conflict in Iraq is of such critical significance.

Here again there is a chance to unify around the UN. Let me make it clear.

There should be a new UN Resolution following any conflict providing not just for humanitarian help but also for the administration and governance of Iraq. That must now be done under proper UN authorisation.

It should protect totally the territorial integrity of Iraq.

And let the oil revenues—which people falsely claim we want to seize—be put in a Trust fund for the Iraqi people administered through the UN.

And let the future government of Iraq be given the chance to begin the process of uniting the nation's disparate groups, on a democratic basis, respecting human rights, as indeed the fledgling democracy in Northern Iraq—protected from Saddam for 12 years by British and American pilots in the No Fly Zone—has done so remarkably.

And the moment that a new government is in place—willing to disarm Iraq of WMD—for which its people have no need or purpose—then let sanctions be lifted in their entirety.

I have never put our justification for action as regime change. We have to act within the terms set out in Resolution 1441. That is our legal base.

But it is the reason, I say frankly, why if we do act we should do so with a clear conscience and strong heart.

I accept fully that those opposed to this course of action share my detestation of Saddam. Who could not? Iraq is a wealthy country that in 1978, the year before Saddam seized power, was richer than Portugal or Malaysia.

Today it is impoverished, 60% of its population dependent on Food Aid.

Thousands of children die needlessly every year from lack of food and medicine.

Four million people out of a population of just over 20 million are in exile.

The brutality of the repression—the death and torture camps, the barbaric prisons for political opponents, the routine beatings for anyone or their families suspected of disloyalty are well documented.

Just last week, someone slandering Saddam was tied to a lamp post in a street in Baghdad, his tongue cut out, mutilated and left to bleed to death, as a warning to others.

I recall a few weeks ago talking to an Iraqi exile and saying to her that I understood how grim it must be under the lash of Saddam.

"But you don't", she replied. "You cannot. You do not know what it is like to live in perpetual fear." And she is right. We take our freedom for granted. But imagine not to be able to speak or discuss or debate or even question the society you live in. To see friends and family taken away and never daring to complain. To suffer the humility of failing courage in face of pitiless terror. That is how the Iraqi people live. Leave Saddam in place and that is how they will continue to live.

We must face the consequences of the actions we advocate. For me, that means all the dangers of war. But for others, opposed to this course, it means—let us be clear—that the Iraqi people, whose only true hope of liberation lies in the removal of Saddam, for them, the darkness will close back over them again; and he will be free to take his revenge upon those he must know wish him gone.

And if this House now demands that at this moment, faced with this threat from this regime, that British troops are pulled back, that we turn away at the point of reckoning, and that is what it means—what then?

What will Saddam feel? Strengthened beyond measure. What will the other states who tyrannise their people, the terrorists who threaten our existence, what will they take from that? That the will confronting them is decaying and feeble.

Who will celebrate and who will weep?

And if our plea is for America to work with others, to be good as well as powerful allies, will our retreat make them multilateralist? Or will it not rather be the biggest impulse to unilateralism there could ever be. And what of the UN and the future of Iraq and the MEPP, devoid of our influence, stripped of our insistence?

This House wanted this decision. Well it has it. Those are the choices. And in this dilemma, no choice is perfect, no cause ideal.

But on this decision hangs the fate of many things.

I can think of many things, of whether we summon the strength to recognise the global challenge of the 21st century and beat it, of the Iraqi people groaning under years of dictatorship, of our armed forces—brave men and women of whom we can feel proud, whose morale is high and whose purpose is clear—of the institutions and alliances that shape our world for years to come.

To retreat now, I believe, would put at hazard all that we hold dearest, turn the United Nations back into a talking shop, stifle the first steps of progress in the Middle East; leave the Iraqi people to the mercy of events on which we would have relinquished all power to influence for the better.

Tell our allies that at the very moment of action, at the very moment when they need our determination that Britain faltered. I will not be party to such a course. This is not the time to falter. This is the time for this House, not just this government or indeed this Prime Minister, but for this House to give a lead, to show that we will stand up for what we know to be right, to show that we will confront the tyrannies and dictatorships and terrorists who put our way of life at risk, to show at the moment of decision that we have the courage to do the right thing. I beg to move the motion.

- **Source:** Tony Blair, "PM Statement Opening Iraq Debate in Parliament," Number10.gov.uk, available at http://www.guardian.co.uk/politics/2003/mar/18/foreignpolicy.iraq1.

- **Analysis:** The United Kingdom has long been the United States' closest NATO ally. It realized that keeping NATO an Atlantic alliance meant preserving its Washington-London axis. If it should be become a European defense force, that axis would shift to Paris-Berlin. Successive British governments have thus supported U.S. policy even when their publics did not.

  In arguing for war with Iraq, Blair trotted out the same arguments advanced by the Bush administration. Iraq possessed or was developing WMD that could be supplied to terrorist organizations. He had flouted UN resolutions and thwarted the work of weapons inspectors even while allowing them into Iraq. The dictator was unreliable and untrustworthy. Finally, Iraq's people suffered under his regime. Parliament supported Blair's call for war.

- **Document 12: President Bush's Address to the Nation at the Start of Hostilities**
- **When:** March 19, 2003
- **Where:** The White House, Washington, DC
- **Significance:** The president addressed the nation to announce the start of hostilities against Iraq.

My fellow citizens, at this hour, American and coalition forces are in the early stages of military operations to disarm Iraq, to free its people and to defend the world from grave danger.

On my orders, coalition forces have begun striking selected targets of military importance to undermine Saddam Hussein's ability to wage war. These are opening stages of what will be a broad and concerted campaign. More than 35 countries are giving crucial support—from the use of naval and air bases, to help with intelligence and logistics, to the deployment of combat units. Every nation in this coalition has chosen to bear the duty and share the honor of serving in our common defense.

To all the men and women of the United States Armed Forces now in the Middle East, the peace of a troubled world and the hopes of an oppressed people now depend on you. That trust is well placed.

The enemies you confront will come to know your skill and bravery. The people you liberate will witness the honorable and decent spirit of the American military. In this conflict, America faces an enemy who has no regard for conventions of war or rules of morality. Saddam Hussein has placed Iraqi troops and equipment in civilian areas, attempting to use innocent men, women and children as shields for his own military—a final atrocity against his people.

I want Americans and all the world to know that coalition forces will make every effort to spare innocent civilians from harm. A campaign on the harsh terrain of a nation as large as California could be longer and more difficult than some predict. And helping Iraqis achieve a united, stable and free country will require our sustained commitment.

We come to Iraq with respect for its citizens, for their great civilization and for the religious faiths they practice. We have no ambition in Iraq, except to remove a threat and restore control of that country to its own people.

I know that the families of our military are praying that all those who serve will return safely and soon. Millions of Americans are praying with you for the safety of your loved ones and for the protection of the innocent. For your sacrifice, you have the gratitude and respect of the American people. And you can know that our forces will be coming home as soon as their work is done.

Our nation enters this conflict reluctantly—yet, our purpose is sure. The people of the United States and our friends and allies will not live at the mercy of an outlaw regime that threatens the peace with weapons of mass murder. We will meet that threat now, with our Army, Air Force, Navy, Coast Guard and Marines, so that we do not have to meet it later with armies of fire fighters and police and doctors on the streets of our cities.

Now that conflict has come, the only way to limit its duration is to apply decisive force. And I assure you, this will not be a campaign of half measures, and we will accept no outcome but victory.

My fellow citizens, the dangers to our country and the world will be overcome. We will pass through this time of peril and carry on the work of peace. We will defend our freedom. We will bring freedom to others and we will prevail.

May God bless our country and all who defend her.

- **Source:** George Bush, "Address to the Nation," March 19, 2003, available at http://georgewbush-whitehouse.archives.gov/news/releases/ 2003/03/20030319-17.html, accessed March 19, 2012.

- **Analysis:** In this speech justification for the war had shifted dramatically. The administration had initially argued that Saddam Hussein's WMD programs and his alleged ties to terrorist organizations posed an immediate threat to U.S. security that must be removed. These arguments had, however, been effectively challenged. In this speech he shifted his emphasis to liberating the Iraqi people from the tyranny of Saddam Hussein, a goal reflected in the name of the mission, "Operation Iraqi Freedom." This final justification came closest to a core reason for the invasion. President Bush and the neocons who supported him saw Iraq as the hub of a new Middle East. A regime in Baghdad loyal to Washington would counterbalance Iran, cease to threaten Israel, provide another secure source of oil, and serve as a shining example of the efficacy of American democracy for the entire region.

- **Document 13: Downing Street Memo**
- **When:** July 23, 2002
- **Where:** London, UK
- **Significance:** This external source supports the conclusion that the determination to invade Iraq predated 9/11.

SECRET AND STRICTLY PERSONAL - UK EYES ONLY
DAVID MANNING

From: Matthew Rycroft
Date: 23 July 2002
S 195 /02
cc: Defence Secretary, Foreign Secretary, Attorney-General, Sir Richard Wilson, John Scarlett, Francis Richards, CDS, C, Jonathan Powell, Sally Morgan, Alastair Campbell

IRAQ: PRIME MINISTER'S MEETING, 23 JULY

Copy addressees and you met the Prime Minister on 23 July to discuss Iraq. This record is extremely sensitive. No further copies should be made. It should be shown only to those with a genuine need to know its contents.

John Scarlett summarised the intelligence and latest JIC assessment. Saddam's regime was tough and based on extreme fear. The only way to overthrow it was likely to be by massive military action. Saddam was worried and expected an attack, probably by air and land, but he was not convinced that it would be immediate or overwhelming. His regime expected their neighbours to line up with the US. Saddam knew that regular army morale was poor. Real support for Saddam among the public was probably narrowly based.

C reported on his recent talks in Washington. There was a perceptible shift in attitude. Military action was now seen as inevitable. Bush wanted to remove

Saddam, through military action, justified by the conjunction of terrorism and WMD. But the intelligence and facts were being fixed around the policy. The NSC had no patience with the UN route, and no enthusiasm for publishing material on the Iraqi regime's record. There was little discussion in Washington of the aftermath after military action.

CDS said that military planners would brief CENTCOM on 1–2 August, Rumsfeld on 3 August and Bush on 4 August.

The two broad US options were:

(a) Generated Start. A slow build-up of 250,000 US troops, a short (72 hour) air campaign, then a move up to Baghdad from the south. Lead time of 90 days (30 days preparation plus 60 days deployment to Kuwait).

(b) Running Start. Use forces already in theatre (3 x 6,000), continuous air campaign, initiated by an Iraqi casus belli. Total lead time of 60 days with the air campaign beginning even earlier. A hazardous option.

The US saw the UK (and Kuwait) as essential, with basing in Diego Garcia and Cyprus critical for either option. Turkey and other Gulf states were also important, but less vital. The three main options for UK involvement were:

(i) Basing in Diego Garcia and Cyprus, plus three SF squadrons.

(ii) As above, with maritime and air assets in addition.

(iii) As above, plus a land contribution of up to 40,000, perhaps with a discrete role in Northern Iraq entering from Turkey, tying down two Iraqi divisions.

The Defence Secretary said that the US had already begun "spikes of activity" to put pressure on the regime. No decisions had been taken, but he thought the most likely timing in US minds for military action to begin was January, with the timeline beginning 30 days before the US Congressional elections.

The Foreign Secretary said he would discuss this with Colin Powell this week. It seemed clear that Bush had made up his mind to take military action, even if the timing was not yet decided. But the case was thin. Saddam was not threatening his neighbours, and his WMD capability was less than that of Libya, North Korea or Iran. We should work up a plan for an ultimatum to Saddam to allow back in the UN weapons inspectors. This would also help with the legal justification for the use of force.

The Attorney-General said that the desire for regime change was not a legal base for military action. There were three possible legal bases: self-defence, humanitarian intervention, or UNSC authorisation. The first and second could not be the base in this case. Relying on UNSCR 1205 of three years ago would be difficult. The situation might of course change.

The Prime Minister said that it would make a big difference politically and legally if Saddam refused to allow in the UN inspectors. Regime change and WMD were linked in the sense that it was the regime that was producing the WMD. There were different strategies for dealing with Libya and Iran. If the political context were right, people would support regime change. The two key issues were whether the military plan worked and whether we had the political strategy to give the military plan the space to work.

On the first, CDS said that we did not know yet if the US battleplan was workable. The military were continuing to ask lots of questions. For instance, what were the consequences, if Saddam used WMD on day one, or if Baghdad did not collapse and urban warfighting began? You said that Saddam could also use his WMD on Kuwait. Or on Israel, added the Defence Secretary.

The Foreign Secretary thought the US would not go ahead with a military plan unless convinced that it was a winning strategy. On this, US and UK interests converged. But on the political strategy, there could be US/UK differences. Despite US resistance, we should explore discreetly the ultimatum. Saddam would continue to play hard-ball with the UN.

John Scarlett assessed that Saddam would allow the inspectors back in only when he thought the threat of military action was real.

The Defence Secretary said that if the Prime Minister wanted UK military involvement, he would need to decide this early. He cautioned that many in the US did not think it worth going down the ultimatum route. It would be important for the Prime Minister to set out the political context to Bush.

Conclusions:

(a) We should work on the assumption that the UK would take part in any military action. But we needed a fuller picture of US planning before we could take any firm decisions. CDS should tell the US military that we were considering a range of options.

(b) The Prime Minister would revert on the question of whether funds could be spent in preparation for this operation.

(c) CDS would send the Prime Minister full details of the proposed military campaign and possible UK contributions by the end of the week.

(d) The Foreign Secretary would send the Prime Minister the background on the UN inspectors, and discreetly work up the ultimatum to Saddam.

He would also send the Prime Minister advice on the positions of countries in the region especially Turkey, and of the key EU member states.

(e) John Scarlett would send the Prime Minister a full intelligence update.

(f) We must not ignore the legal issues: the Attorney-General would consider legal advice with FCO/MOD legal advisers . . .

MATTHEW RYCROFT

- **Source:** Memo from Matthew Rycroft to David Manning, July 23, 2002, available at http://www.pbs.org/newshour/bb/middle_east/jan -june05/memo_6-16.html, accessed December 1, 2011.

- **Analysis:** The United Kingdom, the United States' closest ally, determined to support it against Iraq. In the spring of 2005, this memo was leaked to the *London Times*. Written by a Downing Street foreign policy aide, the memo suggests that the Bush administration had decided upon war with Iraq long before weapons inspectors even returned to Iraq. Tony Blair is the prime minister referred to in the memo.

  The document maintains that that Bush administration was "shopping" intelligence, picking reports that supported the administration's contention that Saddam Hussein had WMD. The memo also reveals that, based on British sources, Iraq's WMD program lagged behind that of Libya, North Korea, and Iran. The British clearly believed that the arguments made for the necessity of war were in fact rationalizations. It also concluded that preparations for war had begun months before Congress was asked to approve the operation.

THE NUCLEAR WEAPONS DEBATE

The administration's case for invading Iraq rested heavily on allegations that Saddam Hussein had or was acquiring WMD, which he might use himself or provide to a terrorist group. Iraq's nuclear capability caused the greatest concern. On April 3, 1991, the UN Security Council passed Resolution 687 setting conditions for a cease-fire in the Gulf War. The resolution required Iraq to refrain from acquiring nuclear weapons technology and charged the International Atomic Energy Agency (IAEA) with dismantling and destroying its program and monitoring compliance with the UN resolution. Iraq halted inspections in 1998. An agreement reached on October 1, 2002, reinstated inspections, which began the following month. On November 8, 2002, the UN Security Council passed Resolution 1441, formally reestablishing the inspection regime by the IAEA. The resolution refers to previous resolutions and details Hussein's refusal to comply with the terms of the original agreement on inspection before reinstating the process.

- **Document 14: Excerpt of Report of the Iraq Verification Mission Activities**
- **When:** January 8, 2003
- **Where:** Vienna, Austria
- **Significance:** This report found no evidence that the Iraqi regime was engaging in prohibited nuclear activity.

14. At this stage, the IAEA is able to report the following progress:
    a. Through access to buildings identified, through satellite imagery, as having been modified or constructed during the period 1998-2002, the IAEA has been able to clarify the nature of activities currently being conducted at such buildings.
    b. Although not complete, significant progress has been made in the verification of Iraq's explanations regarding its attempts to procure high-strength aluminium tubes.
    c. Steps have been taken to clarify the disposition of the HMX that had been subject to verification prior to 1998.

15. To date, no new information of significance has emerged regarding Iraq's past nuclear programme (pre-1991) or with regard to Iraq activities during the period between 1991 and 1998.

16. To date, no evidence of ongoing prohibited nuclear or nuclear-related activities has been detected, although not all of the laboratory results of sample analysis are yet available. It should be noted that IAEA's verification activities serve not only as a mechanism for verifying that Iraq is not currently carrying out any proscribed activities, but equally as an important deterrent to the resumption of such activities by Iraq.

17. The IAEA will endeavour to provide the Security Council as early as possible with credible assurance of the absence of prohibited nuclear and nuclear-related activities in Iraq, but there still remains a significant amount of work to do. While it has been possible to accumulate significant information through field activities, an important part of that information will require additional follow-up before the IAEA is able to draw definitive conclusions.

18. The IAEA's efforts to draw such conclusions will be greatly facilitated by the active cooperation of Iraq, not only in continuing to secure access to locations, but, importantly, in providing documentation, making available Iraqi personnel for interview and encouraging them to accept IAEA modalities for such interviews, and providing the IAEA with any physical evidence which would assist it in reaching its conclusions. To this end, I intend to visit Iraq with the Executive Chairman of UNMOVIC in the third week of this month to discuss with the Iraqi authorities outstanding issues and to impress on them, once more, the importance of their active co-operation.

19. As requested in paragraph 5 of resolution 1441 (2002), IAEA activities and achievements in Iraq during the two months of inspection since 27 November 2002 will be described in greater detail in an update report to the Council to be available by 27 January.

- **Source:** Mohamed ElBaradei, "Status of the Agency's Verification Activities in Iraq as of 8 January 2003," available at http://www.iaea. org/newscenter/statements/2003/ebsp2003n002.shtml, accessed December 1, 2011.

- **Analysis:** The director general reported on the work of the verification mission. The report noted that inspectors found no new evidence of prohibited nuclear activity, although it acknowledged that it did not have full access to all Iraqi facilities. The report called into question the conclusion drawn by the Bush administration. The aluminum tubes referred to were purported by the administration to be for refining uranium, a conclusion that this report and other evidence refutes. While Saddam cooperated to a limited degree with the verification, his failure to co-operate fully provided a plausible argument that he had something to hide. It thus became much easier to argue that Hussein was hoodwinking the inspectors, hiding and/or moving his WMD program so that they could not find it.

- **Document 15: Excerpt of Statement to the Fifty-Eighth Regular Session of the United Nations General Assembly by IAEA Director General Dr. Mohamed ElBaradei**
- **When:** March 2003
- **Where:** New York City
- **Significance:** This report reiterated the conclusion of previous reports that the inspectors had found no evidence of renewed illegal nuclear activity.

Implementation of United Nations Security Council Resolutions Relating to Iraq

After an interruption of nearly four years, last November the Agency resumed verification activities in Iraq under the mandate provided by UN Security Council Resolution 687 and related resolutions. Between November 2002 and March 2003, the Agency sought to determine what, if anything, had changed in Iraq over the previous four years relevant to Iraq's nuclear activities and capabilities.

At the time the Agency ceased its Security Council verification activities in Iraq, we had found no evidence of the revival of nuclear activities prohibited under relevant Security Council resolutions. However, considering our four-year absence, the time available for the renewed inspections was not sufficient for the Agency to complete its overall review and assessment.

The Agency's mandate in Iraq under various Security Council resolutions still stands. In May, the Security Council adopted resolution 1483 in which, inter alia, it expressed its intention to revisit the mandates of the IAEA and the United Nations Monitoring, Verification and Inspection Commission (UNMOVIC). We are awaiting the results of that review and further guidance from the Council. Given the situation in Iraq, I believe it would be prudent for the UN and IAEA inspectors to return to Iraq, to bring the weapons file to a closure—and, through implementation of a Security Council approved plan for long term monitoring, to provide ongoing assurance that activities related to weapons of mass destruction have not been resumed. In the meantime, I trust that the Agency will be kept informed of the outcome of any current inspection activities in Iraq relevant to our mandate, in accordance with Security Council resolution 1441.

- **Source:** Mohamed ElBaradei, "Statement to the Fifty-Eighth Regular Session of the United Nations General Assembly," available at http://www.iaea.org/newscenter/statements/2003/ebsp2003n023.html.
- **Analysis:** The invasion of Iraq brought the verification mission to an end. At the time of this report, however, the mission reiterated the conclusion of the previous one. The inspectors found no evidence of prohibited nuclear activity in Iraq. However, as the Downing Street

memo (**Document 8**) makes clear, the administration had little regard for the United Nations. It considered the organization's approval desirable but not crucial. It could also discredit the report by noting that the inspectors had not had unlimited access to Iraqi facilities.

- **Document 16: Excerpt of *Report on the U.S. Intelligence Community's Prewar Intelligence Assessment on Iraq***
- **When:** July 7, 2004
- **Where:** Washington
- **Significance:** The Senate Select Committee on Intelligence debunked many prewar claims about the state of Iraq's WMD program.

Niger Conclusions

(U) Conclusion 12. Until October 2002 when the Intelligence Community obtained the forged foreign language documents on the Iraq-Niger uranium deal, it was reasonable for analysts to assess that Iraq may have been seeking uranium from Africa based on Central Intelligence Agency (CIA) reporting and other available intelligence. . . .

(U) Conclusion 13. The report on the former ambassador's trip to Niger, disseminated in March 2002, did not change any analysts' assessments of the Iraq-Niger uranium deal. For most analysts, the information in the report lent more credibility to the original Central Intelligence Agency (CIA) reports on the uranium deal, but State Department Bureau of Intelligence and Research (INR) analysts believed that the report supported their assessment that Niger was unlikely to be willing or able to sell uranium to Iraq . . .

(U) Conclusion 14. The Central Intelligence Agency should have told the Vice President and other senior policymakers that it had sent someone to Niger to look into the alleged Iraq-Niger uranium deal and should have briefed the Vice President on the former ambassador's findings. . . .

(U) Conclusion 15. The Central Intelligence Agency's (CIA) Directorate of Operations should have taken precautions not to discuss the credibility of reporting with a potential source when it arranged a meeting with the former ambassador and Intelligence Community analysts. . . .

(U) Conclusion 16. The language in the October 2002 National Intelligence Estimate that "Iraq also began vigorously trying to procure uranium ore and yellowcake" overstated what the Intelligence Community knew about Iraq's possible procurement attempts. . . .

(U) Conclusion 17. The State Department's Bureau of Intelligence and Research (INR) dissent on the uranium reporting was accidentally included in the aluminum tube section of the National Intelligence Estimate (NIE), due in part to the speed with which the NIE was drafted and coordinated. . . .

(U) Conclusion 18. When documents regarding the Iraq-Niger uranium reporting became available to the Intelligence Community in October 2002, Central

Intelligence Agency (CIA) analysts and operations officers should have made an effort to obtain copies. As a result of not obtaining the documents, CIA Iraq nuclear analysts continued to report on Iraqi efforts to procure uranium from Africa and continued to approve the use of such language in Administration publications and speeches. . . .

(U) Conclusion 19. Even after obtaining the forged documents and being alerted by a State Department Bureau of Intelligence and Research (INR) analyst about problems with them, analysts at both the Central Intelligence Agency (CIA) and Defense Intelligence Agency (DIA) did not examine them carefully enough to see the obvious problems with the documents. Both agencies continued to publish assessments that Iraq may have been seeking uranium from Africa. In addition, CIA continued to approve the use of similar language in Administration publications and speeches, including the State of the Union. . . .

(U) Conclusion 20. The Central Intelligence Agency's (CIA) comments and assessments about the Iraq-Niger uranium reporting were inconsistent and, at times contradictory. These inconsistencies were based in part on a misunderstanding of a CIA Weapons Intelligence, Nonproliferation, and Arms Control Center (WINPAC) Iraq analyst's assessment of the reporting. The CIA should have had a mechanism in place to ensure that agency assessments and information passed to policymakers were consistent. . . .

(U) Conclusion 21. When coordinating the State of the Union, no Central Intelligence Agency (CIA) analysts or officials told the National Security Council (NSC) to remove the "16 words" or that there were concerns about the credibility of the Iraq-Niger uranium reporting. A CIA official's original testimony to the Committee that he told an NSC official to remove the words "Niger" and "500 tons" from the speech, is incorrect. . . .

(U) Conclusion 22. The Director of Central Intelligence (DCI) should have taken the time to read the State of the Union speech and fact check it himself. Had he done so, he would have been able to alert the National Security Council (NSC) if he still had concerns about the use of the Iraq-Niger uranium reporting in a Presidential speech. . . .

(U) Conclusion 23. The Central Intelligence Agency (CIA), Defense Hum[an]int [intelligence] Service (DHS), or the Navy should have followed up with a West African businessman, mentioned in a Navy report, who indicated he was willing to provide information about an alleged uranium transaction between Niger and Iraq in November 2002. . . .

(U) Conclusion 24. In responding to a letter from Senator Carl Levin on behalf of the Intelligence Community in February 2003, the Central Intelligence Agency (CIA) should not have said that "DELETED of reporting suggest Iraq had attempted to acquire uranium from Niger," without indicating that State Department's Bureau of Intelligence and Research (INR) believed the reporting was based on forged documents, or that the CIA was reviewing the Niger reporting. . . .

(U) Conclusion 25. The Niger reporting was never in any of the drafts of Secretary Powell's United Nations (UN) speech and the Committee has not uncovered any information that showed anyone tried to insert the information into the speech. . . .

(U) Conclusion 26. To date, the Intelligence Community has not published an assessment to clarify or correct its position on whether or not Iraq was trying to purchase uranium from Africa as stated in the National Intelligence Estimate (NIE). Likewise, neither the Central Intelligence Agency (CIA) nor the Defense Intelligence Agency (DIA), which both published assessments on possible Iraqi efforts to acquire uranium, have ever published assessments outside of their agencies which correct their previous positions. . . .

G. Nuclear Conclusions

(U) Conclusion 27. After reviewing all of the intelligence provided by the Intelligence Community and additional information requested by the Committee, the Committee believes that the judgment in the National Intelligence Estimate (NIE), that Iraq was reconstituting its nuclear program, was not supported by the intelligence. The Committee agrees with the State Department's Bureau of Intelligence and Research (INR) alternative view that the available intelligence "does not add up to a compelling case for reconstitution." . . .

(U) Conclusion 28. The assessments in the National Intelligence Estimate (NIE) regarding the timing of when Iraq had begun reconstituting its nuclear program are unclear and confusing. . . .

(U) Conclusion 29. Numerous intelligence reports provided to the Committee showed that Iraq was trying to procure high-strength aluminum tubes. The Committee believes that the information available to the Intelligence Community indicated that these tubes were intended to be used for an Iraqi conventional rocket program and not a nuclear program. . . .

(U) Conclusion 30. The Central Intelligence Agency's (CIA) intelligence assessment on July 2, 2001 that the dimensions of the aluminum tubes "match those of a publicly available gas centrifuge design from the 1950s, known as the Zippe centrifuge" is incorrect. Similar information was repeated by the CIA in its assessments, including its input to the National Intelligence Estimate (NIE), and by the Defense Intelligence Agency (DIA) over the next year and a half.

( ) PARAGRAPH DELETED

( ) PARAGRAPH DELETED

(U) Conclusion 31. The Intelligence Community's position in the National Intelligence Estimate (NIE) that the composition and dimensions of the aluminum tubes exceeded the requirements for non nuclear applications, is incorrect.

( ) PARAGRAPH DELETED

( ) Conclusion 32. The DELETED intelligence report on Saddam Hussein's personal interest in the aluminum tubes, if credible, did suggest that the tube procurement was a high priority, but it did not necessarily suggest that the high priority was Iraq's nuclear program.

( ) PARAGRAPH DELETED

(U) Conclusion 33. The suggestion in the National Intelligence Estimate (NIE) that Iraq was paying excessively high costs for the aluminum tubes is incorrect. In addition, 7075-T6 aluminum is not considerably more expensive than other more readily available materials for rockets as alleged in the NIE.

( ) PARAGRAPH DELETED

( ) PARAGRAPH DELETED

(U) Conclusion 34. The National Ground Intelligence Center's (NGIC) analysis that the material composition of the tubes was unusual for rocket motor cases was incorrect, contradicted information the NGIC later provided to the Committee, and represented a serious lapse for the agency with primary responsibility for conventional ground forces intelligence analysis.

(U) Conclusion 35. Information obtained by the Committee shows that the tubes were DELETED to be manufactured to tolerances tighter than typically requested for rocket systems. The request for tight tolerances had several equally likely explanations other than that the tubes were intended for a centrifuge program, however.

( ) PARAGRAPH DELETED

( ) PARAGRAPH DELETED

( ) PARAGRAPH DELETED

(U) Conclusion 36. Iraq's attempts to procure the tubes through intermediary countries did appear intended to conceal Iraq as the ultimate end user of the tubes, as suggested in the National Intelligence Estimate (NIE). Because Iraq was prohibited from importing any military items, it would have had to conceal itself as the end user whether the tubes were intended for a nuclear program or a conventional weapons program, however.

( ) PARAGRAPH DELETED

( ) Conclusion 37. Iraq's persistence in seeking numerous foreign sources for the aluminum tubes was not "inconsistent" with procurement practices as alleged in the National Intelligence Estimate (NIE). Furthermore, such persistence DELETED a conventional weapons program than a covert nuclear program.

( ) PARAGRAPH DELETED

( ) PARAGRAPH DELETED

(U) Conclusion 38. The Central Intelligence Agency's (CIA) initial reporting on its aluminum tube spin tests was, at a minimum, misleading and, in some cases, incorrect. The fact that these tests were not coordinated with other Intelligence Community agencies is an example of continuing problems with information sharing within the Intelligence Community.

( ) PARAGRAPH DELETED

( ) PARAGRAPH DELETED

( ) PARAGRAPH DELETED

( ) PARAGRAPH DELETED

(U) Conclusion 39. Iraq's performance of hydrostatic pressure tests on the tubes was more indicative of their likely use for a rocket program than a centrifuge program.

( ) PARAGRAPH DELETED

( ) Conclusion 40. Intelligence reports which showed DELETED were portrayed in the National Intelligence Estimate as more definitive than the reporting showed.

( ) PARAGRAPH DELETED

( ) PARAGRAPH DELETED

( ) Conclusion 41. SENTENCE DELETED in that it was only presented with analysis that supported the CIA's conclusions. The team did not discuss the issues with Department of Energy officials and performed its work in only one day.

( ) PARAGRAPH DELETED

( ) PARAGRAPH DELETED

(U) Conclusion 42. The Director of Central Intelligence was not aware of the views of all intelligence agencies on the aluminum tubes prior to September 2002 and, as a result, could only have passed the Central Intelligence Agency's view along to the President until that time.

( ) PARAGRAPH DELETED

(U) Conclusion 43. Intelligence provided to the Committee did show that Iraq was trying to procure magnets, high-speed balancing machines and machine tools, but this intelligence did not suggest that the materials were intended to be used in a nuclear program.

( ) PARAGRAPH DELETED

(U) Conclusion 44. The statement in the National Intelligence Estimate that "a large number of personnel for the new [magnet] production facility, worked in Iraq's pre-Gulf War centrifuge program," was incorrect.

( ) PARAGRAPH DELETED

(U) Conclusion 45. The statement in the National Intelligence Estimate that the Iraqi Atomic Energy Commission was "expanding the infrastructure—research laboratories, production facilities, and procurement networks—to produce nuclear weapons," is not supported by the intelligence provided to the Committee.

( ) PARAGRAPH DELETED

(U) Conclusion 46. The intelligence provided to the Committee which showed that Iraq had kept its cadre of nuclear weapons personnel trained and in positions that could keep their skills intact for eventual use in a reconstituted nuclear program was compelling, but this intelligence did not show that there was a recent increase in activity that would have been indicative of recent or impending reconstitution of Iraq's nuclear program as was suggested in the National Intelligence Estimate.

( ) PARAGRAPH DELETED

(U) Conclusion 47. Intelligence information provided to the Committee did show that Saddam Hussein met with Iraqi Atomic Energy Commission personnel and that some security improvements were taking place, but none of the reporting indicated the IAEC was engaged in nuclear weapons related work.

- **Source:** *Report on the U.S. Intelligence Community's Prewar Intelligence Assessment on Iraq* (Washington, DC: GPO, 2004), 72–83, 129–42. I have removed sanitized paragraphs, which appear as blacked-over text, indicating excised material with ellipses.

- **Analysis:** As indicated by the deletions noted in the text, much of this report is classified. Even what can be made public, however, challenges the administration's claim that Iraq had tried to buy uranium cake from Niger. On July 7, 2004, the Senate Select Committee on Intelligence released its report on prewar intelligence assessment. The section on Niger completely debunked the assertion that Iraq had tried to buy uranium from the African country, revealed the documents on the transaction as forgeries, and raised concerns about the failure of the CIA to notify the White House about the inaccuracy of the intelligence. It also raised concerns that the Niger claim continued to be used as a justification for war long after its credibility had been destroyed. The document has been heavily sanitized, with entire paragraphs removed between conclusions.

- **Document 17: Excerpt of *Commission on the Intelligence Capabilities of the United States Regarding Weapons of Mass Destruction, Report to the President***
- **When:** March 31, 2005
- **Where:** Washington, DC
- **Significance:** The report declared the prewar intelligence on WMD in Iraq to be "dead wrong."

Mr. President:

With this letter, we transmit the report of the Commission on the Intelligence Capabilities of the United States Regarding Weapons of Mass Destruction. Our unanimous report is based on a lengthy investigation, during which we interviewed hundreds of experts from inside and outside the Intelligence Community and reviewed thousands of documents. Our report offers 74 recommendations for improving the U.S. Intelligence Community (all but a handful of which we believe can be implemented without statutory change). But among these recommendations a few points merit special emphasis.

We conclude that the Intelligence Community was dead wrong in almost all of its pre-war judgments about Iraq's weapons of mass destruction. This was a major intelligence failure. Its principal causes were the Intelligence Community's inability to collect good information about Iraq's WMD programs, serious errors in analyzing what information it could gather, and a failure to make clear just how much of its analysis was based on assumptions, rather than good evidence. On a matter of this importance, we simply cannot afford failures of this magnitude.

After a thorough review, the Commission found no indication that the Intelligence Community distorted the evidence regarding Iraq's weapons of mass destruction. What the intelligence professionals told you about Saddam Hussein's programs was what they believed. They were simply wrong.

As you asked, we looked as well beyond Iraq in our review of the Intelligence Community's capabilities. We conducted case studies of our intelligence agencies' recent performance assessing the risk of WMD in Libya and Afghanistan, and our current capabilities with respect to several of the world's most dangerous state and non-state proliferation threats. Out of this more comprehensive review, we report both bad news and good news. The bad news is that we still know disturbingly little about the weapons programs and even less about the intentions of many of our most dangerous adversaries.

The good news is that we have had some solid intelligence successes—thanks largely to innovative and multi-agency collection techniques.

Our review has convinced us that the best hope for preventing future failures is dramatic change. We need an Intelligence Community that is truly integrated, far more imaginative and willing to run risks, open to a new generation of Americans, and receptive to new technologies.

We have summarized our principal recommendations for the entire Intelligence Community in the Overview of the report. Here, we focus on recommendations that we believe only you can effect if you choose to implement them:

Give the DNI powers—and backing—to match his responsibilities.

In your public statement accompanying the announcement of Ambassador Negroponte's nomination as Director of National Intelligence (DNI), you have already moved in this direction. The new intelligence law makes the DNI responsible for integrating the 15 independent members of the Intelligence Community. But it gives him powers that are only relatively broader than before. The DNI cannot make this work unless he takes his legal authorities over budget, programs, personnel, and priorities to the limit. It won't be easy to provide this leadership to the intelligence components of the Defense Department, or to the CIA. They are some of the government's most headstrong agencies. Sooner or later, they will try to run around—or over—the DNI. Then, only your determined backing will convince them that we cannot return to the old ways.

Bring the FBI all the way into the Intelligence Community.

The FBI is one of the proudest and most independent agencies in the United States Government. It is on its way to becoming an effective intelligence agency, but it will never arrive if it insists on using only its own map. We recommend that you order an organizational reform of the Bureau that pulls all of its intelligence capabilities into one place and subjects them to the coordinating authority of the DNI—the same authority that the DNI exercises over Defense Department intelligence agencies. Under this recommendation, the counterterrorism and counterintelligence resources of the Bureau would become a single National Security Service inside the FBI. It would of course still be subject to the Attorney General's oversight and to current legal rules. The intelligence reform act almost accomplishes this task, but at crucial points it retreats into ambiguity.

Without leadership from the DNI, the FBI is likely to continue escaping effective integration into the Intelligence Community.

Demand more of the Intelligence Community.

The Intelligence Community needs to be pushed. It will not do its best unless it is pressed by policymakers—sometimes to the point of discomfort. Analysts must be pressed to explain how much they don't know; the collection agencies must be pressed to explain why they don't have better information on key topics. While policymakers must be prepared to credit intelligence that doesn't fit their preferences, no important intelligence assessment should be accepted without sharp questioning that forces the community to explain exactly how it came to that assessment and what alternatives might also be true. This is not "politicization"; it is a necessary part of the intelligence process.

And in the end, it is the key to getting the best from an Intelligence Community that, at its best, knows how to do astonishing things.

Rethink the President's daily brief.

The daily intelligence briefings given to you before the Iraq war were flawed.

Through attention-grabbing headlines and repetition of questionable data, these briefings overstated the case that Iraq was rebuilding its WMD programs. There are many other aspects of the daily brief that deserve to be reconsidered as well, but we are reluctant to make categorical recommendations on a process that in the end must meet your needs, not our theories. On one point, however, we want to be specific: while the DNI must be ultimately responsible for the content of your daily briefing, we do not believe that the DNI ought to prepare, deliver, or even attend every briefing. For if the DNI is consumed by current intelligence, the long-term needs of the Intelligence Community will suffer.

There is no more important intelligence mission than understanding the worst weapons that our enemies possess, and how they intend to use them against us. These are their deepest secrets, and unlocking them must be our highest priority. So far, despite some successes, our Intelligence Community has not been agile and innovative enough to provide the information that the nation needs. Other commissions and observers have said the same. We should not wait for another commission or another Administration to force widespread change in the Intelligence Community.

Very respectfully,

Laurence H. Silberman
Co-Chairman

Charles S. Robb
Co-Chairman

Richard C. Levin
John McCain
Henry S. Rowen
Walter B. Slocombe
William O. Studeman
Patricia M. Wald
Charles M. Vest
Lloyd Cutler

- **Source:** "Unclassified Version of the Report of the Commission on the Intelligence Capabilities of the United States Regarding Weapons of Mass Destruction," GPO Access, http://www.gpoaccess.gov/wmd/index.html, accessed July 13, 2011.

- **Analysis:** The report confirmed what many critics of the war had insisted from the beginning: the intelligence on Iraq's WMD program was simply wrong. Inability to get accurate information, lack of inter-agency cooperation, and other structural flaws interfered with the intelligence-gathering and analysis apparatus. The report insisted that there was no deliberate effort to deceive. This conclusion contradicts that of many observers who have concluded that the administration "shopped" for the intelligence it wanted to bolster its case for war.

CHEMICAL AND BIOLOGICAL WEAPONS

Following Iraq's acceptance of Security Council Resolution 687 (April 3, 1991) stipulating conditions for ending the Gulf War, the United Nations set up the UN Special Commission (UNSCOM) "to implement the non-nuclear provisions of the resolution and to assist the International Atomic Energy Agency (IAEA) in the nuclear areas."* In December 1999, the Security Council replaced UNSCOM with the UN Monitoring, Observation, Verification and Inspection Commission (UNMOVIC), which carried out its mandate until the Security Council disbanded it on June 29, 2007. For the first two years of its existence, however, UNMOVIC could do little but monitor Iraqi imports with special attention to dual-use materials (substances with both peaceful and military uses) since Saddam denied it access to Iraq. The Vienna Agreement of September 16, 2002, allowed it to resume activities in-country along with the IAEA. UNMOVIC recommenced work in Iraq on November 27, 2002, and submitted its first report (the 12th since its creation) based on actual inspections conducted on February 28, 2003, just weeks before the invasion.

- **Document 18: Excerpt of *National Intelligence Estimate***
- **When:** 2002
- **Where:** Washington, DC
- **Significance:** This report insisted emphatically that Iraq had significant chemical and biological weapons capability that threatened U.S. interests.

We judge that Iraq has continued its weapons of mass destruction (WMD) programs in defiance of UN resolutions and restrictions. Baghdad has chemical and biological weapons as well as missiles with ranges in excess of UN restrictions; if left unchecked, it probably will have a nuclear weapon during this decade.

We judge that we are seeing only a portion of Iraq's WMD efforts, owing to Baghdad's vigorous denial and deception efforts. Revelations after the Gulf war starkly

---

*UN Security Council Resolution 687 (April 3, 1991)

demonstrate the extensive efforts undertaken by Iraq to deny information. We lack specific information on many key aspects of Iraq's WMD programs.

Since inspections ended in 1998, Iraq has maintained its chemical weapons effort, energized its missile program, and invested more heavily in biological weapons; in the view of most agencies, Baghdad is reconstituting its nuclear weapons program.

Iraq's growing ability to sell oil illicitly increases Baghdad's capabilities to finance WMD programs; annual earnings in cash and goods have more than quadrupled, from $580 million in 1998 to about $3 billion this year.

Iraq has largely rebuilt missile and biological weapons facilities damaged during Operation Desert Fox and has expanded its chemical and biological infrastructure under the cover of civilian production.

Baghdad has exceeded UN range limits of 150 km with its ballistic missiles and is working with unmanned aerial vehicles (UAVs), which allow for a more lethal means to deliver biological and, less likely, chemical warfare agents.

Although we assess that Saddam does not yet have nuclear weapons or sufficient material to make any, he remains intent on acquiring them. Most agencies assess that Baghdad started reconstituting its nuclear program about the time that UNSCOM inspectors departed—December 1998.

How quickly Iraq will obtain its first nuclear weapon depends on when it acquires sufficient weapons-grade fissile material.

If Baghdad acquires sufficient fissile material from abroad it could make a nuclear weapon within several months to a year.

Without such material from abroad, Iraq probably would not be able to make a weapon until 2007 to 2009, owing to inexperience in building and operating centrifuge facilities to produce highly enriched uranium and challenges in procuring the necessary equipment and expertise.

—Most agencies believe that Saddam's personal interest in and Iraq's aggressive attempts to obtain high-strength aluminum tubes for centrifuge rotors—as well as Iraq's attempts to acquire magnets, high-speed balancing machines, and machine tools—provide compelling evidence that Saddam is reconstituting a uranium enrichment effort for Baghdad's nuclear weapons program. (DOE agrees that reconstitution of the nuclear program is underway but assesses that the tubes probably are not part of the program.)

—Iraq's efforts to re-establish and enhance its cadre of weapons personnel as well as activities at several suspect nuclear sites further indicate that reconstitution is underway.

—All agencies agree that about 25,000 centrifuges based on tubes of the size Iraq is trying to acquire would be capable of producing approximately two weapons' worth of highly enriched uranium per year.

In a much less lively scenario, Baghdad could make enough fissile material for a nuclear weapon by 2005 to 2007 if it obtains suitable centrifuge tubes this year and has all the other materials and technological expertise necessary to build production-scale uranium enrichment facilities.

We assess that Baghdad has begun renewed production of mustard, sarin, GF (cyclosarin), and VX; its capability probably is more limited now than it was at the time of the Gulf war, although VX production and agent storage life probably have been improved.

An array of clandestine reporting reveals that Baghdad has procured covertly the types and quantities of chemicals and equipment sufficient to allow limited CW agent production hidden within Iraq's legitimate chemical industry.

Although we have little specific information on Iraq's CW stockpile, Saddam probably has stocked at least 100 metric tons (MT) and possibly as much as 500 MT of CW agents—much of it added in the last year.

The Iraqis have experience in manufacturing CW bombs, artillery rockets, and projectiles. We assess that that they possess CW bulk fills for SRBM warheads, including for a limited number of covertly stored Scuds, possibly a few with extended ranges.

We judge that all key aspects—R&D, production, and weaponization—of Iraq's offensive BW program are active and that most elements are larger and more advanced than they were before the Gulf war.

We judge Iraq has some lethal and incapacitating BW agents and is capable of quickly producing and weaponizing a variety of such agents, including anthrax, for delivery by bombs, missiles, aerial sprayers, and covert operatives.

—Chances are even that smallpox is part of Iraq's offensive BW program.

—Baghdad probably has developed genetically engineered BW agents.

Baghdad has established a large-scale, redundant, and concealed BW agent production capability.

—Baghdad has mobile facilities for producing bacterial and toxin BW agents; these facilities can evade detection and are highly survivable. Within three to six months these units probably could produce an amount of agent equal to the total that Iraq produced in the years prior to the Gulf war.

- **Source:** *National Intelligence Estimate* (Washington, DC: GPO, 2002).

- **Analysis:** The *National Intelligence Estimate* is an annual report on threats facing the United States. The report asserted emphatically the presence of chemical and biological weapons in the Iraqi arsenal. This assertion created a conundrum that the Pentagon never addressed. If Iraqi chemical and biological weapons capability was as great as this report insisted it was, then U.S. troops would have to invade with sufficient protective equipment to counter the threat. Failure of the military to adequately prepare for such an eventuality calls into question how seriously planners took the intelligence in this report. Failure of the Iraqi military to deploy any of its alleged stockpiles of such weapons during the invasion, combined with the lack of protective equipment provided to U.S. soldiers, raises serious questions about the validity of the conclusions in this report.

- **Document 19: Excerpt of Twelfth Quarterly Report of the Executive Chairman of UNMOVIC**
- **When:** May 30, 2003
- **Where:** New York City
- **Significance:** This report challenges the conclusions of the *National Intelligence Assessment* (2002).

---

6. In resolution 1483 (2003) of 22 May 2003, the Security Council reaffirmed the importance of the disarmament of Iraqi weapons of mass destruction and the eventual confirmation of the disarmament of Iraq. In paragraph 11, the Council reaffirmed that Iraq must meet its disarmament obligations, invited the United Kingdom of Great Britain and Northern Ireland and the United States of America to keep the Council informed of their activities in that regard, and underlined its intention to revisit the mandates of UNMOVIC and IAEA as set forth in several earlier resolutions.

7. Since the Commission's work on disarmament in Iraq, which began on 27 November 2002, has been suspended, and since a significant phase of that work has been concluded, the present report provides more detail than previous reports. In addition, the report does not restrict itself to reviewing information from the period 1 March to 31 May 2003 but in a number of places adopts a wider perspective.

8. In the period during which it performed inspection and monitoring in Iraq, UNMOVIC did not find evidence of the continuation or resumption of programmes of weapons of mass destruction or significant quantities of proscribed items from before the adoption of resolution 687 (1991).

9. Inspections uncovered a small number of undeclared empty chemical warheads which appear to have been produced prior to 1990. Those and a few other proscribed items were destroyed.

10. Following a determination by the Commission that the Al Samoud 2 missile system exceeded the range limits set by the Security Council and hence was proscribed, the Commission implemented a programme for destruction. Some 70 missiles and associated equipment were destroyed under Commission supervision before its operations were suspended. At that time, a decision by the Commission was pending as to whether the Al Fatah missile system also exceeded the ranges set by the Council.

11. Inspections and declarations and documents submitted by Iraq, not least during the period under review, contributed to a better understanding of previous weapons programmes. However, the long list of proscribed items unaccounted for and as such resulting in unresolved disarmament issues was not shortened either by the inspections or by Iraqi declarations and documentation. From the end of January 2003, the Iraqi side, which until then had been cooperative in terms of process but not equally cooperative in terms of subsistence, devoted much effort to providing explanations and proposing methods of inquiry into such issues as the

production and destruction of anthrax, VX and long-range missiles. Despite those efforts, little progress was made in the solution of outstanding issues during the time of UNMOVIC operations in Iraq.

12. For example, as described in the present report, extensive excavations undertaken by the Iraqi side and witnessed by inspectors showed that a large number of R-400 bombs declared to have contained biological agents and to have been unilaterally destroyed in 1991 were in fact destroyed. While it was valuable in suggesting the credibility of some information provided earlier, the operation could not verify the total quantities of biological agents destroyed, still less the total quantities produced.

13. Again, with respect to anthrax, the Commission, as it reported, had strong indications—but not conclusive evidence—that all the quantities produced had not been destroyed, and that hence even today such quantities could remain. While the Iraqi side continued to claim that no documentary evidence remained of the destruction operation, it took two different steps in an effort to prove its declaration that all had been destroyed. As described in the present report, the Iraqi side undertook a chemical analysis of soil samples from the site where a quantity of anthrax was declared to have been dumped in 1991. While the results of the analysis were consistent with the declaration that anthrax had been dumped at the site, the study could not provide evidence of the quantities destroyed. The other step taken by the Iraqi side was to supply lists of the persons who in 1991 had been engaged in the operations to destroy anthrax. Regrettably, those lists were received only shortly before the suspension of inspections and the Commission did not have the opportunity to embark on a series of potentially important interviews.

14. By the time inspections were suspended, the Commission had performed a number of inspections to try to verify, as described in the present report, intelligence information that Iraq had mobile units for the production of biological weapons. The Iraqi side denied that any such units existed and provided the Commission with pictures of legitimate vehicles, which they suggested could have been mistaken for mobile units. However, none of the vehicles in those pictures resembles the trucks recently described and depicted by the Coalition.

15. As also described in the present report, the Commission was not able, before the suspension of inspections, to complete its inquiry into the Iraqi programmes of remotely piloted vehicles and unmanned aerial vehicles, notably to establish whether any of them were designed for the dissemination of chemical or biological weapons or had a longer range than was permitted. Extensive Iraqi information on the programme was sent to the Commission as late as 19 March 2003.

16. At the end of the present report, the Commission's readiness for resumed inspection activities is described. Until the Security Council revisits the mandate of the Commission, the resolutions which guided its work until the armed action will continue to be implemented to the extent that they are still relevant and have not been rendered obsolete by resolution 1483 (2003). It is clear that most of the work which the Commission has performed to date relating to the Oil for Food Programme will be phased out, and that as a result some staff will be released. A readiness for possible resumed work in Iraq, for example to confirm findings that may have been made since the end of the Commission's inspections and/or to perform the task of ongoing monitoring and verification, can be maintained with a

somewhat smaller staff than the Commission currently has at its headquarters, thereby reducing costs. However, it would be inadvisable to undertake any drastic overall reduction in the current cadre of staff, which is fully acquainted with the database and vast archives of the United Nations Special Commission (UNSCOM) and UNMOVIC and has broad knowledge of programmes, sites and relevant contacts in Iraq, as well as the logistics of inspection operations.

- **Source:** "Twelfth Quarterly Report of the Executive Chairman of UNMOVIC," United Nations, May 30, 2003, S/2003/580.
- **Analysis:** Since UNMOVIC delivered its report more than a month after the invasion of Iraq, its conclusions had no impact on the decision to invade. However, the report's preliminary findings suggest that Saddam had not restarted his chemical and biological weapons programs. Suspicious materials uncovered during UNMOVIC's first quarter of activity, abbreviated by the need to evacuate the mission before the start of hostilities, appear to have been either dual-use substances or weapons left over from before the Gulf War. Dual-use substances are chemicals that have legitimate industrial or medical uses but that can also be used to make chemical or biological weapons. The same problem of determining purpose exists for dual-use equipment, which can be used for legitimate and illegitimate purposes.

CONGRESSIONAL DEBATE

By the fall of 2002, the Bush administration had laid out its case for war to the American people. It then moved to get congressional approval for the president to go to war at the time of his choosing. With approximately 60 percent of the American people favoring war, Congress approved Operation Iraqi Freedom.

- **Document 20: Congressional Resolution Supporting the Use of Force against Iraq**
- **When:** October 16, 2002
- **Where:** Washington, DC
- **Significance:** This resolution empowered the president to take military action against Iraq.

Resolved by the Senate and House of Representatives of the United States of America in Congress assembled . . .

The President is authorized to use the Armed Forces of the United States as he determines to be necessary and appropriate in order to—

(1) defend the national security of the United States against the continuing threat posed by Iraq; and

(2) enforce all relevant United Nations Security Council resolutions regarding Iraq.

(b) Presidential Determination.—In connection with the exercise of the authority granted in subsection (a) to use force the President shall, prior to such exercise or as soon thereafter as may be feasible, but no later than 48 hours after exercising such authority, make available to the Speaker of the House of Representatives and the President pro tempore of the Senate his determination that—(1) reliance by the United States on further diplomatic or other peaceful means alone either (A) will not adequately protect the national security of the United States against the continuing threat posed by Iraq or (B) is not likely to lead to enforcement of all relevant United Nations Security Council resolutions regarding Iraq; and (2) acting pursuant to this joint resolution is consistent with the United States and other countries continuing to take the necessary actions against international terrorist and terrorist organizations, including those nations, organizations, or persons who planned, authorized, committed or aided the terrorist attacks that occurred on September 11, 2001.

(c) War Powers Resolution Requirements.—

(1) Specific statutory authorization.—Consistent with section 8(a)(1) of the War Powers Resolution, the Congress declares that this section is intended to constitute specific statutory authorization within the meaning of section 5(b) of the War Powers Resolution.

- **Source:** "Authorization for Use of Military Force against Iraq Resolution of 2002. Public Law 107-243," *U.S. Statutes at Large* 116 (2002): 1498.

- **Document 21: Excerpts of Floor Speeches Supporting the Iraq War Resolution**
- **When:** October 10–11, 2002
- **Where:** Washington, DC
- **Significance:** These excerpts reveal which arguments persuaded legislators to support the resolution.

Representative Dennis Hastert (Republican, Illinois)

I rise in support of this resolution, and I urge all of my colleagues to support it. This resolution authorizes the President to use necessary and appropriate military force against Saddam Hussein's regime in Iraq to defend the national security interests of the United States and to enforce the United Nations Security Council resolutions that Saddam Hussein has routinely ignored over the last decade. We take this step knowing that Saddam Hussein is a threat to the American people, to Iraq's neighbors, and to the civilized world at large. . . .

We have a sacred duty to do all that we can to ensure that what happened on September 11 never happens in America again. Some may question the connection between Iraq and those terrorists who hijacked those planes. There is no doubt that Iraq supports and harbors those terrorists who wish harm to the United States. Is there a direct connection between Iraq and al Qaeda? The President thinks so; and based upon what I have seen, I think so also. Should we wait until we are attacked again before finding out for sure; or should we do all that we can to disarm Saddam Hussein's regime before they provide al Qaeda with weapons of mass destruction?

Source: U.S. Congress, *Congressional Record*, 107th Cong., October 2002. Available at http://thomas.loc.gov/cgi-bin/query/R?r107:FLD001:H57191

Representative Henry Hyde (Republican, Illinois)

Permitted to acquire and deploy even more lethal weapons of mass destruction, Saddam Hussein will use those weapons; and he will use them against us and against our allies. Some of us demand a smoking gun before we will approve the use of force. We may well get a smoking city like Hiroshima in place of a gun.

He must not be allowed to gain those nuclear capabilities. We cannot afford another reoccupation of the Rhineland, another gross failure to enforce the basic norms of international order, this time, in a world of weapons of mass destruction and intercontinental ballistic missiles. Saddam Hussein must be disarmed, because the world simply cannot permit this man to obtain usable weapons of mass destruction.

If the international community is so feeble as not to see that this man's threat to peace, justice, and freedom must be confronted boldly and decisively, then the United States and those allies who will stand with us must do the job for our own safety's sake and in defense of the minimum conditions that make a civilized world possible.

The menace posed by Saddam is undeniable, but we are confronted with an even greater danger. Despite clear and repeated warnings, it appears much of the world does not understand that we have entered a wholly new and increasingly perilous era, one with new and harsher rules.

Through repeated usage, the term "weapons of mass destruction" has become almost banal, but the unimaginable destructive power these represent requires our constant focus and the determination to do what we must to defend ourselves.

The problem is not merely that a murderous tyrant such as Saddam may be in possession of these weapons. In the aftermath of September 11, we must accept that he has been joined by many others of an even more fanatical purpose. Terrorists willing to commit suicide in order to kill large numbers of innocents cannot be stopped by the familiar conventions of deterrence. Their possession of weapons of mass destruction must be equated with a certainty that these will be used against us.

Source: U.S. Congress, *Congressional Record,* 107th Cong., October 2002. Available at http://thomas.loc.gov/cgi-bin/query/R?r107:FLD001:H57191

Representative Charles Gilman (Republican, New York)

President Bush has characterized Iraq as part of an "axis of evil" and has identified the key threat from Iraq as its development of weapons of mass destruction and the potential for Iraq to transfer those elements to terrorists. We all know that Iraq has worked to rebuild its weapons of mass destruction programs in the 4 years since the U.N. weapons inspectors were forced to leave Iraq. We know, too, that Saddam is using mobile facilities to hide biological weapons research and even had placed underground some weapons of ass destruction; and there is a growing belief that in a few more years Iraq is going to be able to develop a nuclear weapon, if not sooner.

Mr. Speaker, Iraq has used chemical weapons against its own people, the Kurds, and against Iraq's neighbors in Iran. Moreover, Iraq did not hesitate in 1991 to send Scud missiles to strike at the very heart of Israel. Even if U.N. weapons inspectors return to Iraq, there are no assurances that Iraq is going to become free of weapons of mass destruction. The threat to our Nation's national security interest remains and, hence, this legislative need to provide President Bush with a maximum amount of flexibility to respond to this crisis.

In summation, no other living dictator matches Saddam Hussein's record of waging aggressive war against its neighbors; of pursuing weapons of mass destruction; of using weapons of mass destruction against its own people and other nations; of launching ballistic missiles at its neighbors; of brutalizing and torturing its own citizens; of harboring terrorist networks; of engaging in terrorist acts, including assassination of foreign officials; of violating his international commitments; of lying and cheating and hiding weapons of mass destruction programs; of deceiving and defying the express will of the United Nations over and over again.

As our President has noted in his recent speech to the U.N. General Assembly recently, "In one place, in one regime, we will find all these dangers in their most lethal and aggressive forms." Accordingly, Mr. Speaker, I urge our colleagues to lend their full support to H.J. Res. 114, authorizing the use of U.S. Armed Forces against Iraq....

Source: U.S. Congress, *Congressional Record,* 107th Cong., 2002, H7199. Available at http://thomas.loc.gov/cgi-bin/query/Z?r107:H08OC2-0032, last accessed December 1, 2011.

Senator Hillary Clinton (Democrat, New York)

Today we are asked whether to give the President of the United States authority to use force in Iraq should diplomatic efforts fail to dismantle Saddam Hussein's chemical and biological weapons and his nuclear program....

Now, I believe the facts that have brought us to this fateful vote are not in doubt. Saddam Hussein is a tyrant who has tortured and killed his own people, even his own family members, to maintain his iron grip on power....

It is clear, however, that if left unchecked, Saddam Hussein will continue to increase his capacity to wage biological and chemical warfare, and will keep trying to develop nuclear weapons. Should he succeed in that endeavor, he could alter the political and security landscape of the Middle East, which as we know all too well affects American security.

Now this much is undisputed. The open questions are: what should we do about it? How, when, and with whom?

Some people favor attacking Saddam Hussein now, with any allies we can muster, in the belief that one more round of weapons inspections would not produce the required disarmament, and that deposing Saddam would be a positive good for the Iraqi people and would create the possibility of a secular democratic state in the Middle East, one which could perhaps move the entire region toward democratic reform.

This view has appeal to some, because it would assure disarmament; because it would right old wrongs after our abandonment of the Shiites and Kurds in 1991, and our support for Saddam Hussein in the 1980's when he was using chemical weapons and terrorizing his people; and because it would give the Iraqi people a chance to build a future in freedom.

However, this course is fraught with danger. We and our NATO allies did not depose Mr. Milosevic, who was responsible for more than a quarter of a million people being killed in the 1990s. Instead, by stopping his aggression in Bosnia and Kosovo, and keeping on the tough sanctions, we created the conditions in which his own people threw him out and led to his being in the dock being tried for war crimes as we speak.

If we were to attack Iraq now, alone or with few allies, it would set a precedent that could come back to haunt us. In recent days, Russia has talked of an invasion of Georgia to attack Chechen rebels. India has mentioned the possibility of a preemptive strike on Pakistan. And what if China were to perceive a threat from Taiwan?

So Mr. President, for all its appeal, a unilateral attack, while it cannot be ruled out, on the present facts is not a good option.

Others argue that we should work through the United Nations and should only resort to force if and when the United Nations Security Council approves it. This too has great appeal for different reasons. The UN deserves our support. Whenever possible we should work through it and strengthen it, for it enables the world to share the risks and burdens of global security and when it acts, it confers a legitimacy that increases the likelihood of long-term success. The UN can help lead the world into a new era of global cooperation and the United States should support that goal.

But there are problems with this approach as well. The United Nations is an organization that is still growing and maturing. It often lacks the cohesion to enforce its own mandates. And when Security Council members use the veto, on occasion, for reasons of narrow-minded interests, it cannot act. In Kosovo, the Russians did not approve NATO military action because of political, ethnic, and religious ties to the Serbs. The United States therefore could not obtain a Security Council resolution in favor of the action necessary to stop the dislocation and ethnic cleansing of more than a million Kosovar Albanians. However, most of the world was with us because there was a genuine emergency with thousands dead and a million driven from their homes. As soon as the American-led conflict was over, Russia joined the peacekeeping effort that is still underway.

In the case of Iraq, recent comments indicate that one or two Security Council members might never approve force against Saddam Hussein until he has actually used chemical, biological, or God forbid, nuclear weapons.

So, Mr. President, the question is how do we do our best to both defuse the real threat that Saddam Hussein poses to his people, to the region, including Israel, to the United States, to the world, and at the same time, work to maximize our international support and strengthen the United Nations?

While there is no perfect approach to this thorny dilemma, and while people of good faith and high intelligence can reach diametrically opposed conclusions, I believe the best course is to go to the UN for a strong resolution that scraps the 1998 restrictions on inspections and calls for complete, unlimited inspections with cooperation expected and demanded from Iraq. I know that the Administration wants more, including an explicit authorization to use force, but we may not be able to secure that now, perhaps even later. But if we get a clear requirement for unfettered inspections, I believe the authority to use force to enforce that mandate is inherent in the original 1991 UN resolution, as President Clinton recognized when he launched Operation Desert Fox in 1998.

If we get the resolution that President Bush seeks, and if Saddam complies, disarmament can proceed and the threat can be eliminated. Regime change will, of course, take longer but we must still work for it, nurturing all reasonable forces of opposition.

If we get the resolution and Saddam does not comply, then we can attack him with far more support and legitimacy than we would have otherwise.

If we try and fail to get a resolution that simply, but forcefully, calls for Saddam's compliance with unlimited inspections, those who oppose even that will be in an indefensible position. And, we will still have more support and legitimacy than if we insist now on a resolution that includes authorizing military action and other requirements giving some nations superficially legitimate reasons to oppose any Security Council action. They will say we never wanted a resolution at all and that we only support the United Nations when it does exactly what we want.

I believe international support and legitimacy are crucial. After shots are fired and bombs are dropped, not all consequences are predictable. While the military outcome is not in doubt, should we put troops on the ground, there is still the matter of Saddam Hussein's biological and chemical weapons. Today he has maximum incentive not to use them or give them away. If he did either, the world would demand his immediate removal. Once the battle is joined, however, with the outcome certain, he will have maximum incentive to use weapons of mass destruction and to give what he can't use to terrorists who can torment us with them long after he is gone. We cannot be paralyzed by this possibility, but we would be foolish to ignore it. And according to recent reports, the CIA agrees with this analysis. A world united in sharing the risk at least would make this occurrence less likely and more bearable and would be far more likely to share with us the considerable burden of rebuilding a secure and peaceful post-Saddam Iraq.

President Bush's speech in Cincinnati and the changes in policy that have come forth since the Administration began broaching this issue some weeks ago have made my vote easier. Even though the resolution before the Senate is not as strong as I would like in requiring the diplomatic route first and placing highest priority on a simple, clear requirement for unlimited inspections, I will take the President at his word that he will try hard to pass a UN resolution and will seek to avoid war, if at all possible.

Because bipartisan support for this resolution makes success in the United Nations more likely, and therefore, war less likely, and because a good faith effort by the United States, even if it fails, will bring more allies and legitimacy to our cause, I have concluded, after careful and serious consideration, that a vote for the resolution best serves the security of our nation. If we were to defeat this resolution or pass it with only a few Democrats, I am concerned that those who want to pretend this problem will go way with delay will oppose any UN resolution calling for unrestricted inspections.

This is a very difficult vote. This is probably the hardest decision I have ever had to make—any vote that may lead to war should be hard—but I cast it with conviction.

And perhaps my decision is influenced by my eight years of experience on the other end of Pennsylvania Avenue in the White House watching my husband deal with serious challenges to our nation. I want this President, or any future President, to be in the strongest possible position to lead our country in the United Nations or in war. Secondly, I want to insure that Saddam Hussein makes no mistake about our national unity and for our support for the President's efforts to wage America's war against terrorists and weapons of mass destruction. And thirdly, I want the men and women in our Armed Forces to know that if they should be called upon to act against Iraq, our country will stand resolutely behind them.

My vote is not, however, a vote for any new doctrine of pre-emption, or for unilateralism, or for the arrogance of American power or purpose—all of which carry grave dangers for our nation, for the rule of international law and for the peace and security of people throughout the world.

Over eleven years have passed since the UN called on Saddam Hussein to rid himself of weapons of mass destruction as a condition of returning to the world community. Time and time again he has frustrated and denied these conditions. This matter cannot be left hanging forever with consequences we would all live to regret. War can yet be avoided, but our responsibility to global security and to the integrity of United Nations resolutions protecting it cannot. I urge the President to spare no effort to secure a clear, unambiguous demand by the United Nations for unlimited inspections.

And finally, on another personal note, I come to this decision from the perspective of a Senator from New York who has seen all too closely the consequences of last year's terrible attacks on our nation. In balancing the risks of action versus inaction, I think New Yorkers who have gone through the fires of hell may be more attuned to the risk of not acting. I know that I am.

So it is with conviction that I support this resolution as being in the best interests of our nation. A vote for it is not a vote to rush to war; it is a vote that puts awesome responsibility in the hands of our President and we say to him—use these powers wisely and as a last resort. And it is a vote that says clearly to Saddam Hussein—this is your last chance—disarm or be disarmed.

Thank you, Mr. President. . . .

Source: Floor Speech of Senator Hillary Rodham Clinton on S. J. Res. 45, A Resolution to Authorize the Use of United States Armed Forces Against Iraq. Available at http://www.democraticunderground.com/discuss/duboard.php?az=view_all &address=389x2667891

Senator John McCain (Republican, Arizona)

"The retention of weapons of mass destruction capabilities is self-evidently the core objective of the [Iraqi] regime, for it has sacrificed all other domestic and foreign policy goals to this singular aim." So concludes a recent report by the International Institute for Strategic Studies. The question facing all of us in this body is whether Saddam Hussein's aggressive weapons development, in defiance of the Gulf War cease-fire and a decade of U.N. Security Council resolutions, can stand, when the cost of inaction against this gathering threat could be intolerably high.

I am proud to join Senators Lieberman, Warner, and Bayh in laying down our amendment providing the President the necessary authority to defend the national security of the United States against the continuing threat posed by Iraq and enforce all relevant U.N. Security Council resolutions against Saddam Hussein's regime. I welcome this debate. I am confident it will result in a resounding vote of support for the President as he moves to confront the threat we face in Iraq. I also believe it will be a powerful signal to the world that the American people are united in their determination to meet, and to end, this menace. Our diplomacy at the United Nations will benefit from a strong and bipartisan Congressional vote in favor of this resolution. Our enemies will understand that we are united in our resolve to confront the danger posed by a dictator whose possession of the worst weapons and systematic defiance of every norm the civilized world holds dear threaten all who value freedom and law.

Congress has already spoken on this matter. On August 14, 1998, President Clinton signed into law Senate Joint Resolution 54, which declared that "the Government of Iraq is in material and unacceptable breach of its international obligations" and urged the President "to take appropriate action, in accordance with the Constitution and relevant laws of the United States, to bring Iraq into compliance with its international obligations." On October 31, 1998, the President signed into law the Iraq Liberation Act, which stated that "it should be the policy of the United States to support efforts to remove the regime headed by Saddam Hussein from power in Iraq and to promote the emergence of a democratic government to replace that regime."

Then, as now, Democrats and Republicans recognized the menace posed by Saddam Hussein's arsenal and his ambitions. Unfortunately, after four days of bombing Iraq in Operation Desert Fox in December 1998, the United States and the international community effectively walked away from the Iraq problem, freeing Iraq from a weapons inspection regime that, by that time, had become so compromised by Saddam Hussein's intransigence as to be completely ineffective. Nothing has taken its place over the past four years, even as porous sanctions and illicit oil revenues have enriched the regime. Over this time, Saddam Hussein's threat to the world has grown without hindrance. Regrettably, some of the very same permanent members of the Security Council whose vote for a new resolution on Iraq we are now courting actively conspired against rigorous weapons inspections in Iraq during the 1990s, for reasons that had more to do with their narrow commercial interests than with the world's interest in being rid of the menace posed by Saddam Hussein's weapons of terror.

This threat is not new. Saddam Hussein has been in gross violation of the terms of the cease-fire that ended the Persian Gulf War since that war's end, as a host of United Nations Security Council resolutions passed since 1991 can attest. As *The Economist* has written, "He has treated inspections as a continuation of the Gulf War by other means." After years of stymied efforts to enforce the inspections regime, the international community effectively sanctioned Saddam's impunity after it became clear he would never allow intrusive inspections, and once it became apparent to many Americans that the only way to end his defiance was to end his regime. The withering under U.N. Security Council auspices of the international inspections regime over the course of a decade, and Iraq's decision to even consider renewed inspections only under threat of force today, make clear that unvarnished faith in the ability of the U.N. Security Council or a new corps of inspectors to disarm Saddam's regime is misplaced.

Over the course of this debate, the Senate will consider amendments that would require Security Council authorization before the United States could act to enforce a decade of Security Council resolutions, and that would narrow the focus of American policy to Iraq's disarmament, rather than against the range of Saddam's offenses against his people and his neighbors and the continuing threat his regime itself poses to American national security.

These debates will be important. I believe the President's position will prevail. Congress cannot foresee the course of this conflict and should not unnecessarily constrain the options open to the President to defeat the threat we have identified in Saddam Hussein. Once Congress acts on a resolution, only the President will have to make the choices, with American forces likely deployed in the region to carry out his orders, that will end the threat Saddam Hussein's weapons and his ambitions pose to the world. Congress should give the President the authority he believes he needs to protect American national security against an often irrational dictator who has demonstrated a history of aggression outside his borders and a willingness to use weapons of mass destruction against all enemies, foreign and domestic.

This is not just another Arab despot, not one of many tyrants who repress their people from within the confines of their countries. As *New Yorker* writer Jeffrey Goldberg, who recently traveled across northern Iraq, recently wrote in Slate:

There are, of course, many repugnant dictators in the world; a dozen or so in the Middle East alone. But Saddam Hussein is a figure of singular repugnance, and singular danger. To review: there is no dictator in power anywhere in the world who has, so far in his career, invaded two neighboring countries; fired ballistic missiles at the civilians of two other neighboring countries; tried to have assassinated an ex-president of the United States; harbored al Qaeda fugitives . . . ; attacked civilians with chemical weapons; attacked the soldiers of an enemy with chemical weapons; conducted biological weapons experiments on human subjects; committed genocide; and . . . [weaponized] aflotoxin, a tool of mass murder and nothing else. I do not know how any thinking person could believe that Saddam Hussein is a run-of-the-mill dictator. No one else comes close . . . to matching his extraordinary and variegated record of malevolence.

In light of Saddam Hussein's record of aggression, prohibited weapons development, and consistent rejection of every international obligation imposed on him, I believe the burden of proof in this debate must rest on those who believe inspections could actually achieve the disarmament of Iraq, rather than on those of us who are deeply skeptical that inspections alone could accomplish our common goal. History shows that we will most likely not disarm Iraq without changing the regime in Baghdad—a regime whose continued existence is predicated on possession of weapons of mass destruction. As arms control experts Gary Milhollin and Kelly Motz have noted, "Unless the Iraqi dictator should suddenly and totally reverse course on arms inspection and everything that goes with it, or be forced into early retirement—in other words, unless Saddam Hussein's Iraq ceases to be Saddam Hussein's Iraq—inspections will never work."

Similarly, given the Security Council's failure to enforce its own Article Seven resolutions against Iraq, which are backed by the threat of force and have the sanctity of international law, I believe the burden of proof in this debate must rest on those who can defend the Council's record with regard to Iraq and can convince the rest of us that the Council's judgment, rather than that of our commander in chief, should be the final authority on a matter that so directly affects American security.

Important participants in this debate support the President's determination to use military force to bring about Iraq's disarmament but would constrain the President's authority to act against Iraq to uphold Security Council resolutions related to repression within Iraq, Iraq's support for terrorism, and other issues. This approach would limit the President's authority to achieving only Iraq's disarmament and would explicitly oppose a comprehensive challenge to his tyrannical regime. I believe those who hold this view have an obligation to explain why they would constrain the President's authority to use military force in ways he believes would tie his hands and raise unacceptably high the threshold for ordering military action to defend the national security of the United States.

Others will argue that Saddam Hussein can be deterred—that he is a rational actor who understands that acting on his ambitions will threaten his regime. But deterrence has failed utterly in the past. I fail to see how waiting for some unspecified period of time, allowing Saddam's nuclear ambitions to grow unchecked, will ever result in a stable deterrence regime. Not only would deterrence condemn the Iraqi people to more unspeakable tyranny, it would condemn Saddam's neighbors to perpetual instability. And once Iraq's nuclear ambitions are realized, no serious person could expect the Iraqi threat to diminish. Again, the burden in this debate rests on those who believe American policy has actually been successful in containing the threat Saddam's regime poses to the world.

There is no greater responsibility we face as members of this body than voting to place the country on a course that could send young Americans to war in her defense. All of us must weigh our consciences carefully. Although we may hold different views of how to respond to the threat posed by Saddam Hussein's Iraq, the very fact that we are holding this free debate, and that the fate of nations and peoples other than our own will be determined by the outcome of our actions, serves as a reminder that we are a great nation, united in freedom's defense, and called once again to make the world safe for freedom's blessings to flourish. The quality of our greatness will determine the character of our response.

Source: John McCain, "Statement in Support of the Iraq Resolution," October 11, 2002, available at http://mccain.senate.gov/public/index.cfm ?FuseAction=PressOffice.PressReleases&ContentRecord_id=2526b822-bb60-400e -8cfa-98bd3a9cf5c5&Region_id=&Issue_id=, accessed April 29, 2008.

- **Source:** *See individual speeches.*
- **Analysis:** Republicans who supported the resolution advanced all the arguments the president had made over the previous year. They cited Saddam Hussein's flouting of UN resolutions, his reluctance to cooperate with weapons inspectors, and his violations of the no-fly zones. They also accepted uncritically the arguments that Hussein had restarted his WMD programs and that he had close ties to terrorist organizations. Following 9/11, fear of such weapons falling into terrorist hands provided a powerful inducement to voting for the Iraq War resolution. Few politicians wanted to risk being blamed for another attack.

  Senator Hilary Clinton was representative of those Democratic legislators who reluctantly voted for the resolution. She expressed grave concern for the precedent unilateral, preemptive action might provide for America's adversaries. If the United States could justify invading Iraq because of the potential threat it posed, could not China make the same argument for invading Taiwan? Nevertheless, Senator Clinton believed that failure to pass the resolution would further embolden Saddam Hussein. She may also have been looking ahead to the next president election. If she were to run, she would not wish to be accused of failing to support the resolution.

- **Document 22: Speeches Opposing the Resolution**
- **When:** October 9–10, 2002
- **Where:** Washington, DC

- **Significance:** A small percentage of representatives and senators opposed invading Iraq.

Representative Donald Payne (Democrat, New Jersey)

First of all, let me say from the outset that I oppose a unilateral first-strike attack by the United States without a clearly demonstrated and imminent threat of attack on our soil. The President's resolution does not prove that the United States is in imminent danger of attack, and we in Congress have received no evidence of such an imminent and immediate threat.

If the United States is in fact in danger of immediate attack, the President already has the authority under the Constitution, the War Powers Act, the United Nations Charter, and international law to defend our Nation.

A unilateral first strike would be codified in this resolution. The fact that it could set an example for potential conflicts between India and Pakistan, between Russia and Georgia, between China and Taiwan, and many other corners of the world is something that we have to be concerned about.

Only Congress has the authority to declare war. House Joint Resolution 114 is not a declaration of war, but it is a blank check to use force without moral or political authority of the declaration of war that, for example, Franklin Delano Roosevelt did on December 8 to begin World War II.

Every diplomatic option must be exhausted. This resolution authorizes the potential use of force immediately, long before diplomatic options can be exhausted or even fully explored.

Other governments, including France and Russia, have proposed a two-step process in which the world community renews vigorous and unfettered inspections. This resolution, however, is a one-step process. Rather than letting the United Nations do its work to seek out and destroy weapons through inspections, it places immediate force on the table.

A unilateral first strike would undermine the moral authority of the United States, result in substantial loss of life, destabilize the Middle East region, and undermine the ability of our Nation to address unmet domestic priorities. The President's resolution authorizes all of these outcomes by authorizing and codifying the doctrine of preemption.

This resolution can unleash all these consequences: destabilization of the Middle East; casualties among U.S. troops and Iraqi citizens; a huge cost, estimated at between $100 and $200 billion; and a question about our own domestic priorities, with such a cost looming over our heads.

Further, any post-strike plan for maintaining stability in the region would be costly and would require a long-term commitment. Experts tell us that the United States might have to remain in Iraq for a decade. Such a commitment would drain resources for critical domestic and international priorities. Failure to make such a commitment would leave another post-intervention disaster scene.

We still have the commitment that we were making to Afghanistan, where we said we would rebuild schools and we would repair roads and we would build water treatment plants to bring water out for the people there. We have been unable to do that in Afghanistan; however, now we are moving to Iraq. . . .

Source: "Authorization for Use of Military Force against Iraq," October 9, 2002, available at http://frwebgate2.access.gpo.gov/cgi-bin/waisgate.cgi? WAISdocID=480208413458+0+0+0&WAISaction=retrieve, accessed April 29, 2008.

Representative David Bonior (Democrat, Michigan)

I rise in opposition to this resolution. Our Nation faces a monumental decision, one that could drastically change our lives, harm our national security, and one that could forever shatter the fragile stability that we have carefully rebuilt since September 11.

Thomas Jefferson once said, "War is an instrument entirely inefficient towards redressing wrong and multiplies, instead of indemnifying, losses." Multiplies, instead of indemnifying, losses. We are told this war, this invasion of Iraq, will right the wrongs that Saddam Hussein has created. We are told that this war will help end the evils of terrorism. And we are told that this war will bring peace and regional stability to the Middle East.

I do not share that view. We have to be cognizant of what this war will unleash upon the world. I have never in my 30 years of public life and 26 years of serving here seen the world community so fragile. It is a tinderbox, and a hair trigger waiting to go off could unleash the violence that we all seek to avoid.

I am not ready to alter the course that we have taken since our founding to embrace the preemptive strike doctrine. If we strike first, what kind of message does that send to the tinderboxes of Pakistan and India, China and Taiwan, North and South Korea? Are we prepared to strike first in Iran, in North Korea? Where does it end? The broader global implications will be grave.

Second, I am not ready to act unilaterally and in potential defiance of the United Nations Security Council. Because, by going it alone, what signal do we issue by tossing aside diplomacy? What sirens do we set off by ignoring the rest of the world?

The Reverend Dr. Martin Luther King, Jr., once said, "Destructive means cannot bring about constructive ends." And yet here we are thrown headlong into a decision that could cost thousands and thousands of American men and women their lives, could put our personnel in embassies all over the globe in harm's way, in danger, could unleash another round, another decade of untold suffering among innocent Iraqis, and we are told that we have no other choice.

By rushing into war, we alone will bear the burden of seeing this conflict to its blood end, most likely in the streets of Bagdad among innocent families and U.S. troops engaged in door-to-door combat. By rushing into war, we alone will be responsible for splintering the international coalition that has been built to fight the imminent threat posed by the terrorists, al Qaeda. And by rushing into war we alone will fuel far more extremist passions against the United States, a whole new generation of terrorists bent on our demise.

It will strain our military. It will cost us tens and tens, if not hundreds of millions of dollars, and it will erode any cooperation from Arab and Muslim nations in tracking down and neutralizing the remaining al Qaeda cells. Instead of fighting a war against terrorism, we will have the potential instead of fighting the war against a quarter of the world. I am not ready to support a resolution that could take American people down that road. The sabers continue to rattle, the war drums pound louder every day, and it is quite clear that many people here believe that preparing for war ensures that it will truly happen. . . .

Source: "Authorization for Use of Military Force against Iraq," October 9, 2002, available at http://frwebgate2.access.gpo.gov/cgi-bin/waisgate.cgi?WAISdocID =480208413458+0+0+0&WAISaction=retrieve, last accessed April 29, 2008.

Senator Russell Feingold (Democrat, Wisconsin)

Many of us have spent months reviewing the issue of the advisability of invading Iraq in the near future. From hearings and meetings on the process and the very important role of Congress to the difficult questions of substance, including foreign policy and military implications, after my own review and carefully listening to hundreds of Wisconsin citizens in person, I spoke on the floor on Thursday, September 26, and, Mr. President, I indicated my opposition to the original draft use of force authorization by the President, and I also used that opportunity to raise some very important questions, to which I needed answers before supporting a narrower and more responsible resolution.

Now, after many more meetings and reading articles and attending briefings, listening to my colleagues' speeches, and especially listening to the President's speech in Cincinnati on Monday, Mr. President, I still don't believe that the President and the Administration have adequately answered the critical questions. They have not yet met the important burden to persuade Congress and the American people that we should invade Iraq at this time.

Both in terms of the justifications for an invasion and in terms of the mission and the plan for the invasion, Mr. President, the Administration's arguments just don't add up. They don't add up to a coherent basis for a new major war in the middle of our current challenging fight against the terrorism of al Qaeda and related organizations. Therefore, I cannot support the resolution for the use of force before us.

My colleagues, my focus today is on the wisdom of this specific resolution vis-a-vis Iraq, as opposed to discussing the notion of an expanded doctrine of preemption, which the President has articulated on several occasions. However, I associate myself with the concerns eloquently raised by Senator Kennedy and Senator Byrd and others that this could well represent a disturbing change in our overall foreign and military policy. This includes grave concerns about what such a preemption-plus policy will do to our relationship with our allies, to our national security, and to the cause of world peace in so many regions of the world, where such a doctrine could trigger very dangerous actions with really very minimal justification. . . .

Mr. President, I am increasingly troubled by the seemingly shifting justifications for an invasion at this time. My colleagues, I'm not suggesting there has to be only one justification for such a dramatic action. But when the Administration moves back and forth from one argument to another, I think it undercuts the credibility of the case and the belief in its urgency. I believe that this practice of shifting justifications has much to do with the troubling phenomenon of many Americans questioning the Administration's motives in insisting on action at this particular time.

What am I talking about? I'm talking about the spectacle of the President and senior Administration officials citing a purported connection to al Qaeda one day, weapons of mass destruction the next day, Saddam Hussein's treatment of his own people on another day, and then on some days the issue of Kuwaiti prisoners of war. . . .

I am especially troubled by these shifting justifications because I and most Americans strongly support the President on the use of force in response to the attacks on September 11, 2001. I voted for Senate Joint Resolution 23, the use of force resolution, to go after al Qaeda and the Taliban and those associated with the tragedies of September 11. And I strongly support military actions pursuant to Senate Joint Resolution 23.

But the relentless attempt to link 9-11 and the issue of Iraq has been disappointing to me for months, culminating in the President's singularly unpersuasive attempt in Cincinnati to interweave 9-11 and Iraq, to make the American people believe that there are no important differences between the perpetrators of 9-11 and Iraq.

Mr. President, I believe it is dangerous for the world, and especially dangerous for us, to take the tragedy of 9-11 and the word "terrorism" and all their powerful emotion and then too easily apply them to many other situations—situations that surely need our serious attention but are not necessarily, Mr. President, the same as individuals and organizations who have shown a willingness to fly planes into the World Trade Center and into the Pentagon.

Let me say that the President is right that we've got to view the world, the threats and our own national security in a very different light since 9-11. There are shocking new threats. But, Mr. President, it is not helpful to use virtually any strand of extreme rhetoric to suggest that the new threat is the same as other preexisting threats. Mr. President, I think common sense tells us they are not the same and they cannot so easily be lumped together as the President sought to do in Cincinnati.

Mr. President, I've reviewed the intermittent efforts to suggest a connection of 9-11 and Saddam Hussein or suggest the possibility that such a connection has developed since 9-11. Let me be very clear. If in fact there was a connection in planning together for the 9-11 attack by Saddam Hussein or his agents and the perpetrators of 9-11 and al Qaeda, I've already voted for military action. I have no objection.

But if it is not, if this is premised on some case that has supposedly been made with regard to a subsequent coalition between al Qaeda and the Iraqi government, I think the President has got to do better. He's got to do better than the shoddy piecing together of flimsy evidence that contradicts the very briefings we've received by various agencies, Mr. President.

I'm not hearing the same things at the briefings that I'm hearing from the President's top officials. In fact, on March 11 of this year, Vice President Cheney, following a meeting with Tony Blair, raised fears of weapons of mass destruction falling into the hands of terrorists. He said, "We have to be concerned about the potential"—potential—"marriage, if you will, between a terrorist organization like al

Qaeda and those who hold or are proliferating knowledge about weapons of mass destruction." So in March, it was a potential marriage.

Then the Vice-President said, on September 8, without evidence—and no evidence has been given since that time—that there are "credible but unconfirmed" intelligence reports that 9-11 ringleader Mohammed Atta met with an Iraqi intelligence official several months before 9-11. We've seen no proof of that.

And finally then, the Secretary of Defense follows on September 27 of this year and says, "There is bulletproof evidence of Iraqi links to al Qaeda, including the recent presence of senior al Qaeda members in Baghdad." I don't know where this comes from, Mr. President. This so-called potential marriage in March is beginning to sound like a 25th wedding anniversary at this point.

The facts just aren't there, or at least they have not been presented to me in the situations where they should have been presented to me as an elected Member of this body. In other words, the Administration appears to use 9-11 and the language of terrorism and the connection to Iraq too loosely, almost like a bootstrap.

For example, I heard the President say in Cincinnati that Iraq and al Qaeda both regard us as a common enemy. Of course they do. Well, who else are we going to attack in the near future on that basis alone?

Or do we see an attempt to stretch the notion of harboring terrorists? I agree with the President, if any country is actively harboring or assisting the terrorists involved in 9-11, we have to act against them. But I don't think you can bring within the definition of harboring terrorists the simple presence of some al Qaeda members somewhere in Iraq. After all, Mr. President, apparently we have al Qaeda agents active in our country as well. They are present in our nation as well. How can this be a sufficient basis on its own?

Therefore, Mr. President, without a better case for al Qaeda's connection to Saddam Hussein, this proposed invasion must stand on its own merits, not on some notion that those who question this invasion don't thoroughly condemn and want to see the destruction of the perpetrators of 9-11 and similar terrorist attacks on the United States.

An invasion of Iraq must stand on its own, not just because it is different than the fight against the perpetrators of 9-11 but because it may not be consistent with, and may even be harmful to, the top national security issue of this country. And that is the fight against terrorism and the perpetrators of the crimes of 9-11. . . .

In any event, I oppose this resolution because of the continuing unanswered questions, including the very important questions about what the mission is here, what the nature of the operation will be, what will happen concerning weapons of mass destruction in Iraq as the attack proceeds and afterward, and what the plan is after the attack is over. In effect, Mr. President, we're being asked to vote on something that is unclear. We don't have answers to these questions. We're being asked to vote on something that is almost unknowable in terms of the information we've been given.

In my judgment, the issue that presents the greatest potential threat to U.S. national security, Iraq's pursuit of weapons of mass destruction, has not been addressed in any comprehensive way by the Administration to date. Of course, I know that we don't need to know all the details, and we don't have to be given all the details, and we shouldn't be given all the details. But we've got to be given some kind of a reasonable explanation. Before we vote on this resolution, we need a credible plan for securing W.M.D. sites and not allowing materials of concern to slip away during some chaotic course of action. I know that's a tall order, but, Mr. President, it's a necessary demand.

As I said, I agree with the Administration when it asserts that returning to the same restricted weapons inspection regime of the recent past is not a credible policy for addressing the W.M.D. problem in Iraq. But, Mr. President, there is nothing credible about the we'll-figure-that-out-later approach that we've heard to date. What if actors competing for power in a post-Hussein world have access to W.M.D.? What if there is chaos in the wake of the regime's fall that provides new opportunities for nonstate actors, including terrorist organizations, to bid on the sinister items tucked away in Iraq?

Some would say those who do not unquestioningly support the Administration are failing to provide for our national security. But, Mr. President, I'm sure of this. These issues are critical to that security, and I have yet to get any answers.

Mr. President, we need an honest assessment of the commitment required of America. If the right way to address this threat is through internationally-supported military action in Iraq and Saddam Hussein's regime falls, we will need to take action to ensure stability in Iraq. This could be very costly and time consuming, could involve the occupation—the occupation, Mr. President, of a Middle Eastern country.

Source: Russell Feingold, "Statement of U.S. Senator Russ Feingold on Opposing the Resolution on Authorizing the Use of Force against Iraq," October 9, 2002, available at http://www.senate.gov/~feingold/speeches/02/10/2002A10531.html, last accessed April 29, 2008.

- **Source:** *See individual speeches.*
- **Analysis:** Those who opposed the resolution raised a number of concerns. They questioned the administration's case for war based upon Saddam Hussein's weapons program and his alleged links to al-Qaeda. They also expressed the same reservations about the policy of unilateral preemption expressed by Senator Clinton. Senator Feingold took criticism a step further, calling into question the whole public relations campaign mounted by the Bush administration to justify the war. He noted the constantly changing justifications for war and challenged the conclusion that invading Iraq would in any way contribute to winning the struggle against terrorism.

THE UN DEBATE

Having gained the support of Congress for military action against Iraq, the Bush administration sought approval from the United Nations. Secretary of State Colin

Powell reviewed the litany of complaints against Saddam Hussein. Since coming to power in the 1970s, Hussein had conducted a reign of terror that intensified following the Gulf War. He had crushed uprisings in the Shi'a south and the Kurdish north and extended his formidable system of state surveillance and control. He had used chemical weapons against the Kurds. He had also hampered the work of the monitoring mission. Despite Powell's emphatic arguments, the Security Council refused to authorize military action. As a result, some of the United States' closest allies did not join the coalition that invaded Iraq.

- **Document 23: United Nations Secretary-General Kofi Annan, "I Stand before You Today a Multilateralist," Speech Delivered to the United Nations General Assembly**
- **When:** September 12, 2002
- **Where:** New York City
- **Significance:** The secretary-general argued against unilateral action by member states.

We cannot begin today without reflecting on yesterday's anniversary—and on the criminal challenge so brutally thrown in our faces on 11 September 2001.

The terrorist attacks of that day were not an isolated event. They were an extreme example of a global scourge, which requires a broad, sustained and global response.

Broad, because terrorism can be defeated only if all nations unite against it.

Sustained, because the battle against terrorism will not be won easily, or overnight. It requires patience and persistence.

And global, because terrorism is a widespread and complex phenomenon, with many deep roots and exacerbating factors.

Mr. President, I believe that such a response can only succeed if we make full use of multilateral institutions.

I stand before you today as a multilateralist—by precedent, by principle, by Charter and by duty.

I also believe that every government that is committed to the rule of law at home, must be committed also to the rule of law abroad. And all States have a clear interest, as well as clear responsibility, to uphold international law and maintain international order.

Our founding fathers, the statesmen of 1945, had learnt that lesson from the bitter experience of two world wars and a great depression.

They recognized that international security is not a zero-sum game. Peace, security and freedom are not finite commodities—like land, oil or gold—which one State can acquire at another's expense. On the contrary, the more peace, security and freedom any one State has, the more its neighbours are likely to have.

And they recognized that, by agreeing to exercise sovereignty together, they could gain a hold over problems that would defeat any one of them acting separately.

If those lessons were clear in 1945, should they not be much more so today, in the age of globalization?

On almost no item on our agenda does anyone seriously contend that each nation can fend for itself. Even the most powerful countries know that they need to work with others, in multilateral institutions, to achieve their aims.

Only by multilateral action can we ensure that open markets offer benefits and opportunities to all.

Only by multilateral action can we give people in the least developed countries the chance to escape the ugly misery of poverty, ignorance and disease.

Only by multilateral action can we protect ourselves from acid rain, or global warming; from the spread of HIV/AIDS, the illicit trade in drugs, or the odious traffic in human beings.

That applies even more to the prevention of terrorism. Individual States may defend themselves, by striking back at terrorist groups and at the countries that harbour or support them. But only concerted vigilance and cooperation among all States, with constant, systematic exchange of information, offers any real hope of denying the terrorists their opportunities.

On all these matters, for any one State—large or small—choosing to follow or reject the multilateral path must not be a simple matter of political convenience. It has consequences far beyond the immediate context.

When countries work together in multilateral institutions—developing, respecting, and when necessary enforcing international law—they also develop mutual trust, and more effective cooperation on other issues.

The more a country makes use of multilateral institutions—thereby respecting shared values, and accepting the obligations and restraints inherent in those values—the more others will trust and respect it, and the stronger its chance to exercise true leadership.

And among multilateral institutions, this universal Organization has a special place.

Any State, if attacked, retains the inherent right of self-defence under Article 51 of the Charter. But beyond that, when States decide to use force to deal with broader threats to international peace and security, there is no substitute for the unique legitimacy provided by the United Nations.

Member States attach importance, great importance in fact, to such legitimacy and to the international rule of law. They have shown—notably in the action to liberate Kuwait, 12 years ago—that they are willing to take actions under the authority of the Security Council, which they would not be willing to take without it.

The existence of an effective international security system depends on the Council's authority—and therefore on the Council having the political will to act, even in the most difficult cases, when agreement seems elusive at the outset. The primary criterion for putting an issue on the Council's agenda should not be the receptiveness of the parties, but the existence of a grave threat to world peace.

Let me now turn to four current threats to world peace, where true leadership and effective action are badly needed.

First, the Israeli-Palestinian conflict. Recently, many of us have been struggling to reconcile Israel's legitimate security concerns with Palestinian humanitarian needs.

But these limited objectives cannot be achieved in isolation from the wider political context. We must return to the search for a just and comprehensive solution, which alone can bring security and prosperity to both peoples, and indeed to the whole region.

The ultimate shape of a Middle East peace settlement is well known. It was defined long ago in Security Council Resolutions 242 and 338, and its Israeli-Palestinian components were spelt out even more clearly in Resolution 1397: land for peace; end to terror and to occupation; two States, Israel and Palestine, living side by side within secure and recognized borders.

Both parties accept this vision. But we can reach it only if we move rapidly and in parallel on all fronts. The so-called "sequential" approach has failed.

As we agreed at the Quartet meeting in Washington last May, an international peace conference is needed without delay, to set out a roadmap of parallel steps: steps to strengthen Israel's security, steps to strengthen Palestinian economic and political institutions, and steps to settle the details of the final peace agreement. Meanwhile, humanitarian steps to relieve Palestinian suffering must be intensified. The need is urgent.

Second, the leadership of Iraq continues to defy mandatory resolutions adopted by the Security Council under Chapter VII of the Charter.

I have engaged Iraq in an in-depth discussion on a range of issues, including the need for arms inspectors to return, in accordance with the relevant Security Council resolutions.

Efforts to obtain Iraq's compliance with the Council's resolutions must continue. I appeal to all those who have influence with Iraq's leaders to impress on them the vital importance of accepting the weapons inspections. This is the indispensable first step towards assuring the world that all Iraq's weapons of mass destruction have indeed been eliminated, and—let me stress—towards the suspension and eventual ending of the sanctions that are causing so many hardships for the Iraqi people.

I urge Iraq to comply with its obligations—for the sake of its own people, and for the sake of world order. If Iraq's defiance continues, the Security Council must face its responsibilities.

Third, permit me to press all of you, as leaders of the international community, to maintain your commitment to Afghanistan.

I know I speak for all in welcoming President Karzai to this Assembly, and congratulating him on his escape from last week's vicious assassination attempt—a graphic reminder of how hard it is to uproot the remnants of terrorism in any country where it has taken root. It was the international community's shameful neglect of Afghanistan in the 1990s that allowed the country to slide into chaos, providing a fertile breeding ground for Al Qaeda.

Today, Afghanistan urgently needs help in two areas. The Government must be helped to extend its authority throughout the country. Without this, all else may fail. And donors must follow through on their commitments to help with rehabilitation, reconstruction and development. Otherwise the Afghan people will lose hope—and desperation, we know, breeds violence.

And finally, in South Asia the world has recently come closer than for many years past to a direct conflict between two countries with nuclear capability. The situation may now have calmed a little, but it remains perilous. The underlying cause must be addressed. If a fresh crisis erupts, the international community might have a role to play; though I gladly acknowledge—and indeed, strongly welcome—the efforts made by well-placed Member States to help the two leaders find a solution.

Excellencies, let me conclude by reminding you of your pledge two years ago, at the Millennium Summit, "to make the United Nations a more effective instrument" in the service of the peoples of the world.

Today I ask all of you to honour that pledge.

Let us all recognize, from now on—in each capital, in every nation, large and small—that the global interest is our national interest.

- **Source:** Kofi Annan, "When Force Is Considered, There Is No Substitute for Legitimacy Provided," speech before the United Nations General Assembly, SG/SM/8378, September 12, 2002, http://www.un.org/News/Press/docs/2002/SGSM8378.doc.htm.

- **Analysis:** Although addressed to the General Assembly, Kofi Annan seemed to be aiming his remarks at Washington. The Bush administration's determination to invade Iraq, with or without UN support, was becoming increasingly clear. Annan made an impassioned plea for multilateralism, which he argued lay at the heart of the international system enshrined in the UN charter. He implicitly linked Iraq to two other contemporary conflicts, Afghanistan and Israel-Palestine, both of which were being addressed through UN-sanctioned efforts.

  Annan's admonitions fell on deaf ears. The Bush administration considered UN support a desirable but not a necessary condition for invading Iraq. Failure to get a mandate from the organization for Operation Iraqi Freedom did, however, have one negative impact on the mission. The United States had fewer allies than it might have had, a weakness that limited its ability to handle the occupation and insurgency that followed conventional operations.

- **Document 24: Excerpt of Secretary of State Colin Powell's Presentation to the UN Security Council**
- **When:** February 5, 2003
- **Where:** New York City
- **Significance:** Secretary of State Powell tried unsuccessfully to persuade the Security Council to endorse the U.S.-led invasion of Iraq.

SECRETARY POWELL: Thank you, Mr. President. Mr. President and Mr. Secretary General, distinguished colleagues, I would like to begin by expressing my thanks for the special effort that each of you made to be here today. This is an important day for us all as we review the situation with respect to Iraq and its disarmament obligations under UN Security Council Resolution 1441.

Last November 8, this Council passed Resolution 1441 by a unanimous vote. The purpose of that resolution was to disarm Iraq of its weapons of mass destruction. Iraq had already been found guilty of material breach of its obligations stretching back over 16 previous resolutions and 12 years.

Resolution 1441 was not dealing with an innocent party, but a regime this Council has repeatedly convicted over the years.

Resolution 1441 gave Iraq one last chance, one last chance to come into compliance or to face serious consequences. No Council member present and voting on that day had any illusions about the nature and intent of the resolution or what serious consequences meant if Iraq did not comply.

And to assist in its disarmament, we called on Iraq to cooperate with returning inspectors from UNMOVIC and IAEA. We laid down tough standards for Iraq to meet to allow the inspectors to do their job.

This Council placed the burden on Iraq to comply and disarm, and not on the inspectors to find that which Iraq has gone out of its way to conceal for so long. Inspectors are inspectors; they are not detectives.

I asked for this session today for two purposes. First, to support the core assessments made by Dr. Blix and Dr. ElBaradei. As Dr. Blix reported to this Council on January 27, "Iraq appears not to have come to a genuine acceptance, not even today, of the disarmament which was demanded of it."

And as Dr. ElBaradei reported, Iraq's declaration of December 7 "did not provide any new information relevant to certain questions that have been outstanding since 1998."

My second purpose today is to provide you with additional information, to share with you what the United States knows about Iraq's weapons of mass destruction, as well as Iraq's involvement in terrorism, which is also the subject of Resolution 1441 and other earlier resolutions.

I might add at this point that we are providing all relevant information we can to the inspection teams for them to do their work.

The material I will present to you comes from a variety of sources. Some are U.S. sources and some are those of other countries. Some are the sources are technical, such as intercepted telephone conversations and photos taken by satellites. Other sources are people who have risked their lives to let the world know what Saddam Hussein is really up to.

I cannot tell you everything that we know, but what I can share with you, when combined with what all of us have learned over the years, is deeply troubling. What you will see is an accumulation of facts and disturbing patterns of behavior. The facts and Iraqis' behavior, Iraq's behavior, demonstrate that Saddam Hussein and his regime have made no effort, no effort, to disarm, as required by the international community.

Indeed, the facts and Iraq's behavior show that Saddam Hussein and his regime are concealing their efforts to produce more weapons of mass destruction. . . .

Everything we have seen and heard indicates that instead of cooperating actively with the inspectors to ensure the success of their mission, Saddam Hussein and his regime are busy doing all they possibly can to ensure that inspectors succeed in finding absolutely nothing.

My colleagues, every statement I make today is backed up by sources, solid sources. These are not assertions. What we are giving you are facts and conclusions based on solid intelligence. I will cite some examples, and these are from human sources. . . .

We know that Saddam's son, Qusay, ordered the removal of all prohibited weapons from Saddam's numerous palace complexes. We know that Iraqi government officials, members of the ruling Ba'ath Party and scientists have hidden prohibited items in their homes. Other key files from military and scientific establishments have been placed in cars that are being driven around the countryside by Iraqi intelligence agents to avoid detection. . . .

Thanks to intelligence they were provided, the inspectors recently found dramatic confirmation of these reports. When they searched the homes of an Iraqi nuclear scientist, they uncovered roughly 2,000 pages of documents. You see them here being brought out of the home and placed in UN hands. Some of the material is classified and related to Iraq's nuclear program. . . .

Our sources tell us that in some cases the hard drives of computers at Iraqi weapons facilities were replaced. Who took the hard drives? Where did they go? What is being hidden? Why?

There is only one answer to the why: to deceive, to hide, to keep from the inspectors.

Numerous human sources tell us that the Iraqis are moving not just documents and hard drives, but weapons of mass destruction, to keep them from being found by inspectors. While we were here in this Council chamber debating Resolution 1441 last fall, we know, we know from sources that a missile brigade outside Baghdad was dispersing rocket launchers and warheads containing biological warfare agent to various locations, distributing them to various locations in western Iraq.

Most of the launchers and warheads had been hidden in large groves of palm trees and were to be moved every one to four weeks to escape detection.

We also have satellite photos that indicate that banned materials have recently been moved from a number of Iraqi weapons of mass destruction facilities.

- **Source:** Colin Powell, remarks to UN Security Council, February 5, 2003, available at http://www.state.gov/secretary/former/powell/remarks/2003/17300.htm, last accessed April 24, 2008.

- **Analysis:** Secretary of State Colin Powell presented the U.S. case for military action against Iraq, arguing that Saddam Hussein had failed to comply with UN requirements. Some of the intelligence he used to make his case was later discredited. His inability to identify the sources of the intelligence provided his critics an avenue of attack against his arguments. At the time he made his presentation, planning for the invasion of Iraq was well underway. UN support was desirable but not essential to these plans, as some U.S. allies would not join the coalition without a UN mandate.

- **Document 25: Excerpts of Responses of Security Council Members to Mr. Powell's Remarks**
- **When:** February 5, 2003
- **Where:** New York City
- **Significance:** Secretary Powell failed to persuade the Security Council to pass a resolution in support of war with Iraq.

Mr. Straw (United Kingdom)

We have just heard a most powerful and authoritative case against the Iraqi regime set out by United States Secretary of State Powell. The international community owes him its thanks for laying bare the deceit practised by the regime of Saddam Hussain—and worse, the very great danger which that regime represents.

Three months ago we united to send Iraq an uncompromising message: cooperate fully with weapons inspectors, or face disarmament by force. After years of Iraqi deception, when resolutions were consistently flouted, resolution 1441 (2002) was a powerful reminder of the importance of international law and of the authority of the Security Council itself. United and determined, we gave Iraq a final opportunity to rid itself of its weapons of mass terror, of gases which can poison thousands in one go; of bacilli and viruses like anthrax and smallpox, which can disable and kill by the tens of thousands; of the means to make nuclear weapons, which can kill by the million.

By resolution 1441 (2002), we strengthened inspections massively. The only missing ingredient was full Iraqi compliance—immediate, full and active cooperation. But the truth is—and we all know this—without that full and active cooperation, however strong the inspectors' powers, however good the inspectors, inspections in a country as huge as Iraq could never be sure of finding all Iraqi weapons of mass destruction.

Sadly, the inspectors' reports last week, and Secretary Powell's presentation today, can leave us under no illusions about Saddam Hussain's response. Saddam Hussain holds United Nations Security Council resolution 1441 (2002) in the same contempt as all previous resolutions in respect of Iraq. Let us reflect on what that means: Saddam is defying every one of us, every nation here represented. He questions our resolve and is gambling that we will lose our nerve rather than enforce our will. . . .

There is only one possible conclusion from all of this, which is that Iraq is in further material breach, as set out in United Nations Security Council resolution 1441 (2002). I believe that all colleagues here, all members, will share our deep sense of frustration that Iraq is choosing to spurn this final opportunity to achieve a peaceful outcome. Given what has to follow, and the difficult choice now facing us, it would be easy to turn a blind eye to the wording of resolution 1441 (2002) and hope for a change of heart by Iraq. Easy, but wrong, because if we did so we would be repeating the mistakes of the past 12 years and empowering a dictator who believes that his diseases and poison gases are essential weapons to suppress his own people and to threaten his neighbours, and that by defiance of the United Nations he can indefinitely hoodwink the world.

Mr. Ivanov (Russian Federation)

Russia views today's meeting in the context of the consistent efforts of the Security Council to find a political settlement to the situation surrounding Iraq, on the basis of complete and scrupulous compliance with the relevant resolutions. The unanimous adoption of Security Council resolution 1441 (2002) and the deployment of international inspectors in Iraq have demonstrated the ability of the international community to act together in the interests of attaining a common goal. We are convinced that maintaining the unity of the world community, primarily within the context of the Security Council, and our concerted action, in strict compliance with the Charter of the United Nations and the resolutions of the Security Council, are the most reliable means of resolving the problem of weapons of mass destruction in Iraq through political means.

There is no doubt that we all want to resolve this problem. It was with that in mind that we listened very closely to the presentation given by Secretary of State Powell. Russia continues to believe that the Security Council—and, through it, the entire international community—must have all of the information it needs in order to determine whether or not there are remaining weapons of mass destruction in Iraq. The information given to us today definitely will require very serious and thorough study. Experts in our countries must immediately begin to analyse it and then draw the appropriate conclusions. The main point is that this information must immediately be handed over for processing by the United Nations Monitoring, Verification and Inspection Commission (UNMOVIC) and the International Atomic Energy Agency (IAEA), including through direct on-site verification during the inspections in Iraq. Baghdad must give the inspectors answers to the questions that we heard in the presentation given by the United States Secretary of State. We appeal once again to all States immediately to hand over to the international inspectors any information that can help them discharge their responsible mandate. The information provided today by the United States Secretary of State once again convincingly indicates that the activities of the international inspectors in Iraq must be continued. They alone can say to what extent Iraq is complying with the demands of the Security Council. They alone can help the Security Council work out and adopt carefully balanced decisions—the best possible decisions.

Mr. Galouzeau de Villepin (France)

For now, the inspections regime favoured by resolution 1441 (2002) must be strengthened, since it has not been explored to the end. Use of force can only be a final recourse. Why go to war if there still exists an unused space in resolution 1441 (2002)? Consistent with the logic of that resolution, we must therefore move on to a new stage and further strengthen the inspections. With the choice between military intervention and an inspections regime that is inadequate for lack of cooperation on Iraq's part, we must choose to strengthen decisively the means of inspection. That is what France is proposing today.

Mr. Aldouri (Iraq)

The pronouncements in Mr. Powell's statement on weapons of mass destruction are utterly unrelated to the truth and the reality on the ground. No new information was provided; mere sound recordings cannot be confirmed as genuine. Council members may have seen me smile when I heard some of those recordings; they contain certain words that I will not attempt to translate here. However, those incorrect allegations, unnamed and unknown sources, schemes and presumptions are all in line with United States policy, which is directed towards one known objective.

- **Source:** Transcript of Security Council debate, S/2003/4701.
- **Analysis:** Following Secretary Powell's testimony, the Security Council discussed the matter of Iraq. Only the United Kingdom, represented by foreign secretary Jack Straw, backed the U.S. call for stronger action. Russian Federation foreign minister Igor Ivanov expressed skepticism about the information presented and asked that the U.S. sources be turned over to the UN monitoring group. French foreign minister Galouzeau de Villepin noted that while the developments Secretary Powell noted were troubling, the danger they posed was not imminent, and that strengthening the inspection regime, not immediate military action, was the answer. Iraq's UN representative, Mohammed Aldouri, denied the accusations leveled at his country.

- **Document 26: Joint Statement by Mr. de Villepin, Mr. Ivanov, and Mr. Fischer (France, Russia, and Germany) on Iraqi Sanctions Submitted to the UN Security Council**
- **When:** March 5, 2003
- **Where:** Paris, France
- **Significance:** France, Germany, and Russia declared their opposition to using force against Iraq under the circumstances at the time.

Our common objective remains the full and effective disarmament of Iraq, in compliance with resolution 1441 (2002).

We consider that this objective can be achieved by the peaceful means of the inspections.

We moreover observe that these inspections are producing increasing encouraging results:

- The destruction of the Al-Samoud missiles has started and is making progress;
- Iraqis are providing biological and chemical information;
- The interviews with Iraqi scientists are continuing.

Russia, Germany and France resolutely support Messrs. Blix and ElBaradei and consider the meeting of the Security Council on 7 March to be an important step in the process put in place.

We firmly call for the Iraqi authorities to cooperate more actively with the inspectors to fully disarm their country. These inspections cannot continue indefinitely.

We consequently ask that the inspections now be speeded up, in keeping with the proposals put forward in the memorandum submitted to the Security Council by our three countries. We must:

- Specify and prioritize the remaining issues, programme by programme;
- Establish, for each point, detailed timelines.

Using this method, the inspectors have to present without any delay their work programme accompanied by regular progress reports to the Security Council. This programme could provide for a meeting clause to enable the Council to evaluate the overall results of this process.

In these circumstances, we will not let a proposed resolution pass that would authorize the use of force.

Russia and France, as permanent members of the Security Council, will assume all their responsibilities on this point.

We are at a turning point. Since our goal is the peaceful and full disarmament of Iraq, we have today the chance to obtain through peaceful means a comprehensive settlement for the Middle East, starting with a move forward in the peace process, by:

- Publishing and implementing the roadmap;
- Putting together a general framework for the Middle East, based on stability and security, renunciation of force, arms control and trust-building measures.

- **Source:** United Nations Security Council, S/2003/253, March 5, 2003, available at http://www.un.int/france/documents_anglais/030305 _mae_france_irak.htm.
- **Analysis:** Following 9/11, the United States had enjoyed widespread support from its allies. NATO invoked Article 5 of the Washington Treaty (its founding document) and declared the attack upon one of its members an attack upon all. Both NATO and the United Nations supported military action against Afghanistan, and 47 nations joined the International Stabilization Force.

The plan to invade Iraq elicited far less support. Even the United States' closest allies did not accept the argument that Iraq posed an immediate threat to anyone. While the Russian Federation might be expected to oppose an invasion for cynical reasons, the same could not be said of France and Germany, both of which supported the United States in Afghanistan. As a permanent member of the UN Security Council, Russia could veto any resolution authorizing the use of force against Iraq, so this memorandum virtually guaranteed that the Operation Iraq Freedom would not have a UN mandate.

CONCLUSION

The Bush administration made its case for war in the manner Senator Feingold noted in his speech opposing the Iraq War resolution. Rationale shifted from WMD to terrorist links to humanitarian concerns. However, the letter from the neocons to President Clinton and President Bush's remarks during the 2000 election suggest that his administration had desired to remove Saddam Hussein even before 9/11 provided the pretext for doing so.

2

SHOCK AND AWE

The U.S. military began preparing for a possible invasion of Iraq shortly after 9/11. Because of the long-standing conflict with Saddam, invasion plans had been on the Pentagon drawing board for some time. The latest version had been draw up by the Central Command staff under General Anthony Zinni in 1998. Their plan called for an invasion force of over 400,000, anticipating that a large number of troops would be necessary not to defeat the Iraqi military but to occupy such a large and populous country. The following year, Zinni's staff rehearsed the operational plan in a seminar exercise that predicted many of the problems encountered during the actual occupation of Iraq.

Despite these concerns, Secretary of Defense Donald Rumsfeld insisted on a much smaller invasion force. Operating under the assumption that the Iraqi police and civil service would remain in place and that a new government could quickly be formed, the Pentagon committed enough troops to defeat Saddam Hussein's forces but not enough to occupy and secure the country. While the shortage of troops contributed to the ensuing insurgency, the invasion itself was a masterful joint operation that produced a decisive conventional victory with minimal loss of life on both sides and relatively little damage to Iraqi infrastructure. The ensuing insurgency does not detract from the effectiveness of the conventional war.

THE CONCEPT

The concept of shock and awe developed some time before the Iraq War. The challenge was to achieve decisive results with a massive application of force at key points, not to inflict maximum casualties or physical destruction but to establish psychological dominance over an enemy to such a degree that the enemy would capitulate.

The military concept of effects-based operations (EBO) bore a close relationship to shock and awe. EBO sought to achieve a decisive effect with a limited, highly focused use of force. Instead of degrading enemy capability through long battles of attrition and strategic bombing, military planners sought to incapacitate an enemy through destruction of, for example, his command and control capability. Rather than systematically destroy enemy factories, an EBO air campaign might target electric generating plants, rendering all other manufacturing facilities inoperative.

- **Document 27: Excerpt of *Shock and Awe***
- **When:** 1996
- **Where:** Washington, DC
- **Significance:** This publication explained the concept of shock and awe used in the invasion of Iraq.

The aim of Rapid Dominance is to affect the will, perception, and understanding of the adversary to fit or respond to our strategic policy ends through imposing a regime of Shock and Awe. Clearly, the traditional military aim of destroying, defeating, or neutralizing the adversary's military capability is a fundamental and necessary component of Rapid Dominance. Our intent, however, is to field a range of capabilities to induce sufficient Shock and Awe to render the adversary impotent. This means that physical and psychological effects must be obtained.

Rapid Dominance would therefore provide the ability to control, on an immediate basis, the entire region of operational interest and the environment, broadly defined, in and around that area of interest. Beyond achieving decisive force and dominant battlefield awareness, we envisage Rapid Dominance producing a capability that can more effectively and efficiently achieve the stated political or military objectives underwriting the use of force by rendering the adversary completely impotent.

- **Source:** Harlan K. Ullman and James P. Wade. *Shock and Awe: Achieving Rapid Dominance.* Washington, DC: NDU, 1996, 1–6, available at https://digitalndulibrary.ndu.edu/cdm4/document.php?CISOROOT=/ndupress&CISOPTR=32538&REC=10.

- **Analysis:** Harlan K. Ullman and James P. Wade wrote a study of the concept of shock and awe for the National Defense University. U.S. military thinking in the 1990s was dominated by the Powell Doctrine, a concept developed by General (later Secretary of State) Colin Powell when he was chairman of the Joint Chiefs of Staff. The doctrine required the use of overwhelming force to achieve decisive results against an enemy. The United States and its allies applied this doctrine effectively during the first Gulf War.

  Shock and awe refined this approach. The concept called for the use of decisive force and psychological pressure at key points to achieve the same result with less destruction and loss of life. Targeting enemy communications and command-and-control facilities can incapacitate military forces without destroying them. This approach allows for rapid, decisive results without the undesirable effects of overwhelming military force.

INVASION PLANS

U.S. Central Command, in cooperation with the Pentagon, devised several versions of an Iraq invasion plan, even before the post-9/11 crisis. Operations Plan 1003-98 (OPLAN 1003-98) called for an invasion force of over 400,000 troops and envisioned a protracted postconflict stability operation. General Tommy Franks, who succeeded Anthony Zinni as Central Command (CENTCOM) commander, rejected the plan in favor of one calling for a smaller force, which Rumsfeld whittled down even further. COBRA II, the final version, specified an invasion force of around 150,000 and made little preparation for postwar contingencies.

DID YOU KNOW?

General Tommy Franks

Tommy Franks (b. 1945) was a four-star U.S. Army general who was in charge of U.S. Central Command at the time of the Iraq invasion. Commissioned as a second lieutenant in 1967, Franks served in Vietnam and advanced in rank, holding various positions during the Cold War. He commanded the First Cavalry Division during Operation Desert Storm (1991) and succeeded United States Marine Corps general Anthony Zinni as Central Command (CENTCOM) commander in 2000. Following his retirement in 2003, Franks wrote the best-selling autobiography *American Soldier* (Harper Collins, 2004).

Franks was widely criticized for allowing the Rumsfeld Pentagon to whittle down the size of his Iraq invasion force, a decision he defended as his own in his memoir. A staunch supporter of George W. Bush, Franks received the Presidential Medal of Freedom from him and spoke on his behalf at the 2004 Republican National Convention. In January 17, 2008, the *Army Times* reported that Franks had accepted $100,000 to allow his name to be used by a charity that raised money for wounded veterans, paid out of funds contributed for that purpose. Since retiring he has served on the boards of several foundations.

- **Document 28: Excerpt of Desert Crossing Seminar After-Action Report**
- **When:** June 28–30, 1999
- **Where:** Washington, DC
- **Significance:** The exercise revealed many of the problems that the United States would encounter in Iraq.

Executive Summary

On June 28–30, 1999, The United States Central Command (USCENTCOM) sponsored the Desert Crossing Seminar to identify interagency issues and insights on how to manage change in a post-Saddam Iraq. The Seminar structure focused the participants on crucial interagency issues that would bear on the situation, as well as interagency interests and responsibilities. USCENTCOM briefed a draft plan, known as "Desert Crossing," to participants for discussion of the proposed phases and concepts, as well as the risks, threats, opportunities, and challenges that are likely to be present under those conditions. Over 70 participants, including the Department of State, Department of Defense, National Security Council, and the Central Intelligence Agency took part in the seminar.

Participants were organized into various teams to facilitate development of insights but were not asked to "solve" the problems. In fact, there was a consensus that this seminar should be the beginning of much more robust discussion. The observations below summarize participant views and suggest matters for further deliberation. These views do not represent consensus of the individual participants, the various Departments, agencies, or entities, or the U.S. Government.

Deliberate planning needs to become interagency

Political/Military planning should begin immediately.

The dimensions of preparing a post-Saddam policy for Iraq and the region are vast and complex. Early preparation of a political-military plan as called for in presidential Decision Directive 56 should be a priority. The accompanying policy debate will expose a variety of contentious positions that must be reconciled and managed. Key discussion points include benefits and risks associated with various strategic options; information requirements; and the likelihood that intervention will be costly in terms of casualties and resources.

Regime crisis may require rapid U.S. action on short notice.

When the crisis occurs, policy makers will have to deal with a large number of critical issues nearly simultaneously, including demonstrating U.S. leadership and resolve, managing Iraq's neighbors, and rapid policy formulation. Successfully doing so depends on identifying "Red Lines," the crossing of which is likely to lead to U.S. reaction, in order to facilitate crisis planning. Such Red lines may include large-scale humanitarian crisis, use (or imminent use) of Weapons of Mass Destruction (WMD), or imminent Iraqi attack on a neighboring state.

Regime change may not enhance regional stability.

A change in regimes does not guarantee stability. A number of factors including aggressive neighbors, fragmentation along religious and/or ethnic lines, and chaos created by rival forces bidding for power could adversely affect regional stability. Even when civil order is restored and borders are secured, the replacement regime could be problematic—especially if perceived as weak, a puppet, or out-of-step with prevailing regional governments. These consequences must not be ignored during political-military planning.

> **DID YOU KNOW?**
>
> **United States Central Command (USCENTCOM)**
>
> USCENTCOM is one of six geographic operational commands of the United States. Created on January 1, 1983, CENTCOM included the countries of the Middle East, Central Asia, and East Africa. Responsibility for its African nations (except Egypt) has been transferred to the Africa Command, created in 2007. During the Cold War, the United States concentrated its resources in the European Command and Pacific Command, the two bulwarks against communist aggression. The U.S. Southern Command became more prominent during the conflicts in Latin America during the 1980s. Created in 2002, the U.S. Northern Command is responsible for North America.
>
> The 1986 Goldwater-Nichols Defense Reorganization Act enhanced the role of the unified commands. In an effort to enhance unity of effort, the act gave each combatant commander control over the air force, marine, navy, and army units in their areas of operation during wartime. USCENTCOM came to the fore following the August 1990 Iraqi invasion of Kuwait and has remained the focus of U.S. interest ever since. The wars in Afghanistan and Iraq both fall under its jurisdiction.

WMD issues warrant additional attention.

Participants concluded that U.S. policy in reaction to the use of WMD against U.S. personnel or allies was clear. However, U.S. policy on the possibility of Iraqi use of WMD under other circumstances is ill defined and probably does not address the full range of situations. For example, how should the United States respond to an Iraqi faction that employs WMD against a competing faction or a non-coalition or non-ally neighbor? Although the likelihood of WMD use by Iraq was hotly debated, planners and policy makers should review potential WMD situations now to determine the scale, scope, and nature of such use and the likely U.S. response.

Management of Iran is critical to mission success

Iran's anti-Americanism could be enflamed by a U.S.-led intervention in Iraq.

Iran has substantial interests in developments in Iraq, perhaps its most bitter rival in the region, nor have relations with the United States been any better. The influx of U.S. and other western forces into Iraq would exacerbate worries in Tehran, as would the installation of a pro-western government in Baghdad. More than any other country in the region, the principals were most concerned by how Iran would respond to a U.S.-led intervention in Iraq.

Iran possesses the ability to raise the costs and consequences of intervention.

Many participants felt that Washington should attempt to leverage the crisis to improve the present U.S.-Iran relationship. They believe the worst-case scenario is one in which Iran feels pressured and lashes out asymmetrically in moves that range from harassment of U.S. forces to terrorist attacks. Such attacks will likely shake U.S. determination and perhaps undermine public and political will. To preclude this, the United States and its partners should ensure that Iran does not support counterproductive activities in Iraq and should engage Tehran in a productive fashion wherever possible.

Lifting sanctions on Iran may be part of a full Iraq policy

Whether the lifting of U.S. sanctions will be required to gain Tehran's co-operation is unclear. Some participants expressed the view that the United States should use the possibility of lifting them as an incentive for Iranian cooperation. Other participants expressed concern as to how to control Iran in the long term if it continues its support for terrorism, continues WMD programs, and/or exports its revolutionary principles to other countries in the region once sanctions are lifted.

Ambiguous role of Iraqi opposition clouds U.S. policy development

Lack of information on internal Iraqi opposition conditions severely hampers contingency planning.

The United States lacks sufficient information on individuals and groups within Iraq to plan for, or respond to, Saddam's departure. Information for planning and to facilitate dialog with key internal groups or individuals is currently lacking; the United States does not have a clear understanding of their policies and agendas. The intelligence community should initiate actions to determine potential Iraqi leadership groupings that might "naturally" evolve when Saddam departs and to establish the basic criteria and conditions under which such individuals or groups should be approached.

Iraqi exile opposition weaknesses are significant.

The debate on post-Saddam Iraq also reveals the paucity of information about the potential and capabilities of the external Iraqi opposition groups. The lack of intelligence concerning their roles hampers U.S. policy development. Although participants disagreed as to whether exiled opposition leaders could be useful during the regime transition period, there was no dispute that if the United States were to support them, much must be done in order for these groups to be politically credible within Iraq.

The United States should be prepared to initiate, on short notice, a dialog with leaders of key ethnic groups within Iraq.

A variety of power struggles might occur during the early stages of a post Saddam crisis. Because events are likely to occur rapidly, consideration should be given now to individuals and groups and their policies and agendas in order to develop a range of options. To this end, the United States should initiate, or at least prepare to initiate, dialogs with key leaders in the PUK, KDP, and Shi'a tribes as early as possible.

Coalition dialogue should begin immediately

Active support from coalition partners is critical to mission success.

There are many unknown as to how potential partners think about coalition participation. To facilitate rapid reaction, the United States must begin the process of planning for coalition operations and developing the basis for a coalition now. The risks to U.S. regional interests are too high and events are likely to unfold too rapidly to wait until the crisis begins.

Differing visions of a unified Iraq complicate end-state articulation.

The seminar demonstrated that there are differing visions of what a post-Saddam Iraq should look like to various coalition partners. These differences will complicate developing a common coalition end sate, much less reaching consensus on such a state. This will delay coalition formation during the critical early stages of the crisis and may complicate exit strategies.

Arab coalition may undermine accomplishments of U.S. policy objectives.

A paradox exposed during the Seminar is that while an Arab coalition will be required for legitimacy in the region, such a coalition may make it more difficult for the United States to attain its objectives. Solutions envisioned by U.S. coalition partners (especially our Arab partners) may be significantly different than those envisioned by U.S. planners. For example, the Iraq Liberation Act specifies a democratic outcome that contrasts starkly with the predilections of some Arab governments. Also, some participants believe that no Arab government will welcome the kind of lengthy U.S. presence that would be required to install and sustain a democratic government.

A long-term, large-scale military intervention may be at odds with many coalition partners.

The nature of the region's relationships with the United Sates and other western nations in the post-intervention era are likely to be vastly different. What participated referred to as the "Japanese Option," (long-term presence and directed change) is not likely to be well received by coalition partners. Changes that could result from the intervention at various levels will involve political and military relationships; religious and ethnic conflicts; economic relations; and differing views of social justice. While differences with Arab allies concerning the U.S. presence in the region were managed reasonably well in the past (owing in part to common threats), intervention in Iraq may alter the way these relationships are handled dramatically enough to produce new frictions and conflicts.

Iraq's economic viability is key to long term economic stability

Iraq's stabilization requires debt/claims forgiveness.

Mounting a large intervention will be costly, as regional partners may not be willing to reimburse the United States to the extent that they have in the past. One possibility, using Iraqi oil revenues to pay for the intervention, would come at the expense of long term reconstitution, and may effect regional and global economic stability if oil prices fluctuate too rapidly. Also, Iraq still faces claims estimated at $300 billion as a result of its 1990 invasion of Kuwait. If these claims are relentlessly pursued, economic recovery, and thus stability, may be delayed. Policymakers in the United States and abroad should investigate debt and claims forgiveness, as a stable Iraq can evolve only if it is economically viable.

The relaxation of economic sanctions early in the crisis may be a key determinant in the ability of the United States to influence events in Iraq.

Some seminar participants believed that one of the most important things the United States could do to improve its image in the eyes of the Iraqi people would be the announcement of immediate lifting of economic sanctions early in the transition crisis. The United States should expect immediate pressure from others, including coalition members to lift sanctions, even while the outcome of the internal Iraqi situation is unclear. Seizing the "high ground" and immediately lifting the sanctions upon a change in the Iraqi regime—even if its policies and orientation are unknown—might be advantageous for U.S. interests.

- **Source:** *Desert Crossing Seminar: After-Action Report*, 28–30 June 1999, declassified July 2, 2004, pp. 3-8, available at http://www.gwu.edu/~nsarchiv/NSAEBB/NSAEBB207/Desert%20Crossing%20After%20Action%20Report_1999-06-28.pdf, accessed March 30, 2011.
- **Analysis:** In June 1999, CENTCOM tested the assumptions of OPLAN 1003-98, General Zinni's plan for an invasion of Iraq, in a seminar exercise. The findings of the exercise identified many of the problems that surfaced in postwar Iraq and confirmed the need for a large invasion force. While defeating the Iraqi military might be easy, occupying and governing the country during a transition period would not. The seminar also discovered that maintaining a coalition for a

prolonged nation-building operation would be difficult and that opposition from the Arab world would complicate matters. It also questioned the premise that regime change would enhance regional stability.

The administration, especially the secretary of defense, either did not know of or ignored the findings of the exercise seminar and its prescient conclusions. Determined to avoid a prolonged nation-building operation, the administration wanted a lean invasion force that would overthrow Saddam Hussein and hand power to a democratically elected Iraqi government. They failed to consider, as Zinni's team had, that civil authority might collapse, making it impossible for U.S. forces to fight and leave.

- **Document 29: Excerpt of General Eric Shinseki's Congressional Testimony**
- **When:** February 25, 2003
- **Where:** Washington, DC
- **Significance:** General Shinseki challenged the claim that the Iraq mission could be accomplished with the number of troops that the secretary of defense wanted.

SEN. LEVIN: General Shinseki, could you give us some idea as to the magnitude of the Army's force requirement for an occupation of Iraq following a successful completion of the war?

GEN. SHINSEKI: In specific numbers, I would have to rely on combatant commanders' exact requirements. But I think—

SEN. LEVIN: How about a range?

GEN. SHINSEKI: I would say that what's been mobilized to this point—something on the order of several hundred thousand soldiers are probably, you know, a figure that would be required. We're talking about post-hostilities control over a piece of geography that's fairly significant, with the kinds of ethnic tensions that could lead to other problems. And so it takes a significant ground-force presence.

- **Source:** Hearing of the Senate Armed Services Committee, "The Fiscal Year 2004 Defense Budget," testimony of General Eric Shinseki, February 25, 2003.
- **Analysis:** Whether or not he was familiar with Exercise Desert Crossing, General Shinseki recognized the same issues identified by Zinni's team. Sweeping aside Saddam's forces might be easy, but occupying and stabilizing a country the size of Iraq would be a labor intensive task requiring more troops than the Secretary of Defense wished to commit. Shinseki also recognized the potential for ethnic conflict, which did in fact develop in post-invasion Iraq.

- **Document 30: Excerpt of Testimony of Paul Wolfowitz to the House Committee on the Budget**
- **When:** February 27, 2003
- **Where:** Washington, DC
- **Significance:** In his testimony Wolfowitz rebutted General Shinseki's estimate of troop strength necessary for the Iraq mission.

DEP. SEC. WOLFOWITZ: There has been a good deal of comment—some of it quite outlandish—about what our postwar requirements might be in Iraq. Some of the higher end predictions we have been hearing recently, such as the notion that it will take several hundred thousand U.S. troops to provide stability in post-Saddam Iraq, are wildly off the mark. It is hard to conceive that it would take more forces to provide stability in post-Saddam Iraq than it would take to conduct the war itself and to secure the surrender of Saddam's security forces and his army—hard to imagine.

- **Source:** "Hearing Before the Committee on the Budget, House of Representatives," testimony of Paul Wolfowitz, February 27, 2003.
- **Analysis:** The Department of Defense was furious with General Shinseki for his comments on the number of troops needed to occupy and stabilize Iraq. Donald Rumsfeld wanted to transform the U.S. Army into a smaller, lighter, more mobile force. Transformation would cost money. He did not wish the Pentagon encumbered by an expensive nation-building operation or by the legacy costs (pensions and benefits) of a large deployment. He sent Wolfowitz to Capitol Hill to rebut Shinseki's conclusions.

  Wolfowitz based his claim that it would not take more troops to stabilize Iraq than to conquer it on dubious assumptions. The Department of Defense assumed that the Iraqi administration would remain in place to perform the day-to-day work of government even after Saddam had been removed. They failed to anticipate that government would completely collapse, creating a vacuum to be filled by criminals, insurgents, and foreign terrorists. The wisdom of General Shinseki's testimony and General Zinni's analysis proved more accurate than Wolfowitz's unbridled optimism.

INVASION

The air campaign began on March 19, escalating to "shock and awe" on the night of the ground invasion, March 21. U.S. forces advanced up highways 1, 7, and 8 toward Baghdad while British forces wheeled right to encircle and capture Basra. A planned invasion by the Fourth Infantry Division from the north had to be abandoned when the Turkish government refused permission to use its territory. Joint Special Operations forces did, however, link up with Kurdish Peshmerga forces to attack Kirkuk and Mosul.

American forces faced little resistance from the Iraqi army until they reached the outskirts of Baghdad, where they engaged Republican Guard units. They did, however, face determined and largely unexpected resistance from partisan guerrillas who ambushed them and attacked their long supply lines. This resistance would prove to be a harbinger of worse to come, although most analysts lost sight of the danger in the euphoria following the fall of Baghdad in early April. Mop-up operations followed for the rest of the month. On May 1, 2003, President Bush declared an end to major hostilities on the deck of the aircraft carrier *Abraham Lincoln*.

DID YOU KNOW?

Republican Guard

The Republican Guard was the elite force of Saddam Hussein's army. Created in 1980 as the dictator's bodyguard, the force expanded to two corps at the time of Operation Iraqi Freedom. Carefully screened for loyalty, guardsmen received better equipment, training, and pay than members of the regular army. Saddam used his elite force not only in the Iran-Iraq War and the invasion of Kuwait but to suppress opposition within Iraq. U.S. forces correctly assumed the Republican Guard would put up more of a fight to defend the regime than the rest of the Iraqi military. They were most heavily involved in the fighting outside of Baghdad.

- **Document 31: Excerpt of Transcript of Press Briefing by Secretary of Defense Donald Rumsfeld and Chairman of Joint Chiefs of Staff General Richard Myers**
- **When:** March 21, 2003
- **Where:** Washington, DC
- **Significance:** On the day the ground war began, Rumsfeld explained the goals and objectives of Operation Iraqi Freedom.

Our goal is to defend the American people, and to eliminate Iraq's weapons of mass destruction, and to liberate the Iraqi people. Coalition military operations are focused on achieving several specific objectives: to end the regime of Saddam Hussein by striking with force on a scope and scale that makes clear to Iraqis that he and his regime are finished. Next, to identify, isolate and eventually eliminate Iraq's weapons of mass destruction, their delivery systems, production capabilities, and distribution networks. Third, to search for, capture, drive out terrorists who have found safe harbor in Iraq. Fourth, to collect such intelligence as we can find related to terrorist networks in Iraq and beyond. Fifth, to collect such intelligence as we can find related to the global network of illicit weapons of mass destruction activity. Sixth, to end sanctions and to immediately deliver humanitarian relief, food and medicine to the displaced and to the many needy Iraqi citizens. Seventh, to secure Iraq's oil fields and resources, which belong to the Iraqi people, and which they will need to develop their country after decades of neglect by the Iraqi regime. And last, to help the Iraqi people create the conditions for a rapid transition to a representative self-government that is not a threat to its neighbors and is committed to ensuring the territorial integrity of that country.

- **Source:** Transcript of press briefing by Secretary of Defense Donald Rumsfeld and chairman of the Joint Chiefs of Staff General Richard Myers, March 21, 2003, available at http://www.defense.gov/transcripts/transcript.aspx?transcriptid=2074, accessed April 20, 2011.

- **Analysis:** Rumsfeld repeated the laundry list of reasons for invading Iraq mustered by the administration during the preceding year. In addition to removing what it believed to be threats to U.S. security, the administration now emphasized its desire to provide humanitarian aid to the Iraqi people. The last goal reveals the administration's expectation for the duration of the campaign. It desired a "rapid transition to representative self-government." For such a transition to occur, the bulk of the Iraqi civil service would have to remain in place. Rumsfeld and his associates thus viewed Operation Iraqi Freedom as an elaborate decapitation strike. They would remove Saddam Hussein and his cronies but expected that the government employees who provided vital services would still come to work and do their jobs. This expectation proved totally unfounded.

- **Document 32: Excerpt of Pentagon Briefing on Operation Iraqi Freedom**
- **When:** March 21, 2003
- **Where:** Washington, DC
- **Significance:** This briefing revealed initial progress of the invasion.

Operation Iraqi Freedom, our effort to disarm Iraq and dismantle the Iraqi regime, is fully underway. But before I go into that, I want to recap what has happened in the last 48 hours and how we got to where we are now.

On Wednesday afternoon, we conducted early battlefield preparations by taking out air defense threats, radar communication sites and artillery that could pose a threat to coalition forces. Some of these targets included radars in western Iraq and near Basra in southern Iraq, artillery pieces near Al-Faw and Az Zubay near Kuwait, and surface-to-surface missiles in the south. Later Wednesday evening, coalition forces began inserting Special Operations Forces throughout western and southern Iraq to conduct reconnaissance operations and take down visual observation posts on the southern Iraqi border.

At the same time, as we briefed yesterday, we took advantage of a leadership target of opportunity in Baghdad. Specifically, we struck at one of the residences in southeastern Baghdad, where we thought the leadership was congregated. We also took down—struck intelligence service headquarters in Baghdad and a Republican Guard facility. They were targeted with nearly 40 Tomahawk land attack cruise missiles from coalition ships in the Red Sea and the Persian Gulf. Two Air Force F-117s also dropped precision-guided, 2,000-pound penetration weapons on these leadership targets.

Then yesterday we launched more than 20 TLAMs against eight targets in Baghdad, which included several Baghdad Special Security Organization sites. As most of you know, the Special Security Organization is that organization that protects the senior Iraqi leadership. Also on Thursday, coalition ships launched some 10 TLAMs against three Republican Guard targets in Kirkuk in the north.

In the last 24 hours, Special Forces have seized an airfield in western Iraq and have secured border positions in several key locations. Additionally, Navy Seals and coalition special forces have seized Iraq's two major gas and oil terminals in the northern Persian Gulf. There were embedded media with the Seals, and their reports should be out shortly.

I also have a graphic, I think they'll bring it up—and it's up now; good. Coalition ships boarded three Iraqi tugboats in the Khor Abdullah waterway and found weapons, uniforms and mines. Over 130 mines, including influence mines, were discovered. Our naval vessels are being extra vigilant to ensure the Iraqi Navy has not placed any mines in international waters.

On the ground, as you know, the 1st Marine Expeditionary Force, along with our coalition partners, crossed into Iraq, and they have now secured the port city of Umm Qasar and the al-Faw peninsula. They have also secured the main oil manifolds along the al-Faw waterways, and have moved through the southern Iraqi oil fields. These fields, if we're successful, should be secured sometime later today, and they will be a great resource for the Iraqi people as they build a free society.

Last night, at approximately 10:00 p.m. Eastern Time, the rest of the ground campaign began in earnest when the 3rd Infantry Division rolled into southern Iraq. There's been a lot of reporting on this, of course, with some of the embedded media. At this hour, our ground forces have pushed close to 100 miles inside Iraq.

Since Operation Iraqi Freedom began, coalition aircraft have flown more than 1,000 sorties and dropped scores of precision-guided munitions on Iraqi military targets. I have two gun-camera shots from yesterday; both are from F-14s as they dropped on missile targets in southern Iraq. The first is targeting a missile support vehicle. The second is an Iraqi missile storage facility in Basra. And if you note in the bottom of that picture, you'll see another fire; that was hit from a previous strike from the same flight.

As you've seen from the TV coverage, from embedded media, clearly we're moving towards our objectives, but we must not get too comfortable. We're basically on our plan and moving towards Baghdad, but there are still many unknowns out there.

We have dropped millions of leaflets over Iraq telling the Iraqi people our intentions and asking the Iraqi military to lay down their arms. In fact, some Iraqi soldiers are surrendering and abandoning their positions in the south and also in the north. Clearly, many Iraqi military are heeding our message that it is better to fight for the future of Iraq than to fight for Saddam Hussein.

That brings us up to date. So now, within the last hour, coalition forces have launched a massive air campaign throughout Iraq. Several hundred military targets will be hit over the coming hours, but we're getting into future operations here, and I'm going to let those details be briefed by CENTCOM tomorrow.

- **Source:** General Richard Myers, Department of Defense news briefing, March 21, 2003, available at http://www.defenselink.mil/transcripts/transcript.aspx?transcriptid=2074, accessed May 22, 2008.

- **Analysis:** As the briefing explained, Special Operations forces preceded the conventional units, securing an airfield and oil depots to prevent Saddam Hussein from destroying them. The briefing also identified the leafleting strategy to persuade Iraqi units to defect from their government. This strategy had an unintended consequence. Many Iraqi soldiers did in fact refuse to fight, but they did not return to their barracks as intact units as the United States had expected and desired. They went home as individuals, taking their weapons with them, which would create serious problems once the insurgency began.

- **Document 33: Excerpt of Department of Defense Briefing**
- **When:** March 22, 2003
- **Where:** Washington, DC
- **Significance:** Victoria Clarke and General Stanley McChrystal briefed reporters on the progress of the invasion.

Victoria Clarke: Good afternoon, everybody. First of all, I'd like to welcome Major General McChrystal, who is the vice director for operations on the Joint Staff. I won't quite say he volunteered, but he's going to help out on the briefings.

Although much work lies ahead, and you'll hear us saying that repeatedly, coalition forces are making considerable progress. The oil fields in the south are being saved to benefit the Iraqi people. Coalition forces have the key port of Umm Qasr and are making good progress in Basra. The Iraqi forces, including some leadership, are surrendering and defecting in some numbers. I think we have a few recent images here.

It is only a matter of time before the Iraqi regime is destroyed and its threat to region and the world is ended. As we've made clear from the beginning, this is not a war against a people, a country or a religion, and the Iraqi people who are welcoming coalition forces are clear evidence that they know this to be true.

As operations go forward, we'll continue to take extraordinary care to protect civilians. Our targets are military, and we continue to urge civilians to stay home and away from military assets. Additionally, we are prepared to provide as much humanitarian aid as required when and where it is needed. . . .

General McChrystal: Thank you, Ms. Clarke. . . . Operation Iraqi Freedom continues. A Day began yesterday at 1 p.m. Eastern Standard Time. The goal of the air campaign is to neutralize Iraqi leadership; suppress missile threats to our forces and Iraq's neighbors; support our Special Forces operations; to target Republican Guard, Special Republican Guard and Iraqi Intelligence Service operations as well as be on call for combat air control missions for time-sensitive targeting.

More than 1,000 sorties were flown against several hundred targets across Iraq yesterday. More than 400 Tomahawk cruise missiles were launched from United States Navy and British ships and submarines. Additionally, about 100 air-launch cruise missiles were fired, and 700 precision-guided munitions were dropped by coalition aircraft on targets throughout Iraq.

On the ground, coalition forces continue the main attack towards Baghdad. Ground forces have reached more than 150 miles into Iraqi territory and have crossed the Euphrates River. Coalition forces are advancing north beyond An Nazariyah. As General Franks mentioned, there are between 1,000 and 2,000 Iraqi soldiers who have surrendered and been taken into custody. And although numbers are hard to determine we have seen significant evidence of many Iraqi soldiers simply abandoning their equipment and leaving. Clearly, Operation Iraqi Freedom is moving forward. The success to date is a product of meticulous planning, effective integration of air, maritime, ground and special operations forces, and the impressive accomplishments of the soldiers, sailors, airmen, Marines and Coast Guardsmen of the coalition. But the operation is not over. There's a long way to go, and much of the Iraqi armed forces, highlighted by six Republican Guard divisions and special Republican Guard divisions, who may still fight. So we must remain prepared for potentially tough fights as we move forward.

That said, while the progress and timing of the operation remains impossible to forecast, the outcome is not. With that we'll take your questions.

Q: General, you referred to the one thousand, two thousand approximately Iraqis in custody. What became of the 8,000 members of the 51st who were said to have surrendered yesterday? Were they just allowed to go home? Or what's become of those?

McChrystal: Sir, we are seeing several phenomenon. The commander of the 51st Division, one of the senior leaders, in fact surrendered themselves individually. We also see soldiers essentially leaving the battlefield or melting away. The unit did not surrender en masse. What we have for numbers is, as General Franks outlined this morning, as of this morning between one and two thousand actually in an EPW status. . . .

McChrystal: Sir, trying to predict the conclusion of the operation or reaching Baghdad would be impossible at this point. The forces have moved with impressive speed thus far, as we outlined, and the product of that is where we are. That said, whenever you actually execute a plan the enemy gets a vote. We've still got significant Iraqi forces in front of us. They may fight, they may not. If they fight, there could be a tough battle to be taken. So trying to predict a time would be really difficult. . . .

Q: All along, Defense Secretary Rumsfeld has before this ever started warned that it could take six days, six weeks, or even six months. And this morning in the president's radio address he had again warned that this could take a long time. I wonder if it's time to remind the American people that this may not be wrapped up any time in the next few days—it could be a considerable period?

Clarke: I wouldn't put a timeframe on it, because we just don't know. But we've said from the very beginning, even well before the start of military operations, there are a lot of unknowns. There are a lot of bad things that can happen. And we'll take it one day at a time. And the only thing that is of great certainty is what the outcome is: the end of this regime. . . .

Q: One last thing about the—can you bring us up to date on whatever your state of knowledge is on the Iraqi regime, Saddam Hussein or anyone else in control? Do you know where any of those people are? Is there any evidence that anyone is leaving or defecting or making contact with—

Clarke: I don't have information about specific individuals, but I'll repeat what I said before: We continue to see evidence of confusion, of not a real solid grip on the command and control aspects that you would expect at this time. . . .

Q: Torie, and general, either one of you—can you tell us how far shock and all has gone? Is there more shock and all left? Are we going to see more today? If you don't want to put a specific on it, but is there some left in the barrel there?

McChrystal: Yes, sir, there's as much left in the barrel as required. The air campaign has been directed at a number of targets, importantly at the beginning the Iraqi command and control capability, the regime leadership, and then weapons of mass destruction and their capability to execute those. And that's tied to command and control as well. It will continue to target additional parts of the force as long as resistance is there to include Republican Guards and special Republican Guards, the intelligence. It is—we are waiting to get the feedback on how well that's working, and there is a lag time in that. We are hitting targets effectively and with precision, and pleased with that. But it takes a little while, as Torie just described, to get the feedback on how much we've affected it—because we know they have redundant capabilities in many areas. . . .

Q: (Inaudible)—over the last month we've had (inaudible) about 3,000 precision-guided bombs would rain down on Baghdad on the first night. This is the New York Times put that in play. Your math lays out maybe a thousand weapons at most, if conservatively. Was that the—was the original plan a much greater number, or was this always kind the state of play, roughly a thousand or so? Because that set the stage for this expectations of shock, awe, whatever you want to call it.

McChrystal: Sir, a couple things. First is, to go back in shock and awe as a concept, the idea is very precise, and some people I think misinterpreted shock and awe for a wave of fire and huge destruction. In fact, in an effects-based campaign, as this was, we can achieve much shock and awe by hitting just critical points. In fact, a perfect shock and awe would hit as few as possible to create those effects.

So, the answer is, we believe we are having effect, but it's tough to do that. Whether it will go forward in numbers—

Q: Could I have a follow-up?

Clarke: Well, let me just add on one point to that. If you go back to our objectives, our objective very clearly is to break the back of the Iraqi regime while causing as little collateral damage as possible. That's what our objective is. What is so important about the plans is its ability to scale-up and scale-down. . . .

Q: What role with SOF are we playing? Is SOF playing the same role as it did in Afghanistan? . . .

McChrystal: Sir, the role is different but the same. They are leveraging combat power. The key role of Special Operating Forces is to take very mature, well trained people and leverage power, i.e., it's not desirable that they get in direct firefights themselves, but instead they use air, they work with coalition allies, they use information. And a small force has a disproportionate effect on the battlefield. And that's what we're having right now. . . .

Q: Can you talk to us about the strategy of dealing with a large city like Basra, and then basically sealing it off once you have destroyed the organized force, and then moving rapidly beyond—same strategy today in Al Nazariyah—the risk that you take of having potentially a hostile city behind you, several of them, as you stretch out your lines of communication and resupply? High-risk strategy?

McChrystal: It depends upon the situation, sir. And I'd let General Franks characterize it in each case. Clear, we try to avoid combat in cities because of the effect on civilians and potential damage to infrastructure as well. In cases where we can bypass or isolate and continue the operation forward and hope then that that element or that location falls without pitched combat, I think that's in everyone's best interest. And the commander on the ground weighs whether or not the enemy forces in the city are any kind of threat to his lines of communication. . . .

Q: General, we saw some early morning bombing over Baghdad at dawn Baghdad time. Should we take from that that you're now confident enough you have taken down the air defense system enough over Baghdad and over Iraq to have daylight bombings?

McChrystal: Ma'am, we have the capability to operate any time. We still respect the air defenses in the Baghdad area. And of course as you know was known as the super "missile engagement zone," or MEZ. But the air defense is there already—an integrated system of air defense artillery, radars, command and control communications and surface-to-air missiles. If you can take down parts of that and degrade it, then it gets more feasible to operate effectively in day or night. We are still respectful of what they have.

Q: And if I could also follow up. Secretary Rumsfeld yesterday again spoke about communications that elements of the administration have had with Iraqi leadership, and that that was key to your decision-making on going forward in the campaign if they were to surrender that might be a good sign. Has there been any sign beyond the Republican Guard that you spoke about that any member of the senior leadership in Iraq was responding to the overtures from the Bush administration?

Clarke: I'd say two things. One, for quite some time now, with a variety of tools— the president of the United States speaking very openly, the leaflets, the commando solo—a variety of ways, a variety of conversations and discussions, we have been communicating with the leadership saying, End this now—save your lives, save the Iraqi people's lives. So we have communicated with them consistently over a range—with a range of tools—and we'll continue to do this. I am not going to characterize individual conversations, but discussions are ongoing, and there is still an opportunity for some people to do the right thing. . . .

Q: Can you get into the weapons of mass destruction sites? They were listed the first night of the air campaign. How many were struck? What do you expect was there? Are there chem, bio or long-range missiles? And did you use any special kinds of weaponry—incendiary devices, for example, to take them out?

Clarke: If you go back to what Secretary Rumsfeld talked about yesterday, and General Franks went through it again today, clearly one of our top priorities, one of our top objectives is to find and destroy the WMD. There are a number of sites. I won't go into details which ones they are, where they are, but it is a—

Q: More than 10? Less than a hundred?

Clarke: No, I will not give you a ballpark, but I will do two things. One is just underscore what a priority that is for us; and, two, try to manage expectations. We know with great certainty the Iraqi regime was extraordinarily skilled at hiding the stuff, at dispersing the stuff in very small amounts in underground bunkers. So I want to manage expectations. It could be difficult to find and exploit this stuff.

Q: Any kind of special bombs and missiles used to take some of this stuff out, incendiary type weapons?

McChrystal: And that's a great question. In fact the whole weaponeering process that we use in our very, very meticulous targeting process identifies every target—identifies the best munition to use. In some cases a munition that might potentially help destroy any agents that might be there is an option. There are many other options. But in addition to the correct munition from that standpoint, we also balance that against potential collateral damage, potential unintended casualties of civilians. So a lot goes into the calculus that determines exactly what munition is used.

Q: When you mention the hard target category of weapons of mass destruction and the capability to execute them, what are you really talking about? Do you—can you explain that? Because I don't think you're actually bombing stocks of chemical weapons. What are you bombing?

McChrystal: That's a—I would not go into the specifics exactly, but we are taking great care not to achieve a negative effect with something we're trying to hit.

Q: Did you hope to see some of these sites with ground troops as opposed to bombing it because of the concern maybe about some sort of a chemical plume, let's say, or something?

McChrystal: I think exactly. Every weapon of mass destruction location has its own inherent built-in danger to it, either if it's stored incorrectly—even just going in. And so as we go after each of those, we'll look to secure them and we'll look to then render them safe in a very—in a way that's not dangerous for our coalition forces going in, or to the surrounding area.

Q: Clearly some you feel safe to bomb as opposed to seize?

McChrystal: I won't—I won't identify which we might feel safe to bomb and which we wouldn't.

Q: General, you said that the troops are making good progress, but by the evidence of the names that were read at the beginning of this press briefing, apparently it's not a complete rollover. Can you give us any idea where the coalition forces are meeting the most resistance? And can you give us any details of what the fighting has been like?

McChrystal: I would leave it to CENTCOM to describe that, because I think they'd do it better that we have. I think the speed of the advance will indicate that any engagements there have been have been settled fairly rapidly. . . .

Q: Is there any evidence so far that any of the resistance encountered by advancing troops has been directed from Baghdad, or perhaps are the units on the ground responding to standing orders in place? And then, also, have U.S. forces encountered any caches of WMD of any kind?

McChrystal: We have found no caches of weapons of mass destruction to date. It is difficult to say what causes the engagements from the Iraqi forces. . . .

- **Source:** Victoria Clarke and Major General Stanley A. McChrystal, Department of Defense briefing, March 22, 2003, available at http://www.defenselink.mil/transcripts/transcript.aspx?transcriptid=2077, accessed May 23, 2008.
- **Analysis:** Reporters wanted as much detail on the U.S. advance as the Pentagon could provide. Ms. Clarke and General McChrystal understandably refused to provide such detail, which might benefit the enemy. They indicated that the invasion was proceeding well but that the situation was fluid and its course unclear, though the final outcome was not in doubt.

  A very interesting discussion of WMD ensued. Here the briefers' vagueness appeared to stem less from reluctance to provide operational details that might aid the enemy than from genuine ignorance. This discussion provided yet further evidence that the WMD threat had been exaggerated by the Bush administration.

- **Document 34: Excerpt of Department of Defense Briefing**
- **When:** March 28, 2003
- **Where:** Washington, DC
- **Significance:** One week into the war, Secretary of Defense Donald Rumsfeld and General Richard Myers briefed the press on progress to date.

One week and a few minutes ago, the air war began in Iraq. So Operation Iraqi Freedom is now just a little over one week old. In that brief period of time, the coalition forces have made solid progress. And interestingly, in that short period of a week, we have seen mood swings in the media from highs to lows to highs and back again, sometimes in a single 24-hour period.

For some, the massive TV—the massive volume of television—and it is massive— and the breathless reports can seem to be somewhat disorienting. Fortunately, my sense is that the American people have a very good center of gravity and can absorb and balance what they see and hear. Often when General Myers and I go from the building up to the Hill to brief, by the we get there, questions are posed about columns of things flying down someplace and something having happened, which is reported by a person who saw it on the ground, which has not even been reported back yet to the Pentagon. So it's—it is a very different kind of a circumstance.

In less than a week, despite high wind gusts and sandstorms that can turn day into night, coalition forces have moved across more than 200 miles of Iraqi territory and are now just some 50 miles south of Baghdad. They've secured Iraq's southern oil

DID YOU KNOW?

Fedayeen Saddam

The Fedayeen Saddam was a paramilitary force created by Saddam Hussein's son Uday in 1995. These members of the Ba'ath party served as regime thugs, squelching opposition within Iraq. Saddam Hussein expanded the force once it became clear the United States intended to invade Iraq. He planned to use them as guerrillas to attack coalition forces and disrupt logistics. They had little success but contributed significantly to the chaos of postwar Iraq, not merely for what they did but for the perception they created in Washington. The presence of some 5,000 Fedayeen reinforced the notion that the growing resistance to the occupation was the work of regime diehards rather than a complex insurgency involving Shi'a and Sunni Iraqis bolstered by foreign *mujahedeen*.

fields, we believe successfully, and have completed the de-mining of the port. The British ship *Sir Galahad* docked there this morning and began off-loading some 200-plus tons of humanitarian aid. I'm told that in the southern oil fields they found a number of wells with wires and timers, the explosives having not yet been put in place, nor triggered off. Fortunately, the wells seem to have been protected.

The 173rd Airborne has been deploying into the North, and coalition forces have launched successful attacks on terrorist targets. In the West, they have had good success dealing with the regime's ability to threaten neighboring countries from that part of Iraq. Each day more coalition forces flow into the country. Each day more Iraqi forces surrender. The regime knows this. Already they have deployed death squads into Iraqi cities to terrorize civilians and to try to prevent them from welcoming coalition forces, to try to compel the regular army to fight by putting guns to their head, because they know that—the only way to force them to fight for Saddam Hussein. I urge the Iraqi people being threatened in the cities to try to remember the faces and the names of the death squad enforcers. Their time will come, and we will need your help and your testimony.

These death squads report to the Hussein family directly. Their ranks are populated with criminals released from Iraqi prisons. They dress in civilian clothes and operate from private homes, confiscated from innocent people, and try to blend in with the civilian population. They conduct sadistic executions on sidewalks and public squares, cutting the tongues out of those accused of disloyalty and beheading people with swords. They put on American and British uniforms to try to fool regular Iraqi soldiers into surrendering to them, and then execute them as an example for others who might contemplate defection or capitulation.

Their name, Fedayeen Saddam, is a lie, because their purpose is certainly not to make martyrs of themselves, but to make martyrs of innocent Iraqis opposed to Saddam's rule. But we will take them at their word, and if their wish is to die for Saddam Hussein, they will be accommodated.

As the regime deploys death squads to slaughter its own citizens, coalition forces are working to save Iraqi lives. We do this because, unlike Saddam Hussein's regime, our nation and our people value human life. We want the Iraqi people to live in freedom so they can build a future where Iraq's leaders answer to the Iraqi people instead of killing the Iraqi people.

There are some who suggest that the U.S. and its coalition partners are not destroying Iraqi cities and are not destroying the Iraqi people, and that this somehow could reflect a lack of will or a lack of determination on the part of the coalition. The opposite is true. It is precisely because of our overwhelming power and our certainty of victory that we believe we can win this war and remove the regime while still striving to spare innocent lives. Our military capabilities are so devastating and precise that we can destroy an Iraqi tank under a bridge without damaging the bridge. We do not need to kill thousands of innocent Iraqis to remove Saddam Hussein from power. At least that's our belief. We believe we can destroy his institutions of power and oppression in an orderly manner.

The tactics employed by the Iraqi regime, by contrast, hiding behind women and children, murdering civilians, these are not signs of strength. They're sign of weakness and of desperation.

The outcome of this conflict is not in doubt. The regime will be removed. But for our coalition of free people, we believe it is important not just to win, but to win justly. The power of our coalition derives not simply from the vast overwhelming force at our disposal, but from the manner in which we employ that force. The Iraqi people will see how we employ our force and know that we are coming not to occupy their country, not to oppress them, but to liberate their country.

Finally, before I turn to General Myers, a few words of caution.

First, to the officials of the Iraqi regime: The defeat—your defeat is inevitable and you will be held accountable for your conduct in this war. The coalition POWs that you are holding must be treated according to the Geneva Conventions. And any Iraqi officials involved in their mistreatment, humiliation or execution will pay a severe price.

And to Iraq's neighbor, Syria: We have information that shipments of military supplies have been crossing the border from Syria into Iraq, including night-vision goggles. These deliveries pose a direct threat to the lives of coalition forces. We consider such trafficking as hostile acts and will hold the Syrian government accountable for such shipments.

Last, the entrance into Iraq by military forces, intelligence personnel, or proxies not under the direct operational control of General Franks will be taken as a potential threat to coalition forces. This includes the Badr Corps, the military wing of the Supreme Council on Islamic Revolution in Iraq. The Badr Corps is trained, equipped and directed by Iran's Islamic Revolutionary Guard, and we will hold the Iranian government responsible for their actions, and will view Badr Corps activity inside Iraq as unhelpful. Armed Badr Corps members found in Iraq will have to be treated as combatants.

General Myers.

Myers: Thank you, Mr. Secretary.

Operation Iraqi Freedom continues. More than 270,000 coalition forces are deployed in support of combat operations, with approximately one-third of those already inside Iraq.

Our ground operations are continuing to push north with Marine, armored, and infantry forces poised near Baghdad.

The slide on the screen shows the now approximately 35 to 40 percent of Iraq, Iraqi territory, where Saddam's regime has lost control. In just eight days of operations, coalition forces are located throughout that entire shaded area that you see there on the screen. And while there will continue to be sporadic, even serious engagements in those areas, the regime does not control them. And they're, again, annotated by the highlighted color there.

The air campaign continues as well. We flew almost a thousand sorties over Iraq yesterday, mostly against Iraqi regime leadership and command and control targets, ballistic missile threats and major communication nodes.

As you'll see on the slide now, we have air supremacy over approximately 95 percent of Iraq. The area over Baghdad and just north we are not yet calling our skies. While we've been flying freely over Baghdad, we have some surface-to-air missiles system—missile systems currently unlocated in that area.

That said, since the beginning of operations, our forces have fired more than 650 Tomahawk missiles and dropped more than 5,000 precision-guided munitions.

Overall, our plans are on track. We are degrading Iraqi forces, particularly the Republican Guard, by air, and that's fixed wing and rotary wing. And we will engage them with the full weight of our combat power at a time and place of our choosing.

As we've said before from up here, we're going to be engaged in a difficult fight ahead, but the outcome is certain. We will disarm Iraq and remove the current regime from power.

And finally today, I have three videos and one more picture slide.

The first video is of an F-16 delivering precision-guided munitions against enemy troops in western Iraq that were firing mortars at Special Operations forces.

The second video is of an AV-8B Harrier dropping a precision-guided weapon on a tank in the open, south of al-Amarah.

And the last video is of a Predator firing a Hellfire missile at an Iraqi communication dish outside the Ministry of Information yesterday in Baghdad. As you'll see when the tape ends and freezes, you'll see that the dish is in a parking lot actually some distance from the ministry building. The ministry building's there at the edge, off to the right, right lower edge.

Also in our last picture slide here, the image depicts military equipment dispersed in residential areas. The red dots indicate location of military equipment in this neighborhood, and we've highlighted just four of them in the yellow boxes. This neighborhood is located approximately 30 miles south of Baghdad, in the proximity of the Medina Republican Guard division. This image up here is a tank on a transporter that's in the middle of a neighborhood. They have some armored personnel carriers here that are in neighborhood streets. We have handouts, so you can see these better, probably when we give you the handouts. The upper right is a tank on a residential street. In the lower right are armored vehicles in trees.

And with that, we'll take your questions.

Q: General Myers, I'd like to ask about reports that the Republican Guard divisions, Medina south of Baghdad and the Hammurabi west of Baghdad, are perhaps physically realigning themselves for defensive or other reasons. And do you have any sign at all that these people are beginning to actually don chemical weapons suits? There's been a report to that effect.

Myers: The only thing that I have on the chemical suits are the over 3,000 or 3,000 suits, new suits that were found, I think, in An Nasiriyah, I think is where they were found by the Marines when they went in the Ba'ath Party headquarters. And that was also where they found weapons, and they found people, of course, I think

170 of them they rounded up, and they also found uniforms, Iraqi uniforms they had taken off. That's the only suits that I'm aware of at this time.

And we do have some indications that some of the Republican Guard divisions are relocating. And exactly where, we're just going to wait and see.

Q: Does it appear that it's because they have been hit too hard. Is this a defensive thing, or are they moving—are they moving the Hammurabi down to support the Medina?

Myers: The Republican Guard has not gone on the offense yet. They are dug in, disbursed. That's quite possibly Republican Guard there in that neighborhood. I've got to be careful if I confirm that or not, but in that neighborhood. So they could be consolidating to make a defense. It doesn't make any difference. The outcome is going to be certain, as I said. They'll make—we're making plans right now, and we'll attack when we're ready. . . .

Q: Mr. Secretary, I'd like to ask you about your statement about military supplies moving across the border from Syria. You described those as hostile acts. Are they subject to military action in response if that continues?

Rumsfeld: There's no question but that to the extent military supplies or equipment or people move across borders between Iraq and Syria, that it vastly complicates our situation. And that is why I said what I said.

Q: But so are you threatening military action against Syria?

Rumsfeld: I'm saying exactly what I said. It was carefully phrased. . . .

Q: Mr. Secretary, General Wallace was predominantly quoted today, saying that this may be a longer war than the commanders had thought and that this was not the enemy that we war-gamed against. It seems to contradict some of the statements that have been made from the podium here and the podium in Doha. Can you reconcile the two views?

Rumsfeld: Well, I didn't read the article; I saw the headline. And I've seen a lot of headlines that don't fit articles. Someone coming down here told me that he also said that we're about where we expected to be, which is generally what General Franks is saying. I suppose everyone can have their own view.

Q: Well, I wasn't there, of course, but the article quotes him as saying that this is going to be a longer war than had been anticipated.

Rumsfeld: Does it have quotes saying that?

Q: Yes. It says the enemy we're fighting is not the enemy we war-gamed—"the enemy we're fighting is different from the one we war-gamed against."

Rumsfeld: Yeah, well, as far as I'm concerned, it seems to me a careful reading of Amnesty International or the record of Saddam Hussein, having used chemical weapons on his own people as well as his neighbors, and the viciousness of that regime, which is well known and documented by human rights organizations, ought not to be surprised.

Q: Can I follow up on that, sir?

Q: Mr. Secretary, as you know, there has been some criticism, some by retired senior officers, some by officers on background in this building, who claim that the war plan that is in effect is flawed and our number of troops on the ground is too light, supply lines are too long and stretched too thin. Would you give us a definitive statement, if you would, to the effect that you agree that the war plan is sound and that this criticism is unfounded, or that there's some substance to it?

Rumsfeld: Well, we're one week into this, and it seems to me it's a bit early for history to be written, one would think. The war plan is Tom Franks' war plan. It was carefully prepared over many months. It was washed through the tank with the chiefs on at least four or five occasions.

Myers: Exactly—more, more.

Rumsfeld: It has been through the combatant commanders. It has been through the National Security Council process. General Myers and General Pace and others, including this individual, have seen it in a variety of different iterations. When asked by the president or by me, the military officers who've reviewed it have all said they thought it was an excellent plan. Indeed, adjectives that go beyond that have been used, quite complimentary. . . .

Myers: Ivan, you know, there's that old adage that you probably know as well, that no plan, no matter how perfect, survives first contact with the enemy. I think some of that was shown in the way we orchestrated the opening moments of this conflict. I don't think anybody expected it to come out—be laid out the way it was. And that wasn't exactly according to the plan, but it had the flexibility inherent.

So I stand by this plan. I think General Franks put together a good plan. I'll give you a definitive statement: I think it's a brilliant plan. And there will be—there's branches and sequels to everything that might possibly happen, but the plan is sound, it's being executed and it's on track. And that's essentially what General Wallace said, too. He said we're about where we expected to be. That's one of his quotes as well. . . .

Q: Could you, General Myers, on that same subject, maybe narrate for us what we've seen in the last week from your perspective, particularly on the ground: with the fast punch up north, what the purpose of that was, and if it's shaken out the way you thought it would; stringing the Marines out behind to protect the lines of communication, how that's going; and then the effects-based air targeting. So if you could—the problem I think we're all running up against is we talk to a lot of retired officers, who may be Gulf War focused or Kosovo focused, and this is very different. And can you explain to us why it's different and how it's different and how that's stacking up against what you expected to see at this point?

Myers: I guess I can try, and the secretary, please help me on this as we go through it. But in 36 hours, we're on the outskirts of Baghdad. You know, it took 38 days of air war before for the 100 hours of the ground war to take place last time. So it's a much different objective, much different way of addressing a much different problem. . . .

Q: Mr. Secretary, last time we met with you, you were asked if the supply lines were stretched or vulnerable, and actually you both said no. And you also said the Fedayeen Saddam were onesies and twosies. Do you still stand by both those statements?

Myers: I just said that I think the attacks on the lines of communication with our—inside our forces have not been militarily significant, and we're dealing with the death squad attacks on those lines of communication. There have not been regular army forces, I don't think, attacking those lines, unless it's been close to one of the major population hubs. But they're being dealt with. There have been some battles that have been bravely fought by our folks, and they have dispatched the enemy, in many cases quite quickly.

Rumsfeld: I'd have to go back and see what we actually said, but—

Q: You said onesies and twosies—

Rumsfeld: Let me respond. I'd have to go back and see what we said and what the context was. But my recollection is, we said that—not that there were only onesies and twosies in terms of the Fedayeen Saddam. We know the numbers there; there's somewhere between 5,000 and 25,000 in the country, depending on how you characterize them. But what we said was the attacks outside of cities have been relatively small, as the general said. And I suspect that's what we actually said.

Q: Mr. Secretary, you've said that the military outcome of this is certain, and I'm sure that not too many people doubt that. But what does seem uncertain at the moment are the mood of the Iraqi people and whether or not—despite whatever dislike they have for Saddam Hussein, whether they will welcome American and British forces as liberators. Is it possible that you've miscalculated the desire of the Iraqi people to be liberated by an outside force and that because of their patriotism or nationalism, that they'll continue to resist the Americans, even after you prevail militarily?

Rumsfeld: Jamie, don't you think it's a little premature—the question? We'll know the answer to that. As portions of the country are liberated, we'll have people on the ground, embedded with our forces, who will have a chance to see what happens and see how they feel about it. Why do we want to guess?

What we do know is that people behave fairly rationally, and if they have a gun to their head, and they're told, "Don't surrender," and they're told, "Don't assist the coalition forces coming in, or we will kill you," and then they go and kill somebody and execute him in front of everybody else to make sure everyone really got the message, it's not surprising that people's behavior is one of caution.

Now the other part of the answer to your question, it seems to me, is also self-evident. And that is, there is not "an Iraqi people." There are Iraqi individual people, and they're going to be all across the spectrum! The ones who were close to Saddam Hussein and been getting the Mercedes cars and all the good food—they're going to be unhappy, and they're not going to prefer that we're there. The people that he's repressed and threatened to kill and whose children have been killed by him—they'll probably have a somewhat different view. Will there be people in the middle who are ambivalent? Sure. They'll be all across the spectrum. But we've—we don't need to try to answer those questions. We have time. We'll see what happens. . . .

- **Source:** Department of Defense briefing, March 28, 2003, available at http://www.defense.gov/transcripts/transcript.aspx?transcriptid=524, accessed March 20, 2012.
- **Analysis:** During the question-and-answer period, Rumsfeld came under criticism for sending in too few troops to deal with widely

dispersed, irregular forces. Despite conclusive evidence that he pressured CENTCOM to reduce the size of the invasion force, Rumsfeld insisted that the war plan was General Franks's. He also faced pressing questions on the strength and activities of irregular Iraqi forces, such as the Fedayeen Saddam. He had initially claimed that the resistance was minor, but it had proven to be more serious. Both Secretary Rumsfeld and General Myers defended their previous conclusions that guerrilla resistance was generally on a small scale.

- • **Document 35: Excerpt of Department of Defense Briefing by Secretary Rumsfeld and General Myers**
- • **When:** April 1, 2003
- • **Where:** Washington, DC
- • **Significance:** Two weeks into Operation Iraqi Freedom it was becoming increasingly clear that some of the assumptions behind the invasion plan were not panning out.

Rumsfeld: Good afternoon. We are certainly grateful for the brilliant and courageous rescue of Sergeant—correction—Pfc. [Private First Class] Jessica Lynch, who was being held by Iraqi forces in what they called a "hospital." And we thank all of those who were involved in the planning and execution of the mission. We're grateful to have her back, to be sure. It was a superb rescue effort by truly outstanding and courageous teams. The celebration of her rescue is, of course, tempered by the knowledge that others still remain in enemy hands. To the families of those coalition forces missing in action or held prisoner by the Iraqi regime, know that your loved ones are not forgotten, that our forces are doing everything possible to find them and to bring them home safely.

It's now 14 days since coalition forces entered Iraq, and they are closing on Baghdad. They've taken several outlying areas and are closer to the center of the Iraqi capital than many American commuters are from their downtown offices.

As the coalition continues to close on Baghdad, there likely will be difficult days ahead, but the regime is under increasing pressure. Their Republican Guard forces are being defeated by coalition airstrikes and by effective ground engagements. The Baghdad and Medina Divisions have suffered serious blows. Some units are laying down their arms and surrendering to coalition forces, wisely choosing not to die fighting for a doomed regime.

Coalition forces have caused such attrition to the Republican Guard units ringing the capital that the regime has been forced to backfill its Baghdad defenses with regular army units, forces that they have historically considered less reliable, which is a sign that they know they're in difficulty. Key bridges over the Tigris and Euphrates Rivers have been taken by coalition forces. This, of course, eases the approach to Baghdad.

Like the southern oil fields, our forces are finding some bridges wired for demolition, but not yet detonated. Perhaps those responsible for destroying the bridges heard the message in coalition leaflets and radio broadcasts and have heeded our warnings. Or perhaps coalition advance has been so rapid that they were taken by surprise. We may never know which.

What we do know is that the strategy is working. The coalition has secured the majority of Iraq's oil wells for the Iraqi people, secured key roads and bridges leading the Baghdad, and has now arrived near the regime's doorstep, all in less than two weeks.

As the battle unfolds, it's becoming increasingly clear to Iraqis who is a friend and who is an enemy of Muslim people. In Najaf, for example, Saddam's forces seized a mosque that is one of the most important religious sites of Shi'a Muslims and they used it for cover as they fired at coalition forces. Coalition forces naturally would tend to want to respond to firing on their positions. But they did not. They held their fire. They protected the mosque from destruction. Soon after, a prominent Iraqi cleric, the Grand Ayatollah Sistani, took the courageous step of instructing the population to remain calm and not to interfere with coalition actions.

Truth be told, while coalition forces have taken extraordinary measures to protect innocent civilians in this war, Saddam Hussein has sent death squads to massacre innocent Iraqi Muslims. Indeed, Saddam Hussein has killed more Muslim people than perhaps any living person on the face of the earth. The day is fast approaching when his murderous rule will end. Let there be no doubt, the most dangerous fighting may very well be ahead of us. And by its conduct in this war, the Iraqi regime has shown that there is no depth to the brutality to which they will not sink.

The regime has been weakened, to be sure, but it is still lethal, and it may prove to be more lethal in the final moments before it ends. For the senior leadership there is no way out. Their fate has been sealed by their actions. The same is not true for the Iraqi armed forces. Iraqi officers and soldiers can still survive and help to rebuild a free Iraq if they do the right thing. They must now decide whether they want to share the fate of Saddam Hussein, or whether they will they save themselves, turn on that condemned dictator, and help the forces of Iraq's liberation. I must say, however, that given the conduct of the Iraqi regime, it increasingly seems that Iraq is running out of real soldiers, and soon all that will be left are war criminals.

Gen. Myers.

Myers: Thank you, Mr. Secretary.

Coalition ground, air, maritime and special forces have made remarkable progress in the first two weeks of Operation Iraqi Freedom. And I know that Gen. Brooks at CentCom headquarters over in theater gave an excellent operational lay down this morning. And things are progressing well. But I'd like to caution all that there still is much more work to be done. And there's no doubt that some of it's going to be very, very difficult.

We are continuing to move toward our objectives. As you see in this chart, the Iraqi regime has—no longer controls about 45 percent of Iraq. And coalition forces are on the outskirts of Baghdad.

Air strikes continue. In the last 24 hours coalition air forces have flown more than 1,000 sorties over Iraq. Since the war began we have fired over 725 Tomahawks and dropped over 12,000 precision-guided munitions. We essentially control over 95 percent of Iraqi airspace.

Now let me show you a pre- and post-strike image of some recent strikes. These images are of Special Republican Guard military barracks located on the edge of the Saddam International Airport just outside Baghdad. And that's the post-strike image.

We are also conducting helicopter strikes on Republican Guard armor, and I have some recent video that captures the success of advancing forces. The video shows three short clips of Apache helicopters destroying Iraqi tanks and anti-aircraft missile launchers southwest of Baghdad. . . .

And with that, we'll take your questions. . . .

Q: Mr. Secretary, you referred to some of the Republican Guard forces laying down arms. Can you tell us whether some of them have actually been withdrawn deliberately back into the city limits where—and does Saddam and his—do they have central control over the forces that are in the city, as opposed to those that are out in the field?

Rumsfeld: We've had pretty good visibility, but cloud cover has resulted in a situation we don't have perfect visibility. And if I dropped a plumb line through everything I've read on this subject, my impression is that it's all of the above; that the—some forces have in fact retreated into cities, others have just left and gone home, still others have surrendered, still others are still there fighting and have been reinforced both with remnants of other Republican Guard units and also regular army forces.

Q: Mr. Secretary, you said a couple of months ago that Iraq is running out of real soldiers and that all that will be left are war criminals. Is that a warning that if these military leaders don't give up now that they'll be considered war criminals or is that an appeal to surrender?

Rumsfeld: I guess it's a reflection of what's taking place there. There are any number of soldiers that are behaving as soldiers, and they have been either surrendering, been captured or been killed or they're still there fighting. There are others who have left and gone into a different mode where they are in civilian clothes and they are operating out of cities and they are putting themselves in close proximity to schools, hospitals, mosques and the like, and conducting themselves less as soldiers and more as war criminals. I don't want to get into any legal definitions, but there's no question but that the things—the execution of Iraqi people, the execution of others is certainly not something that soldiers do. . . .

Q: We've heard a lot from people going on about securing the southern oil fields, but not very much about what's going on in the north to try to secure those fields. Could you comment on that and on the activities in the north generally?

Rumsfeld: We have a lot of Special Forces up there. The British have been up there, as well, from time to time. We have—the 173rd [Airborne Brigade] is there. And we have excellent relationships with the two Kurdish groups and are—and as a matter of fact, have conducted a combined operation with them on some facilities and suspected poison sites in the country. The oil wells, as I recall, Dick, run pretty much just outside the green line—just south of the green line.

Myers: They do, and then sort of north and south around Kirkuk, as well. So they're exactly in that area.

Rumsfeld: And needless to say, we have to assume that they've been wired with explosives, as some were in the south. We also would like very much to get in there and be able to assure that they are not damaged and cause a major environmental problem. And Gen. Franks has ways of doing that at the right time. . . .

Q: Gen. Myers?

Q: Mr. Secretary?

Q: Gen. Myers, factoring in the air campaign that has taken out a lot of the Republican Guard divisions to the south, there are some U.S. commanders who are expressing surprise at the lack of resistance that they're seeing as they're rolling to Baghdad. Is your perception that there is a tactic—

Rumsfeld: Who is expressing that?

Q: Some commanders on the ground, from embedded reporters talking to them. Is there a tactic, do you feel, by the Iraqis to draw coalition forces into the city to try to do an urban warfare scenario?

Myers: Let me just say we talked about—we've talked to—no. I think if you look at the way the combat is being conducted, we are—coalition forces are—destroying most of the equipment associated with these Republican Guard divisions. A lot of the people have been killed. A lot of the people that come out after dark to attack our tanks, that might be a line in the shadows—the death squads and those sorts of folks—a lot of them have been killed as well. So it doesn't appear—we know that they're dispersing, sometimes with equipment, and our forces are smart enough to figure out that you don't want to get in where you could be enveloped somehow. So they're taking all that into account.

Rumsfeld: We know they have a series of things that they plan to do as the first don't succeed and then they have other things they will do. But to call it a ploy, after they've been decimated and had their effectiveness reduced, in terms of their equipment, from a hundred percent down to somewhere in some cases 15 percent or 20 percent or 40 percent or 55 or 75 percent, it's hardly a ploy. The air power has been very effective and the ground action has been very effective. . . .

Q: Gen. Myers, I wanted to take you back to a the old issue of urban conflict, urban warfare, as it sees imminent, there may be a conflict there. Can you give the public a sense of how the U.S. has advanced from the days of—you may think of the battle of Hue in Vietnam, or Stalingrad and the Mesopotamia. There's images of apocalyptic urban conflict. Can you give us a sense of the model you've used to game this out in terms of the blend of lethal, nonlethal. How might it be different, this great urban conflict people have envisioned?

Myers: Well, first of all, you never know, I mean, how it's going to come out. The tactical situation could be very different from what we suppose, and so, I mean, you're just going to have to be ready for lots of things. But you've got a city of Baghdad, you've got about 5 million residents, half of whom are Shi'a that have been persecuted by the regime, probably will not be friendly to the regime. They're basically on the eastern half of the city. You would have to—you could assume that they might be helpful.

When you get to the point where Baghdad is basically isolated, then what is the situation you have in the country? You have a country that Baghdad no longer controls, that whatever is happening inside Baghdad is almost irrelevant compared to what's going on in the rest of the country. What's going on in the rest of the country? Well, you have the southern oil fields; we'll see about the north. You have the face now of a—by this time, probably, of an Iraqi administration, interim administration, some form of people standing up now starting to work the post-conflict governance. It will take some time, but you'll have that.

So you're going to have Baghdad isolated, you're going to have half the population that probably wants nothing to do with the folks—the oppressive regime. And then you'll start working at it as you can. But one of the things you can do is be patient about that. So this notion of a siege, and so forth, I think is not the right mental picture. . . .

Q: Mr. Secretary, do you have any information that would lead you to believe that a third party, perhaps a foreign government, such as France or Russia, might be encouraging what's left of Saddam's regime to just hang on in hopes of cutting some kind of a deal? And is there any deal available to them, short of their end?

Rumsfeld: The answer is yes and no. There's no question but that some governments are discussing, from time to time, some sort of a—cutting a deal. And the inevitable effect of it, let there be no doubt, is to give hope and comfort to the Saddam Hussein regime, and give them ammunition that they can then try to use to retain the loyalty of their forces with hope that one more time maybe he'll survive, one more time maybe he'll be there for another decade or so, for another 17 or 18 U.N. resolutions.

And as to the second question, there's not a chance that there's going to be a deal. It doesn't matter who proposes it, there will not be one. . . .

Q: . . . Do you have any information that substantiates some of the accounts we're hearing of her heroic effort to hold out and expending all of her ammunition before she was captured? Is there any evidence that she was tortured or mistreated? And is she a witness to any war crimes, specifically the execution of any American prisoners?

Rumsfeld: Gen. Myers and I get briefed on these types of things and there's an orderly process for debriefing and discussing them. And I have no intention of discussing it piecemeal. . . .

Q: Gen. Myers, can I take you back to a couple points? When you talked about the strategy of approaching Baghdad a couple of minutes ago, you talked about moving forward; isolating the regime, I think, is what you said; and then, you know, an interim government authority would begin to emerge.

But what you didn't mention in that was the removal of the current regime in that scenario. So what I'm wondering is if you're looking at a solution here of sort of terrific simplicity. You just go to Baghdad, isolate the regime and establish this interim authority, and you're de facto in charge and then work on removing the regime after that.

Myers: You may have a regime. You may not. I use the term "irrelevant" because at this point they're not going to be able to communicate with the people of Iraq. That will all be shut down. They won't be able to communicate within certain parts of Baghdad, and you'll continue to ensure that happens. You know, there's— we would control the water, the electricity, things like that. I'm not suggesting any of that would be turned off, turned on. It just would depend on the tactical situation.

So they become an entity, perhaps, if there's anybody left, if they haven't all run. Of course, there's lots of reports of people already leaving Baghdad. But whatever remnants are left would not be in charge of anything except their own defense. And it would be fairly small compared to the rest of the country and what's happening.

Q: And if I could just ask you a follow-up, you both mentioned your concerns, I believe, about the Shi'a population on the east side of Baghdad. Now that you've put that on the table, is there any plan or possibility for the U.S. military to provide protection to those people, now that you've put the risk on the table here?

Myers: That gets into future operational planning, which I think we probably shouldn't talk about. . . .

Q: Mr. Secretary, I presume you're pleased, but are you also puzzled by the fact that the Iraqis haven't used any chemical or biological weapons? And do U.S. forces have any special way to respond militarily if such an attack should be launched, or is the threat of war crimes trials the strongest deterrent?

Rumsfeld: Well, needless to say, the last thing anyone would want to see is chemical weapons used in this conflict. We've always believed that the chances of their being used increase the closer that coalition forces got to Baghdad. I suspect that the regime has a dilemma. If, on the one hand, they are holding out hope with their people that there might be a deal cut, the use of chemical weapons would certainly end that prospect. And—

Q: (Inaudible)—

Rumsfeld: Just a minute. And that being the case, they have to be balancing that. Do they want to not use all their weapons and hope that they can get a deal, when it's not even a remote possibility, or will they go ahead and use them and totally eliminate the perception in their people that he might survive, because once he uses those, it's pretty clear there can't be a deal? So that's the dilemma I suspect he faces.

Q: And Gen. Myers—

Q: Is there a special military response to the chemical weapons—

Rumsfeld: We've allowed as how we thought that they'd best not use those weapons. And I don't want to go beyond that. . . .

Q: It's been seven or 10 days since there's been much discussion about contact with Iraqi commanders in hopes that they might turn. Is that no longer a productive enterprise, or do you still have some hope that once you get to Baghdad you may be able to persuade—

Rumsfeld: There are still contacts and you never know. Until people decide that for sure he's going to go, and they are not at risk from the Special Republican Guard or the SSO or the Fedayeen Saddam of shooting them if they do try to make a deal, it won't happen. At that moment where they're convinced he is going to go, and they do want to be helpful, then they're going to have to figure out a way to live and not get shot by some of the folks that have been infiltrated into their operations. And as I say, discussions still continue. . . .

Q: Have you seen any indications from Iran or Syria that they've heeded your warning, or are ignoring your warning? And please be as specific as possible. And Gen. Myers, your thoughts on progress on the friendly fire front. Is it better or worse this time around, or about what you expected?

Rumsfeld: I have no way of knowing what Iran's reaction was, but I have not seen anything recently on the part of Iran that was—I don't know if you have, either—that is terribly disturbing. We do—we have seen that Syria is continuing to conduct itself the way it was prior to the time I said what I said. . . .

Q: Mr. Secretary, you and Gen. Myers have said that the most dangerous fighting may lie ahead. Wouldn't it be more accurate to say the most unpredictable phase lies ahead? Because we don't know what we'll find in Baghdad, whether the regime has lost control, whether there will be a coup, chemical weapons attacking the people. And doesn't that present the most challenging phase yet in terms of our planning?

Rumsfeld: It's interesting how people tend to always start where we are. Predictability. What was not predictable when we started? It was not predictable that we would be able to save the southern oil wells. It was not predictable whether we'd be able to prevent Scuds from going into Jordan or Saudi Arabia or Israel. It was not predictable whether or not there would be a massive humanitarian crisis, as there was in 1991. It was not predictable whether there would be massive refugee flows into neighboring countries and causing great difficulties for them. It was not predictable whether our forces gathering in Kuwait conceivably could have been hit with chemical weapons in that location.

There has been a whole series of things, unpredictables, unknowables, that had to be addressed by Gen. Franks, that he addressed very thoughtfully, that he fashioned a plan to deal with. And because of the success of his plan, he has in fact avoided any number of risks and dangers that he had to take into account and that concern all of us.

So, no, I would not say that the future is necessarily less predictable than the past. I think the past was not predictable when it started.

Q: (Off mike)—is this a highly unpredictable phase we're entering? And how does that complicate the planning now?

Rumsfeld: In this business, everyone goes to school on everyone else, from the first day. They react to what we do. We react to what they do. The plan is adjusted, and the plans are made, and excursions are developed and, the good Lord willing, serious problems are averted and avoided.

The—I guess I'll stand—what I said. I believe that what I said is correct: that we have faced this whole series of risks, very serious risks and dangers, from the beginning, and a good many of them have thus far been avoided. We still have the risk of the northern oil fields, to be sure. We still have—nothing's ever over till it's over. But sure, there are difficult days ahead.

Is it more or less unpredictable than it was 12, 14 days ago? I think not.

- **Source:** Department of Defense briefing, April 1, 2003, available at http://www.defenselink.mil/transcripts/transcript.aspx?transcriptid=2244, accessed May 26, 2008.

- **Analysis:** After providing an overview of operations to date, Secretary Rumsfeld and General Myers took questions. Discussion focused on the perplexing lack of resistance by regular Iraqi units and a corresponding rise in irregular operations. Rumsfeld downplayed the importance of these irregulars, calling them "war criminals" and "death squads." The administration would continue to echo this unfounded optimism throughout the spring and summer, characterizing a growing insurgency as futile resistance by Ba'ath Party holdouts. The briefers bristled at the suggestion that their plan for regime change was "terribly simplistic," a charge that proved well founded.

DID YOU KNOW?

Jessica Dawn Lynch

Jessica Lynch (b. 1983) was a private first class in the U.S. Army Quartermaster Corp during the invasion of Iraq. She became first a minor celebrity and then the center of controversy after Iraqi forces ambushed and destroyed her convoy near Nasiriyah on March 23, 2003. Lynch sustained serious injuries when her Humvee overturned. Iraqi soldiers took her to a nearby hospital, where U.S. special forces rescued her on April 1.

The story quickly spread that Lynch had fought tenaciously until she ran out of ammunition. This story proved to be false. Lynch herself testified before Congress that she never fired a shot because her M-16 jammed. Some analysts accused the Pentagon of deliberately promulgating the heroic version of events to bolster morale, but these allegations have never been proven. Lynch never encouraged the stories and was quite honest about what had occurred. Rick Bragg published an authorized biography of Lynch in November 2003, *I Am a Soldier Too: The Jessica Lynch Story* (Knopf, 2003).

This briefing also addressed the famous (or infamous) Jessica Lynch story. Private Jessica Lynch was captured by Iraqi forces when her supply convoy was attacked. Popular accounts credit her with heroic resistance as she used up all of her ammunition in a failed attempt to save herself and protect her comrades. Rumsfeld refused to deny these stories, even though they proved wildly exaggerated.

- **Document 36: Department of Defense Briefing**
- **When:** April 7, 2003
- **Where:** Washington, DC
- **Significance:** Less than three weeks after the start of the ground offensive, U.S. troops engaged in mop-up operations in Baghdad while British forces secured Basra.

Rumsfeld: Good afternoon. Coalition forces are operating in and around Baghdad on the ground, in the air. The regime's leaders are increasingly isolated. The circle is closing, and their options are running out.

As his regime collapses around him, the question is asked, where is he? There are three possibilities: He's either dead or injured or not willing to show himself.

We may not know if or where he is, but we do know that he no longer runs much of Iraq. His forces continue to surrender and capitulate. His regime is running out of real soldiers. And soon, all that will be left will be the war criminals.

In the south, the UK forces now control much of Basra. They're performing well in liberating the city from the regime death squads that have terrorized the local population for some days now. We believe that the reign of terror of "Chemical Ali" has come to an end. To Iraqis who have suffered at his hand, particularly in the last few weeks in that southern part of the country, he will never again terrorize you or your families.

Despite the dire predictions about the forces and the plan, coalition forces have come a long way in a short time. But there is dangerous and difficult work ahead. As the forces continue their work, I want to remember the U.S. forces who have given their lives in this struggle. The names are on the screen behind me. They volunteered to risk their lives for a cause they believed in. Their sacrifice has helped protect their fellow countrymen and the world from a very dangerous regime. And it will soon be giving the gift of freedom to the long-oppressed Iraqi people. We're deeply grateful for their service and their sacrifice, and our hearts and prayers go out to their families and their loved ones. . . .

Myers: Thank you, Mr. Secretary. The 85 brave U.S. service members killed in Operation Iraqi Freedom remind us of the heavy price we often pay for freedom. They are indeed American heroes, and we will not forget their sacrifice or their families' sacrifice. And as the secretary said, we should also remember those missing or being held prisoner. Our thoughts are with you and your families, and I can guarantee you we will make every effort to find you and return you safely home.

Also, more than 150 have been wounded in battle. And as the secretary said, I was out at Walter Reed when he was over at Bethesda Hospital. I met some of these brave Americans yesterday. Each and every time I visit them, I guess I'm amazed at their dedication and their strength. Often, their primary concern is to want to rejoin their comrades as quickly as possible. So, I think we all thank them for their inspiration and their service to our nation. And to their families, as well, we thank them, many of whom were there yesterday. . . .

Operation Iraqi Freedom continues. The battlefield has certainly shifted since the last time we were at this podium on Thursday. We have over 340,000 coalition forces in the region, more than 125,000 inside Iraq. We've secured Baghdad International Airport and have begun using it for coalition missions. We've secured most of the major roads into and out of Baghdad. We've visited two of Saddam's presidential palaces. Republican Guard divisions have only been able to conduct sporadic attacks on our forces. Of the 800-plus tanks they began with, all but a couple of dozen have been destroyed or abandoned. We have more than 7,000 enemy prisoners of war. We are restoring power to cities throughout southern Iraq. And we're delivering a growing amount of humanitarian relief to the Iraqi people in various locations.

Iraqi citizens are assisting coalition forces in identifying locations of weapons caches, as well as the hideouts of the remaining elements of the Fedayeen Saddam and the Ba'ath Party members.

But as I did on Thursday, I need to add a caution to this discussion, because there's still much more work to be done, and some of it will no doubt be very, very difficult.

In the last 24 hours, coalition air forces have flown more than 1,000 sorties over Iraq. Since the war began we have fired 750 Tomahawks and dropped over 18,000 precision-guided munitions. . . .

Rumsfeld: Yes?

Q: Mr. Secretary, I'd like to ask you about a report that Reuters has from an embedded reporter in Karbala. Quoting a spokesperson for the 101st Airborne Division, they're saying that the substances found at a training camp in central Iraq between Karbala and Hilla apparently include nerve agents sarin and tabun, and the blister agent lewisite, and that preliminary tests indicate that they are WMD, but that traces are being sent back to the United States for final testing. Could you give us your comment on that, sir? And might this be the smoking gun that you've been looking for?

Rumsfeld: Once we decided to put reporters in with units that were out, it was obvious that they would be there when things were discovered and that they would report on them, which is fine. And they've reported what sounded—I haven't seen the report, but it sounded—you used the word "apparently" and you used the word "preliminary," so it sounds like a very responsible report. We don't do that. We have to recognize that almost all first reports that we get turn out to be wrong. There tend to be changes in them. And as a result, we have to take our time and look at it. I don't know, Dick, how many of these things we've seen in the last couple of years, but literally dozens and dozens and dozens of instances where the first report comes in—and perfectly good reporting—but it's wrong. And therefore, we don't do that.

We don't do first reports and we don't speculate. And I can tell you it takes days to get samples of things from wherever they are in the battlefield into a first place where they take a look, and then to a second place where things get checked. And I think that the prudent thing in a case like this would be to kind of let the thing play itself out and we'll see what's—we'll eventually know.

Yes?

Q: Given the intense skepticism by many governments around the world about the U.S. government's WMD case, are there procedures in place to establish, in the event you do find something, what in civilian law enforcement would be called a chain of custody?

Rumsfeld: Yes. To the extent you can do that on the battlefield, the answer is yes. We've got people who have been alerted to the importance of chain of custody, and they're attentive to that and will be to the extent that it's possible in a battlefield environment.

Yes?

Q: General Myers, I wanted to follow up on that line of questioning. Back on February 5th, Colin Powell, in his case before the U.N., specifically alluded to a missile unit, an Iraqi missile unit that had been moved to the west that had launchers and biological warheads. He used that as a piece of proof. Has the U.S. been tracking that unit? And do you have any insight into the whereabouts of that one very specific example of WMD weaponry?

Myers: I'm trying—Tony, I'm trying to recall his specific example. I can't connect it to other intel that I know right now. But I know we were tracking—at the time Secretary Powell was speaking, we were talking about some FROGs, short-range, surface-to-surface missiles moved up into the northeast. We had had some movements to the south. I'm not sure about the warheads.

Q: This is a specific example of moving to the west—

Myers: I'd have to go look at it. Are you talking about moving to another country?

Q: No, no, western Iraq. Warheads with biological agent and missile launchers. He used that as a primary example.

Myers: I'd have to check the wording. I'll get back to you on that.

Q: Has anything been found in the west even comparable—even similar—to that type of weaponry?

Myers: As the secretary said, we've done several sensitive-site exploitations in the west and in other parts of Iraq. And we've really focused hard on delivery means; we've really paid a lot of attention to delivery means, trying to preclude their use on U.S. and other coalition forces.

Q: Mr. Secretary, what can you tell us about the presence of exiled Iraqis in southern Iraq in some kind of military role, and the presence of Ahmed Chalabi among them? Does that signify any broader role for him after this is over?

Rumsfeld: No, I wouldn't think so. The Iraqi people are going to sort out what their Iraqi government ought to look like, and that is very clear. What's happening is that the United States has done a variety of different things. We've been working with two Kurdish groups in the north and have Special Forces with them, and they've been cooperating on various things, the PUK [Patriotic Union of Kurdistan] and the other one.

Myers: The KDP [Kurdistan Democratic Party].

Rumsfeld: KDP, yeah. The other thing that's been going on is we trained some folks who were Iraqis, and have brought them in to assist. And then there has been this group that you described, that has moved south and is involved. There are also, I think, four Shi'a groups that are involved in various ways. So there are, you know, six, eight, 10 different activities going on the part of people who are Iraqis—either Kurds or Shi'a or expatriates or people from within the country. And that's a good thing. They can be very helpful to us in a variety of ways, and we appreciate it.

Q: Are they offering direct military assistance? In other words, are they engaging in combat-related activities?

Rumsfeld: There is no question but that there are some that are doing that.

Q: Mr. Secretary?

Q: Mr. Secretary, I'd like to ask you about the British gains in Basra over the last 24 hours or so. To what extent do you think that might accelerate the erosion of resistance in Baghdad and advance your case there?

Rumsfeld: Oh, it's unclear. I don't know how good the communications are between Basra and Baghdad at the present time. A good deal of the communications in the country are out, in terms of telephone lines and radio and some television. There's some spotty local television in places. But I just don't know how good the communications happen to be, so I think it's a little premature to know.

Q: Mr. Secretary, do you want to comment on these reports that either State Department personnel or General Garner's people have nominated particular names, and you have vetoed those nominations and suggested ones of your own?

Rumsfeld: Sure, I'd be happy to. I have not read a lot of these articles, although I've been told that there are—somewhere, there's a hemorrhaging of these articles that seem to be flying around.

The short answer to it is that the president has asked us to put in place an activity. Jay Garner is the person who has been helping us with that. It has currently moved from the United States to Kuwait, and it will eventually move into Iraq. There are people from the Department of Agriculture, from the Department of Interior, from the Department of Defense, there are people from the Department of State, there are people from outside the government who are helping with it. And my understanding is that they've sorted through most of the jobs and that they're now either in route or there, and will be beginning that process of trying to help—well, for example, take an agriculture ministry. They'll be trying to help figure out what do you do with the agriculture-related ministries in Iraq and how do you fix that so that it goes forward. Which people can you use, which people don't want you to—do you not want to use? And we'll have Americans along with other coalition partners and, eventually, additional coalition partners involved.

The thought is that within a relatively short period of time, a number of those ministries could be put into the hands of Iraqis, the ones that—for example, not the defense department for a bit and certainly not the intelligence services. But there are some activities that it might very well be proper to move over to Iraqis as soon as possible. And that's sort of who's going to do what is taking place and my understanding is it's pretty well sorted through. I just—I don't know all the details, but I think it's pretty well agreed and decided. . . .

Q: . . . one elements of the Congress have voted against funding the Pentagon effort for reconstruction, saying that should be a State Department effort, and there is the controversy about the United Nations taking a leading role in it. Are you—

Rumsfeld: You know, what's happened here is we've seen people go from debating the war plan they haven't read, and the number of troops and all of that, now they're debating the form of the government, which no one has decided, and what the post–Saddam Hussein regime exercise, activity, organization ought to look like. And I can tell you we've spent a lot of time thinking about it. There's very good people from all the departments. In the last analysis, it's the president's policy, and whatever is put forward by the Congress by way of money will be expended in a way that the president decides should be expended. And what we're going to try to do is to do it in a way that makes sense for the people of Iraq.

Q: So you are opposed then, sir—just to make sure I understand—to the congressional vote taking away funding, the reconstruction of Iraq, from the Pentagon? You want to see that stay here?

Rumsfeld: All I can tell you is the president made a recommendation, and that is his preference. And we'll see what the Congress ultimately decides. But in the last analysis, it doesn't matter which pocket it's in. It will be spent in the way that the president feels is appropriate to the circumstance. . . .

Q: Mr. Secretary, when would you declare victory? Must Saddam Hussein be captured or killed, or can you declare victory when Baghdad is basically under—and the government is under—your control?

Rumsfeld: That's a tough question. And my guess is, it would be later rather than sooner, simply because it's a big country, and the idea that you could conclude that the kinetic aspects were over without having really done a good deal of work around the country, it seems to me, would be inappropriate, and it conceivably also would be misleading, which would be unfortunate.

Second, I don't think it would necessarily hinge on Saddam Hussein. At that point where he is not running his country, the regime has been changed. At that point where the coalition forces have the ability to move around the country in relative safety, and assure that humanitarian assistance can come in, and that internally displaced people can go home, and that we can go about our task trying to gather up the people who can tell us where the weapons of mass destruction caches are and where the documentation is, and then have the time to go do that, it seems to me that that takes a little bit of time. So I wouldn't think that there would be a likely early declaration of that type. . . .

Q: . . . you indicated—you indicated earlier that the stabilization process, which you hope to initiate rather quickly under General Garner, as you said, perhaps the agriculture department under Iraqis, but not—but not defense and

Rumsfeld: General Garner—let me finish. General Garner is not there to do the stabilization. General Franks will do the stabilization. General Garner's activity is a civil administration activity. And it involves the reestablishment of an Iraqi government; it involves seeing that the humanitarian assistance takes place, seeing that all of those kinds of civil, non-military, non-stabilization, non-security issues are addressed in a thoughtful and energetic way. . . .

- **Source:** Department of Defense briefing, April 7, 2003, available at http://www.defenselink.mil/transcripts/transcript.aspx? transcriptid=2316, accessed May 26, 2008.

- **Analysis:** The issue of WMD refused to die. If chemical and biological weapons had been such a concern, reporters asked, why had little or no evidence of them been found? Rumsfeld insisted that it was too early to draw any conclusions.

  One of the more interesting exchanges concerned the role of Jay Garner, head of the Office of Humanitarian Aid and Reconstruction. The office had been sent up only a few months before the invasion. Rumsfeld had never liked it, in part because he disliked the whole idea of nation building and in part because he wished to control all aspects of the Iraq mission. Rumsfeld's response to the question about funding and stabilization operations revealed his views on this subject. He insisted that General Franks was in charge of stabilization. After the invasion, the Coalition Provisional Authority headed by L. Paul Bremer would completely undercut Garner's efforts.

- **Document 37: Excerpt of President Bush's Remarks to the Crew of the USS *Abraham Lincoln***
- **When:** May 1, 2003
- **Where:** USS *Abraham Lincoln*, off the coast of California
- **Significance:** The president used this occasion to declare the Iraq mission accomplished.

THE PRESIDENT: Thank you all very much. Admiral Kelly, Captain Card, officers and sailors of the USS *Abraham Lincoln*, my fellow Americans: Major combat operations in Iraq have ended. In the battle of Iraq, the United States and our allies have prevailed. (Applause.) And now our coalition is engaged in securing and reconstructing that country.

In this battle, we have fought for the cause of liberty, and for the peace of the world. Our nation and our coalition are proud of this accomplishment—yet, it is you, the members of the United States military, who achieved it. Your courage, your willingness to face danger for your country and for each other, made this day possible. Because of you, our nation is more secure. Because of you, the tyrant has fallen, and Iraq is free. (Applause.)

Operation Iraqi Freedom was carried out with a combination of precision and speed and boldness the enemy did not expect, and the world had not seen before. From distant bases or ships at sea, we sent planes and missiles that could destroy an enemy division, or strike a single bunker. Marines and soldiers charged to Baghdad across 350 miles of hostile ground, in one of the swiftest advances of heavy arms in history. You have shown the world the skill and the might of the American Armed Forces.

This nation thanks all the members of our coalition who joined in a noble cause. We thank the Armed Forces of the United Kingdom, Australia, and Poland, who shared in the hardships of war. We thank all the citizens of Iraq who welcomed our troops and joined in the liberation of their own country. And tonight, I have a special word for Secretary Rumsfeld, for General Franks, and for all the men and women who wear the uniform of the United States: America is grateful for a job well done. (Applause.)

The character of our military through history—the daring of Normandy, the fierce courage of Iwo Jima, the decency and idealism that turned enemies into allies—is fully present in this generation. When Iraqi civilians looked into the faces of our servicemen and women, they saw strength and kindness and goodwill. When I look at the members of the United States military, I see the best of our country, and I'm honored to be your Commander-in-Chief. (Applause.)

In the images of falling statues, we have witnessed the arrival of a new era. For a hundred of years of war, culminating in the nuclear age, military technology was designed and deployed to inflict casualties on an ever-growing scale. In defeating Nazi Germany and Imperial Japan, Allied forces destroyed entire cities, while enemy leaders who started the conflict were safe until the final days. Military power was used to end a regime by breaking a nation.

Today, we have the greater power to free a nation by breaking a dangerous and aggressive regime. With new tactics and precision weapons, we can achieve military objectives without directing violence against civilians. No device of man can remove the tragedy from war; yet it is a great moral advance when the guilty have far more to fear from war than the innocent. (Applause.)

In the images of celebrating Iraqis, we have also seen the ageless appeal of human freedom. Decades of lies and intimidation could not make the Iraqi people love their oppressors or desire their own enslavement. Men and women in every culture need liberty like they need food and water and air. Everywhere that freedom arrives, humanity rejoices; and everywhere that freedom stirs, let tyrants fear. (Applause.)

We have difficult work to do in Iraq. We're bringing order to parts of that country that remain dangerous. We're pursuing and finding leaders of the old regime, who will be held to account for their crimes. We've begun the search for hidden chemical and biological weapons and already know of hundreds of sites that will be investigated. We're helping to rebuild Iraq, where the dictator built palaces for himself, instead of hospitals and schools. And we will stand with the new leaders of Iraq as they establish a government of, by, and for the Iraqi people. (Applause.)

The transition from dictatorship to democracy will take time, but it is worth every effort. Our coalition will stay until our work is done. Then we will leave, and we will leave behind a free Iraq. (Applause.)

The battle of Iraq is one victory in a war on terror that began on September the 11, 2001—and still goes on. That terrible morning, 19 evil men—the shock troops of a hateful ideology—gave America and the civilized world a glimpse of their ambitions. They imagined, in the words of one terrorist, that September the 11th would be the "beginning of the end of America." By seeking to turn our cities into killing fields, terrorists and their allies believed that they could destroy this nation's resolve, and force our retreat from the world. They have failed. (Applause.)

In the battle of Afghanistan, we destroyed the Taliban, many terrorists, and the camps where they trained. We continue to help the Afghan people lay roads, restore hospitals, and educate all of their children. Yet we also have dangerous work to complete. As I speak, a Special Operations task force, led by the 82nd Airborne, is on the trail of the terrorists and those who seek to undermine the free government of Afghanistan. America and our coalition will finish what we have begun. (Applause.)

From Pakistan to the Philippines to the Horn of Africa, we are hunting down al Qaeda killers. Nineteen months ago, I pledged that the terrorists would not escape the patient justice of the United States. And as of tonight, nearly one-half of al Qaeda's senior operatives have been captured or killed. (Applause.)

The liberation of Iraq is a crucial advance in the campaign against terror. We've removed an ally of al Qaeda, and cut off a source of terrorist funding. And this much is certain: No terrorist network will gain weapons of mass destruction from the Iraqi regime, because the regime is no more. (Applause.)

In these 19 months that changed the world, our actions have been focused and deliberate and proportionate to the offense. We have not forgotten the victims of September the 11th—the last phone calls, the cold murder of children, the searches in the rubble. With those attacks, the terrorists and their supporters declared war on the United States. And war is what they got. (Applause.)

Our war against terror is proceeding according to principles that I have made clear to all: Any person involved in committing or planning terrorist attacks against the American people becomes an enemy of this country, and a target of American justice. (Applause.)

Any person, organization, or government that supports, protects, or harbors terrorists is complicit in the murder of the innocent, and equally guilty of terrorist crimes.

Any outlaw regime that has ties to terrorist groups and seeks or possesses weapons of mass destruction is a grave danger to the civilized world—and will be confronted. (Applause.)

And anyone in the world, including the Arab world, who works and sacrifices for freedom has a loyal friend in the United States of America. (Applause.)

Our commitment to liberty is America's tradition—declared at our founding; affirmed in Franklin Roosevelt's Four Freedoms; asserted in the Truman Doctrine and in Ronald Reagan's challenge to an evil empire. We are committed to freedom in Afghanistan, in Iraq, and in a peaceful Palestine. The advance of freedom is the surest strategy to undermine the appeal of terror in the world. Where freedom takes hold, hatred gives way to hope. When freedom takes hold, men and women turn to the peaceful pursuit of a better life. American values and American interests lead in the same direction: We stand for human liberty. (Applause.)

The United States upholds these principles of security and freedom in many ways—with all the tools of diplomacy, law enforcement, intelligence, and finance. We're working with a broad coalition of nations that understand the threat and our shared responsibility to meet it. The use of force has been—and remains—our last resort. Yet all can know, friend and foe alike, that our nation has a mission: We will answer threats to our security, and we will defend the peace. (Applause.)

Our mission continues. Al Qaeda is wounded, not destroyed. The scattered cells of the terrorist network still operate in many nations, and we know from daily intelligence that they continue to plot against free people. The proliferation of deadly weapons remains a serious danger. The enemies of freedom are not idle, and neither are we. Our government has taken unprecedented measures to defend the homeland. And we will continue to hunt down the enemy before he can strike. (Applause.)

The war on terror is not over; yet it is not endless. We do not know the day of final victory, but we have seen the turning of the tide. No act of the terrorists will change our purpose, or weaken our resolve, or alter their fate. Their cause is lost. Free nations will press on to victory. (Applause.)

Other nations in history have fought in foreign lands and remained to occupy and exploit. Americans, following a battle, want nothing more than to return home. And that is your direction tonight. (Applause.) After service in the Afghan—and Iraqi theaters of war—after 100,000 miles, on the longest carrier deployment in recent history, you are homeward bound. (Applause.) Some of you will see new family members for the first time—150 babies were born while their fathers were on the Lincoln. Your families are proud of you, and your nation will welcome you. (Applause.)

We are mindful, as well, that some good men and women are not making the journey home. One of those who fell, Corporal Jason Mileo, spoke to his parents five days before his death. Jason's father said, "He called us from the center of Baghdad, not to brag, but to tell us he loved us. Our son was a soldier."

Every name, every life is a loss to our military, to our nation, and to the loved ones who grieve. There's no homecoming for these families. Yet we pray, in God's time, their reunion will come.

Those we lost were last seen on duty. Their final act on this Earth was to fight a great evil and bring liberty to others. All of you—all in this generation of our military—have taken up the highest calling of history. You're defending your country, and protecting the innocent from harm. And wherever you go, you carry a message of hope—a message that is ancient and ever new. In the words of the prophet Isaiah, "To the captives, 'come out,'—and to those in darkness, 'be free.' "

Thank you for serving our country and our cause. May God bless you all, and may God continue to bless America. (Applause.)

- **Source:** George W. Bush. *Public Papers of the Presidents of the United States: George Bush, 2003.* Book I, 410–413. Washington, DC: GPO, 2003.

- **Analysis:** The appearance on the *Abraham Lincoln* was a carefully staged event in which the president landed on the flight deck in a two-person combat aircraft. His remarks clearly indicate a perception of Iraq as a conventional war to be followed by a mopping-up operation. The comparison of Operation Iraqi Freedom with the defeat of Germany and Japan suggests how the administration considered the next phase of operations would proceed. A military government supervised German and Japanese bureaucrats who performed the routine tasks of administration. The administration believed the occupation of Iraq would unfold in a similar manner. The president also dismissed continued irregular warfare as the work of regime holdouts.

CONCLUSION

The United States invaded Iraq with a smaller number of troops than many military planners wanted. The invasion force had no trouble brushing aside Hussein's forces, although it did encounter heavier fighting as it approached Baghdad. The critics, however, proved to be correct in their conclusion that the coalition would have too few troops to control the country once conventional operations ceased. The predictions in General Zinni's invasion exercise proved to be all too accurate.

3

RECONSTRUCTION

During Operation Iraqi Freedom, the U.S.-led coalition made a concerted and largely successful effort to minimize casualties and avoid damage to Iraqi infrastructure. However, failure to plan and prepare adequately for a postconflict stability operation contributed to an atmosphere of anarchy following the collapse of the regime. Rather than remain at their posts as U.S. planners had anticipated, police and other civil servants deserted en mass, creating a vacuum that coalition forces could not fill. Ordinary Iraqis vented years of pent-up rage and deprivation in an orgy of looting and violence. The United States had too few troops to maintain law and order, and those available lacked training, equipment, and a proper mandate for civil policing. Looters emptied government buildings of all valuables and even stripped wiring from electric generating plants, causing extensive damage to an infrastructure weakened by years of sanctions and neglect. Delays in planning for postwar reconstruction compounded by this wanton destruction delayed restoration of vital services, fueling frustration on which a growing insurgency fed. U.S. mistakes compounded these problems.

ANTICIPATING THE PROBLEM

Even before widespread looting severely damaged Iraq's already fragile infrastructure, studies gauged the scope, challenges, and cost of reconstruction. They foresaw formidable challenges requiring a costly effort unfolding over several years. Wishing to avoid nation-building, the Bush administration ignored such forecasts.

- **Document 38: Excerpt of *Reconstructing Iraq: Insights, Challenges, and Missions for Military Forces in a Post-Conflict Scenario***
- **When:** February 2003
- **Where:** Carlisle Barracks, PA
- **Significance:** This Strategic Studies Institute study published a month before the invasion estimated the cost of reconstruction and the need for an international effort to meet it.

The Requirement for Large-Scale Economic Assistance to Iraq

Iraq is a country with important natural resources which is, nevertheless, stricken by poverty as a result of recent historical events. Ten years of sanctions followed upon the heels of the Gulf War in 1991. Earlier, from 1980–88, Iraqis were absorbed in an extremely bloody war with Iran. While Saddam initially attempted to fund both war requirements and social spending during the conflict with Iran, circumstances forced him to shift to a total war economy by 1981. If the United States assumes control of Iraq, it will therefore assume control of a badly battered economy.

Upon ousting Saddam, the United States will then have responsibility for providing some level of comfort and subsistence to Iraq's impoverished population. Based on the people's current plight, these tasks will be exceptionally challenging. Moreover, regional or international public opinion will have little tolerance for a lethargic aid program under which people starve while waiting for relevant bureaucracies to work out their problems. Any incidents of suffering, neglect, or U.S. indifference can be expected to come to the prompt attention of the regional and international media.

Some of the economic burden of rebuilding the country may be borne by reliance on the Iraqi oil industry. It is doubtful, however, that oil wealth will pay for all of Iraq's reconstruction needs, even if the oil infrastructure survives the war relatively intact. Estimates of the cost of rebuilding range from $30 to $100 billion and do not include the cost of occupation troops.[92] Such troops will be maintained as a separate expense from that of reconstruction and are not expected to be maintained through Iraqi revenues. Moreover, Iraq also has an exceptionally heavy burden of debt, the management of which was one of Saddam's major reasons for invading Kuwait in 1990. On the plus side, Iraq does have a well-educated population that could participate in reconstruction efforts. It is not clear what the condition of the Iraqi oil industry will be in the aftermath of war with a U.S.-led coalition. If Saddam perceives his regime as crumbling, he could order the destruction of the wells just as he did with the Kuwaiti oil wells in 1991.[93] While the destruction of Kuwaiti wells may have had some military utility in obscuring ground targets from allied aircraft, Saddam's primary motive for this action was probably revenge. Should his regime face certain destruction, it is likely that Saddam will at least consider the destruction of the Iraqi oil fields, rather than leave them for a successor regime. It is also possible that Saddam will destroy other Iraqi infrastructure targets if he can.[94]

The destruction of some or even most of Iraq's oil infrastructure would delay the ability of a successor government to generate revenue, but the oil wells could not be rendered permanently unusable. The experience of repairing the Kuwaiti oil wells suggests that deeply damaged facilities can be repaired in a reasonable period of time with current technology. Sabotage would of course remain a serious threat well into the occupation and this would require substantial efforts at security by either occupation forces or their indigenous allies. Additionally, economic shortfalls could come at a time of critical need due to the expected creation of large numbers of displaced persons (DPs) and internally-displaced persons (IDPs) during the war. The exact number of IDPs is impossible to predict because it depends on the nature and progress of the war. A worst case analysis would suggest IDPs in the millions.[95] Also, tuberculosis, cholera, and typhoid are already prevalent in Iraq, and the health crisis in that country could only be further aggravated due to war. Medical crises are extremely likely in postwar Iraq.

[92.]"After the Fall," [*U.S. News and World Report*, December 2, 2002] p. 23.

[93.]Christopher Cooper, "A Burning Issue About Iraq: Will Hussein Set Oil Ablaze?" *Wall Street Journal*, November 27, 2002, internet edition.

[94.]Bradley Graham, "Scorched Earth Plans in Iraq Cited," *Washington Post*, December 19, 2002, p. 1.

[95.]Displaced persons were an immense problem after World War II. It took many years to resettle them, and many never could return home.

Winning the Peace in Iraq

The occupation of Iraq involves a myriad of complexities arising from the political and socio-economic culture of that country. This situation is further complicated by the poor understanding that Westerners and especially Americans have of Iraqi political and cultural dynamics. The society is exceptionally difficult for Westerners to penetrate and the factions and fragmentations are extraordinarily complex. While Americans often define themselves by a national creed dating back to the 1770s, Iraqis have no such creed and define themselves through tribe, ethnicity, and religion. Moreover, the redispositions and concerns of the Iraqis, not the values of their occupiers, will need to be addressed to build a viable new society. Any culturally based efforts by the United States to assume away differences between Americans and Iraqis can only doom the effort for social rebuilding.

The possibility of the United States winning the war and losing the peace in Iraq is real and serious. Rehabilitating Iraq will consequently be an important challenge that threatens to consume huge amounts of resources without guaranteed results. The effort also threatens to be a long and painful process, but merely "toughing it out" is not a solution. The longer the occupation continues, the greater the potential that it will disrupt society rather than rehabilitate it. Thus, important and complex goals must be accomplished as quickly as possible. However, a withdrawal from Iraq under the wrong circumstances could leave it an unstable failed state, serving as a haven for terrorism and a center of regional insecurity or danger to its neighbors. The premature departure of U.S. troops could also result in civil war.

Successfully executing the postwar occupation of Iraq is consequently every bit as important as winning the war. Preparing for the postwar rehabilitation of the Iraqi political system will probably be more difficult and complex than planning for combat. Massive resources need to be focused on this effort well before the first shot is fired.

Thinking about the war now and the occupation later is not an acceptable solution. Without an overwhelming effort to prepare for occupation, the United States may find itself in a radically different world over the next few years, a world in which the threat of Saddam Hussein seems like a pale shadow of new problems of America's own making.

- **Source:** Conrad C. Crane and W. Andrew Terrill. *Reconstructing Iraq: Insights, Challenges, and Missions for Military Forces in a Post-Conflict Scenario.* Carlisle Barracks, PA: Strategic Studies Institute of U.S. Army War College, 2003, 39–41.

- **Analysis:** This assessment painted a daunting picture of the challenges facing the United States during its occupation of Iraq. The authors anticipated the possibility of widespread destruction but did not identify its cause. They feared that Saddam Hussein would destroy oil wells as he had done before retreating from Kuwait in 1991. They did, however, correctly conclude that winning the peace would require a massive infusion of aid and a sustained U.S. presence. Withdrawing before stabilizing the country, the study warned, could result in Iraq plunging into civil war.

Like the conclusions drawn by General Zinni's "Exercise Desert Crossing," this study was ignored by the Rumsfeld Pentagon. The secretary of defense wanted nothing to do with a protracted nation-building operation, which would take resources away from his pet project, restructuring the U.S. military. He expected a pro-U.S. Iraqi government to take over after a short period of transition.

- **Document 39: Excerpt of Interagency Briefing on Humanitarian Assistance for Iraq**
- **When:** February 24, 2003
- **Where:** Washington, DC
- **Significance:** The document revealed the administration's perceptions about the nature and extent of the humanitarian crisis in Iraq, how it should be addressed, and who would address it.

> ## DID YOU KNOW?
>
> ### U.S. Agency for International Development (USAID)
>
> The U.S. Agency for International Development is an independent agency of the U.S. government charged with distributing nonmilitary foreign aid. Created in 1961 by the Foreign Assistance Act, USAID receives foreign policy guidance from the secretary of state. It funds programs to promote economic growth, trade, and agricultural development, supports improved health care, and fosters democracy. USAID also works to prevent conflict and delivers humanitarian aid in crises. Since 2003, USAID has funded $7.4 billion dollars worth of projects on aid and development in Iraq.

Participants:

Elliott Abrams—NSC Senior Director for Near East and North Africa;

Andrew Natsios—Administrator of The U.S. Agency for International Development;

Gene Dewey—Assistant Secretary of State for The Bureau of Population, Refugees and Migration;

Ron Adams—Deputy Director of The Pentagon Office of Reconstruction and Humanitarian Assistance;

Joe Collins—Deputy Assistant Secretary of Defense for Stability Operations;

Robin Cleveland—Associate Director for National Security Programs

MR. ABRAMS: We go into a situation where we recognize that military action in Iraq, if it is necessary, could have adverse humanitarian consequences. And we've been planning, therefore, over the last several months, an inter-agency effort to prevent or at least to mitigate any such consequences.

We're going into a situation where there are a number of humanitarian problems. About 60 percent of Iraqis, the U.N. estimates, are completely dependent on the food distributions of the Oil For Food program for their food supply, and many other Iraqis are at least partly dependent. There are roughly 800,000 displaced persons inside Iraq, and 740,000, it is estimated, who are refugees in nearby countries.

We also know that conflict can have a number of humanitarian effects. It can increase the number of displaced persons. It can interrupt the Oil For Food distribution of food. It can disrupt electricity supplies. It can lead U.N. and NGO workers to evacuate. Some have already evacuated. We believe that the International Red Cross will not evacuate, and stay during the conflict.

How much displacement will there be? How much of an impact on the humanitarian situation would a conflict have? To a substantial degree, the answer to that question depends on the regime. Does it use weapons of mass destruction? Are there efforts against their own oil wells, such as they did in Kuwait, when they set the oil wells on fire. Other efforts to cause, deliberately cause flooding. Other efforts to encourage ethnic violence or to destroy their own infrastructure. Those are questions we're not going to be able to answer at this time. We'll see.

But in dealing with them, the strategy we have for humanitarian relief has six key principles, and I think you've got those before you. The first is to try to minimize the displacement and the damage to the infrastructure and the disruption of services. And the military campaign planning has had—has been tailored to try to do that, to try to minimize the impact on civilian populations.

We have what is called the humanitarian mapping program, in which the U.S. military has gone to very great lengths to work with humanitarian organizations, international agencies to locate humanitarian sites, key infrastructure, cultural and historical sites, and to protect them to extent that that's possible.

We recognize the potential for Saddam Hussein to target his own civilian population, he certainly has in the past—and campaign planning has aimed, to the extent possible, to deny him that capability. We hope to discourage population displacement through—partly through an information campaign, and partly by efforts to provide aid rapidly and restore public services rapidly—for example, electricity, water supply, the Oil for Food Program, itself, and I'll come back to that.

Second principle, to rely primarily on civilian relief agencies. And civilian agencies and personnel are in the lead in all the coordinating and planning that we've been doing for about—I'd say about four months. As a kind of offshoot of the deputies committee, Robin Cleveland and I have co-chaired an interagency group that has been doing this relief and reconstruction planning.

We want to rely primarily on civilian international organizations, which is the standard practice in situations like this: U.N. agencies; NGOs; other governments and their civilian agencies. OFDA, the Office of Foreign Disaster Assistance, and the Refugee Bureau at State, PRM, have been meeting with representatives of the international aid community for several months now.

These organizations—the U.N. agencies, the NGOs—have enormous expertise and capacity. And we're going to try to facilitate and fund their efforts to the greatest extent possible. We welcome U.N. planning—and there has been a considerable amount of U.N. planning by the specialized agencies to play a key role in Iraq, as they do generally, when there are humanitarian crises. And we will be trying to support and facilitate their activities.

The role of the U.S. military is not to take a lead role in humanitarian relief activities. It is to facilitate early secure access, to create a humanitarian space, to provide information for U.S. civilian teams—civilian relief agencies—to fulfill their humanitarian mandates. There will probably be circumstances where there is no U.N. agency or NGO or civilian capability of any kind at a very early moment if conflict happens. And there, the military may be actually required to provide limited relief because there's no alternative. And with the guidance and assistance of USG civilian relief experts, they'll have to do that. We're going to anticipate that any such period would be short, and that civilian relief agencies would be able to get into those areas quickly.

Third principle, effective civil military coordination. We have been training and preparing a 60-person DART team, disaster assistance response team, which is really about the largest we've ever had. And it would enter liberated areas of Iraq in co-ordination with U.S. military forces, to, first of all, make an assessment of what are the—what is the humanitarian situation, to coordinate then U.S. government relief activities that try to resolve whatever problems there are. They will be capable of immediate, in the field grant making. And their job is also liaison with the military, other donors, NGOs, international organizations.

The DART itself is made up of professionals in the field of humanitarian emergencies from several U.S. civilian agencies. And we'll have—there will be a number of DART teams in the field. Andrew Natsios can say more about that. There are other coordination structures, humanitarian operations centers and civil military operation centers, being established in the region with the cooperation of several neighboring governments.

The government of Kuwait, for example, has made available a large facility to support a humanitarian operation center in Kuwait City. The job there is information sharing coordination, deconflicting efforts between U.S. military and Kuwaiti officials, U.S.-civilian representatives, U.N. agencies, international organizations, NGOs, coalition partners. The job of the humanitarian operation center is to gather them in one place so they can all coordinate what they are doing.

It is not a replacement for the U.N., which has its own coordinating structure through OCHA, the coordinator for humanitarian affairs. But it is a supplement to that. Fourth principle, facilitating IO and NGO operations. We will provide civilian experts to be the liaison with international organizations and NGOs, and to support and staff these coordination centers—the humanitarian operation center in Kuwait and the civil military operation centers—so that they are—this is a customary pattern for NGOs and international organizations to work with the civilian side of U.S. government and they'll continue to do that.

And one of the things that our civilians can do by their own connection with the U.S. military is to provide information about access to particular geographical locations, security in those areas, and information about the populations in those areas that the U.S. military may have found. The DART staff is the primary contact for international organizations and NGOs in the field.

NGOs have raised the question of licensing, because due to the sanctions regime that are in place—the U.N. sanctions, the U.S. sanctions on Iraq—it has been difficult in some cases for them to undertake the planning they want to do. For example, they may want to go to Iraq. And we've had cases where they have been slowed down, so we have been streamlining the OFAC, Office of Foreign Asset Control, licensing procedures to expedite the issuance of licenses to NGOs so that they can operate inside Iraq.

State and USAID now have blanket licenses that cover agencies, NGOs that have received grants from them, from State or AID. And NGOs working in areas of Iraq that are not controlled by the Saddam Hussein regime and those who are only conducting assessments in the country will also have an expedited registration process.

We've given money, we have provided funding to relief agencies so that they can plan, hire staff and pre-position supplies. The Refugee Bureau at State has provided over $15 million to international agencies for pre-positioning and for contingency planning. Most of that to the U.N. High Commissioner for Refugees.

AID has provided over $9 million to a variety of agencies for contingency planning, including $2 million to UNICEF and $5 million to the World Food Program. AID is in discussions with international organizations to provide an additional $56 million soon.

We've also encouraged other donors. And a number of governments have come forward to pledge millions of dollars to—mostly to U.N. agencies and to some NGOs.

Fifth, pre-positioning U.S. government relief supplies and response mechanisms. We have been stockpiling blankets, water, ladders, shelter supplies, medicines, other relief items at this point to serve about a million people—the material in question worth about $12 million. And we're trying to forward-deploy those stockpiles into the region. One example, there are 46, 40-foot long containers of relief supplies en route to warehouses in the Gulf. We are stockpiling and pre-positioning humanitarian daily rations. You may remember those from Afghanistan and previous situations. This is a ration for one person for one day—the equivalent in calories of three meals. And we're getting up to about 3 million of those pre-positioned.

And we are preparing to undertake immediate rehabilitation and reconstruction efforts to deliver essential services to the Iraqi people. And that means critical infrastructure, health facilities, water and sanitation systems. And electricity is key in all of those.

Finally, sixth, support the resumption of the ration-distribution system. That's a very important item. As I noted at the beginning, about 60 percent of Iraqis depend on it for their food. It is an immensely complex system that is run very competently by the U.N. and by the Iraqis. There are at the ground level about 55,000 ration agents. Iraqis get a ration booklet which tells them which day of the month their family should go to the distribution point, usually a local grocer, to pick up their rations for the month. We will make an effort to get that system up and running again if there is a conflict, and if we are in that situation.

We want to disrupt that system as little as possible, and get it back on its feet as soon as possible. And that is something that a lot of U.S. agencies are thinking about. We recognize that that is a critical aspect of—a critical aspect of the humanitarian situation in Iraq.

- **Source:** "Press Briefing on White House Inter-Agency Humanitarian Reconstruction Issues," February 24, 2003, available at http://www .usaid.gov/press/speeches/2003/sp030224.html, accessed June 4, 2008.

- **Analysis:** This document reveals that the administration did anticipate the need for a humanitarian effort in the aftermath of the invasion, although they underestimated its extent. However, as this briefing indicates, U.S. officials saw short-time humanitarian relief rather than long-term nation building as their major concern. They also insisted that the humanitarian effort be civilian and anticipated an extensive international effort to supplement U.S. contributions. The United Nations and other agencies did become involved, but the deteriorating security situation soon made it impossible for them to work effectively. In the end, U.S. taxpayers footed a much larger bill than anyone anticipated.

THE REALITY OF POSTWAR IRAQ

The wildly optimistic nature of administration forecasts for the scope and cost of humanitarian assistance soon became clear. Far from remaining at their posts, Iraqi police and civil servants abandoned them. The coalition was totally unprepared to fill the vacuum they left. The resulting chaos made a shambles of an already seriously compromised infrastructure and increased exponentially the cost of getting the country back on its feet.

- **Document 40: Excerpt of Secretary of Defense Donald Rumsfeld and General Richard B. Myers, Department of Defense News Briefing**
- **When:** April 11, 2003
- **Where:** Baghdad
- **Significance:** The secretary faced intense questioning about lawlessness in Iraq and his alleged failure to plan for such an eventuality.

Rumsfeld: . . . The scenes we've witnessed in Baghdad and other free Iraqi cities belie the widespread early commentary suggesting that Iraqis were ambivalent or even opposed to the coalition's arrival in their country. I think it's fair to say that they were not ambivalent or opposed, but they were understandably frightened of the regime of Saddam Hussein and the retaliation or retribution that they could have suffered. And now, as their fear of the former Iraqi dictator lessens, the true sentiments of a large majority, I believe, of the Iraqi people are surfacing. And I think it's increasingly clear that most welcome coalition forces and see them not as invaders or occupiers, but as liberators.

The images of thousands of cheering Iraqis, celebrating and embracing coalition forces, are being broadcast throughout the world, including the Arab world. And possibly for the first time, Arab people are seeing the people of Iraq waving American flags and thanking the men and women in uniform for risking their lives to free them from tyranny. I think it's important that that message be seen, for America is a friend of Arab people. And now, finally, Arab people are hearing the same message, not from U.S. officials, but from their fellow Arabs, the liberated people of Iraq.

Meanwhile, we're working to expand the flow of free information to the Iraqi people. We're moving a ground station to Baghdad to expand the coverage area for radio and television broadcasts. We've begun broadcasting a one-hour news program and are moving to restore Iraqi radio and television networks. We're doing this because access to free information is critical to building a free society.

At the same time, we're working with free Iraqis, those in liberated areas, and those who have returned from abroad, to establish—begin the process of establishing—an interim authority which will help pave the way for a new Iraqi government, a government that will be chosen by the Iraqi people, not by anyone else, and based on democratic principles and peaceful coexistence with its neighbors and with the world. The makeup of this interim authority and the government that emerges from it will be decided by the free Iraqi people.

In areas where the war is winding down, coalition forces are bringing humanitarian aid and are working with a number of international organizations in other countries to deliver food, water, medicine and other necessities. . . .

Q: Mr. Secretary, you spoke of the television pictures that went around the world earlier of Iraqis welcoming U.S. forces with open arms. But now television pictures are showing looting and other signs of lawlessness. Are you, sir, concerned that what's being reported from the region as anarchy in Baghdad and other cities might wash away the goodwill the United States has built? And, are U.S. troops capable of or inclined to be police forces in Iraq?

Rumsfeld: Well, I think the way to think about that is that if you go from a repressive regime that has—it's a police state, where people are murdered and imprisoned by the tens of thousands—and then you go to something other than that—a liberated Iraq—that you go through a transition period. And in every country, in my adult lifetime, that's had the wonderful opportunity to do that, to move from a repressed dictatorial regime to something that's freer, we've seen in that transition period there is untidiness, and there's no question but that that's not anyone's choice.

On the other hand, if you think of those pictures, very often the pictures are pictures of people going into the symbols of the regime—into the palaces, into the boats, and into the Ba'ath Party headquarters, and into the places that have been part of that repression. And, while no one condones looting, on the other hand, one can understand the pent-up feelings that may result from decades of repression and people who have had members of their family killed by that regime, for them to be taking their feelings out on that regime.

With respect to the second part of your question, we do feel an obligation to assist in providing security, and the coalition forces are doing that. They're patrolling in various cities. Where they see looting, they're stopping it, and they will be doing so. The second step, of course, is to not do that on a permanent basis but, rather, to find Iraqis who can assist in providing police support in those cities and various types of stabilizing and security assistance, and we're in the process of doing that.

Q: How quickly do you hope to do that? Isn't that a pressing problem?

Rumsfeld: Wait. Wait. But in answer to your—direct answer to your question— are we concerned that this would offset it, the feeling of liberation—suggests that,

"Gee, maybe they were better off repressed." And I don't think there's anyone in any of those pictures, or any human being who's not free, who wouldn't prefer to be free, and recognize that you pass through a transition period like this and accept it as part of the price of getting from a repressed regime to freedom. . . .

Rumsfeld: Let me say one other thing. The images you are seeing on television you are seeing over, and over, and over, and it's the same picture of some person walking out of some building with a vase, and you see it 20 times, and you think, "My goodness, were there that many vases?" [Laughter.] "Is it possible that there were that many vases in the whole country?"

Q: Do you think that the words "anarchy" and "lawlessness" are ill-chosen—

Rumsfeld: Absolutely. I picked up a newspaper today and I couldn't believe it. I read eight headlines that talked about chaos, violence, unrest. And it just was Henny Penny—"The sky is falling." I've never seen anything like it! And here is a country that's being liberated, here are people who are going from being repressed and held under the thumb of a vicious dictator, and they're free. And all this newspaper could do, with eight or 10 headlines, they showed a man bleeding, a civilian, who they claimed we had shot—one thing after another. It's just unbelievable how people can take that away from what is happening in that country!

Do I think those words are unrepresentative? Yes.

Q: Mr. Secretary, could I follow that up? . . . I think the question is, if you—if a foreign military force came into your neighborhood and did away with the police, and left you at the mercy of criminals, how long would you feel liberated?

Rumsfeld: Well, that's a fair question. First of all, the foreign military force came into their neighborhood and did not do away with any police. There may have been some police who fled, because the people didn't like them, and because they'd been doing things to the people in the local community that the people wanted to have a word with them about. But we haven't gone in and done away with any police. In fact, we're looking for police in those villages and towns who can, in fact, assist in providing order, to the extent there are people who can do it in a manner that's consistent with our values. . . .

Q: Given how predictable the lack of law and order was, as you said, from past conflicts, was there part of General Franks' plan to deal with it? And—

Rumsfeld: Of course.

Q: Well, what is it?

Rumsfeld: This is fascinating. This is just fascinating. From the very beginning, we were convinced that we would succeed, and that means that that regime would end. And we were convinced that as we went from the end of that regime to something other than that regime, there would be a period of transition. And, you cannot do everything instantaneously; it's never been done, everything instantaneously. We did, however, recognize that there was at least a chance of catastrophic success, if you will, to reverse the phrase, that you could in a given place or places have a victory that occurred well before reasonable people might have expected it, and that we needed to be ready for that; we needed to be ready with medicine, with food, with water. And, we have been.

And, you say, "Well, what was it in the plan?" The plan is a complex set of conclusions or ideas that then have a whole series of alternative excursions that one can do, depending on what happens. And, they have been doing that as they've been going along. And, they've been doing a darn good job.

Q: Yes, but Mr. Secretary, I'm asking about what plan was there to restore law and order?

Rumsfeld: Well, let's just take a city. Take the port city, Umm Qasr—what the plan was. Well, the British went in, they built a pipeline bringing water in from Kuwait; they cleared the mine of ports [sic]; they brought ships in with food; they've been providing security. In fact, they've done such a lousy job, that the city has gone from 15,000 to 40,000. Now think of that. Why would people vote with their feet and go into this place that's so bad? The reason they're going in is because there's food, there's water, there's medicine and there's jobs. That's why. The British have done a fantastic job. They've done an excellent job.

And, does that mean you couldn't go in there and take a television camera or get a still photographer and take a picture of something that was imperfect, untidy? I could do that in any city in America. Think what's happened in our cities when we've had riots, and problems, and looting. Stuff happens! But in terms of what's going on in that country, it is a fundamental misunderstanding to see those images over, and over, and over again of some boy walking out with a vase and say, "Oh, my goodness, you didn't have a plan." That's nonsense. They know what they're doing, and they're doing a terrific job. And it's untidy, and freedom's untidy, and free people are free to make mistakes and commit crimes and do bad things. They're also free to live their lives and do wonderful things, and that's what's going to happen here. . . .

Q: There's some additional specificity here. While you have just expressed yet again your dismay at the international news media, in fact, the reporting does factually show there are some certain number of Iraqi citizens that have spoken on-camera quite directly about their own concerns about the safety and security in Baghdad and that situation. There have also been absolutely verified reports that it is not just regime targets but indeed hospitals, banks, other facilities essential to society. The ICRC has been on TV today saying that hospitals are being looted, not regime targets you're speaking of, and that they can't even get there to resupply these essential hospitals.

Now, my question is, General Brooks said this morning that the military—U.S. military—did not want to reconstruct the Iraqi police force in Baghdad because the feeling of the U.S. military is that that the Iraqi police force has been operating against the U.S. military. He didn't feel that was a secure solution. So with some specificity, what type of Iraqi force can you bring to bear in Baghdad to have Iraqis help restore security? And, what types of specific tasks are you now going to assign the U.S. military to do to help restore the situation, which the people of Baghdad appear to be concerned about?

Rumsfeld: Well, hospitals. No, let's go back to what you said about people.

You could take a camera and a microphone, and stick it in front of a thousand people in Iraq today, and you could find someone saying every single thing you've said and every single thing I've said. You're going to find it all across the spectrum. You know, it's the facts on the ground where a person is that determines how they feel about it. And, there are some very dangerous places in that country and some very difficult situations.

And, there is no question but there is a hospital that was looted. There also is this fact. The Saddam Hussein regime and the Ba'ath Party put their headquarters in hospitals all over that country. They have been doing it systematically. Have we been complaining about that? Have we been photographing that? Have we been bemoaning that? No! Why? Because there wasn't a free press. You couldn't get in to do it; you'd get thrown out. You'd get thrown in jail if you were an Iraqi and you tried to do it.

A hundred and twenty-three schools were Ba'ath Party headquarters. Is that a good thing to do to a school? Is that a good thing to do to a hospital? No. But was there any complaint about it? No, there was no complaint. Is it true that a hospital was looted? Yes. Is that unfortunate? Yes. Do we have medicines and medical supplies coming in behind to help the people in those situations? You bet we do.

Q: But I guess what I'm not hearing here is, either one of you gentlemen, what tasks, with some specificity if you can, what U.S. military forces in Baghdad will now be doing to help calm the situation, or do you just—

Rumsfeld: They're already doing it. They're already going to hospitals that are being looted and stopping it. If you look carefully, you'll see images of people being arrested for looting, and they're walking out with those little white things on their wrists and said "Don't do that." And, they take them out of there and they tell them to go someplace else. And, that's happening all over the place. . . .

Rumsfeld: Our folks are operating to the extent they can in Baghdad in creating a presence and dissuading people from looting. And, for suddenly the biggest problem in the world to be looting is really notable. . . .

Q: If I may, Secretary Rumsfeld—Terry Call from the [inaudible word] Newspaper Group—let me ask a question that is relevant to your duties as Secretary of Defense, of—and General Myers, as the chairman, for a very successful military operation. And, that relevant question is, could both of you address how consistent with your optimistic and most hopeful results has the military operation been to date? And correspondingly, do you and General Myers have the same confidence, in a straightforward way, that the rebuilding of Iraq as a successful society, with American assistance, will be consistent, as you've tried to describe to the group here?

Are we—[off mike]—militarily, sir, as you expect in six months we may be regarding the civil affairs matters?

[Pause.]

Rumsfeld: I had a list, a long list, of three or four, five, six pages of things that could go wrong, because I tend to be conservative and cautious. And I looked it over this morning, and a number, a large number, haven't happened bad. . . .

Some of them are still open—that could still go bad. There's no question about that. There's still some tough stuff ahead, and—but one has to say that the speed that was used and the care that was used in the targeting, and the tactical surprise that was achieved by starting the ground war before the air war, undoubtedly contributed to the fact that a number of those things didn't happen bad. The oil wells weren't all blown up, and there's not a major humanitarian crisis, despite the fact that someone's looting someplace. There were not large refugee numbers. There were not large internally displaced people numbers. So we feel good about that.

The task we've got ahead of us now is an awkward one, because you have to go from a transition—from a repressed regime to an unrepressed regime that is free to do good things and also do bad things, and we're going to see both. And, we expect that, and we also expect people to report both. That's fine.

But as we go through this, I feel that we've got a group of wonderful people who have thought this through, that are engaged in the process, that have done the planning that will see that the kinds of food, and medicine, and water, and assistance that are needed will happen. Will it be perfect? No. Will it be bumpy? Sure. How do you go from—take a—look at every other country that's done this. Look at East Germany, and Romania, and the Soviet Union, pieces of that—it isn't an easy thing to do. And, we can't do it for them; the Iraqi people are going to have to do this, in the last analysis. We can help, and we want to create an environment that is as secure as possible, and that is as stable as possible, so that they can find their sea legs, if you will, and get themselves on a path to the future. . . .

Q: Mr. Secretary, why don't you just update us a little bit on what progress you're making, if any, on some of the unfinished missions you outlined the other day, specifically accounting for senior regime leadership, such as the ones on these playing cards that were distributed today, the search for weapons of mass destruction, and what about the American prisoners of war? Can you tell us you're making any progress on any of those three fronts?

Rumsfeld: I think, I hope when I spoke those words that I prefaced it by saying the first task is to prevail in this conflict and to stop the forces of Saddam Hussein in the areas that they continue to operate in, and to reduce the violence. That is the principal assignment. And, then to point out how much work was still ahead of us, I listed all of these six, eight, 10 things that are on our priority list. They will, of necessity, follow along behind, although, as I said, when there happens to be a weapon of mass destruction suspect site in an area that we occupy, and if people have time, they'll look at it. And, then they'll send things out to be examined and looked at. We clearly have people dedicated to trying to find the prisoners of war, ours and others from the '91 war. And as we are successful in any of those things, we'll report them. Undoubtedly, there will be embedded reporters there when they happen and will report them.

But I don't have anything particular to note, except that there are documentations that have been retrieved and they are being looked at. We are looking for people. We continue to look for people who can help us find the people we want to find, and people who can help us find the weapon sites of interest and people who can help us find records, for example, of Ba'ath Party members and the like. But I don't have anything of note to report. . . .

Q: Sir, I had a follow-up on the weapons of mass destruction issue. We keep hearing "results are pending, results are pending" of these early finds. What can—

Rumsfeld: Of which one of this—

Q: Well, the finding weapons of mass destruction. Here's my question: What can you guarantee the U.S. public and a skeptical world that U.S. soldiers will eventually find, without any shadow of a doubt in your mind, by way of raw agents, weapons facilities? And how long should they wait before they start making conclusions that maybe the U.S. didn't have the evidence in the first place? . . .

Rumsfeld: You said how long should they wait, how should they—before they lose—I've got a lot of confidence in the American people. . . .

Secretary Powell presented a presentation to the United Nations and the world. He laid out intelligence community estimates from the Central Intelligence Agency, and there is not a doubt but that we will, over a period of time, find people who can tell us where to go look for those things. We are not going to find them, in my view, just as I never believed the inspectors would, by running around seeing if they can open a door and surprise somebody and find something, because these people have learned that they can live in an inspection environment—the Iraqis did; they functioned in that environment, they designed their workplaces to do that. Things were mobile, things were underground, things were in tunnels, things were hidden, things were dispersed. Now, are we going to find that? No. It's a big country. What we're going to do is we're going to find the people who will tell us that, and we're going to find ways to encourage them to tell us that.

- **Source:** DoD News Briefing—Secretary Rumsfeld and Gen. Myers, United States Department of Defense, http://www.defense.gov/ Transcripts/Transcript.aspx?TranscriptID=2367, accessed July 13, 2011.

- **Analysis:** Rumsfeld faced intense, at times hostile questions from a press corps wanting to know why the situation in Iraq had deteriorated. The secretary attacked the media for its focus on the negative and bristled at suggestions that he had no plan for dealing with looters. He tried to deflect questions by insisting that a newly liberated country was bound to face problems. He compared the situation in Iraq to that facing the newly independent countries of Eastern Europe after the collapse of communism, overlooking the fact that none of them faced such a complete collapse of government or such extensive looting.

  The secretary tried to deflect criticism by noting the crowds cheering their U.S. liberators. He attributed looting and violence to pent-up rage vented by a newly freed people against their erstwhile oppressors. One reporter challenged this interpretation, noting that looting had gone far beyond government buildings. Repeatedly asked about his plan for dealing with the situation, Rumsfeld explained that he had considered numerous contingencies, some of which had occurred. U.S. forces, he insisted, were working to restore law and order in Iraq.

- **Document 41: Excerpt of Hearing of Senate Foreign Relations Committee on Iraq Reconstruction**
- **When:** June 12, 2003
- **Where:** Washington, DC

- **Significance:** The transcript of this hearing revealed that administration forecasts for postwar Iraq had proven grossly inaccurate and that the United States now faced a complex and expensive reconstruction mission.

OPENING STATEMENT OF SENATOR RICHARD G. LUGAR

This is the third in a series of hearings on post-conflict Iraq. During our first two hearings, administration witnesses identified the needs and problems in re-building Iraq and outlined the administration's responses. Those hearings gave the American public and Congress insight into complex decisions involved in formulating U.S. policies in post-conflict Iraq.

Today, the Foreign Relations Committee will hear from expert witnesses from outside the Bush administration. We welcome Ambassador Peter Galbraith, from the National Defense University, Dr. Geoffrey Kemp, Director of Regional Strategic Programs at the Nixon Center, and Ambassador Frank G. Wisner, a co-chair of the Council on Foreign Relations Task Force, which recently published the Report: "Iraq: The Day After."

Each of these experts has a wealth of experience and knowledge on Iraq, the Middle East region, and U.S. foreign policy. We have asked them to examine U.S. policy and plans in Iraq from three perspectives:

First, how should the United States deal with domestic issues in Iraq and in other Middle Eastern countries? In particular, how can we promote the prospects for democracy, stability, and economic reform?

Second, what are the repercussions of U.S. policies in Iraq on regional political and economic issues, on traditional regional alignments, and on the evolving Middle East peace process?

Finally, what is the likely impact of our policies in Iraq on broader foreign policy concerns, including the war on terrorism; non-proliferation efforts; and our relations with the United Nations, NATO allies, and other nations?

The ramifications of U.S. policies in Iraq go far beyond the Iraqi people or Iraqi territory. Nations throughout the Middle East, including regimes that have supported terrorists, are assessing how U.S. and coalition reconstruction of Iraq will affect their own interests. An American presence in Iraq that is devoted to achieving democracy and a healthy economy puts enormous pressure on states in the region to undertake reform. It improves our ability to encourage the transformation of repressive countries such as Iran and Syria and to promote the liberation of minorities across the Middle East. The achievement of democracy and a sound economy in Iraq could dispel growing anti-Americanism and dampen Islamic extremism and terrorism. It could raise expectations in the region for general economic growth, personal freedom, and women's rights. By improving U.S. credibility and underscoring the benefits of participation in the global community, success in Iraq could also provide added impetus for a permanent diplomatic resolution to the Arab-Israeli conflict.

But these opportunities will not be realized if we fail in Iraq. In the worst case, an ineffective or unsuccessful reconstruction effort in Iraq could lead to sustained civil unrest or even open civil war between ethnic or religious factions. In that event, Middle East states might become more repressive and entrenched, their populations more divided and extremist. Anti-American sentiments, already festering, could spread, leading to an increased threat of terrorism.

As we work to reconstruct Iraq, we must prepare for unintended consequences of our efforts. If U.S. policies inspire more agitation for democracy in Iran, for instance, a crackdown by the mullahs might ensue. In Egypt, Jordan, and Saudi Arabia, while reformers may be strengthened, existing divisions may be intensified, leading to instability in countries that have long been friends of the United States. These states already face demographic pressures, stagnant economic growth, uncertain political succession, and smoldering regional disputes, which threaten to undercut stability. None of this should dissuade us from pursuing the most aggressive and effective reconstruction and reform agenda possible in Iraq, but we must be flexible enough to deal with problems and consequences throughout the region.

Achieving ambitious goals in Iraq and the Middle East will require that we act with both patience and a sense of urgency. We must understand that our prospects for success depend greatly on what we do for the next several months. Right now, we are at a critical stage in Iraqi reconstruction, and no expense should be spared to show signs of progress and to demonstrate our commitment. But we also must keep in mind Deputy Secretary Wolfowitz's admonition to avoid unrealistic expectations. Success may not be instant, and we have to be prepared to stay in Iraq as long as necessary to win the peace. If the international community knows that the United States will not run out of patience in Iraq, we will find it easier to generate contributions that reduce our burdens and to gain support for our diplomatic initiatives.

The military victory in Iraq has presented us with a once-in-a-generation opportunity to help remold the Middle East. We must speak frequently to the American people about the costs and benefits of seizing this opportunity. Historically, Americans have been anxious to disengage from postwar commitments. This impulse is understandable, but in the case of Iraq we do not have the luxury of disengaging after the battles have been fought. It would be irresponsible—and contrary to our own national security interests—to walk away from Iraq before it becomes a dependable member of the world community. We would provide an incubator for terrorist cells and activity. . . .

The Chairman, It's my privilege to turn now to the distinguished ranking member, Senator Biden, for his opening statement. . . .

OPENING STATEMENT OF SENATOR JOSEPH R. BIDEN, JR.

Mr. Chairman, I join you in welcoming our distinguished witnesses today. . . .

Before the war we heard a great deal of discussion of the so-called "democracy domino theory." I'd like to hear what impact our witnesses think the war has had on regional attitudes toward democracy. What is the best way to advance democracy throughout the region?

I'd also like to hear the assessment of our witnesses regarding the reconstruction effort in Iraq. Ambassador Wisner chaired a Council on Foreign Relations Task

Force that produced a first-rate planning document for post-Saddam Iraq. Ambassador Galbraith, who served on the Committee staff for several years, was recently on the ground in Iraq for three weeks. And Dr. Kemp has consulted closely with Europeans and Arabs on the Iraq issue.

Where in your judgment could we be doing better? Have we done enough to involve our friends and allies in the reconstruction and peacekeeping effort? What sort of political process would you design for the post-conflict transition? There is a lot of ground to cover and I look forward to your testimony. . . .

STATEMENT OF HON. PETER W. GALBRAITH, DISTINGUISHED FELLOW, INSTITUTE FOR INTERNATIONAL AND STRATEGIC STUDIES, NATIONAL DEFENSE UNIVERSITY, WASHINGTON, DC

Ambassador Galbraith. Mr. Chairman, Senator Biden, Senator Feingold, Senator Alexander, as a former staff member of this committee, it is, of course, a real honor to be invited back to testify. I consider that the work I did for this committee in the 1980s and 1990s, documenting the atrocities of the Saddam Hussein regime, to have been some of the most important of my career. And what I talk about today draws on 20 years of experience with Iraq, as well as a 3-week trip I took shortly after American forces entered Baghdad, from April 13 to May 2 of this year.

I would note, for the record, that while I'm an employee of the Department of Defense at the National Defense University, my views do not necessarily reflect the views of those institutions.

Operation Iraqi Freedom has transformed Iraq. Even Iraqis opposed to the American occupation embrace the result—that is the removal of Saddam Hussein. And, in 3 weeks, I saw many scenes of joyful liberation. Shi'ites exuberantly marching on a pilgrimage to Karbala, that had been banned for 27 years; Kurds posing for family pictures on ruined Iraqi tanks; picnickers playing soccer in the grounds of one of Saddam Hussein's vast palaces in Mosul; and ex-political prisoners banging away at toppled statues of the fallen dictator. . . .

Unfortunately, U.S. goals in Iraq have been, in my view, seriously undermined by the conduct of the immediate postwar period. This includes the failure to stop the catastrophic looting of Baghdad, the slow pace of restoring essential services, and an uncertain and confused approach to postwar governance.

When the United States entered Baghdad on April 9, it entered a city largely undamaged by a carefully executed military campaign. However, in the 3 weeks following the U.S. takeover, unchecked looting effective gutted every important public institution in the city, with the notable exception of the oil ministry. . . .

The physical losses include the National Library, which was looted and burned—equivalent to our Library of Congress, it held every book published in Iraq, all newspapers from the last century, as well as rare manuscripts; the Iraqi National Museum, where the losses number in the thousands, not as bad as we originally thought, but still large, and, in value, well over $100 million; banks; hospitals and public-health institutions; the universities in Baghdad and Mosul, where it's not just the equipment and furniture that was gone, but decades of academic research; and government ministries, almost all of which were looted and/or burned.

Even more surprising, the United States failed to secure sites related to Iraq's weapons of mass destruction program or obvious locations holding important intelligence. Ten days after the Marines took over Baghdad, looters were banging open safes and setting fires in Iraq's unguarded Foreign Ministry. Important sites related to Iraq's WMD program, such as the Iraqi version of the Centers for Disease Control, or the Tuwaitha Nuclear Facility, were left unguarded and were looted.

There is a remote chance that dangerous biological or radiological material could end up in the hands of terrorists. But what is fairly certain is that the United States lost vital information related to WMD procurement, Iraqi foreign-intelligence activities, and possible links to al-Qaeda. I have described this in more detail in my prepared statement.

The looting was both predictable—it happened in 1991—and at least partially preventable. In spite of meticulous planning for the warfighting, I saw no evidence of any plan to secure critical sites. Obviously, U.S. forces could not protect everything, but even the more limited forces that entered Baghdad could have protected more.

The looting cost billions in property damage, demoralized educated Iraqis with whom we will want to work, and undermined Iraqi confidence and respect for the occupation authorities. This has complicated the task of the coalition provisional authority and, in my view, has likely increased the risk to U.S. personnel in the country.

The fall of Saddam Hussein has left a political vacuum that the U.S. civilian authorities were slow to fill. General Garner did not arrive in Baghdad until 13 days after the Marines entered the city, and did not effectively set up operations for days after that. Even today, staff of the coalition provisional authority remain ensconced behind concertina wire in Saddam's palaces, traveling around Baghdad only with full military escort.

The lack of preparation and planning, as well as the much-publicized bureaucratic battles between agencies of the U.S. government, have created confusion in the minds of Iraqis, and undermined confidence in the coalition. Early on, Garner and his team moved to reappoint prominent Ba'athists to top positions. Then, on May 16, Ambassador Bremer announced that all senior Ba'athists were disqualified from top posts. Similarly, General Garner traveled around Iraq promising that a representative assembly would soon be named to choose a provisional government. Ambassador Bremer reduced the Iraqi participation in the new administration to a small appointed advisory council. These radical changes in course contribute to an impression of incoherence.

The first weeks of the U.S. occupation have shown the limits of American power in Iraq, and the missteps have served to limit American power in the country. In my judgment, any occupying power has a relatively short window before the goodwill generated by liberation is replaced by anger and frustration at the inevitable lack of progress in improving the quality of life for the people of the country. For the reasons outlined above, the United States may have an especially short window in Iraq. . . .

The long-term challenge facing the United States in Iraq is developing a democratic political system while holding the country together. Decades of dictatorship have contributed to a crisis of identity within Iraq that cannot be wished away. While there are many Sunni and Shi'ite Arabs who proudly consider themselves

Iraqi, many other Shi'ites look at themselves primarily through the prism of their religion.

As an oppressed majority, many feel it is their turn to run the country on their own. The Ba'ath ideology encouraged Arabs to think of themselves less as Iraqis and more as part of the larger Arab nation. Sunni Arabs, now fearful of losing their historic privileges, may again find pan-Arabism an attractive alternative to minority status within Iraq.

For the last 12 years, four million Kurds have governed themselves in a de facto independent state protected by the United States and Great Britain. With their own elected parliament and having enjoyed relative freedom and prosperity, the Kurds have no desire to return to control from Baghdad. . . .

STATEMENT OF DR. GEOFFREY KEMP, DIRECTOR, REGIONAL STRA-TEGIC PROGRAMS, THE NIXON CENTER, WASHINGTON, DC

Dr. Kemp. Thank you, Mr. Chairman. . . .

Most troubling of the [recent] events, of course, are the problems of how to reconstitute Iraq's military forces and bring law, order, and a better quality of life to the citizens of Baghdad, Basra, and other Iraqi cities. Particularly difficult is the need to bring responsible Iraqi's into the decision making process while assuring a balance of representative leaders within Iraq's diverse population. How to deal with the majority Shi'a population is probably the most complicated task.

Now, when we go and look at the regional issues and how Iraq affects that, I think it's important to remember that there were lots of benefits for Iraq's regional neighbors while he was in power, because so long as he was in power, he posed no direct military threat to his neighbors, thanks to U.N. sanctions and the formidable U.S. presence in the region and the enforcement of the northern and southern no-fly zones. Iraq's oil exports were contained by lack of investment and the U.N. Oil for Food Program. A tight, but by no means foolproof, embargo on military supplies assured that Iraq's conventional weapons were not in good condition.

Nevertheless, under these constrained circumstances, Saddam retained enough internal power to rigidly control his country and prevent large-scale instability. These conditions suited a number of neighbors, especially Syria, Turkey, Jordan, Iran, and Saudi Arabia. Farther afield, traditional rivals of Iraq, such as Egypt, did not have to share the limelight with the leader of Baghdad, who was isolated in Arab circles and unable to exert Iraq's traditional influences on Arab politics. Many countries, directly or indirectly, profited from the flourishing black market trade with the Saddam regime. With the coalition victory, these perks have all ended.

So several realities must be acknowledged at the outset, particularly when discussing short-term conditions. Until Saddam and his entourage are found dead or alive, and the issue of Iraq's WMD is resolved, and the day-to-day conditions of Iraq is improved, it would be premature to pass judgment on what has happened since the war, except in the short term. Postwar scenarios are always messy. And while clearly there was a lack of foresight and preparation for the aftermath of Saddam Hussein, perhaps because his army collapsed so quickly, Iraq is very much a work in progress and, therefore, requires the most careful scrutiny by the U.S. Congress and the American public; hence, the reason I'm so pleased you're having these hearings.

This is the time to look at the facts on the ground and interpret them in a sound and sober manner. No one, anymore, doubts the effectiveness of U.S. military power in destroying regimes such as the Taliban and the Iraqi Ba'athists. But the early mistakes of the administration in handling the postwar reconstruction need to be fixed quickly.

At this time, post-Saddam Iraq does not look like post-war Germany or Japan; it looks more like Afghanistan or Bosnia. The coming months will be decisive in determining whether or not a brilliant military campaign and faulty postwar policies can be formulated into a successful outcome. . . .

PREPARED STATEMENT OF GEOFFREY KEMP, DIRECTOR OF REGIONAL STRATEGIC PROGRAMS, THE NIXON CENTER

BACKGROUND

In the months preceding the Iraq war, an intense international debate took place on the wisdom and consequences of using military forces to overthrow Saddam Hussein. One issue on which supporters and most opponents of the war concurred was that the United States and its allies would defeat the Iraqi armed forces, and that the most difficult problems were likely to arise following victory. This prediction was correct. The short-term glory of a quick, decisive and remarkably effective military victory has been replaced by a more sober realization of America's long-term strategic commitments to the region. . . .

Most troubling for the administration are the difficult questions of how to reconstitute Iraq's military forces and bring law, order and a better quality of life to the citizens of Baghdad, Basra and other Iraqi cities. Particularly difficult is the need to bring responsible Iraqis into the decision-making process while assuring a balance of representative leaders within Iraq's diverse population. How to deal with the majority Shi'a population is the most important and most complicated task. If a moderate Shi'a leadership emerges that is supportive of democracy and not an Islamic state, the repercussions in the neighborhood could be far reaching and could eventually pose a major challenge to Iran's conservative mullahs. For this reason hardline elements in Iran will continue to interfere in Iraq and this raises the risks of a U.S.-Iran confrontation.

From Washington's perspective, the most dangerous scenario would be successful military or terror operations against U.S. or British forces in Iraq. This would require the allies to take a tougher line and deploy additional military forces at the very time Iraq's residual security forces are in limbo. This, in turn, will undermine hopes for the speedy establishment of a representative Iraqi regime and the drawing down of occupation forces.

For the foreseeable future the U.S. will have to sustain a major military presence in the region if it wishes to protect vital interests. It will require patience and it will be costly and increasingly controversial. If the White House handles this mandate poorly, the Middle East could prove to be a political nightmare for yet another American president.

PREPARED STATEMENT OF HON. FRANK G. WISNER, VICE CHAIRMAN, EXTERNAL AFFAIRS, AMERICAN INTERNATIONAL GROUP

IRAQ, THE MIDDLE EAST, AND U.S. POLICY: GETTING IT RIGHT

Thank you for the opportunity to discuss with you today, Iraq, the Middle East, and U.S. Policy. . . .

What is clear is that Iraq's future will have significant consequences far beyond its borders. An unstable chaotic Iraq will spill its problems across boundaries and draw neighbors in to fill the power vacuum. A stable democratic Iraq, on the other hand, has the potential to set a political example for the rest of the region and become an engine of economic growth. To help Iraq achieve this latter vision, America must be clear in its goals and steadfast in its commitment. We must be mindful of regional dynamics, cognizant of the interests of others and honest about our own limitations.

IRAQ—NEXT STEPS

Establish law and order. The lack of law and order in Iraq threatens to destabilize the entire region. And it threatens to destroy the tolerance of the Iraqi population for the continuing U.S.-led military presence inside Iraq. Rampant violence, score-settling, and political uncertainty are allowing elements of the old regime to reconstitute, criminal groups to flourish, and compelling ordinary citizens to take matters into their own hands. Public security must be established and services restored for people to return to work and get Iraq moving again. Without sustained law and order, the loftier goals that we set for the region will be nothing more than fanciful fleeting dreams.

A robust, multinational security presence throughout Iraq's main population centers is required to establish basic security and deal with holdouts from the Ba'athist regime. Iraq's security forces need retraining and de-politicization. The task of building a new political order in Iraq must be shared with the United Nations, and our allies and partners who maintain constabulary and deployable national police forces. NATO's support of the Polish-led multilateral security force is a step in the right direction.

Articulate a vision. The Administration needs to articulate a more detailed vision for what it wants to foster in post-Saddam Iraq. The undertaking before us is truly massive, and we need to set realistic, achievable goals that can be readily understood, accepted, and embraced by the citizens of Iraq, America and the region.

The long-term goal for Iraq continues to be a sovereign, democratic, economically vibrant country, at peace with its neighbors and free of weapons of mass destruction. It will take years to achieve this, beyond the timeframe of an American occupation. But America must commit to stay in Iraq long enough to plant the seeds that sets Iraq on the right course. At local levels, communities should be organized to facilitate the handing over of political and economic responsibilities. At the national level, a consensus among Iraq's disparate communities and those committed to a modern, secular state, respectful of its religious heritages will serve the country well.

Including others. The U.S. vision must be as inclusive as possible. Iraq's neighbors have a vital stake in Iraq's success. They are well aware that chaos in their backyard is troubling on its face, but could also translate into chaos at home. Our partners in Europe and the Muslim world can provide much needed security capabilities and help remove the lingering suspicion that America is set to conquer Iraq. Over time, international support will allow America to reduce its profile and restore confidence in our role in the region. Whereas the Iraqi war divided us; the pursuit of stability can help reunite us, even though the latter effort may take time.

There also must be active consultations among the U.S., Iraqis, their Arab neighbors, Iran, Turkey, our European Allies as well as other members of the Security Council. The goal should be to bring as many international partners as possible into the effort of rebuilding Iraq and promoting a more secure Middle East. As we saw in the run-up to the war, the failure to confront differences and disputes up front, had disastrous implications for several of our country's most important relationships and gave rise to outright attempts to thwart our objectives.

GETTING IT RIGHT IN THE MIDDLE EAST

Setting clear and achievable goals. The defeat and subsequent collapse of Iraq confirmed America's military prowess. In the aftermath of the military phase, we have seen ample reason to fear that while we have won the war, we may lose the peace. Washington's commitment to improve the lives of Iraqi citizens must remain paramount.

- **Source:** Hearing of the Senate Foreign Relations Committee on Iraq Reconstruction, June 12, 2003, available at http://frwebgate.access. gpo.gov/cgi-bin/getdoc.cgi?dbname=108_senate_ hearings&docid=f:90076.wais, accessed June 7, 2008.

- **Analysis:** Just weeks after President Bush declared "mission accomplished," the problems of postwar Iraq and the administration's failure to prepare adequately for them had become painfully obvious. Looters had destroyed much of Iraq's already fragile infrastructure. The country's three main ethnic groups were not cooperating with one another or with the U.S.-led coalition. The Kurds in the north had enjoyed de facto autonomy for a decade and had no desire to be subordinated to Baghdad. The Sunni minority resented loss of its privileged status, and the Shi'a majority believed it should rule the country.

  The regional situation proved equally troubling. Arab regimes privately applauded the removal of Saddam Hussein while publically criticizing the U.S.-led invasion, but the Arab street opposed any Western intervention in the region. Iraq had historically balanced Iran, which now threatened to emerge as the regional power. Syria could be expected to support insurgents in Iraq and provide them a safe haven. The need to create a stable, pro-American state capable of defending itself was thus paramount.

  All the experts who addressed Congress at this hearing agreed on the need for a sustained U.S. presence in Iraq. The follow-on mission would require maintenance of law and order, humanitarian assistance, and rebuilding. No one yet mentioned "counterinsurgency," which remained a taboo subject in the Pentagon. Resistance had yet to reach the level of insurgency, but it would soon do so.

- **Document 42: Excerpt of Report Presented to Senate Foreign Relations Committee by John Hamre, President of CSIS**
- **When:** July 23, 2003
- **Where:** Washington, DC
- **Significance:** The report revealed that Iraqi reconstruction would be more complicated and expensive than anticipated.

EXECUTIVE SUMMARY

Rebuilding Iraq is an enormous task. Iraq is a large country with historic divisions, exacerbated by a brutal and corrupt regime. The country's 24 million people and its infrastructure and service delivery mechanisms have suffered decades of severe degradation and under-investment. Elements of the old regime engage in a campaign of sabotage and ongoing resistance, greatly magnifying the "natural" challenges of rebuilding Iraq. Given the daunting array of needs and challenges, and the national security imperative for the United States to succeed in this endeavor, the United States needs to be prepared to stay the course in Iraq for several years.

The next 12 months will be decisive; the next three months are crucial to turning around the security situation, which is volatile in key parts of the country. All players are watching closely to see how resolutely the coalition will handle this challenge. The Iraqi population has exceedingly high expectations, and the window for cooperation may close rapidly if they do not see progress on delivering security, basic services, opportunities for broad political involvement, and economic opportunity. The "hearts and minds" of key segments of the Sunni and Shi'a communities are in play and can be won, but only if the Coalition Provisional Authority (CPA) and new Iraqi authorities deliver in tort order. To do so, the CPA will have to dramatically and expeditiously augment its operational capacity throughout the country, so that civilian-led rebuilding can proceed while there are still significant numbers of coalition forces in Iraq to provide maximum leverage over those who seek to thwart the process.

To succeed, the United States and its allies will need to pursue a strategy over the next twelve months that: recognizes the unique challenges in different parts of the country; consolidates gains in those areas where things are going well; and wins hearts and minds even as it decisively confronts spoilers.

Seven major areas need immediate attention.

1. The coalition must establish public safety in all parts of the country. In addition to ongoing efforts, this will involve: reviewing force composition and structure, as well as composite force levels (U.S., coalition, and Iraqi) so as to be able to address the need for increased street-level presence in key conflictive areas; quickly hiring private security to help stand up and supervise a rapid expansion of the Iraqi Facility Protection Service, thereby freeing

thousands of U.S. troops from this duty; ratcheting up efforts to recruit sufficient levels of international civilian police through all available channels; and, launching a major initiative to reintegrate "self-demobilized" Iraqi soldiers and local militias.

2. Iraqi ownership of the rebuilding process must be expanded at national, provincial, and local levels. At the national level ensuring success of the newly formed Iraqi Governing Council is crucial. This will require avoiding overloading it with too many controversial issues too soon. The natural desire to draw anger away from the coalition by putting an Iraqi face on the most difficult decisions must be balanced with a realistic assessment of what the council can successfully manage. At the provincial and local levels, coalition forces and the CPA have made great progress in establishing political councils throughout the country, but they need direction and the ability to respond to local needs and demands. To achieve this, local and provincial political councils need to have access to resources and be linked to the national Iraqi Governing Council and the constitutional process.

3. Idle hands must be put to work and basic economic and social services provided immediately to avoid exacerbating political and security problems. A model economy will not be created overnight out of Iraq's failed statist economic structures. Short-term public works projects are needed on a large scale to soak up sizable amounts of the available labor pool. Simultaneously, the CPA must get a large number of formerly state-owned enterprises up and running. Even if many of them are not competitive and may need to be privatized and downsized eventually, now is the time to get as many people back to work as possible. A massive micro-credit program in all provinces would help to spur wide-ranging economic activity, and help to empower key agents of change such as women. The CPA must also do whatever is necessary to immediately refurbish basic services, especially electricity, water, and sanitation.

4. Decentralization is essential. The job facing occupation and Iraqi authorities is too big to be handled exclusively by the central occupying authority and national Iraqi Governing Council. Implementation is lagging far behind needs and expectations in key areas, at least to some extent because of severely constrained CPA human resources at the provincial and local levels. This situation must be addressed immediately by decentralizing key functions of the CPA to the provincial level, thereby enhancing operational speed and effectiveness and allowing maximum empowerment of Iraqis. The CPA must rapidly recruit and field a much greater number of civilian experts to guide key governance, economic, social, justice, and also some security components of the occupation.

5. The coalition must facilitate a profound change in the Iraqi national frame of mind—from centralized authority to significant freedoms, from suspicion to trust, from skepticism to hope. This will require an intense and effective communications and marketing campaign, not the status quo. The CPA needs to win the confidence and support of the Iraqi people. Communication—between the CPA and the Iraqi people, and within the CPA itself—is insufficient so far. Drastic changes must be made to immediately improve the daily

flow of practical information to the Iraqi people, principally through enhanced radio and TV programming. Iraqis need to hear about difficulties and successes from authoritative sources. Secondly, the CPA needs to gather information from Iraqis much more effectively—through a more robust civilian ground presence, "walk-in" centers for Iraqis staffed by Iraqis, and hiring a large number of Iraqi "animators" to carry and receive messages. Thirdly, information flow must be improved within the CPA itself through an integrated operations center that would extend across both the civilian and military sides of the CPA, and by enhancing cell-phone coverage and a system-wide email system that could ease the timely dissemination of information to all CPA personnel.

6. The United States needs to quickly mobilize a new reconstruction coalition that is significantly broader than the coalition that successfully waged the war. The scope of the challenges, the financial requirements, and rising anti-Americanism in parts of the country make necessary a new coalition that involves various international actors (including from countries and organizations that took no part in the original war coalition). The Council for International Cooperation at the CPA is a welcome innovation, but it must be dramatically expanded and supercharged if a new and inclusive coalition is to be built.

7. Money must be significantly more forthcoming and more flexible. Iraq will require significant outside support over the short to medium term. In addition to broadening the financial coalition to include a wider range of international actors, this means the President and Congress will need to budget and fully fund reconstruction costs through 2004. The CPA must be given rapid and flexible funding. "Business as usual" is not an option for operations in Iraq, nor can it be for their funding.

The enormity of the task ahead must not be underestimated. It requires that the entire effort be immediately turbo-charged—by making it more agile and flexible, and providing it with greater funding and personnel.

- **Source:** John Hamre, "Field Review of Iraq, July 17, 2003," presented to Committee on Foreign Relations of the U.S. Senate, July 23, available at http://frwebgate.access.gpo.gov/cgi-bin/getdoc.cgi?dbname =108_senate_hearings&docid=f:90883.wais, accessed, June 9, 2008.
- **Analysis:** This report echoed the conclusions of other experts that the coalition faced a daunting reconstruction task. The report also noted the close connection between security on the one hand and humanitarian assistance and reconstruction on the other. Relief work cannot be done in an atmosphere of anarchy. Civilian organizations lacked the means to provide their own security. The coalition, which consisted overwhelmingly of U.S. forces, would have to protect them and restore law and order.

While the report did not specifically mention insurgency, it expressed growing concern for Iraqi attitudes. Chronic unemployment fed resentment. The Coalition Provisional Authority (CPA), which now governed Iraq, lacked legitimacy, and the international community had not been as forthcoming with donor aid as had been hoped. All of these weaknesses would have to be addressed to recoup the situation.

- **Document 43: Excerpt of Prepared Testimony of Andrew Natsios, Presented to the House Appropriations Foreign Operations Subcommittee**
- **When:** September 30, 2003
- **Where:** Washington, DC
- **Significance:** The director of USAID provided an overview of the agency's work in Iraq.

> ## DID YOU KNOW?
>
> ### Coalition Provisional Authority (CPA)
>
> The CPA governed Iraq for the first year of the occupation. Formed on April 21, 2003, the body performed executive, legislative, and judicial function until June 28, 2004, when it handed over these responsibilities to a newly elected Iraqi government. The CPA replaced the Office for Reconstruction and Humanitarian Assistance, formed in January 2003 under the leadership of Jay Garner. Garner had headed the CPA for less than a month when L. Paul Bremer III replaced him on May 11, 2003.
>
> Controversy plagued the CPA from its inception. In June 2003 Bremer issued orders to disband the Iraqi armed forces and to bar former Ba'ath Party members from holding office. The CPA was also criticized for poor oversight of the reconstruction effort. The formation of an Iraqi government eliminated the need for an interim governing body, so the CPA was dissolved in June 2004.

Mr. Chairman, thank you for this opportunity to speak with you and members of the Committee in support of the President's supplemental request and the U.S. Government's considerable accomplishments in Iraq and Afghanistan....

As the Committee has requested, my testimony will focus on what USAID has done thus far with funds already provided by the Congress. I will begin my presentation today with Iraq and then make some comments on Afghanistan.

USAID provides vital reconstruction and rehabilitation assistance to Iraq. USAID is investing resources in planning, staffing, managing, implementing, and evaluating reconstruction and rehabilitation programs to advance the Coalition Provisional Authority (CPA) strategic plan for Iraq and improve the wellbeing of the Iraqi people.

Today I would like to provide you a clear sense of our many accomplishments, our immediate next steps, USAID's organizational presence in Iraq, and the challenges we face in the current operating environment.

USAID Works to Advance the CPA Strategy

We support the CPA strategic plan for Iraq. The CPA strategy has four objectives, none of which can be pursued in isolation and all of which lead to the return home of U.S. troops and a transition to national governance of Iraq by Iraqis sooner rather than later:

security, which determines the speed with which we can advance reconstruction and build up institutions of good governance;

essential services, which are a major priority for the people of Iraq;

the economy, which requires considerable assistance before the country can realize its potential for economic growth; and

governance, which requires a rapid development of institutions and values to support democratic government.

Our USAID mission in Iraq reports to Ambassador Bremer and the Coalition Provisional Authority and, through him, to the emerging Iraqi government and the Iraqi people.

USAID's Accomplishments and Next Steps in Iraq

Before combat started, USAID was involved in planning efforts to respond to potential humanitarian needs in Iraq, and an inter-agency Disaster Assistance Response Team (DART), the largest in U.S. history, had pre-positioned humanitarian commodities in the region for up to 1,000,000 internally displaced people. This DART team entered Iraq on March 27, before the cessation of combat and before the fall of Baghdad. USAID obligated hundreds of millions of dollars in food and other humanitarian assistance before the war had ended.

On May 2, one day after the President declared the end of major combat operations, USAID began directing assistance to the most immediate post-conflict needs in Iraq. Our DART team provided urgent assistance to displaced people and linked the humanitarian community and Coalition Forces, facilitating their delivery of food, medicines and clean drinking water. The DART team included an Abuse Prevention Unit deployed to protect vulnerable Iraqis and to help the CPA preserve evidence such as mass grave sites of past abuse by Saddam's regime.

USAID undertook rapid assessments of Iraqi needs and immediately began programming resources. USAID programmed over $400 million through UN agencies to ensure that the food distribution system was restarted and people did not go hungry, including many displaced people who had not been receiving food rations. The transition was so smooth that the media paid little attention to it.

Our field mission in Iraq is delivering reconstruction, rehabilitation, and humanitarian relief assistance through approximately 45 grants and contracts to American non-profit organizations and firms. While our $680 million contract with Bechtel captures the media spotlight, it certainly does not define our engagement with the Iraqi people. We have tapped into the innovation and expertise of a number of American firms. Through grants to American groups such as the International Rescue Committee, International Medical Corps, Mercy Corps, Save the Children, World Vision, Cooperative Housing Foundation International, and CARE and international organizations such as UNICEF, the World Food Program and the World Health Organization, USAID is engaging Iraqis neighborhood by neighborhood, providing basic services and helping Iraqi communities to help themselves.

USAID works to ensure that U.S. assistance benefits the average Iraqi citizen and encourages cooperation among ethnic and religious groups on Iraqi society.

Infrastructure

Let me touch on our progress in reconstructing and rehabilitating seven key components of Iraq's infrastructure: electricity, water and sanitation, the Umm Qasr seaport, the Baghdad and Basrah airports, bridges, railroads, and telecommunications.

Electricity is critical for economic development, Iraqi livelihoods, and a sense of normalcy in Iraq. On September 28, national electrical generation was at 3,927 megawatts, the highest level produced since before the war at approximately 89% of pre-conflict levels. Under an agreement between the Iraqi Commission of Electricity, the U.S. Army Corps of Engineers, Bechtel, USAID, and CPA, responsibilities for procuring parts and materials are divided according to the predominant capability of each agency.

Water and sanitation prevent disease and meet an essential human need. USAID support to water and sanitation projects has benefited over 14.5 million Iraqis. Among other things, we have helped Iraqi municipal governments repair over 1,700 pipe breaks in Baghdad's water network, increasing water flow by 200,000 cubic meters per day; we have rehabilitated 70 of Baghdad's 90 non-functioning waste pumping stations; and we began installing generators at 37 Baghdad water facilities and pumping stations, to ensure continuous water supply, even in the event of an electrical grid failure. Through our non-governmental partners, we support projects meeting the immediate water needs of Iraqis in urban and rural communities throughout the country. These projects will help to reduce the incidence of water-borne disease and mortality by bringing safe drinking water to thousands of children and their families, in many cases to villages that have been forced to go without water for years.

Seaport access is critical to the timely flow of humanitarian and reconstruction materials and kick starting the Iraqi economy. Together with the CPA regional coordinator, I opened Umm Qasr port to commercial traffic June 17, and the first test of passenger vessel docking was completed July 16. Working with our counterpart, the Iraqi Port Authority, port tariffs have been approved and applied on June 20, opening the way towards financial sustainability for port operations. Major dredging activities—USAID has also supported the removal of vessels, 250 pieces of unexploded ordinance, and about 4 million cubic meters of silt—are complete and the port is able to handle deep-draft ships at all 21 berths. Generators have been installed, restoring power to most parts of the port. Over 500,000 metric tons of cargo passed through the port in August, and work on the grain-receiving facility is complete. USAID contractor Bechtel is awaiting the arrival of a grain ship to test the system and turn it over to the Grain Board. When operational, it will be able to process up to 600 metric tons of grain an hour.

Airports will enhance commercial productivity and help integrate Iraq and its economy into the global community. USAID has completed infrastructure work at Baghdad International Airport. This included repairing a terminal and the administration offices; installing power generators; and repairing sewage pumps. USAID investments in the Basrah International Airport have included repairing the runway and installing baggage x-ray units, toilets, and passenger lounges.

Bridges are critical to economic development, regional integration, transportation. The USAID mission in Iraq has worked with our implementation partners to complete construction of a 1.5-kilometer, four-lane bypass for the damaged Al-Mat Bridge—a key bridge needed for humanitarian efforts. Our partners have completed 36 detailed bridge assessments and are working with the Iraqi Ministry of Public Works and Iraqi firms to reconstruct three priority bridges.

Railroads link the Umm Qasr port to grain mills and are also important to Iraq's economy and integration. USAID contractor Bechtel completed an evaluation of the Iraqi railroad system on June 25 and repairs to tracks leading out of Umm Qasr port are underway. Work on railways is an integrated U.S.-Iraqi effort: Bechtel contributes project management, material and parts while the Iraqi Railway Administration contributes equipment and labor. This approach brings Iraqis into the rebuilding process and lowers project costs. Bechtel is also reviewing assessments from rail construction equipment manufacturers with Iraqi Republic Railways personnel.

Telecommunications investments will enable private, commercial, and official communications throughout Iraq, serving the people, business, and the government. USAID contractor Bechtel has awarded sub-contracts for 12 containerized telephone switches and one satellite gateway for international telephone calls. The projects will restore international calling for Iraq and reconnect all 240,000 phone lines in Baghdad presently without service, returning the city to pre-conflict level of 540,000 operational phone lines. Alongside Bechtel, Iraqi Telephone and Postal Company employees are constructing foundations, splicing cables, and testing lines prior to the arrival of the switches. In addition, Bechtel is repairing the fiberoptic backbone from Mosul in the north to Umm Qasr in the south, connecting Baghdad to 20 cities in Iraq and benefiting 70% of all Iraqis.

Next Steps in Infrastructure

Let me briefly tell you about our next steps in infrastructure. In collaboration with the CPA, USAID has begun or will work to:

increase Iraq's daily national power generation to 6,000 MW prior by the summer of 2004;

increase potable water flow to east Baghdad by 45%, benefiting approximately 2.5 million people, rehabilitate eight water treatment and pump stations in the south, and establish a water system in Mosul with an independent, 24 hour water supply;

manage customs, immigration and security for shipping cargo; purchase cranes and equipment to increase port capacity; and gradually pass on control of the port of Umm Qasr to the Iraqi people;

rehabilitate Baghdad International Airport's control tower and building (restoring the air and ventilation system, floors, ceilings, walls, the customs section, and security gates), and continue rehabilitating at Basrah Airport; and

install 12 telephone switches between late October through mid-January, approximately one every week; and complete repairs to the nation's fiberoptic network from north of Mosul, through Baghdad and Nasiriyah to Umm Qasr by November 2003; and repair of the 2,000 km fiber optic cable that will connect 20 cities to Baghdad and benefit 70% of Iraq's population.

Economic Reform and Democratic Governance

Promoting national security, supporting CPA objectives, and expressing American values in the huge project of Iraqi reconstruction requires that our government invest heavily in economic governance, and social programs as well as infrastructure. Working with the CPA and the emerging Iraqi government and in consultation with the Congress, USAID is applying its development expertise and investing in several inter-related economic and social sectors. We are working under the direction of the CPA in implementing economic governance, local governance, education, health, community action, and agriculture programs in Iraq.

Economic rehabilitation is essential to economic growth. The CPA has asked USAID to provide technical support in 17 priority areas in economic governance. Our counterparts in this critical effort include the Iraqi Central Bank, Iraqi state-owned enterprises, and the Ministries of Finance, Trade, Agriculture, and Industry. These priority areas include: introduction of a new currency, credit for small businesses, improvement to commercial legislation, coordination of a national employment program, bank-to-bank payment system, new tax policies, and effective budget planning. USAID and its partner, BearingPoint, are playing a key supporting role in supporting the currency exchange operation and are developing a bank-to-bank payment system that will allow 80 banks to conduct business by mid-October. We are also assisting the CPA in the management of its micro-lending program and are evaluating private sector and investment-related commercial laws.

Agriculture sustains rural people, contributes to the economy, and feeds the nation; trauma to the southern marshlands has left deep scars that we are helping to heal. In collaboration with the Iraqi Ministries of Trade and Agriculture and Irrigation, a four-person USAID-supported technical team traveled in June to the southern marshes, a region devastated by Saddam Hussein's brutal regime, to determine the feasibility of providing irrigation and restoring the marshes. This visit to the marshlands was the first on-the-ground scientific assessment in more than two decades. The team met with marsh dwellers to assess social and economic conditions, and their conversations revealed repeated displacement, persecution and destruction. Residents suffer from a lack of public health services and clean drinking water.

Iraq's agricultural capacity was devastated by Saddam's regime. Competitive bids for an agriculture rehabilitation contract, which will target the small private farmer, are under internal USAID technical evaluation and will soon be awarded. USAID also works with the CPA and the U.N. World Food Program to ensure the smooth transition to Iraqi management of the delivery of food baskets to about 27 million Iraqis each month. We are also helping the CPA to encourage domestic food production.

Local governance creates demands for democracy, the equitable distribution of resources, and provides local populations with basic services. Iraqis are experiencing new freedoms. For the first time, the Iraqi people have the freedom to vote and run for office. Together with CPA and civil affairs officers, we have designed an interim local government structure to represent the population in the Baghdad metropolitan area. Just through our work alone, more than 200 neighborhood advisory councils have been established, representing more than half of Iraq's people and all of Baghdad's 88 neighborhoods. This neighborhood council program is being established in 14 other governorates across the country. These councils are coordinating the provision of essential services. USAID is also partnering with the CPA, coalition forces, Iraqi provincial and municipal governments and others to deliver essential services, promote Iraqi citizen participation in decision making at the grass roots level, and assist with budget development and payroll management. Through our partners, USAID has also awarded over 830 Rapid Response Grants, totaling over $40 million. These grants are increasing Iraqi participation in local governance, promoting civil society, human rights, and gender equality in Iraq. USAID has provided over 40 "Ministries in a Box." These deliver essential supplies and equipment to Iraqi Ministries and government offices, including the Ministries of Justice, Irrigation, Foreign Affairs, Labor, Health and Finance and eight Baghdad municipality headquarters.

Community action helps communities to help themselves. Five USAID non-governmental partners have established offices in 9 major Iraqi cities throughout Iraq. These five Community Action Program partners have identified more than 390 community activities that promote improved local governance. Nearly 7 million Iraqi people have already benefited. Our collective efforts include: the organization of 74 Iraqi counterpart community associations to direct activities focusing on repair of sewage treatment plants, neighborhood clean-up, road repairs, school renovation, water sanitation, and medical facilities; construction of a Community Market Place, with an estimated 250,000 residents benefiting; clean up of medical waste disposal sites and education of medical personnel on proper disposal methods; water sanitation programs; and hospital and kindergarten renovation.

Education is a basic service that promotes economic growth, supports democracy, and inspires hope. USAID, the Iraqi Ministry of Education, and our partners have inventoried all 3,900 secondary schools in areas with a permissive security environment, and we are on target in most areas to supply secondary schools with desks, supplies, and school materials by the time classes start on October 4. We have exceeded CPA's target of renovating 1,000 schools in time for the first day of school; we have renovated 1,500 schools. In addition to that achievement, we have approved 89 grants worth over $1.2 million to refurbish schools and re-equip Education Offices in each governorate, and we have supported UNESCO in undertaking a review with Iraqis of 98 math and science textbooks. More than 5.6 million math and science books—all free of Saddam's propaganda—are being printed and delivered to students. More than 1.5 million secondary students will receive student supply kits in time for school. We have selected five sites for an accelerated learning program and conducted a survey of out-of-school Iraqi children at each site. Alongside the Ministry of Education we have helped create a plan for the national exam process, including schedule and security requirements, and we are concluding a $20 million grant competition program for U.S. universities to partner with Iraqi universities.

Health is an immediate and basic human need. USAID is applying its extensive expertise in international public health to the health challenges faced by Iraqi citizens today. USAID and the Iraqi Ministry of Health are working to develop a national health strategy for Iraq which will include our plan to reduce the shamefully high child mortality rates. Together with our partners, we have also rehabilitated 20 delivery rooms in care centers serving 300,000 residents in Basrah. An additional 29 hospital rehabilitations have been completed in other areas and 131 more are planned or underway; 600 primary health centers have been re-equipped. We have awarded grants to the Iraqi Doctors and Nurses associations to help revitalize the Iraqi medical system; distributed most of three million packets of Oral Re-hydration Salts to children with diarrhea; and provided 2.5 kilograms of supplementary food rations to more than 100,000 pregnant, nursing mothers and malnourished children under 5 years. We have procured 4.2 million vaccinations, with approximately 1.4 million children vaccinated through July during monthly immunization days; provided assistance to more than 168 hospitals and clinics and 82 primary health care centers; and evaluated 18 national and regional public health laboratories for equipment needs. We have completed our rehabilitation of the National Polio Laboratory. Training for community outreach is critical, and we have trained more than 2,000 health workers to provide life-saving services for malnourished children; training for additional 8,000 health workers is underway through our partner, UNICEF.

Next Steps in Economic and Social Programs

The stability and prosperity of Iraq and the wellbeing of the Iraqi people require continued investments in economic and social rehabilitation and development programs. Here is an outline of our immediate plans. We are in the process of helping to:

support CPA in replacing the existing Iraqi currencies with a single new currency; support CPA and Iraqi evaluation of strategic alternatives for the disposition of state owned enterprises; oversee the design and management of credit facilities for small Iraqi businesses; and review and recommend changes to key commercial laws.

promote political and social stability by helping Baghdad neighborhood advisory councils provide affordable, high-quality public services to citizens; help Baghdad officials in developing Baghdad's first openly-approved budget; develop emergency communications packages that will reconnect nine key central government ministries to the local governorate offices; and assess rehabilitation needs of municipal fire departments in five cities.

return to the Southern Marshes to assist marsh dwellers by providing economic opportunities and improve marshland management; and implement an agricultural assistance program to address urgent agricultural rehabilitation needs, enhance food security, and support the development of competitive agro-enterprise and agricultural markets.

accelerate the formation of community associations and improve their ability to manage municipal infrastructure, rehabilitate roads and schools, and repair irrigation systems.

print and distribute 5.6 million math and science textbooks in October; train tens of thousands of teachers and administrators across Iraq.

rehabilitate 21 referral hospitals, 50 public health centers, 20 delivery rooms and 35 hospitals in Baghdad by April 2004; continue to conduct monthly National Immunization Days; and increase efficiency of drug distribution to 157 outpatient health facilities in Baghdad.

USAID Presence in Iraq

USAID began operations in Iraq before hostilities in Iraq ended and officially opened a USAID Mission there on July 27. USAID plans, delivers, and evaluates in collaboration with the CPA to manage this large reconstruction and rehabilitation portfolio with a workforce of approximately 57 USAID officers and associated direct staff. Our implementation partners currently deliver services with a total workforce in Iraq of approximately 600 personnel. Together with our implementation partners, we are employing approximately 55,000 Iraqis in our reconstruction efforts.

USAID Mission headquarters are in Baghdad, and we maintain offices in Hillah, Basrah, Mosul, and Arbil.

Security

USAID and its implementing partners face a fluid environment and significant security challenges in the neighborhoods, villages, and towns of Iraq. The bombings of the United Nations building illustrate the extent to which the civilian reconstruction of Iraq continues to face violent opposition. However, USAID personnel have operated effectively in 12 hot war zones in recent years without casualties. Our personnel travel in armored vehicles, and these vehicles have saved lives in both Iraq and Afghanistan.

I have met with the elders of Iraqi towns and villages where we are successfully working together using the same community development approaches we apply around the world. These communities showed me how they are organizing to protect their infrastructure themselves from sabotage and terrorism. Meanwhile, we are increasing power reliability and reducing security costs by disconnecting some plants from the vulnerable power grid and installing smaller generators at each facility. This will make sewer and water treatment plants independent of the power grid and much easier to protect from terrorist attacks.

Donor Coordination

USAID is lending its extensive expertise in donor coordination to our government's fundraising effort. U.S. assistance to Iraq is coordinated with donors at the field level and in Washington, and many USAID partners coordinate their activities on the ground, real-time, with other organizations providing assistance. USAID continues to encourage multilateral funding of education, health care, electricity, water, sewage, and telecommunications projects, among others.

USAID is working to improve conditions in Iraq and contribute to our nation's vision of an Iraq that is a sovereign, stable, prosperous, and democratic country at peace with the United States and with the world.

- **Source:** Prepared statement of Andrew Natsios, director of USAID, presented to the House Appropriations Foreign Operations Subcommittee, September 30, 2003.
- **Analysis:** By the fall of 2003, even the most enthusiastic supporters of Operation Iraqi Freedom had to admit that the coalition faced a growing insurgency complicated by sectarian violence, foreign terrorist activity, and crime. Andrew Natsios, the head of the U.S. Agency for Inter-

national Development, had the unenviable task of requesting more funds for an operation that was supposed to be winding down. He mustered an impressive array of numbers to demonstrate the accomplishments of the CPA to date but did not indicate how these results compared to the level of need. No amount of obfuscation, however, could hide the fact that most Iraqis experienced a significant drop in quality of life.

WASTE, FRAUD, AND ABUSE

Recognizing the scope and cost of humanitarian aid and reconstruction was but the first step in meeting Iraqi needs. The United States and its coalition partners found themselves chasing a speeding train as they tried to ramp up the relief and reconstruction effort in the face of a deteriorating security situation. The pace at which the government issued contracts to deal with the situation invited abuse. The reconstruction effort had to be monitored, mistakes corrected, and wrongdoers held accountable.

- **Document 44: Excerpt of Hearings before the Committee on Government Reform of the House of Representatives**
- **When:** March 11, 2004
- **Where:** Washington D.C.
- **Significance:** Between March and July 2004, the committee held hearings on the contracting process for Iraq reconstruction. Democratic members raised serious concerns about the process as indicated by the opening statement of Senator Henry Waxman (Democrat, California), the ranking minority member.

[Opening Statement of Henry Waxman, Democrat, California]

The subject we are going to consider, contracting in Iraq, urgently needs congressional oversight. It is an issue that has crucial implications for the success of our efforts in Iraq and for U.S. taxpayers. Usually I keep my remarks short at committee hearings, but today I am going to speak at some length in this opening statement.

I have been investigating contracting in Iraq for many months and I believe few of my colleagues understand just how big a mess this administration has created. I want to explain to the members of this committee and the public what is going wrong and why.

The problem starts with the procurement strategy that the administration is using in Iraq. It is profoundly flawed. . . .

2,300; 2,300 is the number of discrete reconstruction projects that the coalition provisional authority is planning to do in Iraq. . . . zero, is the number of projects that will be subject to competitive bidding.

Instead of promoting competition, the administration is giving contractors monopolies over huge sectors of the reconstruction effort. One company,

DID YOU KNOW?

Halliburton

Halliburton Corporation is the second largest oil services company in the world. From 1995 to 2000, Dick Cheney served as its chief executive officer. Halliburton subsidiaries, most notably Kellogg, Brown and Root (KBR), received billions of dollars in contracts for Iraq. Although Cheney retired from Halliburton to run for vice president, he continued to receive deferred severance payments from the company while in office. His connections to Halliburton led to allegations of conflict of interest, especially because many of Halliburton's contracts were no-bid, cost-plus projects. Halliburton was accused of overcharging for work it preformed and for not performing some of the work for which it had been paid. Neither the company nor any of its members has been prosecuted for wrongdoing in Iraq.

Halliburton, gets all work related to oil reconstruction in southern Iraq. Another company, Parsons, gets all work related to oil reconstruction in northern Iraq. And they never have to bid against each other for any specific project. The administration has a procurement strategy that intentionally shields contractors from competition.

Think about this: For nearly a year both Halliburton and Bechtel have had enormous operations in Iraq. Both companies can do virtually the same work. But never once have they had to compete against each other for a specific project. This is a great deal for Bechtel and Halliburton, but it is an absolutely horrendous deal for the taxpayers.

These problems are compounded by the fact that many of the contracts that are being issued are cost-plus contracts. Under a cost-plus contract, the more the contractor bills, the more money the contractor makes. That is why cost-plus contracts are notoriously prone to abuse.

In the absence of competition to discipline the process and to hold down prices, the taxpayer has to rely on contracting officers working for the Defense Department to keep prices reasonable. These officials are supposed to scrutinize the proposals submitted by Halliburton and other contractors and reject those that are loaded up with unnecessary expenses. But they are inexperienced and overworked.

Representative John Dingell and I asked GAO to investigate what kind of job the Defense Department is doing managing the largest contract in Iraq, Halliburton's LOGCAP contract. The contract alone is worth over $4 billion to Halliburton.

GAO told us that the Army Central Command in Kuwait has not made cost control a priority. GAO found that the Army does not have the expertise or the personnel in Kuwait needed to ensure that taxpayers are not being overcharged. According to the General Accounting Office, inexperienced reservists are being sent to Kuwait and given key oversight responsibilities. A 2-week training course on contract management is the only preparation they receive.

GAO told us that in one instance the Army approved a LOGCAP contract worth $587 million to Halliburton in just 10 minutes. The documentation for this mammoth contract was just six pages long. In essence, this administration's approach to contractors like Halliburton is "trust but don't verify." ...

It is not just the government auditors who are complaining about Halliburton's practices. Halliburton's own internal auditors have said that the company procedures are, "antiquated" and that it has, "weak internal controls."

Last month, my staff was contacted by two former Halliburton procurement officers. They described company practices that systematically overcharge the taxpayer on hundreds of routine requisitions every day. When they tried to protest, they were ignored. They said that the company's motto was "Don't worry about price. It's cost-plus."

Well, it's very hard to get details from the administration about the specific amounts Halliburton is charging for particular projects. The White House, Secretary of Defense, and the USAID all have an aversion to any form of oversight. When Representative Dingell and I wrote letters raising significant issues, they were almost always ignored. But we have been able to penetrate one particular contract, Halliburton's contract to import fuel from Kuwait into Iraq; and what we have learned is that Halliburton and its obscure subcontractor, Altanmia, have been gouging the taxpayer. . . .

I firmly believe that Congress has an important oversight role to play in ensuring the wise expenditure of taxpayers' dollars. Part of the problems that we are experiencing can be attributed to the lack of vigorous congressional oversight. But I'm encouraged by the recent steps that Chairman Davis has taken. He has joined me in requesting the DCAA audit documents. He scheduled this hearing, and he has promised to hold another hearing hopefully by the end of April. This is not easy for him to do, and I am sure it will alienate many in the administration, but I commend him for the steps that he is taking, even as I will be pressing him to take more. In closing, let me say that I look forward to today's hearing and the opportunity to hear from and question the distinguished witnesses before us.

Thank you, Mr. Chairman.

- **Source:** Excerpt of hearings before the Committee on Government Reform, House of Representatives, March 11, 2004, available at http://frwebgate.access.gpo.gov/cgi-bin/getdoc.cgi?dbname=108 _house_hearings&docid=f:96407.wais, accessed May 31, 2011.

- **Analysis:** To expedite reconstruction the administration allowed the issuing of no-bid, cost-plus contracts. Under normal circumstances, companies must compete with one another, submitting competitive bids for government work. The government then issues the successful company a fixed-price contract under which it receives the amount it bid regardless of any unexpected costs it incurs. This competitive approach provides a powerful incentive for contractors to keep costs down. No-bid contracts were awarded without a competitive bidding process; cost-plus contracts covered unforeseen increases in costs and guaranteed the bidder's profit. No-bid, cost-plus contracts, invited waste, fraud, and abuse. Absence of transparency in issuing them and lack of sufficient oversight compounded congressional concerns.

- **Document 45: Excerpt of *Special Inspector General for Iraq Reconstruction: Quarterly Report to Congress***
- **When:** July 30, 2004
- **Where:** Washington, DC
- **Significance:** This report validated the concerns raised by Congressman Waxman in **Document 44**.

DID YOU KNOW?

Special Inspector General for Iraq Reconstruction (SIGIR)

The Office of the Special Inspector for Iraq Reconstruction was created by an act of Congress in October 2004. SIGIR replaced the CPA as the body responsible for overseeing the U.S.-funded Iraq Reconstruction Fund. On January 20, 2004, Stuart W. Bowen, Jr., was appointed to the post of CPA inspector general. He has served as SIGIR since the creation of the position. SIGIR answered directly to Congress, to which it submitted quarterly reports. It reported administratively to the secretaries of defense and state. Bowen and his office identified waste, fraud, and abuse in Iraq.

These are some of the CPA-IG's specific findings to date:

- A CPA-IG audit found that the CPA Comptroller created policies and regulations that, although well intended, did not establish effective funds controls and accountability over $600 million in DFI funds held as cash available for disbursement. This included $200 million held by the Comptroller in Baghdad and over $400 million with appointed agents. Although the CPA-IG did not identify any actual losses of cash, the $600 million under the control of the Comptroller was susceptible to fraud, waste, and abuse.
- A CPA-IG audit of accountable property in Baghdad found that the management and record-keeping for accountable property needed improvement. CPA auditors in Baghdad estimated that accountable property items valued at approximately $11.1–26.2 million may have been unaccounted for at the time of the audit.
- The CPA-IG identified 178 major contracts awarded in 2003 and 2004, each valued at more than $5 million. The CPA-IG verified contract data for 164 of the 178 contracts. Of the 178 contracts, 14 were not located during the review. Based on a review of the 164 major contracts, the percentage of total value of contracts awarded through full and open competition increased from 25% in 2003 to 99% in 2004, while those awarded on a sole source basis decreased from 66% to 1%.
- A CPA-IG investigation uncovered evidence of manipulation in the award of a security contract. The resulting CPA general counsel review led to the revocation of the $7.2 million award, recovery of the $2.3 million advance payment, and the removal of a senior advisor.
- In the course of an ongoing fraud investigation, the CPA-IG found weak contract monitoring, including numerous deficiencies in a contract for oil pipeline repair. The Program Management Office issued a deduction of more than $3.3 million for improper charges because contractors were not in the field conducting the work specified in the contract.

- **Source:** *Special Inspector General for Iraq Reconstruction: Quarterly Report to Congress, July 30, 2004.* Washington, DC: GPO, 2004, p. 1, available at http://www.hsdl.org/?view&doc=75376&coll=limited, accessed June 2, 2011.
- **Analysis:** Only one-quarter of the contacts issued in 2003 were open and competitive. As the report noted, the situation had improved in 2004 when 99 percent of all new contracts let were open and competitive.

The government was, however, stuck with the early cost-plus contracts still in effect. The report also noted that auditing and oversight were still not adequate to ensure taxpayer money was well spent.

- **Document 46: Excerpt of "Status of Iraq Reconstruction"**
- **When:** July 2005
- **Where:** Washington, DC
- **Significance:** The report noted persistent challenges of reconstruction and the high cost that insecurity added to the effort.

As the reconstruction effort in Iraq matures and shifts focus from planning and design to implementation and handover, U.S. agencies must ensure that their efforts leave the Iraqis with a firm foundation on which to build. During this reporting period, the SIGIR continued to conduct discussions and interviews with key members of Iraq reconstruction management teams in Baghdad and Washington, D.C. Based on first-hand knowledge of the current situation in Iraq, existing SIGIR initiatives, and continuing oversight work, the SIGIR is actively pursuing two emerging issues:

- *Cost to complete*: Can the U.S. government agencies managing Iraq reconstruction projects produce reliable estimates of the costs of completing those projects (and thus avoid over-obligating funds)?
- *Sustainability*: Can reconstruction projects funded by the U.S. government be sustained after handover to the Iraqis?

A failure on either of these points puts at risk the important legacy of success that the U.S. intends to leave. As of July 5, 2005, approximately *75% of the $18.4 billion IRRF had been obligated, and 35% had been disbursed.* During this quarter, the SIGIR increased efforts to address a persistent set of challenges facing the agencies and organizations involved in Iraq reconstruction:

- *Strategy and Interagency Coordination*: At least a dozen offices representing six U.S. agencies directly spend money from the IRRF. There is minimal, if any, integration among the various systems that these offices use to manage information on contracting, finance, and projects.
- *Program Management*: Inadequate processes, systems, documentation, training, and internal controls are regularly cited in oversight reports on Iraq reconstruction. To make informed, effective decisions, management requires more reliable data.
- *Acquisition and Contract Management*: The SIGIR is concerned that insufficient internal controls have created conditions for mismanagement, inefficiencies, and ineffectiveness in acquisition and contract management.
- *Human Resources*: The SIGIR has observed that Iraq reconstruction efforts continue to be hampered by high turnover of key personnel and vacancies in critical positions.

- *Security:* Providing security continues to exact a heavy cost on Iraq reconstruction, slowing reconstruction efforts and reducing the potential impact of reconstruction.

The threat to life and property from continuing insurgent attacks remains a major impediment to the reconstruction and rehabilitation of Iraq. As of June 30, 2005, 330 contractors had been killed in Iraq. During this reporting period, the total number of Defense Base Act insurance claims grew by more than 30%, and death claims rose by 20%. The rising number of claims underscores both the danger inherent in reconstruction activities and the continuing costs arising from the current environment.

- **Source:** *Special Inspector General for Iraq Reconstruction: Quarterly Report to Congress, July 30, 2005.* Washington, DC: GPO, 2004, 3–4, available at http://www.hsdl.org/?view&doc=75370&coll=limited, accessed June 2, 2010.
- **Significance:** The report revealed the tremendous sums being spent on Iraq reconstruction on top of the high and increasing costs of coping with a raging insurgency. The security situation added to reconstruction costs through the insurance and death benefit claims for contract workers and their companies' need to pay private security firms to protect them. The report raised a serious concern over the effectiveness and sustainability of reconstruction projects. It also noted a lack of coordination among various agencies overseeing the reconstruction effort. This problem no doubt led to duplication of effort and waste.

- **Document 47: Excerpt of *Special Inspector General for Iraq Reconstruction: Quarterly Report to Congress***
- **When:** October 30, 2005
- **Where:** Washington, DC
- **Significance:** The report identifies a serious reconstruction gap.

The Reconstruction Gap

On October 18, 2005, the Inspector General appeared before the House Government Reform Subcommittee on National Security, Emerging Threats, and International Relations. In his testimony, the Inspector General highlighted a growing area of concern—the *reconstruction gap.* SIGIR defines the reconstruction gap as the difference between the number of projects that the United States originally proposed to build in Iraq and the number of projects that the United States will ultimately complete. When the U.S.-led portion of Iraq's reconstruction concludes, many planned projects will remain on the drawing board for execution by other funding sources. The reconstruction gap is the result of a number of factors:

- dramatically increased spending for security needs
- increased costs of materials, particularly in the oil sector
- increased costs arising from project delays
- cost overruns
- multiple reprogrammings of reconstruction priorities
- needed increases in spending for sustainment

The United States has appropriated nearly $30 billion for reconstruction projects in Iraq. Nearly all of the U.S. appropriated dollars—more than 93%—have already been committed to programs and projects. More than 25% of these funds have been spent on security costs related to the insurgency, which has proportionately reduced funds for other reconstruction projects.

- **Source:** *Special Inspector General for Iraq Reconstruction: Quarterly Report to Congress, October 30, 2005.* Washington, DC: GPO, 2005, 3, available at http://www.hsdl.org/?search&offset=0&submitted =Search&collection=public&so=date&creatormore=true&creator =Bowen%2C+Stuart+W.&fct&page=1, accessed June 4, 2011.
- **Analysis:** This report painted a disturbing picture of an inefficient and wasteful reconstruction effort. A quarter of all reconstruction dollars allocated had been spent on security. The insurgency no doubt con-tributed to project delays and increased cost of materials as well. The reference to "multiple reprogrammings [*sic*] of reconstruction prior-ities" suggests that the poor cooperation and lack of unity of effort raised in an earlier report had not been remedied.

- **Document 48: Excerpt of *Special Inspector General for Iraq Reconstruction: Quarterly Report to Congress***
- **When:** July 30, 2006
- **Where:** Washington, DC
- **Significance:** This report identified accomplishments and noted con-tinuing problems with reconstruction.

During this quarter, the U.S. reconstruction effort in Iraq achieved some impor-tant milestones: production of electricity and oil climbed above pre-war levels for the first time in over a year, with electricity output exceeding 5,000 megawatts and oil production reaching 2.5 million barrels per day. The watershed event of this year, however, occurred in May, when the first permanent, democratically-elected government of Iraq took office. Iraq's new unity government now faces many

DID YOU KNOW?

Provincial Reconstruction Teams (PRTs)

PRTs are small operational units of the U.S. Department of State. Comprised of military and civilian specialists from various government departments and agencies (USAID, Justice Department, etc.), PRTs work closely with Iraqi provincial and local officials on a variety of political and economic development projects. They dispense reconstruction funds with the goal of capacity building, enabling Iraqi leaders to provide services to their own people. While the goal is to keep civilian members to the fore, the military takes the lead in areas of high insecurity.

daunting tasks, including improving security, sustaining the infrastructure, and fighting corruption. . . .

At the end of June 2006, $18.94 billion of the Iraq Relief and Reconstruction Fund (IRRF 1 & 2) had been obligated, and $14.85 billion had been expended. The U.S. government's authority to obligate the remaining funds in the IRRF expires September 30, 2006, so any IRRF dollars not under contract by that date will revert to the U.S. Treasury. U.S. contracting entities in Iraq are now focused on rapidly obligating the balance of the IRRF. Security problems continue. Recurring violence in Iraq continues to impede reconstruction efforts, slowing progress on projects, restricting the movement of personnel, and diverting dwindling resources. The lethal environment limits the important work of the U.S. Provincial Reconstruction Teams (PRTs). . . .

Corruption threatens to undermine Iraq's democracy. Iraqi officials estimate the cost of corruption at $4 billion a year, and the Commission for Public Integrity has more than 1,400 criminal cases, involving about $5 billion. A poll conducted this quarter found that one-third of Iraqis reported that they have paid bribes for products or services this year. More resources and stronger support will be needed for Iraq's anticorruption entities to battle corruption effectively. SIGIR sees positive signs in the Iraqi Prime Minister's recent words of support for anticorruption efforts. Additionally, the U.S. Mission in Iraq concurred with (and is implementing) the recommendations in SIGIR's audit of the U.S. anticorruption capacity-building program, which means more resources will be devoted to this important issue. . . .

In an audit of transition planning completed this quarter, SIGIR noted that coordination among agencies managing the transition of the reconstruction program needs coordinating among agencies, centralizing reporting, and managing ministry advisors. It must be empowered to do more to bring all operating agencies together to effect a successful transition. . . .

The fall of Saddam's regime ended four decades of a state controlled economy, leaving local officials, many of whom lacked experience, to manage the delivery of provincial government services. Programs to assist these officials in developing management skills are a priority. The PRT program embodies this priority, helping local officials to improve their capacities to govern by teaching them to promote security, rule of law, political participation, and economic development. Currently, the PRTs face serious challenges, including security threats, insufficient staffing, and limited resources. SIGIR has announced an audit of the PRT program, which will examine their effectiveness. . . .

A significant development this quarter was the Iraqi government's request to the UN for help in securing a financial compact with the international donor community. Under this compact, Iraq will pledge to implement reforms in exchange for political and economic support. The compact's goal is to provide a financial framework for the transformation of Iraq's economy and its integration into the regional and global economies. The compact is expected to energize the next phase of reconstruction in Iraq.

- **Source:** *Highlights of Special Inspector General for Iraq Reconstruction: Quarterly Report to Congress, July 30, 2006,* available at http://www. hsdl.org/?view&doc=75367&coll=limited, accessed June 4, 2011.
- **Analysis:** In addition to identifying accomplishments and challenges, this report contained two other salient conclusions. First, it noted the serious problem of corruption in Iraq. In addition to the waste and abuse of no-bid, cost-plus contracts, outright theft by Iraqi officials siphoned billions of dollars from aid and reconstruction programs. Endemic corruption resulted from a corresponding problem: lack of oversight.

  The report also noted an initiative focused on delivering services to the provinces. Saddam Hussein had concentrated government resources on Baghdad and other key cities to the neglect of outlying areas. The coalition began to address this inequity through the use of PRTs. These teams concentrated on restoring basic services to local communities.

- **Document 49: Excerpt of *Special Inspector General for Iraq Reconstruction: Quarterly Report to Congress***
- **When:** October 30, 2006
- **Where:** Washington, DC
- **Significance:** The report reveals continued problems with construction amid a deteriorating security situation.

Challenges Confronting Transition

As the U.S.-led phase of Iraq reconstruction nears its conclusion, it is vital that the Iraqi government attract broader international donor and private-sector support to finance continued development and reconstruction efforts. The Iraqi government faces several serious challenges to this endeavor.

Deteriorating Security Situation

Continued violence and the resulting lack of security have seriously impeded progress on reconstruction programs, causing construction delays, preventing travel to project sites, increasing security costs, and endangering the lives of contractors. Baghdad suffered the most acute security problem this quarter. The electricity sector was especially hard hit. Recent attacks on power lines providing electricity to Baghdad isolated the capital from the national power grid, and power-line repair continues to be difficult. Iraq's Minister of Electricity recently stated: Every day

I send repair teams, but they can't get to the area: there are too many insurgents . . . I've spoken to [everyone] . . . no one can help.

Weak Iraqi Capital Budget Execution

The execution of the Iraqi capital budget for 2006 is well behind schedule. Many government ministries, particularly the Ministry of Oil, are seemingly unable to obligate capital funds to programs and projects. SIGIR is concerned that, unless the Iraqi government demonstrates an ability to spend its own funds more effectively, international donors will likely be reluctant to provide further financial support to Iraq.

Transparency and the Fight against Corruption

SIGIR continues to support Iraq's anticorruption institutions. This quarter, SIGIR worked to build support for the Board of Supreme Audit, the Commission on Public Integrity, and the inspectors general of the Iraqi ministries. Without visible and authoritative oversight, corruption could derail Iraq's efforts to rebuild and sustain itself.

Incomplete Transfer of U.S. Assets to Iraqi Ministries

The asset recognition and transfer process, begun in 2005 to catalogue and transfer IRRF assets to the Iraqi government, appears to have broken down. The Iraqi government and the U.S. Embassy must work together to complete the asset transfer process and ensure that Iraq is in a position to take responsibility for IRRF facilities and inventories.

The Year of Transition Enters the Fourth Quarter

Foremost among the challenges confronting transition this quarter was the U.S. government's effort to ensure the obligation of remaining money in the Iraq Relief and Reconstruction Fund (IRRF) by the September 30, 2006 statutory deadline. As of October 18, 2006, SIGIR had yet to obtain complete information on this effort, but it appears that the goal of full and effective obligation of the IRRF was met.

- **Source:** *October 30, 2006 Special Inspector General for Iraq Reconstruction Report to Congress*, available at http://www.sigir.mil/publications/ quarterlyreports/October2006.html, accessed March 20, 2012.
- **Analysis:** Issued at the height of the insurgency, this report painted a bleak picture of the situation in Iraq. Insurgents were targeting the Baghdad power grid, disrupting its already compromised service. Corruption and lack of transparency continued to plague operations. In addition to being rife with corruption, the Iraqi government proved incapable of taking responsibility for managing key sectors of its own economy.

Tired of hearing his negative reports, the Bush administration tried to prevent renewal of the Special Inspector General for Iraq Reconstruction, whose congressional mandate was to expire in October 2007. However, congressional support for the office was too strong. Democratic gains in the 2006 midterm election made it impossible to prevent the position being renewed.

- **Document 50: Excerpt of Testimony by Special Inspector General for Iraq Reconstruction Stuart W. Bowen, Jr., to House Committee on Homeland Security**
- **When:** June 19, 2007
- **Where:** Washington, DC
- **Significance:** The SIGIR explained the problem of corruption in Iraq.

Chairman Scott, Ranking Member Forbes, and members of the Subcommittee, thank you for this opportunity to address you today on the work of the Office of the Special Inspector General for Iraq Reconstruction.

To ensure accurate context, permit me to outline several points essential to understanding the challenges of investigating and prosecuting fraud in Iraq.

First, corruption *within* the Iraqi government, indeed within the fabric of Iraqi society, is a serious problem that inhibits progress on many fronts in Iraq. This is widely recognized by the Government of Iraq and the international community. In our quarterly reports, SIGIR has called Iraq's endemic corruption problem a "second insurgency."

I returned last month from my 16th trip to Iraq and, during my visit, I met with the Commissioner of Public Integrity, who heads the institution created by the CPA to increase accountability for public corruption in Iraq—and the President of the Board of Supreme Audit, the analogue to the Government Accountability Office, which has existed in Iraq for many decades. The Iraqi anti-corruption authorities again emphasized to me the widespread nature of the problem of corruption, which stretches across the government, afflicting virtually every ministry. And they outlined for me the difficulties they face in implementing their respective anti-corruption mandates.

The CPI Commissioner told me that he currently has 2,000 cases involving $5 billion in alleged corruption. And the President of the Board of Supreme Audit has hundreds of audits ongoing. In virtually every case, he is uncovering a lack of accountability. Let me emphasize that the CPI and the BSA oversee *Iraqi* money —not U.S. money—that is missing or has been stolen from *Iraqi* programs.

During my visit, I was informed about political interference with the work of Iraqi investigators and prosecutors. For example, I learned that Ministers and former Ministers are exempt from prosecution unless the assent of the Prime Minister is obtained; and each Minister is entitled, under an Iraqi criminal code provision, to immunize selectively ministry employees from being held accountable for corruption.

Iraq must make progress on rule of law enforcement, in general, and corruption, in particular; political interference with fighting corruption remains a problem, undermining the effectiveness of the developing rule of law system and consequently eroding the Iraqi people's confidence in their government.

Iraq is a sovereign state. The role of the United States thus is to *encourage* the development of an efficient Iraqi justice system. We do this for its own sake and for the sake of maintaining and building upon the efforts made, at great cost in blood and treasure, by Americans and Iraqis since the liberation of Iraq.

SIGIR's specific role in this process has been to review the effectiveness of United States efforts to improve the rule of law system and to build up the corruption-fighting capacity of the Iraqi government.

On July 28, 2006, SIGIR released a survey on this subject and found that American efforts were funded at a very modest level, given the scope of the problem, receiving about $65 million (about three-tenths of one percent of our total reconstruction spending). My auditors found that American efforts have not been sufficiently coordinated and focused and that more adequate leadership and organization was needed. The U.S. Embassy has responded to some of these concerns since the review was released. SIGIR will soon release another review on the issue, updating our previous report.

SIGIR has a continuing investigative responsibility to detect and investigate malfeasance in American relief and reconstruction programs in Iraq. As part of this effort, we have developed good working-level and leadership-level relationships with the CPI and the BSA. We coordinate with these Iraqi agencies whenever we come across evidence of potential wrongdoing by Iraqis. SIGIR, of course, concentrates its law enforcement efforts on American targets and works with the Department of Justice in their effective prosecution.

My *second* point is that *the incidence of corruption within the U.S. reconstruction program*—judging from those cases that we have uncovered thus far—*appears to constitute a relatively small component of the overall American financial contribution to Iraq's reconstruction.* Based on the work of our 18 career investigators on SIGIR staff, I believe that losses to American taxpayers from fraud within reconstruction programs will likely amount to a relatively small component of the overall investment in Iraq, totaling in the tens of millions (rather than hundreds of millions or billions, as is sometimes imagined). However, the fact that the fraud we have detected is relatively small (to date) does not diminish the aggressiveness with which SIGIR pursues allegations of fraud in Iraq. We have found egregious incidents of fraud. And in partnership with the Department of Justice, SIGIR has produced clear results in prosecutions and convictions.

For example, in January, two individuals were sentenced to prison as a result of SIGIR investigations. In early February, indictments were announced of five more individuals, resulting from SIGIR investigations. To date, SIGIR has opened over 300 cases, and we have over 70 ongoing investigations. Thirty-two of those cases are under prosecution at the Department of Justice.

We believe that the publicity our enforcement actions have received has helped to deter misconduct in the U.S reconstruction program. And we also believe that enforcement will be an increasingly important part of SIGIR's mission over the next

18 months. Moreover, in the course of this year, we expect to produce concrete investigative results as significant current cases come to fruition.

SIGIR remains committed to a robust, deterrent presence in Iraq as long as our temporary organization exists. Today, I have five investigators on the ground in Iraq investigating fraud. Although there are other law enforcement agencies fighting fraud in Iraq, SIGIR has maintained over the past three years the largest contingent of fraud investigators in Iraq. My investigators travel the country under dangerous conditions, pursuing leads, interviewing witnesses, and piecing together evidence on a wide variety of cases. Their work also takes them to other countries in the region. Of note, SIGIR is currently reducing its overall personnel "footprint" in Baghdad in conjunction with the reduction in spending of appropriated dollars on Iraq reconstruction.

One of the most important aspects of our investigative efforts is the development of task-force relationships with other agencies involved in oversight in Iraq, including my colleagues from the Office of Inspector General of the Department of Defense and the Defense Criminal Investigative Service, as well as the Federal Bureau of Investigation. SIGIR has 16 investigators in Arlington, and we are participating in the new Joint Operations Center located at the FBI to coordinate and enhance fraud investigations in Iraq.

SIGIR's first task force was the Special Investigative Task Force for Iraq Reconstruction (SPITFIRE), and it combined the efforts of the Internal Revenue Service, the Department of Homeland Security, Immigrations and Customs enforcement office, the FBI and the Department of State Office of Inspector General. That task force was able to effectively pursue the Bloom-Stein conspiracy that my auditors uncovered in Hillah, Iraq—a very egregious kickback and bribery scheme involving over $10 million in reconstruction funds that Philip Bloom, the contractor, and Robert Stein, the Coalition Provisional Authority comptroller for that region, engineered for their own criminal ends. SPITFIRE continues its work today; and we continue to pursue a number of leads that arose from the Bloom-Stein case.

The other major task-force initiative that SIGIR has initiated with the FBI is the International Contract Corruption Task Force (ICCTF). ICCTF prompted the creation of the Joint Operations Center mentioned above, which is producing the effective collection and coordination of investigative leads and source development. Although I am not at liberty to discuss details of these cases, I am very pleased with the very significant progress the JOC investigators have made, news of which I expect to be forthcoming later this year.

Along with SIGIR, the ICCTF includes the U.S. Army's Criminal Investigative Division's Major Procurement Fraud Unit, the Defense Criminal Investigative Service, the FBI, and the inspectors general of the Department of State and the Agency for International Development.

SIGIR is also part of the DOJ National Procurement Fraud Task Force. We continue to work closely with DOJ in the investigation and prosecution of our cases.

Finally, to coordinate efforts in oversight in Iraq, I formed the Iraq Inspector Generals' Council (IIGC) three years ago, which brings together every agency with oversight authority in Iraq for a meeting every quarter. The IIGC exists to deconflict and coordinate the member agencies' oversight efforts in Iraq.

SIGIR is not limiting its efforts just to addressing contractor misconduct through the criminal justice system. We also refer cases to the U.S. government's administrative debarment and suspension processes. To date, the competent oversight authorities have, through established rules that preserve due process, suspended 17 companies and individuals, debarred ten, and have another nine pending debarments.

To date, SIGIR has produced 13 quarterly reports, 86 audit reports, and 90 inspection reports. Our auditors and inspectors regularly refer investigative leads to our investigators some of which have developed into very significant cases. The Bloom-Stein case is just one example.

SIGIR's three lessons-learned reports produced to date have provided recommendations on policies designed to improve economy, efficiency and effectiveness for the Iraq program and for future reconstruction and stabilization operations. The reports have prompted the introduction of reform measures in the Congress that will improve contracting processes. SIGIR is at work on a lessons-learned capping report, which will be produced at the end of this year. It is my hope that our lessons learned reports will prompt reforms that will improve the capacity of law enforcement to deter crime.

Mr. Chairman, with respect to H.R. 400, Representative Abercrombie's bill entitled the "War Profiteering Prevention Act of 2007," our position is essentially what it was when we were asked to reflect on its counterpart at a Senate hearing this past March. SIGIR remains a strong proponent of legislation that would strengthen efforts to punish fraud or abuse in contracting programs in Iraq or elsewhere. We look forward to working with the Department of Justice to enforce H.R. 400, should it become law. We are, however, unaware of instances where the Justice Department was unable to prosecute, under existing law, on the facts we developed in our investigations.

One of our responsibilities in Iraq is to encourage efficiency in the reconstruction effort. In that role, we have prompted management to seek the widest possible participation by business enterprises (especially Iraqi firms) in reconstruction. The security risks in Iraq are self-evident, and thus the risks to any business enterprise operating in such an environment are mammoth. International companies likely will not get into the business of reconstruction in Iraq without incentives that render the risk-taking worthwhile. This reality should figure in the development of legislation that affects contracting in Iraq or similarly insecure environments.

- **Source:** Stuart W. Bowen Jr., "War Profiteering and Other Contractor Crimes Committed Overseas," statement before the U.S. House of Representatives Committee on the Judiciary Subcommittee on Crime, Terrorism, and Homeland Security, June 19, 2007, available at http://www.sigir.mil/reports/pdf/testimony/SIGIR_Testimony_07-012T.pdf, accessed June 12, 2008.

- **Analysis:** SIGIR identified two types of corruption plaguing the Iraq reconstruction effort. U.S. contractors and personnel accounted for a small percentage of the fraud. Iraqi officials did most of the stealing.

Mr. Bowen identified steps being taken to address the problem. He also noted that these efforts encountered interference from elements within the Iraqi government. Given Iraq's lack of experience with democratic government, this problem should have come as no surprise.

- **Document 51: Excerpt of Press Briefing on the Status of Iraq Reconstruction**
- **When:** February 2008
- **Where:** Baghdad
- **Significance:** This report documented a significant improvement in the reconstruction effort.

This penultimate quarter of the Year of Transfer witnessed the emergence of nascent normalcy in Iraq. As U.S. reconstruction assistance continued to target civil and military capacity building, Iraq achieved progress on the security, political, and economic fronts. Violent incidents dropped to their lowest levels since 2004; the long-awaited Provincial Election Law finally passed; and commercial activity, spurred by Iraq's oil-revenue windfall, continued to increase. But, as General Ray Odierno, the new Commanding General, Multi-National Force–Iraq (MNF–I), recently noted, Iraq "was a failed state [in 2006]. In 2008, it's a fragile state. We've got to move it to a stable state." To sustain progress in this direction, Iraq must improve its provision of security and essential services, such as electricity, potable water, sewage systems, and health care services.

Iraq's nascent normalcy follows upon—and, to some extent, stems from—the completion and transfer of most of the significant U.S. relief and reconstruction projects. Almost exactly five years ago, the Congress appropriated more than $18 billion to the Iraq Relief and Reconstruction Fund (IRRF) to support the ambitious Coalition Provisional Authority (CPA) rebuilding program. On September 30, 2008, the authority of U.S. agencies to obligate IRRF funds for new obligations expired. At that point, over 97% was obligated, and nearly 94% was spent. The $17.94 billion Iraq Security Forces Fund (ISFF) also is drawing down, with $3.85 billion left to obligate and $6.90 billion to expend. The Department of State's (DoS's) Economic Support Fund (ESF) and the Department of Defense's (DoD's) Commander's Emergency Response Program (CERP) have $1.81 billion and $0.88 billion left to expend, respectively. In sum, about $10.72 billion of the four major U.S. reconstruction funds has yet to be expended, and $5.26 billion remains unobligated.

- **Source:** *Special Inspector General for Iraq Reconstruction: Quarterly Report to Congress, October 30, 2008. Washington, DC: GPO, 2008, 2, available at http://www.sigir.mil/files/quarterlyreports/October2008/ Report_-_October_2008.pdf#view=fitm, accessed June 8, 2011.*

- **Analysis:** Halfway through the "year of transition," the year of the surge strategy, SIGIR presented his most optimistic report to date. He described the situation in Iraq as one of "nascent normalcy," noting that the country had progressed from being a failed state in 2006 to a stable state in 2008. The improved security situation had contributed significantly to the success in reconstruction. The process was, however, far from complete.

    Most analysts agree that 2007 through 2008 was a turning point in the Iraq War. Future reports by SIGIR would reflect the same cautiously optimistic view of the situation. The problems of waste and corruption would continue but improve. The SIGIR's office was a positive innovation of the Iraq experience worth repeating in future efforts.

- **Document 52: Excerpt of Testimony of Special Inspector General for Iraq Reconstruction to Congress**
- **When:** March 25, 2009
- **Where:** Washington, DC
- **Significance:** The SIGIR provided a succinct overview of the reconstruction effort to date.

The original reconstruction plan—developed in 2002 and early 2003—envisaged a very narrow program that would focus on repairing war damage and averting humanitarian disasters. That plan was quickly superseded by a much larger vision, embodied in the occupation executed by the Coalition Provisional Authority. The CPA envisaged a $20 billion reconstruction effort—ten times larger than the originally planned investment—and the amount we have appropriated for Iraq to date ($50 billion) is about 25 times greater than what we originally anticipated.

Before the initial U.S. reconstruction efforts in Iraq had an appreciable effect, a lethal insurgency erupted derailing much of what had been planned. The CPA's strategy did not focus on security—it focused on big infrastructure projects. But a lack of security in 2003–2004 significantly slowed the reconstruction program. The situation that dominated Iraq through 2005–2006 was ameliorated only after a substantial military and civilian surge in 2007, deploying many more troops and new counterinsurgency tactics—such as "Money as a Weapons System"—that suppressed the insurgency and allowed the balance of the U.S. reconstruction effort to proceed in a relatively more secure environment.

In retrospect, the failure to adapt the reconstruction effort earlier to a counterinsurgency strategy that eventually worked is responsible in part for the considerable waste of reconstruction resources that occurred.

Before the 2007 counterinsurgency program, SIGIR had pointed out—in Lessons Learned reports and many individual audits and inspections—steps to improve the operation of the reconstruction program. . . .

Most of these recommendations were effectively implemented by agency management or departmental leadership. We also have seen commendable success evolve from the recommendation that contracting focus more on awards to Iraqis with the substantial growth of the Iraqi First program managed by the Joint Contracting Command—Iraq/Afghanistan. SIGIR's call for more support for training and deploying a civilian reserve corps to assist in post-conflict contingencies added impetus to the effort that led the Congress to pass the Reconstruction and Stabilization Civilian Management Act, which this Committee included in last year's NDAA. But our work still is turning up program weaknesses: an upcoming SIGIR audit will reveal that our asset-transfer and asset-sustainment recommendations have still not been effectively implemented.

The Iraq program failed to satisfy a first principle for successful reconstruction contingencies—ensuring sufficient security. In fact, the United States undertook complicated public works projects in very unstable places like Fallujah in 2004 and Basra in 2005. This led to an enormous waste of resources as projects could not progress due to unsafe environments but contractors were still being paid.

Taken as a whole, the U.S. reconstruction program has not met the goals set by the CPA in 2003 on the infrastructure front but has made great strides toward meeting them on the security front, after an enormous increase in funding for the Iraq Security Forces Fund.

The shortfalls on the reconstruction side stem, to a significant degree, from the lack of a system within the U.S. government for managing contingency relief and reconstruction operations. The lack of a good management framework meant that there were ineffective lines of authority and accountability among and between military and civilian organizations. This led to a lack of unity of command and weakened the program's unity of effort.

- **Source:** Hearing before House Committee on Armed Services, March 25, 2009, available at http://www.sigir.mil/files/testimony/ SIGIR_Testimony_09-002T.pdf#view=fit, accessed June 9, 2011.

- **Analysis:** In his testimony, the SIGIR provided a succinct but comprehensive overview of the reconstruction effort. He identified continuing problems with the effort, including waste, fraud, and corruption. He also detailed reform recommendations and noted that most had been implemented. Unfortunately, millions of dollars of taxpayer money had been wasted before meaningful change occurred. His testimony framed a lengthy report on lessons learned from the Iraq experience.

  In particular the SIGIR noted the failure to connect the reconstruction effort with the counterinsurgency campaign. Effective counterinsurgency requires addressing the root causes of unrest. Most people support insurgents because of discontent over their own situation. The coalition found itself in a reinforcing cycle of failure in Iraq. As long as aid and reconstruction stalled, people would support the insurgents. Insurgent violence, made possible by popular support, in turn made reconstruction difficult. Linking the two efforts from the outset instead of belatedly would have been more effective.

CONCLUSION

Despite the warnings of many experts, the administration failed to appreciate the degree and extent of damage to Iraqi infrastructure. Failure to prepare for the dire circumstances of postwar Iraq encouraged the climate of unrest that fueled the insurgency. Ramping up the relief and reconstruction effort belatedly was inefficient and costly. No-bid, cost-plus contracts encouraged waste, fraud, and abuse, as did the nature of Iraqi politics. The coalition eventually recouped the situation but not before millions of taxpayer dollars had been wasted.

4

FROM CONVENTIONAL TO UNCONVENTIONAL WAR

U.S. Central Command had opted for an invasion plan requiring enough troops to defeat Iraq's conventional forces in a rapid campaign but not enough to occupy and pacify the country. The Pentagon planned to hand over responsibility for internal security to police and military units expected to remain intact and at their posts. This assumption precluded preparations for an internal security mission. Few troops had the equipment, training, or experience necessary to handle the widespread looting and unrest that followed the collapse of Hussein's regime. Refusal to acknowledge or even recognize signs of a growing insurgency allowed organized resistance to take root and develop. The ill-advised decision to demobilize the Iraqi army and bar former Ba'ath Party members above a certain rank from holding political or administrative office made matters worse.

Even when the signs of a growing insurgency became so clear that even the Rumsfeld Pentagon could not ignore them, the U.S. military found itself ill prepared to counter the threat. With little or no strategic guidance, commanders tried to make the best of a bad situation. Lacking sufficient troops to saturate the country and live among the Iraqi people and with no real experience of counterinsurgency (COIN) operations, U.S. forces adopted a largely conventional approach to unconventional war, exacerbating the deteriorating security situation. Overemphasis on capturing or killing insurgents put pressure on units to round up bad guys and their supporters, an approach that led to the infamous Abu Ghraib prison scandal. Trying to pacify too large an area with too few troops produced excesses born of frustration, such as the murders in Haditha.

From trial, error, and study of past campaigns, the U.S. military finally developed tactics, which it captured in the first major revision of COIN doctrine since the Vietnam War. Good tactics do not a strategy make, however. The administration had a vision of a prosperous, secure, democratic Iraq, but no effective plan for realizing it. The White House issued its "Strategy for Victory in Iraq" in the fall of 2005, but little progress occurred until General David Petraeus took command of coalition forces and implemented the troop surge in combination with the Anbar awakening.

ESCALATING VIOLENCE

The situation in Iraq deteriorated throughout the summer and fall of 2003. By the end of the year not even the most strident optimist could deny that coalition forces faced a full-blown, complex insurgency with many actors. Muqtada al-Sadr's Mahdi Army operated in the Sadr City neighborhood of Basra and throughout much of the south. Sunni insurgents operated in an area of central Iraq known as the "Sunni triangle." At the same time foreign fighters poured into Iraq from around the Arab world. Each threat required a different response. The United States deployed more and more troops to Iraq as casualties mounted.

- **Document 53: Captured Internal Security Memorandum**
- **When:** April 3, 2003

- **Where:** Baghdad
- **Significance:** The memorandum documents the presence of foreign fighters in Iraq.

Republic of Iraq
Presidential Headquarters
Department of Public Security
SECRET
Date: 2 April, 2003

The Secretary
Headquarters of the Republic

Subject: Volunteers

With reference to our letter number 190 of 29/3/2003, we wish to inform the respected headquarters of the following:

1. The total number of volunteers up to 28/3/2003 reached 646, which includes two Turks, two Saudis, three each of the following nationalities: Jordanians, Algerians, Lebanese and the rest are Syrians. They were all sent to the concerned authorities in the Ministry of Defense, as directed.

2. We noticed an accumulation of Arab volunteers who ended up being inhabited in [ineligible name] Hotel, in Baghdad. There was talk amongst them that they came here as volunteered to fight, but they were not sent to any fighting battle, in spite of their being here for a long time since their arrival in the country.

With appreciation, we remain
The Manager,
Department of Public Security

Page 2 of 19

In the name of Allah, The Merciful, The Beneficent

Department of Public Security   Internal Memorandum

TO: The (respectable) General Manager
FROM: Manager of Tracking and Coordination
Subject: Volunteers
Date: 30/3/2003

- **Source:** Larry Diamond, Senior Fellow of the Hoover Institution, testimony of Larry Diamond to the Senate Foreign Relations Committee, May 19, 2004.
- **Analysis:** After the fall of Baghdad the United States captured numerous Iraqi government documents. This memorandum documents the arrival of foreign fighters. As occurred following the 1979 Soviet

DID YOU KNOW?

Mujahedeen

Loosely translated from Arabic, *mujahedeen* means "holy warrior." During the Afghan war against the Soviets (1979–1989) the term referred to Arab men who journeyed to Pakistan to fight alongside the Afghans against the invaders. Among these fighters was the son of a wealthy Saudi businessman—Osama bin Laden. Bin Laden and his associates founded al-Qaeda to assist Muslims under threat in other countries. He offered an army of *mujahedeen* to defend Saudi Arabia and expel Saddam Hussein from Iraq in 1990 and 1991. When the U.S.-led coalition invaded Iraq in 2003 it created another conflict that attracted foreign *mujahedeen*. Many of these foreign fighters joined al-Qaeda for Jihad in the Land of the Two Rivers, better known as al-Qaeda in Iraq. These *mujahedeen* eventually became so unpopular with Iraqis that the United States allied with former Iraqi insurgents in the Anbar Awakening to expel the hated foreigners.

invasion of Afghanistan, foreign *mujahedeen* traveled to Iraq to fight the U.S. invaders. They joined local insurgents and foreign terrorist groups to complicate an already difficult security situation.

- **Document 54: Anbar Directorate Security Report**
- **When:** March 31, 2003
- **Where:** Baghdad
- **Significance:** The memorandum documents foreign fighters entering Iraq via Syria.

The Syrian authorities prevented the Syrian citizens among the volunteers from entering the nation until they obtain official passports and tickets.

The number of volunteers who entered the country until today 03/31/2003 is (2500) volunteers. When these volunteers were blocked by the Syrian authorities, they organized demonstrations denouncing the American aggression in the area of Bukmal. They vilified the Arab leaders and paid tribute to President Saddam Hussein.

The Syrian Red Crescent brought considerable amount of medical assistance and food into the country and delivered them to the Iraqi Red Crescent representatives in al-Qa'im bordering complex.

Among the assistance there were two ambulances. Several Iraqi families entered the country through the Passports office in al-Qa'im. These families were in Syria for jihad purposes against the American invaders.

- **Source:** Anbar Directorate security report, March 31, 2003. Available at http://%3AFiraqslogger.powweb.com/%2Fdownloads/%2FP_4287 _Vol_5.zip%3FPHPSESSID%3Dc5aa4044714cf600c5a3785c5c8aefed &ei=dAsUT5z0L-fY0QGYoZzEAw&usg=AFQjCNEOpftW4Xk5X Dc7qoUdwC68CMpfMQ, last accessed January 16, 2012.
- **Analysis:** This document reveals that the number of foreign fighters entering the country was considerably higher than the number given in **Document 53**. It also reveals the dilemma faced by Syria. Its people clearly favored allowing *mujahedeen* to cross into Iraq, but the Syrian government rightly feared the implications of aiding those that the U.S. deemed terrorists. Indeed, some members of the Bush administration spoke of a "left turn" addition to the Iraq invasion plan. They proposed advancing westward (left) into Syria after taking Baghdad.

- Document 55: Excerpt of Testimony of Larry Diamond to the Senate Foreign Relations Committee
- When: May 19, 2004
- Where: Washington, DC
- Significance: An advisor to the CPA assesses the security situation.

Chairman Lugar, Senator Biden, Distinguished Members, Ladies and Gentlemen:

As you all well understand, the United States now faces a perilous situation in Iraq today. Because of a long catalogue of strategic and tactical blunders, we have failed to come anywhere near meeting the post-war expectations of Iraqis for security and post-conflict reconstruction. Although we have done many good things to eliminate tyranny, to rebuild infrastructure, and to help construct a free society and democratic political system, the overall ineptitude of our mission to date leaves us—and Iraq—in a terrible bind. If we withdraw our military forces precipitously in this security vacuum, we will leave the country at the mercy of a variety of power-hungry militias and criminal gangs, and Iraq will risk a rapid descent into one or another form of civil war. If the current situation persists, we will continue fighting one form of Iraqi insurgency after another with too little legitimacy, too little will, and too few resources. There is only one word for a situation in which you cannot win and you cannot withdraw: quagmire. We are not there yet, but we are close.

The scope for a good outcome has been greatly reduced as a result of the two insurgencies that we now confront in Iraq. One of these, in the Sunni heartland, has been festering since the end of the war, but has picked up deadly momentum in recent months and then took on a new ferocity with the grisly murder of the four American contractors in Fallujah on March 31. The other, in the Shiite heartland, broke out shortly thereafter when the radical young Shiite cleric, Muqtada al-Sadr, launched a violent uprising after the Americans badly bungled the long-delayed imperative of confronting his violent network. Add to this the awful news of grotesque humiliation of Iraqi prisoners by our own forces, and you have a profoundly deteriorating and potentially disastrous situation for the United States.

I will not dwell long on how we got to this perilous point, but a few observations are necessary. In any situation of occupation or imperial dominion, there is always a tension between control and legitimacy. The less control you have or can impose as an occupying power, the more you need legitimacy and voluntary cooperation. In many parts of its colonial empire, Britain addressed this challenge through the system of "indirect rule," which used local rulers to maintain control and gradually devolved more power through elections and local self-rule. As a result of this, Britain needed less troops relative to population than other colonial powers. United Nations peace implementation missions have addressed this problem in part through the mobilization of international legitimacy, via UN Security Council resolutions, and in part by developing explicit and transparent timetables for the transfer of power back to the people through elections. But even in these UN or other international trustee missions, success has depended in part on the presence of a sufficiently large and robust international force to keep (and in some instances impose) peace.

In Iraq, we have had too little legitimacy, but also in some ways too little control as well. We insisted on maintaining full political control from the start, but we did not have sufficient control on the ground, through adequate military force, to make our political and administrative control effective. Thus we could not meet popular expectations for the restoration of security and basic services like water and electricity (though progress we did make on all of those fronts). Because we did not deliver rapidly enough (and it could never truly have been rapidly enough to meet the inflated public expectations), because it was always an American administrator out in front decreeing and explaining, and because the Iraqi people did not see new Iraqi political leaders exercising much effective responsibility, the American-led occupation quickly developed a serious and growing legitimacy deficit.

Many things could have relieved this deficit. For example, if we had pushed more reconstruction funding out to local military commanders, through the rather effective CERP (Commanders' Emergency Reconstruction Program) channel, and if we had given some real authority and funding to the local and provincial councils we were establishing around the country, Iraqis might have seen more progress and found emerging new forms of Iraqi authority with which they could identify. We might have also made more progress by organizing actual elections, however imperfect, at the local level where the people were ready for it and the ration-card system provided a crude system for identifying voters. In the few places where this mechanism was employed, it worked acceptably well—before CPA ordered that no more direct elections be held (for fear of giving the impression that it would be possible to hold national elections soon—which it would not have been). Even so, the local governance teams did a pretty good job in many cases of finding ways to choose, and then later "refresh", the provincial and local councils. Sadly, the CERP funding was terminated prematurely, and the Local Government Order, defining the powers of provincial and local governments, sat around at CPA for months in various states of development and imminent release, while the local councils dawdled and dithered without much of anything to do, and ominously in some cases, without getting paid for months at a time. Within the CPA itself, I think historians will find that there was an obsession with centralized control, at the cost of the flexibility and devolution that might have gotten things done more quickly and built up more legitimacy.

So we had serious problems of security, reconstruction delivery, and legitimacy. We failed to ameliorate these by putting enough resources in (particularly enough troops) and by giving Iraqis early on more control over their own affairs. Now we are transferring control soon to Iraqis, and that is truly the only hope for rescuing a rapidly deteriorating situation. But in transitional politics, as in all other politics, timing is crucial, and what could be achieved by a certain initiative at one moment in time may no longer be possible months or years later, when the parameters have shifted and the scope for building a moderate center may have been lost. . . .

All counter-insurgency efforts ultimately depend on winning the larger political and symbolic struggle for "hearts and minds." Though he has gained in popular support in recent weeks, Muqtada Sadr—a fascist thug with only the thinnest Islamist religious credentials, who is reviled by much of the Shiite population and religious establishment—cannot win the broad bulk of Iraqi "hearts and minds," even in the Shiite south. Neither can the diehard Ba'athist remnants of Saddam's regime, who, in connivance with external jihadists such as Al-Qaeda, have been driving the insurgency in the Sunni center of the country. Indeed, one of the fascinating, potentially destructive, but also potentially positive elements in the fluid political situation we confront is that there is no coherent political and military force in Iraq that is capable of rallying, and for any meaningful period of time, sustaining broad popular support.

No single force can win in Iraq, but the United States could lose, and very soon. Even before the outbreak of the scandal over US forces' degrading, disgraceful abuse of Iraqi prisoners at the Abu Ghraib prison, Iraqi patience with the American occupation was dwindling rapidly. More and more Iraqis have been coming around to the view that if we cannot give them security, jobs, and electricity, why should they continue to suffer the general humiliation and countless specific indignities of American forces occupying their land?

What seemed possible six weeks ago, and certainly three months ago, is not necessarily feasible today. Clearly, the option of sending in significantly more troops to combat the insurgency and defeat the diehard and spoiler elements is dead. It is now clear that the Bush Administration—which has never been honest with itself or the American people about what would be needed to succeed in Iraq—is not going to up the ante for the United States in that kind of way in an election year. Moreover, even introducing two more divisions—which would still leave our overall troop strength far below the 250,000 or so that many military experts believed was the minimum necessary to bring and maintain order in post-war Iraq—would so strain the capacity of our armed forces that it would require drastic measures.

So we are stuck in Iraq for the moment with too few troops to defeat the insurgency and way too many for a growing segment of deeply disaffected Iraqi public opinion. Thus we have basically opted to live with the city of Fallujah under the control of insurgents, hoping the Iraqi force we have quickly stood up there will at least contain and dampen down the problem. And we are slowly trying to take back some of the facilities and installations that Muqtada Sadr's al-Mahdi Army has seized in the past few weeks and months, while so far avoiding a decisive confrontation with Muqtada himself (so as not to inflict civilian casualties or damage the religious shrines). If there is any chance of decent governance emerging in Iraq in the near to medium term, I believe we are going to have to defeat the insurgency of the Mahdi army. But we can only do so if we work with Iraqi Shiites of at least somewhat more moderate and pragmatic political orientations, and most of all with Ayatollah Sistani. No Iraqi commands a wider following of respect and consideration, and has more capacity to steer political developments away from violence and extremism, than Sistani, who insists on free elections as the basis of political legitimacy.

In fact, there are many Iraqi forces with whom we can work. But the tragedy is that the most democratic among them do not have sizable armed militias at their command, and for the most part, have not had the money, time, training, and skill to build up broad bases of support. At least four political parties represented on the Governing Council do have some basis of support in the country. The problem is that two of these are the ruling parties of the semi-autonomous Kurdistan region, the PUK (Patriotic Union of Kurdistan) and the KDP (the Democratic Party of Kurdistan), and their influence largely ends at the borders of that region, while the other two forces, SCIRI and Da'wa, are backed in various ways by the Iranian regime and, despite the moderation they have evinced in Baghdad, appear to favor one or another form of Islamic fundamentalist regime. Each of these four parties has its own militia with probably at least 10,000 fighters, and in the case of the two Kurdish Peshmerga forces, maybe each several times that number.

If Iraq has elections with these forces, and many other private armed forces, controlling various strongholds, and without a superior neutral force on the ground to rein them in, the elections are not going to be free and fair. There will be a war for dominance along the margins of different strongholds, opposing candidates will be assassinated, electoral officials will be intimidated, ballot boxes will be stolen—it will be a nasty business. Beyond this, there is the danger that if the militias are not demobilized before the Americans withdraw, other political forces would arm in self-defense, or more precisely—if you consider that in many parts of rural Iraq, every male over 14 already has a Kalishnikov (or at least older) rifle—they will acquire heavy weapons, in preparation for the coming war for Iraq. Then you would have a truly awful mess, in which different parties, tribes, and alliances would have their own armies contesting violently for local, regional, and perhaps ultimately national dominance, with every neighboring country in the region intervening on behalf of its favored group or groups. This would be what Thomas Friedman calls "Lebanon on steroids"—a hellish (and possibly like Lebanon, protracted) civil war in which no central government could exert coherent authority.

Such a scenario could spawn disastrous humanitarian and political consequences. There would be thousands, possibly tens or even hundreds of thousands, of Iraqi casualties. In the chaos, terrorism and organized crime would thrive. Anti-Americanism, which is already gaining momentum in Iraq, would take on an entirely new breadth and intensity. We would be blamed for this, even if the instigators were more properly located in Syria, Saudi Arabia, and most of all Iran.

The only alternative to civil war or another truly brutal and total dictatorship is a political system based on some kind of constitutional, consensual power-sharing bargain. Any plan to break up the country, explicitly or implicitly, into its constituent ethnic or religious pieces will inevitably bring massive bloodshed, much of it regionally driven. And any effort to simply hand power over to a reconstructed Baathist dictatorship would be violently, and I am sure successfully, resisted by both the Kurds and the Shia. Any scenario that is even vaguely positive—that avoids the disaster of total war or total dictatorship—must involve key elements of democracy: negotiations, mutual concessions and compromise, delineation of individual and group rights, sharing and limiting of power, and elections in which different political parties and independents contest to determine who will exercise power....

What Is To Be Done?

The only way out of this mess is a combination of robust, precise, and determined military action to defeat the most threatening, anti-democratic insurgency—led by Muqtada Sadr and his Mahdi Army—combined with a political strategy to fill the legitimacy vacuum as rapidly as possible.

The Bush Administration has taken two vital steps in the latter regard. First, it has sought to improve the international legitimacy of our mission, and our ability to find a transitional solution that will be credible and acceptable to the largest possible number of Iraqis—by giving the United Nations and its special envoy, Lakhdar Brahimi, a leading role in the process. Ambassador Brahimi is an extraordinarily able, imaginative, and fair-minded mediator; I could not imagine a better candidate for this arduous task. One reason why he is the right person for the job is that he has a habit of doing something elementary that our own CPA has not done often and well enough: listening to Iraqis themselves, and as wide a range of Iraqi opinion as possible.

The second essential, correct decision of the Administration is to hold to the June 30 deadline for transferring power to an Iraqi interim government. One of the few positive things that has been suppressing Iraqi frustration and even rage over the occupation has been the prospect of a return to Iraqi sovereignty on June 30, and the promise of elections for a transitional government within seven months after that. It is vital that we adhere to the June 30 deadline. There is no solution to the dilemma we are in that does not put Iraqis forward to take political leadership responsibility for the enormous challenges of governance the country confronts. They cannot do it alone, but they must take the lead, and Iraqis must see that Iraqis are taking the lead. We should stop talking about "limited sovereignty." Iraqis have suffered enough humiliation. They need the dignity of knowing that they will be able to assert control over their own future after June 30, even if this will obviously be limited on the security side by the presence of some 150,000 international troops.

We need to embrace a number of other steps that will advance three key principles or goals: building legitimacy for the transitional program, increasing the efficacy of emergent Iraqi control, and improving the security situation in a more lasting way. All three of these goals require an intensive effort at rebuilding the now decimated, fragmented, and demoralized Iraqi state.

Here, briefly, are my recommendations:

1. **Disavow any long-term military aspirations in Iraq.** We should declare unambiguously that we will not seek any permanent American military bases in Iraq. (No Iraqi parliament in the near term is going to approve such a treaty, anyway). Iraqis fear that we harbor long-term imperial intentions toward their country. This would help to allay this fear.

2. **Establish a clear date for an end to the military occupation.** We should declare that when Iraq is at peace and capable of fully providing for its own security, we intend to withdraw all American forces from Iraq. We should set a target date for the full withdrawal of American forces. This may be three or four years in the future, but setting such a date will convince Iraqis that we are serious about leaving once the country is secure—that the occupation, in every respect, will come to a definite end.

3. **Respond to the concerns about Iraqi detainees.** We need an independent investigation of the treatment of Iraqi detainees, with international participation, and we should release as many detainees as possible for whom we do not have specific evidence or a strong and credible suspicion of involvement in insurgent

or criminal activity. This has been a profound grievance of Iraqis virtually since the end of the war, and it has been a major factor feeding the Sunni insurgency.

4. **Reorganize and accelerate recruitment and training of the new Iraqi police and armed forces.** Police training in particular has been an astonishing disaster. There is no hope of avoiding renewed oppression and/or civil war in Iraq unless we can stand up Iraqi police and armed forces that are independent of party and religious militias and answerable to the new, and ultimately democratically elected, Iraqi government. We can no longer allow ourselves to be hampered by divided responsibilities, bureaucratic face-saving, and resource constraints. We must find the best, most experienced experts and give them all the resources they need to get the job done.

5. **Proceed vigorously with our plan for disarmament, demobilization, and reintegration (DDR) of the principal armed militias into the police and armed forces.** There cannot be free and fair elections in Iraq—or even sustainable peace—if the most powerful forces in the country are a variety of competing and antidemocratic religious and political party militias. The most radical and antidemocratic militias, particularly Muqtada Sadr's Mahdi Army, must be isolated, confronted, and defeated—disarmed by force, or the credible threat of force. With the militias of the Kurdish Peshmerga, SCIRI, Dawa, and other political parties that have indicated their willingness to play in the political game, we need to complete negotiations that have now been underway for several months. We will have a much stronger hand in these negotiations if we compel the Mahdi Army to disarm, rather than offering to merge it into the new police and armed forces. Outside of Kurdistan, which is a special case, militia fighters should be merged into the new police and armed forces as individuals, not as organized units with their command structures intact.

6. **Get more money flowing to our Iraqi allies.** In particular, we should increase the pay of the Iraqi Army and police, giving them a stronger incentive to risk their lives to join up and stick with us. We might also want to increase the pay of the provincial and local councils, and most of all, we should make sure that all of these Iraqis who are part of the newly reemerging Iraqi state get paid in a timely fashion.

There are several other steps we can take to address our debilitating deficits of legitimacy with the Iraqi people and the international community:

7. **Make the new Iraqi Interim Government dependent on some expression of popular consent.** It is a pity that time did not permit the proposed Iraqi national conference and consultative assembly to be chosen well before June 30, so that one of these two more representative bodies could have elected the presidency council, the prime minister, and the cabinet. However, it is vital that the plans for indirect election of these bodies proceed after June 30. Once the consultative assembly is chosen by a large national conference, it should have the ability to interpellate [sic] the prime minister and cabinet ministers, and even to remove them, at least through a "constructive vote of no confidence" (which brings down the government only if there is a simultaneous majority vote for a new government).

8. **Aim as much as possible for instruments of democratic control, even in the interim period.** I do not think the Governing Council should continue in its current form. It has its own severe legitimacy problems, due to widespread Iraqi perceptions of its inefficacy and corruption. If some members of this Council have real bases of popular support, they should be able to demonstrate this within the national conference, to win election to the consultative assembly, and to exercise influence through that more democratic means. And one or members of the GC may wind up being appointed to positions in the presidency council or the new government.

9. **Provide for the appointment of an Iraqi Supreme Court, according to the Transitional Administrative Law, as soon as there is a consultative assembly that could confirm the appointments.** If the spirit and practice of constitutionalism is to develop in Iraq, it must do so from the beginning of the reemergence of Iraqi self-rule. The Prime Minister, Cabinet, or Presidency Council should not each decide for itself what is constitutional. There must be a neutral arbiter, and it should no longer be the US or the UN. The TAL provides for the Iraqi Higher Judicial Council to propose three nominees for each of the nine vacancies on the Supreme Court, with the Presidency Council then nominating and the transitional parliament confirming. This new method would involve only a minor modification to be codified in the TAL Annex.

10. **Codify the domestic and international arrangements for Iraq in a new UN Security Council Resolution.** This resolution should recognize the Iraqi Interim Government and its right to name its own representation at the UN. Beyond this, however, a UN Security Council resolution should also recognize whatever temporary "status of forces agreement" is reached between the US and the Interim Government, hopefully with UN mediation or participation. UN involvement and recognition of this element might then make it possible for a number of other countries to contribute troops to help maintain peace and security in Iraq until the country can fully manage its own security.

11. **We should do something in this period to acknowledge the grievances over the Transitional Administrative Law.** The TAL is the most liberal and progressive basic governance document anywhere in the Arab world. Iraqis can take great pride in many of its features, such as the bill of rights. However, there is intense controversy over a number of its provisions, including the degree of minority rights and the balance of power between the center and the provinces and regions. At a minimum, **we should emphatically acknowledge that the TAL is only a temporary document,** that Iraqis will be fully free and sovereign to write a new permanent constitution (and this declaration could also be incorporated into a new UN Security Council Resolution). It might be possible, however, to go further, and encourage the key parties to negotiate soon, in the Annex to the TAL, some modest amendments that might address some of the most serious objections that have been raised.

Finally, we need to continue to think act more innovatively in the quest to build as democratic a political system as possible.

12. **We should invest in supporting moderate, secular Shi'a** who draw support from parties, movements, and associations that don't have muscular militias. Hopefully, a fair process of selection of national conference participants will put many of these new faces forward.

13. **We urgently need to level the playing field with respect to political party funding.** The big parties either sit on huge resources, or are getting lavish funding from neighboring states, particularly Iran. More independent and democratic political parties are begging us for support. As soon as an Independent Iraqi Electoral Administration is established, we should help it create a transparent fund for the support (in equal amounts) of all political parties that pass a certain threshold of demonstrated popular support, and we should fund it generously (perhaps with an initial infusion of $10 to 20 million). Unless the gross imbalance in access to funding is established, there will not be anything approaching free and fair elections.

(Larry Diamond, Senior Fellow at the Hoover Institution, served as a senior advisor to the Coalition Provisional Authority in Baghdad from January to March 2004)

- **Source:** Testimony of Larry Diamond, Senior Fellow of the Hoover Institution, to the Senate Foreign Relations Committee, May 19, 2004.

- **Analysis:** Larry Diamond was a senior fellow at the Hoover Institution and senior advisor to the CPA. His conservative bona fides did not inhibit his scathing critique of Operation Iraqi Freedom. He noted that the United States in Iraq suffered from a legitimacy gap and a control gap. One year after the invasion it had become increasingly difficult to sustain the image of coalition forces as liberators. The United States had enough troops in country to anger the Iraqi people but not enough to provide them security.

  While Diamond did recognize the existence of a growing insurgency, he did not accurately assess its nature. He dismissed Muqtada al-Sadr as a thug and seriously underestimated the degree of the support he enjoyed among the Shi'a of Iraq. He also dismissed Sunni insurgents as disgruntled Ba'ath Party members. He outlined a series of steps to be taken to recoup the situation, primary among them handing responsibility for managing Iraq to its new interim government, scheduled to take office in late June 2004, and training more Iraqi security forces.

DID YOU KNOW?

Muqtada al-Sadr

Muqtada al-Sadr (b. 1973) is a leader of the Iraqi Shi'a community. His father, Mohammad Sadiq al-Sadr, was a grand ayatollah murdered by Saddam Hussein. Although he lacked his father's religious credentials, Muqtada emerged as an influential Shi'a leader after the U.S. invasion. Operating out of his support base in the Sadr City district of Baghdad, he organized the Mahdi Army, which fought against the Americans from 2003 to 2008, when he ordered it to disarm. In June 2011, he threatened renewed violence should U.S. forces stay beyond their announced withdrawal date even if requested to stay by the Iraqi government.

- **Document 56:** *Prospects for Iraq's Stability: A Challenging Road Ahead*
- **When:** 2007
- **Where:** Washington, DC
- **Significance:** The report painted a bleak picture of the security situation in Iraq.

Key Judgments

Iraqi society's growing polarization, the persistent weakness of the security forces and the state in general, and all sides' ready recourse to violence are collectively driving an increase in communal and insurgent violence and political extremism. Unless efforts to reverse these conditions show measurable progress during the term of this Estimate, the coming 12 to 18 months, we assess that the overall security situation will continue to deteriorate at rates comparable to the latter part of 2006....

The challenges confronting Iraqis are daunting, and multiple factors are driving the current trajectory of the country's security and political evolution.

- Decades of subordination to Sunni political, social, and economic domination have made the Shia deeply insecure about their hold on power. This insecurity leads the Shia to mistrust US efforts to reconcile Iraqi sects and reinforces their unwillingness to engage with the Sunnis on a variety of issues, including adjusting the structure of Iraq's federal system, reining in Shia militias, and easing de-Baathification.
- Many Sunni Arabs remain unwilling to accept their minority status, believe the central government is illegitimate and incompetent, and are convinced that Shia dominance will increase Iranian influence over Iraq, in ways that erode the state's Arab character and increase Sunni repression.
- The absence of unifying leaders among the Arab Sunni or Shia with the capacity to speak for or exert control over their confessional groups limits prospects for reconciliation. The Kurds remain willing to participate in Iraqi state building but reluctant to surrender any of the gains in autonomy they have achieved.
- The Kurds are moving systematically to increase their control of Kirkuk to guarantee annexation of all or most of the city and province into the Kurdistan Regional Government (KRG) after the constitutionally mandated referendum scheduled to occur no later than 31 December 2007. Arab groups in Kirkuk continue to resist violently what they see as Kurdish encroachment.
- Despite real improvements, the Iraqi Security Forces (ISF)—particularly the Iraqi police—will be hard pressed in the next 12–18 months to execute significantly increased security responsibilities, and particularly to operate independently against Shia militias with success. Sectarian divisions erode the dependability of many units, many are hampered by personnel and equipment shortfalls, and a number of Iraqi units have refused to serve outside of the areas where they were recruited.

- Extremists—most notably the Sunni jihadist group al-Qa'ida in Iraq (AQI) and Shia oppositionist Jaysh al-Mahdi (JAM)—continue to act as very effective accelerators for what has become a self-sustaining inter-sectarian struggle between Shia and Sunnis.
- Significant population displacement, both within Iraq and the movement of Iraqis into neighboring countries, indicates the hardening of ethno-sectarian divisions, diminishes Iraq's professional and entrepreneurial classes, and strains the capacities of the countries to which they have relocated. The UN estimates over a million Iraqis are now in Syria and Jordan.

The Intelligence Community judges that the term "civil war" does not adequately capture the complexity of the conflict in Iraq, which includes extensive Shia-on-Shia violence, al-Qa'ida and Sunni insurgent attacks on Coalition forces, and widespread criminally motivated violence. Nonetheless, the term "civil war" accurately describes key elements of the Iraqi conflict, including the hardening of ethno-sectarian identities, a sea change in the character of the violence, ethno-sectarian mobilization, and population displacements.

Coalition capabilities, including force levels, resources, and operations, remain an essential stabilizing element in Iraq. If Coalition forces were withdrawn rapidly during the term of this Estimate, we judge that this almost certainly would lead to a significant increase in the scale and scope of sectarian conflict in Iraq, intensify Sunni resistance to the Iraqi Government, and have adverse consequences for national reconciliation.

- If such a rapid withdrawal were to take place, we judge that the ISF would be unlikely to survive as a non-sectarian national institution; neighboring countries—invited by Iraqi factions or unilaterally—might intervene openly in the conflict; massive civilian casualties and forced population displacement would be probable; AQI would attempt to use parts of the country—particularly al-Anbar province—to plan increased attacks in and outside of Iraq; and spiraling violence and political disarray in Iraq, along with Kurdish moves to control Kirkuk and strengthen autonomy, could prompt Turkey to launch a military incursion.

A number of identifiable developments *could* help to reverse the negative trends driving Iraq's current trajectory. They include:

- *Broader Sunni acceptance of the current political structure and federalism* to begin to reduce one of the major sources of Iraq's instability.
- *Significant concessions by Shia and Kurds* to create space for Sunni acceptance of federalism.
- *A bottom-up approach*—deputizing, resourcing, and working more directly with neighborhood watch groups and establishing grievance committees— to help mend frayed relationships between tribal and religious groups, which have been mobilized into communal warfare over the past three years.

A key enabler for all of these steps would be stronger Iraqi leadership, which could enhance the positive impact of all the above developments.

Iraq's neighbors influence, and are influenced by, events within Iraq, but the involvement of these outside actors is not likely to be a major driver of violence or the prospects for stability because of the self-sustaining character of Iraq's internal sectarian dynamics. Nonetheless, Iranian lethal support for select groups of Iraqi Shia militants clearly intensifies the conflict in Iraq. Syria continues to provide safehaven for expatriate Iraqi Bathists and to take less than adequate measures to stop the flow of foreign jihadists into Iraq. . . .

A number of identifiable internal security and political triggering events, including sustained mass sectarian killings, assassination of major religious and political leaders, and a complete Sunni defection from the government have the potential to convulse severely Iraq's security environment. Should these events take place, they could spark an abrupt increase in communal and insurgent violence and shift Iraq's trajectory from gradual decline to rapid deterioration with grave humanitarian, political, and security consequences. Three prospective security paths might then emerge:

- *Chaos Leading to Partition.* With a rapid deterioration in the capacity of Iraq's central government to function, security services and other aspects of sovereignty would collapse. Resulting widespread fighting could produce *de facto* partition, dividing Iraq into three mutually antagonistic parts. Collapse of this magnitude would generate fierce violence for at least several years, ranging well beyond the time frame of this Estimate, before settling into a partially stable end-state.
- *Emergence of a Shia Strongman.* Instead of a disintegrating central government producing partition, a security implosion could lead Iraq's potentially most powerful group, the Shia, to assert its latent strength.
- *Anarchic Fragmentation of Power.* The emergence of a checkered pattern of local control would present the greatest potential for instability, mixing extreme ethno-sectarian violence with debilitating intra-group clashes.

- **Source:** *Prospects for Iraq's Stability: A Challenging Road Ahead* (Washington, DC: NIC, 2007).
- **Analysis:** Conditions in Iraq had deteriorated to the point where a de facto partition of the country seemed possible, perhaps even likely. Shi'a and Sunni communities battled one another while they fought the United States and its allies. The Kurds feared any government dominated by either group. Complete partition would create three weak states in a volatile region of the world. Federation with local autonomy for the country's three main groups made sense but was hard to achieve. The Shi'a majority, long dominated by the Sunnis, believed their time to rule had come. The Sunnis resented loss of their traditional status and power, and the Kurds had been quasi-independent, thanks to a U.S.-enforced no-fly zone in place over their territory since 1991. As the report indicated, effective government required compromises by all three parties.

DID YOU KNOW?

L. Paul Bremer III

L. Paul ("Jerry") Bremer III (b. 1941) served as special envoy and head of the Coalition Provisional Administration of President George W. Bush from May 2003 to June 2004. Prior to serving in Iraq, Bremer held junior appointments in the State Department during the administration of Richard Nixon and more senior positions under President Ronald Reagan, including ambassador at large for counterterrorism. He also had extensive experience in the private sector. During his time in Baghdad, chronicled in his memoir *My Year in Iraq*, Bremer functioned as de facto president of the country. Bremer made many controversial decisions, none more so than de-Ba'athification and disbanding the Iraqi military.

- **Document 57: Excerpt of Transcript of Videoconference Briefing on Iraqi Reconstruction by L. Paul Bremer III**
- **When:** June 12, 2003
- **Where:** Baghdad
- **Significance:** The head of the coalition provisional authority commented on the deteriorating security situation.

Q: . . . Ambassador Bremer, Martha Raddatz from ABC News. Can you talk about what sort of organized resistance you're seeing in Iraq, how large that resistance is, and who you believe is behind it?

Bremer: Yes. We are certainly seeing some organized resistance, particularly in the area west of Baghdad and the area north of Baghdad. Now, I want to qualify that by saying we do not see signs of central command and control direction in that resistance at this point. That is to say, these are groups that are organized, but they're small; they may be five or six men conducting isolated attacks against our soldiers.

We are clearly on the lookout to see if this evolves into a more organized, more broadly and centrally directed resistance. But for the time being, it appears that these are small groups, usually Ba'athists or Fedayeen Saddam; in some cases they may be officers of the Republican Guard. And we are going to have to continue to deal with them in a military fashion, as we are now doing.

Q: They are small groups of five or six men. Are these small groups of five or six men connected in a larger way?

Bremer: Well, that's what I meant by saying we don't yet have evidence of central command and control. They look to be groups who have spontaneously come together and are attacking us. They may be colleagues from the Ba'ath movement, they could be several people from the Fedayeen Saddam or from the Republican Guards. But we do not at the moment see evidence of central command control of these groups. I certainly wouldn't exclude it, but we don't have the evidence yet.

Q: There's no evidence that Saddam Hussein is directing any of it?

Bremer: No. . . .

Q: Ambassador, Bret Baier with Fox News Channel. I have two questions, and I'll ask them separately, if I may.

First, you've said that you believe the attacks on U.S. troops are from Ba'ath Party loyalists, Fedayeen Saddam and Iraqi Republican Guards that may have been sticking around. Within the last 24 hours there's been this strike on what CENTCOM calls a terrorist training camp in the West. Any new information about that and possibly that foreign fighters have been involved in attacks on U.S. forces? That's my first question.

Bremer: Well, it's really not appropriate for me to comment on ongoing military operations. We have had in the past some evidence of extremist operations, some of which might be classified as terrorist, in Iraq. We do have clear evidence of some Sunni extremism in the area to the west of Baghdad. Whether that turns out to have been involved in the operation you're talking about is a matter still, I think, to be determined.

And we do have clear evidence of Iranian interference in the affairs of Iraq. Of course, Iran is still—correctly, in my view—identified as the world's leading sponsor of terrorism. There was an Ansar al-Islam terrorist camp, as you will remember, at the beginning of the war, in the North. We are very attentive to the possibility of those people flowing back into Iraq, and we'll obviously take the appropriate steps if we get evidence that that's happening.

- **Source:** "Briefing on Coalition Post-war Reconstruction and Stabilization Efforts," June 12, 2003, available at http://www.defenselink.mil/transcripts/transcript.aspx?transcriptid=2737, accessed June 16, 2008.
- **Analysis:** Ambassador Bremer's remarks are noteworthy for what they did not say. While he recognized the violence going on in Iraq, he failed to understand fully who perpetrated it. Former Ba'ath Party members and foreign fighters did join the fray, but the Shi'a and Sunni insurgencies involved many more local people angry over the occupation and frustrated with a standard of living and services that had fallen below what Saddam Hussein had provided.

- **Document 58:** Excerpt of Transcript of Videoconference with General Raymond Odierno, Commander, Fourth Infantry Division
- **When:** June 18, 2003
- **Where:** Baghdad
- **Significance:** General Odierno dismissed growing insurgent violence as disorganized and of no military significance.

Q: Martha Raddatz from ABC News. Could you give us more information on the resistance you're facing? You're saying you're facing almost daily contact with paramilitaries, Fedayeen Saddam. How big a problem is this? If you can quantify it in any way about how much resistance you're getting; how many more people are out there who you believe are resisting? And also, if you could give us more detail about these new groups—I believe you said Snake Party and New Return—how they formed, and how big they are and where they are?

Odierno: We are seeing military activity throughout our zone. But I really qualify it as militarily insignificant. They are very small, they are very random, they are very ineffective. I believe there's three groups out there right now. Basically, there is a group of ex-Saddam Ba'ath Party loyalists. In addition, there are some Islamic fundamentalists. And then there are just some plain Iraqis who are poor and are being paid to attack U.S. forces. All of these attacks are uncoordinated. They are very ineffective and, in my mind, really do not have much effect on U.S. forces.

And if you are—on a daily basis, you will see that 99 percent of the area is free, clear, and the citizens go about every day, doing their business, without interruption.

Q: If I could, the military insignificance—I believe 11 soldiers have been killed in the last three weeks. So clearly they're having a rather profound effect.

And also, you talk about them not being organized, and yet you say they're just plain Iraqis who are being paid. Who's paying them, if they're not organized?

Odierno: My guess is, they're being paid by ex-Ba'ath Party loyalists, who are paying people to kill Americans.

And I want to make sure—first, I want to comment on the 11 individuals that have been killed. I will never downplay Americans being killed in combat. It is a very significant sacrifice, especially for their families. And that is significant to an individual's family, and I would never say anything different from that.

But from a military perspective, it is insignificant. They're having no impact on the way we conduct business on a day-to-day basis in Iraq.

- **Source:** "Maj. Gen. Odierno Videoteleconference from Baghdad," June 18, 2003, http://www.defenselink.mil/transcripts/transcript.aspx ?transcriptid=2757, accessed June 16, 2008.

- **Analysis:** General Odierno's comments reveal how little the United States understood about the deteriorating security situation. His insistence that attacks were the work of disgruntled holdouts from Saddam's regime was less a conclusion based on evidence than a political mantra of the Bush administration. Odierno dismissed the violence as "militarily insignificant" when in fact it showed signs of escalating. One of the reporters pointed out the profound contradiction in his statement. How could a weak and disorganized insurgency deploy paid fighters with such deadly effect? Failure to take the insurgent threat seriously delayed development of an effective COIN campaign.

- **Document 59:** Excerpt of Department of Defense Briefing by General Richard Myers, Chairman of the Joint Chiefs of Staff, and Secretary of Defense Donald Rumsfeld
- **When:** June 24, 2003
- **Where:** Washington, DC
- **Significance:** The Pentagon continued to deny the existence of an insurgency.

Q: Oh, General Myers, then. General Myers, you've said that U.S. troops are having considerable success inside Iraq. Yet in the past 24 hours, there were 25 separate attacks against U.S. forces, six Brits were killed in two separate attacks down near Basra, and there was a rocket attack on the civilian mayor's office at Fallujah. That doesn't sound like success. Do you—can you tell us what the U.S. military thinks is happening? Is there an increase in the tempo of attacks? Are they better coordinated today, those conducting the attacks? Or is there a change in their strategy?

Myers: First of all, as we look at this, we look at trends, of course. And—but you've got to be careful of the snapshots you take. And there has been a lot of action lately, a lot of it instigated, as I was talking about in my remarks—a lot of it instigated by coalition forces.

I think the basic analysis, notwithstanding what happened in the last 24 hours or 48 hours, is that the security situation is a little uneven in the country in the north and the south, relatively secure in the Sunni area, central-west and northwest of Baghdad, where you have the biggest issues. I think it's undetermined at this point how coordinated these efforts are. We know that there are Ba'ath Party members that don't want this country to go to a democratic form of government that they don't want. They prefer to return to the old ways. And so, they are still out there. There are other paramilitaries, probably, that have joined them. How organized is yet to be determined, and that's one of the things, of course, we've got intel—intelligence looking at.

Q: We were told last week it was not organized by General Odierno of the 4th Infantry Division. Now, you're saying it's uncertain?

Myers: I'd say at this point, it's uncertain. That's right. I mean, things—you can expect things to change on the ground over there, and they may be changing. But I can't—it's hard to say one way or the other at this point.

Rumsfeld: The other reason you may be able to find a seam between what the general said and what Dick Myers said is because he may be referring to a certain area.

Q: Well, his area's the size of West Virginia.

Rumsfeld: I understand. That does not naysay what I just said to you. People may—you may see things that appear to be coordinated in a particular area that are not coordinated throughout the entire country, which is a country the size of California.

- **Source:** "DoD News Briefing—Secretary Rumsfeld and Gen. Myers," June 24, 2003, http://www.defenselink.mil/transcripts/transcript.aspx?transcriptid=2760, accessed June 16, 2008.
- **Analysis:** Reporters continued to challenge assertions that the mounting violence in Iraq was the sporadic work of disorganized regime holdouts. The Pentagon adamantly refused to accept clear and mounting evidence of a complex insurgency developing in the country. In this briefing Rumsfeld and Myers deflected questions by insisting that the pattern of violence was uneven, with most areas remaining peaceful.

- **Document 60:** Excerpt of Presidential Press Conference
- **When:** July 2, 2003
- **Where:** Washington, DC
- **Significance:** Asked about those who attacked Americans in Iraq, President Bush made his famous "bring them on" challenge.

Q: Mr. President, a posse of small nations—like the Ukraine and Poland—are materializing to help keep the peace in Iraq. But with the attacks on U.S. forces and the casualty rates rising, what is the administration doing to get larger powers, like France and Germany and Russia, to join the American occupation there?

THE PRESIDENT: Well, first of all, we'll put together a force structure who meets the threats on the ground. And we've got a lot of forces there, ourselves. And as I said yesterday, anybody who wants to harm American troops will be found and brought to justice. There are some who feel like that if they attack us that we may decide to leave prematurely. They don't understand what they're talking about, if that's the case.

Let me finish. There are some who feel like—that the conditions are such that they can attack us there. My answer is, bring them on. We've got the force necessary to deal with the security situation. Of course we want other countries to help us— Great Britain is there, Poland is there, Ukraine is there, you mentioned. Anybody who wants to help, we'll welcome the help. But we've got plenty tough force there right now to make sure the situation is secure. We always welcome help. We're always glad to include others in. But make no mistake about it—and the enemy shouldn't make any mistake about it—we will deal with them harshly if they continue to try to bring harm to the Iraqi people.

I also said yesterday an important point, that those who blow up the electricity lines really aren't hurting America, they're hurting the Iraq citizens; their own fellow citizens are being hurt. But we will deal with them harshly, as well.

- **Source:** Presidential press conference, July 2, 2003, http://www. whitehouse.gov/news/releases/2003/07/20030702-3.html, June 16, 2008.
- **Analysis:** Unlike the invasion of Afghanistan, Operation Iraqi Freedom lacked a UN mandate and NATO approval. Consequently, many of the allies that backed the United States in Afghanistan declined to join the coalition in Iraq. The president assured the American people that while he welcomed allies, the United States had plenty of troops to deal with internal security in Iraq. He insisted that attacks would not force the United States to withdraw. His "bring them on" remark would prove to be bitterly ironic and provide grist for the insurgents' propaganda mill.

- **Document 61: Excerpt of Statement of General Tommy Franks to Congress**
- **When:** July 9, 2003
- **Where:** Washington, DC
- **Significance:** Like Myers and Rumsfeld, General Franks refused to acknowledge the deteriorating security situation.

Although security continues to improve, portions of Iraq are now, and will remain for some time, dangerous. The term "stability operations" does not infer that combat actions have ended. Military forces are still required to set conditions that enable progress. As we move forward, the composition and size of our forces will change to match emerging requirements. Factors that influence our force mix will include Coalition force contributions, threat, and success in fielding Iraqi police forces, security, and the New Iraqi Army.

Integration of Coalition forces is a major near-term effort. The United Kingdom and Poland are committed to leading Divisions in Southern Iraq, and many partner nations have offered forces to fill those units. Deployment of those forces has already begun. We continue discussions with India and Pakistan. At this moment, 19 Coalition partners are on the ground in support of military operations in Iraq, with deployment pending for 19 additional countries. An additional 11 nations are conducting military to military discussions with respect to possibly deploying forces to Iraq in support of stability and security operations.

At this point some 35,000 police have been hired. This fills about half of the requirement nationwide. Throughout the country, many of these law enforcement officers are conducting joint patrols with U.S. military forces, and we will ultimately transition responsibility for security and stability to the Iraqis. In the near-term, we must build upon the momentum we have generated in this area. Creation of the New Iraqi Army is moving forward. The plan envisions three divisions located near Mosul, Baghdad, and Basrah to provide territorial defense and conduct stability operations. In the first year, the goal is to field approximately nine battalions. Initially, Iraqi forces will focus on performing security functions at fixed sites, convoy security, and border control. As it develops, this force will work with Coalition forces to contribute to stability and security throughout Iraq.

Underlying all security functions is the need to continue humanitarian assistance and the conduct of civil-military operations to improve the quality of life for the Iraqi people. In this regard, our regional allies have been invaluable. Neighboring nations have provided hospitals, medical supplies, water, food, and expertise in beginning the rebuilding process. The fact that there has been no humanitarian disaster in Iraq; no widespread outbreak of disease, hunger, refugees or displaced persons; or any of the other predicted consequences of war is due, in large part, to the generosity of our allies. The CPA and Coalition forces will continue to work in concert with international and non-governmental agencies to reverse the result of years of neglect by a brutal regime.

- **Source:** Statement of General Tommy R. Franks to Senate Committee on Foreign Relations, July 9, 2003.
- **Analysis:** The retiring commander of the U.S. Central Command pointed to continued progress in Iraq. While he recognized the continued need for a stability operation, Franks emphasized that instability was confined to specific areas. He did not acknowledge the deteriorating security situation or mention the word *insurgency*. He did, however, note the need for increased policing. Finally, Franks emphasized that Iraq's problems resulted from years of neglect and brutality by the regime of Saddam Hussein. He did not admit any deleterious effect of U.S. actions.

- **Document 62: Excerpt of Presidential Statement on Progress in Iraq**
- **When:** July 23, 2003
- **Where:** Washington, DC
- **Significance:** The president continued to blame the violence on regime holdouts, whom he said would soon be eliminated.

Saddam Hussein's regime spent more than three decades oppressing Iraq's people, attacking Iraq's neighbors, and threatening the world's peace. The regime tortured at home, promoted terror abroad, and armed in secret. Now, with the regime of Saddam Hussein gone forever, a few remaining holdouts are trying to prevent the advance of order and freedom. They are targeting our success in rebuilding Iraq, they're killing new police graduates, they're shooting at people that are guarding the universities and power plants and oil facilities.

These killers are the enemies of Iraq's people. They operate mainly in a few areas of the country. And wherever they operate, they are being hunted, and they will be defeated. Our military forces are on the offensive. They're working with the newly free Iraqi people to destroy the remnants of the old regime and their terrorist allies.

Yesterday, in the city of Mosul, the careers of two of the regime's chief henchmen came to an end. Saddam Hussein's sons were responsible for torture, maiming and murder of countless Iraqis. Now, more than ever, all Iraqis can know that the former regime is gone and will not be coming back.

- **Source:** President's remarks during visit of L. Paul Bremer, July 23, 2003, http://www.whitehouse.gov/news/releases/2003/07/20030723-1 .html, accessed June 16, 2008.
- **Analysis:** Despite mounting casualties and growing evidence of a complex insurgency, the president insisted that regime holdouts perpetrated the violence. He also claimed that they operated "mainly in a few areas of the country," neglecting to point out that these areas were

the most heavily populated. Coalition forces, he maintained, remained on the offensive and would soon kill or capture the remaining malcontents. The president pointed to the recent operation that killed Saddam Hussein's two sons as a case in point.

MAKING A BAD SITUATION WORSE

Failure to understand and acknowledge the nature of the threat made it difficult for the United States to develop an effective strategy for restoring order and providing security to the Iraqi people. U.S. forces compounded this mistake with errors of commission, actions that antagonized locals and exacerbated the deteriorating security situation. These failures included administrative decisions by the CPA, mistreatment of Iraqis, and the overreliance on firepower to which conventional armies are prone. These mistakes contributed to a legacy of bitterness and resentment U.S. forces struggled to live down.

- **Document 63: Excerpt of CPA Order Number 1: De-Ba'athification of Iraqi Society**
- **When:** May 16, 2003
- **Where:** Baghdad
- **Significance:** Head of the CPA L. Paul Bremer removed Ba'ath party members from positions in government and banned them from holding future office.

Pursuant to my authority as Administrator of the Coalition Provisional Authority (CPA), relevant U.N. Security Council resolutions, and the laws and usages of war,

Recognizing that the Iraqi people have suffered large scale human rights abuses and depravations over many years at the hands of the Ba'ath Party,

Noting the grave concern of Iraqi society regarding the threat posed by the continuation of Ba'ath Party networks and personnel in the administration of Iraq, and the intimidation of the people of Iraq by Ba'ath Party officials,

Concerned by the continuing threat to the security of the Coalition Forces posed by the Iraqi Ba'ath Party, I hereby promulgate the following:

Section 1

Disestablishment of the Ba'ath Party

1) On April 16, 2003 the Coalition Provisional Authority disestablished the Ba'ath Party of Iraq. This order implements the declaration by eliminating the party's structures and removing its leadership from positions of authority and

responsibility in Iraqi society. By this means, the Coalition Provisional Authority will ensure that representative government in Iraq is not threatened by Ba'athist elements returning to power and that those in positions of authority in the future are acceptable to the people of Iraq.

2) Full members of the Ba'ath Party holding the ranks of 'Udw Qutriyya (Regional Command Member), 'Udw Far' (Branch Member). 'Udw Shu'bah (Section Member), and 'Udw Firqah (Group Member) (together, "Senior Party Members") are herby removed from their positions and banned from future employment in the public sector. These Senior Party Members shall be evaluated for criminal conduct or threat to the security of the Coalition. Those suspected of criminal conduct shall be investigated and, if deemed a threat to security or a flight risk, detained or placed under house arrest.

3) Individuals holding positions in the top three layers of management in every national government ministry, affiliated corporations and other government institutions (e.g., universities and hospitals) shall be interviewed for possible affiliation with the Ba'ath Party, and subject to investigation for criminal conduct and risk to security. Any such persons detained to be full members of the Ba'ath Party shall be removed from their employment.

- **Source:** "Coalition Provisional Authority Order Number 1: De-Ba'athification of Iraqi Society," May 16, 2003, available at http://www.iraqcoalition.org/regulations/20030516_CPAORD_1_De-Ba_athification_of_Iraqi_Society_.pdf, accessed June 18, 2008.

- **Analysis:** De-Ba'athification was the most controversial decision made by Bremer. With a single stroke of the pen he removed thousands of Iraqis from their posts, depriving them of their livelihoods and turning potential allies into implacable enemies willing to back the insurgents. The CPA failed to understand that most people joined the Ba'ath Party for the same reason most Soviet citizens joined the Communist one. Hope of economic and social advantage rather than ideological conviction motivated them. Had the newly independent countries of Central and Eastern Europe excluded former communists from government, they would have had few people qualified to run departments and agencies. Iraq faced the same problem.

  The error of de-Ba'athification soon became obvious as it contributed directly to the escalating violence. Controversy still surrounds who exactly authorized the order. Some argue that Bremer acted on his own initiative. Others maintain he merely implemented White House policy.

- **Document 64: Excerpt of Coalition Provisional Order Number 2**
- **When:** May 23, 2003

- **Where:** Baghdad
- **Significance:** Bremer dissolved the Iraqi military without paying them.

Pursuant to my authority as Administrator of the Coalition Provisional Authority (CPA), relevant U.N. Security Council resolutions, including Resolution 1483 (2003), and the laws and usages of war,

Reconfirming all of the provisions of General Franks' Freedom Message to the Iraqi People of April 16, 2003,

Recognizing that the prior Iraqi regime used certain government entities to oppress the Iraqi people and as instruments of torture, repression and corruption,

Reaffirming the Instructions to the Citizens of Iraq regarding Ministry of Youth and Sport of May 8, 2003,

I hereby promulgate the following:

Section 1

Dissolved Entities

The entities (the "Dissolved Entities") listed in the attached Annex are hereby dissolved. Additional entities may be added to this list in the future.

Section 2

Assets and Financial Obligations

1) All assets, including records and data, in whatever form maintained and wherever located, of the Dissolved Entities shall be held by the Administrator of the CPA ("the Administrator") on behalf of and for the benefit of the Iraqi people and shall be used to assist the Iraqi people and to support the recovery of Iraq.

2) All financial obligations of the Dissolved Entities are suspended. The Administrator of the CPA will establish procedures whereby persons claiming to be the beneficiaries of such obligations may apply for payment.

3) Persons in possession of assets of the Dissolved Entities shall preserve those assets, promptly inform local Coalition authorities, and immediately turn them over, as directed by those authorities. Continued possession, transfer, sale, use, conversion, or concealment of such assets following the date of this Order is prohibited and may be punished.

Section 3

Employees and Service Members

1) Any military or other rank, title, or status granted to a former employee or functionary of a Dissolved Entity by the former Regime is hereby cancelled.

2) All conscripts are released from their service obligations. Conscription is suspended indefinitely, subject to decisions by future Iraq governments concerning whether a free Iraq should have conscription.

3) Any person employed by a Dissolved Entity in any form or capacity, is dismissed effective as of April 16, 2003. Any person employed by a Dissolved Entity, in any form or capacity remains accountable for acts committed during such employment.

4) A termination payment in an amount to be determined by the Administrator will be paid to employees so dismissed, except those who are Senior Party Members as defined in the Administrator's May 16, 2003 Order of the Coalition Provisional Authority De-Ba'athification of Iraqi Society, CPA/ORD/2003/01 ("Senior Party Members") (See Section 3.6).

5) Pensions being paid by, or on account of service to, a Dissolved Entity before April 16, 2003 will continue to be paid, including to war widows and disabled veterans, provided that no pension payments will be made to any person who is a Senior Party Member (see Section 3.6) and that the power is reserved to the Administrator and to future Iraqi governments to revoke or reduce pensions as a penalty for past or future illegal conduct or to modify pension arrangements to eliminate improper privileges granted by the Ba'athist regime or for similar reasons.

6) Notwithstanding any provision of this Order, or any other Order, law, or regulation, and consistent with the Administrator's May 16, 2003 Order of the Coalition Provisional Authority De-Ba'athification of Iraqi Society, no payment, including a termination or pension payment, will be made to any person who is or was a Senior Party Member. Any person holding the rank under the former regime of Colonel or above, or its equivalent, will be deemed a Senior Party Member, provided that such persons may seek, under procedures to be prescribed, to establish to the satisfaction of the Administrator, that they were not a Senior Party Member.

- **Source:** "Coalition Provisional Authority Order Number 2: Dissolution of Entities," May 23, 2003, available at http://www.iraqcoalition .org/regulations/20030823_CPAORD_2_Dissolution_of_Entities_with _Annex_A.pdf, accessed June 16, 2008.

- **Analysis:** Almost as damaging as de-Ba'athification, the decision to disband the Iraqi armed forces contributed significantly to the growing insurgency. Prior to and during the invasion, the coalition urged Iraqi forces not to resist, promising that they would be looked after. Many simply abandoned their units, returning home with their weapons. Not only were they not recalled, but they received no compensation, being left to fend for themselves in a country with 60+ percent unemployment. Some of these disgruntled veterans supported or even joined the insurgency.

- **Document 65: Excerpt of "The Insurgency," Multinational Forces Iraq Report**
- **When:** August 20, 2007
- **Where:** Baghdad

- **Significance:** This report revealed the nature of what analysts now called a "complex insurgency."

The Insurgency

The insurgency in Iraq consists of myriad anti-Iraqi Forces and their supporters who are engaged in guerilla warfare against Coalition and Iraqi security forces and use terrorism to strike fear in the Iraqi populace. Their tactics include, but are not limited to, suicide bombings, improvised explosive device attacks, kidnapping, rudimentary sniper techniques, mortar attack, rocket attacks, and murder.

Insurgent activity is centered in the Sunni-dominated parts of Iraq, primarily the areas to the northwest of Baghdad and between the cities of Tikrit, Ramadi, Samarra and Fallujah. Sunni Arabs, including Ba'athist and former elements of Saddam Hussein's regime, Saddamists, sometimes collaborate with international Sunni Arab terrorist networks, providing funds and guidance across family, tribal, religious and peer group lines. The foreigners include jihadists led by Abu Musab al-Zarqawi's terrorist network, al-Qaida in Iraq, AQI. Together, these groups work to perpetuate a reign of terror designed to breed havoc in Iraq.

Some of these anti-government elements are clearly groups drawn from the former regime, the Ba'th Party, the paramilitary Fedayeen, and the Republican Guard. Some are anti-Saddam nationalist groups with no desire to see Saddam restored but resentful of U.S. and Western presence; others are Islamist groups, some members of which have been trained overseas or are foreign nationals, the latter including Syrians, Saudis, Yemenis, and Sudanese. Some activities have been the work of criminals or criminal organizations, large numbers of criminals being released at the end of the war and some certainly hiring themselves out for attacks on Coalition forces.

Other Iraqi jihadists groups are active, notably Ansar al-Sunnah, which operates primarily in Kurdish-dominated northern Iraq. The foreign jihadists enter Iraq from Saudi Arabia, Syria, Jordan, and Iran.

Most of the victims of jihadists suicide bombings have been civilians, innocent bystanders. This has been especially true since Coalition and Iraqi security forces developed tactics and deployed better equipment to protect themselves from the attacks. Among the Sunnis, a variety of groups have been identified. They are united only in the sense of having what have been called "negative" goals in opposition to U.S. presence; in seeking some return to the former status quo in which the Sunni minority have exercised power since the Ottoman period.

There are also armed militias attached to the two main Shiite political parties, the Supreme Council for the Islamic Revolution in Iraq and al-Dawa, and there is clearly potential for Shiite participation in violence. The pattern of Iraqi activity thus far looks remarkably similar to that in Palestine with roadside bombs, which have also been used by Hezbollah in Lebanon, and other so-called improvised explosive devices; ambushes of soft-skinned vehicles; opportunistic rocket-propelled grenade and shooting attacks on military personnel; attacks on civilian members of the Coalition authorities and foreign personnel working in some way for the Coalition; attacks on Iraqi "collaborators," most recently police and army recruits, and attacks on economic targets such as power stations, oil installations, and pipelines. There has also been an increase in the number of attacks upon "soft" targets, principally civilian gatherings.

Terrorist Organizations

Al-Qaeda Organization in the Land of the Two Rivers

Mujahideen Shura Council

Ansar al-Sunnah

Islamic Army in Iraq

Although some named terrorist groups operate in Iraq, these categories are constantly shifting. The following is a brief introduction to some of the most well-known terrorist groups in Iraq.

A. al-Qaida Organization in the Land of the Two Rivers

(al-Qaida in Iraq—AQI)

Al-Qaida Organization in the Land of the Two Rivers (AQI) is the name of the terrorist group led by Abu Musab al-Zarqawi before being killed in a coalition forces airstrike on June 7, 2006.

Abu Ayyub al-Masri replaced al-Zarqawi as leader of the group whose name implies that they consider themselves as the center of Jihadist activities in Iraq.

The goals of this group are to overthrow the Iraqi government and establish an Islamic state in Iraq by forcing out the U.S.-led coalition. Elements of the Kurdish Islamist group Ansar al-Islam, and indigenous Sunni Iraqis form the ranks of this group.

AQI has issued claims of responsibility in Iraq for attacks on American and Iraqi security forces, often claiming several attacks in one day. The group uses a variety of tactics that include RPG attacks against armored vehicles, guerilla style attacks by armed militants, suicide bombings, and the kidnapping and beheadings of foreigners.

Al-Qaida in the land of the Two Rivers, which is believed to derive most of its domestic support from Sunni Arabs, has focused on attacking Shiite Arabs and the fledgling Iraqi police force. This group is blamed for the bombing of a Shia shrine in Samarra in February of 2006 and June of 2007, which set off a series of deadly reprisal killings between Sunnis and Shias.

In addition to these frequent smaller scale attacks in Iraq, the group claimed responsibility for the bombing of three hotels in Amman, Jordan that left 67 people dead and injured more than 150.

In January 2006, the group was one of six insurgent organizations to unify under the Mujahideen Shura Council. As of now, all attacks perpetrated by al-Qaida in Iraq are claimed in the name of the Council.

B. Mujahideen Shura Council

The Mujahideen Shura Council, "Freedom Fighter Consultation Council," is an umbrella organization made up of several terrorist groups in Iraq, including AQI.

The Mujahideen Shura Council first appeared in spring 2005 when it claimed the kidnapping of Australian citizen Douglas Wood. Wood was a contractor with the American firm Bechtel. The group demanded the departure of all foreign forces in

Iraq. Wood was freed by Iraqi forces in an operation in June 2005 after being held several weeks.

Despite the high-profile nature of this incident, the Council did not claim responsibility for any more attacks for several months.

In January 2006, several Sunni insurgent groups announced that they were joining to form the Mujahideen Shura Council. They claimed to unite in order to continue the struggle and force out the "invading infidels." The groups that formed the council included: al-Qaida Organization in the Land of the Two Rivers, Jaish al-Taifa al-Mansoura, al-Ahwal Brigades, Islamic Jihad Brigades, al-Ghuraba Brigades, and Saraya Ansar al-Tawhid.

The idea of the Council is to unify insurgent efforts in Iraq against government and Coalition forces. It may also be an attempt to mend a rift between various Sunni insurgent groups. But it is clearly an attempt to unify disparate groups with a radical Sunni ideology driven to destroy the Iraqi government and its international support.

The formation of the Council is also possibly to shore up support for the insurgency by distancing itself from the extremely violent tactics and targeting of innocent Iraqis by al-Qaida. The Council allows AQI to continue its methods without claiming direct responsibility. It is now the organization claiming attacks by its member factions. Thus, the goals of the Council and its members are the same: the removal of U.S. troops from Iraq and the formation of an Islamic government in place of the current government.

C. Ansar al-Sunnah

Ansar al-Sunnah ("Followers of the Tradition") is a group of Iraqi Jihadists attempting to establish an Islamic state with Shariah law in Iraq. They aim to achieve this by defeating Coalition Forces in the country. To them, Jihad in Iraq is obligatory for all Muslims, and anyone opposed to Jihad is their enemy. The group's membership is varied, but includes radical Kurds in the Ansar al-Islam, foreign al-Qaida and other Sunni terrorists.

The Ansar al-Sunnah has targeted coalition military, Iraqi soldiers and governmental institutions, and other political establishments in Iraq which the group treats as puppet regimes of American occupation. The group claims many attacks, many of which are unsubstantiated.

Ansar al-Sunnah has reportedly teamed up with the banned Arab Socialist Ba'ath Party and AQI where they pledge to continue and increase attacks on the coalition and Iraqi government forces.

D. Islamic Army in Iraq

The Islamic Army in Iraq, IAI, conducts a brutally violent campaign against foreigners within Iraq, specifically anyone believed to be cooperating with the U.S.-led coalition. IAI has been implicated in several gruesome beheading deaths. The terrorist group aims to drive all U.S. and related Coalition forces, both military and civilian, from Iraq. But IAI does not limit its attacks to just these groups; it has also murdered French journalists, Pakistani contractors, an Italian journalist, and Macedonian citizens working for a U.S. company.

In the past, IAI has kidnapped individuals or groups of people and then made demands impossible to meet. Frequently, these demands are indirectly related to the kidnapping victims. For example, IAI captured Enzo Baldoni, an Italian journalist who also volunteered for the Red Cross in Iraq. IAI demanded that Italy withdraw all troops from Iraq or Enzo Baldoni, both an independent journalist and humanitarian volunteer, would be killed. Italy did not recall its troops and Baldoni was murdered. This is a common tactic of IAI. The Islamic Army in Iraq has also attacked French civilians in retaliation for France's law regarding headscarves in schools. IAI does not limit its terrorist attacks to non-Iraqis; the group has also executed Iraqi people who join Iraq's police and military services.

According to old statements by the leader of the Islamic Army in Iraq, the group has thousands of terrorists in its ranks. The group's leader also claims that the group is predominantly Iraqi, not foreign-born. Statements released in November 2004 announced that the Islamic Army in Iraq has collaborated with Ansar al-Sunnah and AQI.

- **Source:** "The Insurgency," August 20, 2007, available at http://www.mnf-iraq.com/index.php?option=com_content&task=view&id=729&Itemid=45, accessed June 18, 2008.

- **Analysis:** Written at the height of the insurgency, this report revealed what was just beginning to develop during the summer of 2003. Its conclusions reveal the absurdity of viewing the escalating violence as the work of holdouts from Saddam's regime who refused to accept that they had lost. While no one could have easily grasped the full extent of the growing resistance during the early days of the occupation (al-Qaeda in Iraq had not even formed yet), its outlines were becoming increasingly clear. The experience of Afghanistan following the 1979 Soviet invasion should have provided clues for what to expect. Foreign *mujahedeen*, some funded by the United States, poured into the country to oppose what they saw as an attack upon a Muslim community.

- **Document 66: Excerpt of "Terrorist Tactics," Multinational Forces Iraq Report**
- **When:** January 3, 2007
- **Where:** Baghdad
- **Significance:** This report revealed the tactics used by insurgents against coalition forces and Iraqi citizens.

Iraqi guerilla attacks against Multi-National Force— Iraq, Iraqi government and commercial targets typically take the following forms:

- Attacks on convoys and patrols using improvised explosive devices
- Ambushes on Coalition forces with small arms and/or rocket propelled grenade fire and hit-and-run mortar strikes on Iraqi government, Iraqi security forces, and MNF-I bases are also common.

- Sabotage of oil pipelines and other infrastructure is another tactic often used
- Assassination of Iraqis cooperating with the Coalition forces and Iraqi government
- Suicide bombings targeting international organizations, Coalition forces, Iraqi police, hotels, etc.
- Kidnapping and murder of private contractors working in Iraq for Iraqi government, MNF-I, or for commercial entities.
- Kidnapping private Iraqi citizens as a fundraising tactic.

Improvised Explosive Devices

The majority of insurgent attacks come in the form

> **DID YOU KNOW?**
>
> **Improvised Explosive Devices (IEDs)**
>
> IEDs are homemade bombs used with devastating effect in Iraq. The insurgents often used ordinance (e.g., artillery shells) rigged with a variety of detonators and placed along roads to destroy convoy vehicles or along the paths of foot patrols to kill soldiers. IEDs range from the very primitive to the very sophisticated, using a variety of explosives and detonators. Iraqi insurgents also used IEDs for propaganda purposes, filming attacks and posting the videos on the Internet to gain support for the insurgency.

of IEDs targeting Iraqi and Coalition convoys and patrols. Most IEDs are made from leftover munitions and foreign explosive materials which are often hastily put together. Vehicle borne IEDs, VBIEDs, are devices that use a vehicle as the package or container of the device. These IEDs come in all shapes and sizes, from small sedans to large cargo trucks. There have even been instances of what appeared to be generators, donkey-drawn carts, and ambulances used to attempt attacks on Coalition forces and the new Iraqi government.

With high levels of sectarian violence in 2006, suicide bombs and VBIEDs, car bombs, are increasingly targeting Iraqi civilians.

The Internet and Psychological Warfare

Terrorism has often been conceptualized as a form of psychological warfare, and terrorists have certainly sought to wage such a campaign through the Internet. There are several ways for terrorists to do so. They can use the Internet to spread disinformation, to deliver threats intended to distill fear and helplessness, and to disseminate horrific images of recent actions, such as beheadings of foreign hostages in Iraq. The insurgents and terrorists in Iraq wage battles with traditional guerilla means as well as by employing psychological warfare on the Internet. Many terrorist groups use message boards, online chat, and religious justifications for their activities. Sites also often provide histories of their host organizations and activities.

- **Source:** "Terrorist Tactics," January 3, 2007, available at http://www .usf-iraq.com/?option=com_content&task=view&id=727&Itemid =44, accessed June 18, 2008.
- **Analysis:** Tactics used by the insurgents became clear sooner than did a picture of the organizations employing them. Ambushes, sniping, and IEDs caused the most casualties. As the report noted, the target list expanded as the insurgency expanded, with Iraqis increasingly victimized. IEDs also became more sophisticated and powerful. Insurgent or terrorist tactics had several purposes. They sought to force a U.S. withdrawal by making the cost in blood and treasure of staying in Iraq

unacceptably high for the U.S. public. They also sought to intimidate any Iraqis who considered supporting the occupiers. Finally, they wished to provoke conventional troops into overreacting to provocation. Return fire that killed innocent civilians would increase support for the insurgency.

- **Document 67: Excerpt of U.S. Army Report on Abu Ghraib Prisoner Abuse**
- **When:** May 2004
- **Where:** Baghdad
- **Significance:** The report found both individual wrongdoing and institutional failures in the infamous abuse scandal.

ARTICLE 15-6 INVESTIGATION OF THE 800th MILITARY POLICE BRIGADE

BACKGROUND

1. (U) On 19 January 2004, Lieutenant General (LTG) Ricardo S. Sanchez, Commander, Combined Joint Task Force Seven (CJTF-7) requested that the Commander, US Central Command, appoint an Investigating Officer (IO) in the grade of Major General (MG) or above to investigate the conduct of operations within the 800th Military Police (MP) Brigade. LTG Sanchez requested an investigation of detention and internment operations by the Brigade from 1 November 2003 to present. LTG Sanchez cited recent reports of detainee abuse, escapes from confinement facilities, and accountability lapses, which indicated systemic problems within the brigade and suggested a lack of clear standards, proficiency, and leadership. LTG Sanchez requested a comprehensive and all-encompassing inquiry to make findings and recommendations concerning the fitness and performance of the 800th MP Brigade.

2. (U) On 24 January 2003, the Chief of Staff of US Central Command (CENTCOM), MG R. Steven Whitcomb, on behalf of the CENTCOM Commander, directed that the Commander, Coalition Forces Land Component Command (CFLCC), LTG David D. McKiernan, conduct an investigation into the 800th MP Brigade's detention and internment operations from 1 November 2003 to present. CENTCOM directed that the investigation should inquire into all facts and circumstances surrounding recent reports of suspected detainee abuse in Iraq. It also directed that the investigation inquire into detainee escapes and accountability lapses as reported by CJTF-7, and to gain a more comprehensive and all-encompassing inquiry into the fitness and performance of the 800th MP Brigade.

3. (U) On 31 January 2004, the Commander, CFLCC, appointed MG Antonio M. Taguba, Deputy Commanding General Support, CFLCC, to conduct this investigation. MG Taguba was directed to conduct an informal investigation under AR

15-6 into the 800th MP Brigade's detention and internment operations. Specifically, MG Taguba was tasked to:

a. (U) Inquire into all the facts and circumstances surrounding recent allegations of detainee abuse, specifically allegations of maltreatment at the Abu Ghraib Prison (Baghdad Central Confinement Facility (BCCF));

b. (U) Inquire into detainee escapes and accountability lapses as reported by CJTF-7, specifically allegations concerning these events at the Abu Ghraib Prison;

c. (U) Investigate the training, standards, employment, command policies, internal procedures, and command climate in the 800th MP Brigade, as appropriate;

d. (U) Make specific findings of fact concerning all aspects of the investigation, and make any recommendations for corrective action, as appropriate.

4. (U) LTG Sanchez's request to investigate the 800th MP Brigade followed the initiation of a criminal investigation by the US Army Criminal Investigation Command (USACIDC) into specific allegations of detainee abuse committed by members of the 372nd MP Company, 320th MP Battalion in Iraq. These units are part of the 800th MP Brigade. The Brigade is an Iraq Theater asset, TACON to CJTF-7, but OPCON to CFLCC at the time this investigation was initiated. In addition, CJTF-7 had several reports of detainee escapes from US/Coalition Confinement Facilities in Iraq over the past several months. These include Camp Bucca, Camp Ashraf, Abu Ghraib, and the High Value Detainee (HVD) Complex/Camp Cropper. The 800th MP Brigade operated these facilities. In addition, four Soldiers from the 320th MP Battalion had been formally charged under the Uniform Code of Military Justice (UCMJ) with detainee abuse in May 2003 at the Theater Internment Facility (TIF) at Camp Bucca, Iraq.

5. (U) I began assembling my investigation team prior to the actual appointment by the CFLCC Commander. I assembled subject matter experts from the CFLCC Provost Marshal (PM) and the CFLCC Staff Judge Advocate (SJA). I selected COL Kinard J. La Fate, CFLCC Provost Marshal to be my Deputy for this investigation. I also contacted the Provost Marshal General of the Army, MG Donald J. Ryder, to enlist the support of MP subject matter experts in the areas of detention and internment operations.

6. (U) The Investigating Team also reviewed the Assessment of DoD Counter-Terrorism Interrogation and Detention Operations in Iraq conducted by MG Geoffrey D. Miller, Commander, Joint Task Force Guantanamo (JTF-GTMO). From 31 August to 9 September 2003, MG Miller led a team of personnel experienced in strategic interrogation to HQ, CJTF-7 and the Iraqi Survey Group (ISG) to review current Iraqi Theater ability to rapidly exploit internees for actionable intelligence. MG Miller's team focused on three areas: intelligence integration, synchronization, and fusion; interrogation operations; and detention operations. MG Miller's team used JTF-GTMO procedures and interrogation authorities as baselines.

7. (U) The Investigating Team began its inquiry with an in-depth analysis of the Report on Detention and Corrections in Iraq, dated 5 November 2003, conducted by MG Ryder and a team of military police, legal, medical, and automation experts. The CJTF-7 Commander, LTG Sanchez, had previously requested a team of subject matter experts to assess, and make specific recommendations concerning detention

and corrections operations. From 13 October to 6 November 2003, MG Ryder personally led this assessment/assistance team in Iraq.

ASSESSMENT OF DoD COUNTER-TERRORISM INTERROGATION AND DETENTION OPERATIONS IN IRAQ (MG MILLER'S ASSESSMENT)

1. (S/NF) The principal focus of MG Miller's team was on the strategic interrogation of detainees/internees in Iraq. Among its conclusions in its Executive Summary were that CJTF-7 did not have authorities and procedures in place to affect a unified strategy to detain, interrogate, and report information from detainees/internees in Iraq. The Executive Summary also stated that detention operations must act as an enabler for interrogation.

2. (S/NF) With respect to interrogation, MG Miller's Team recommended that CJTF-7 dedicate and train a detention guard force subordinate to the Joint Interrogation Debriefing Center (JIDC) Commander that "sets the conditions for the successful interrogation and exploitation of internees/detainees." Regarding Detention Operations, MG Miller's team stated that the function of Detention Operations is to provide a safe, secure, and humane environment that supports the expeditious collection of intelligence. However, it also stated "it is essential that the guard force be actively engaged in setting the conditions for successful exploitation of the internees."

3. (S/NF) MG Miller's team also concluded that Joint Strategic Interrogation Operations (within CJTF-7) are hampered by lack of active control of the internees within the detention environment. The Miller Team also stated that establishment of the Theater Joint Interrogation and Detention Center (JIDC) at Abu Ghraib (BCCF) will consolidate both detention and strategic interrogation operations and result in synergy between MP and MI resources and an integrated, synchronized, and focused strategic interrogation effort.

4. (S/NF) MG Miller's team also observed that the application of emerging strategic interrogation strategies and techniques contain new approaches and operational art. The Miller Team also concluded that a legal review and recommendations on internee interrogation operations by a dedicated Command Judge Advocate is required to maximize interrogation effectiveness.

IO COMMENTS ON MG MILLER'S ASSESSMENT

1. (S/NF) MG Miller's team recognized that they were using JTF-GTMO operational procedures and interrogation authorities as baselines for its observations and recommendations. There is a strong argument that the intelligence value of detainees held at JTF-Guantanamo (GTMO) is different than that of the detainees/internees held at Abu Ghraib (BCCF) and other detention facilities in Iraq. Currently, there are a large number of Iraqi criminals held at Abu Ghraib (BCCF). These are not believed to be international terrorists or members of Al Qaida, Anser Al Islam, Taliban, and other international terrorist organizations.

2. (S/NF) The recommendations of MG Miller's team that the "guard force" be actively engaged in setting the conditions for successful exploitation of the internees would appear to be in conflict with the recommendations of MG Ryder's Team and AR 190-8 that military police "do not participate in military intelligence supervised interrogation sessions." The Ryder Report concluded that the OEF template whereby military police actively set the favorable conditions for subsequent interviews runs counter to the smooth operation of a detention facility.

REPORT ON DETENTION AND CORRECTIONS IN IRAQ (MG RYDER'S REPORT)

1. (U) MG Ryder and his assessment team conducted a comprehensive review of the entire detainee and corrections system in Iraq and provided recommendations addressing each of the following areas as requested by the Commander CJTF-7:

a. (U) Detainee and corrections system management

b. (U) Detainee management, including detainee movement, segregation, and accountability

c. (U) Means of command and control of the detention and corrections system

d. (U) Integration of military detention and corrections with the Coalition Provisional Authority (CPA) and adequacy of plans for transition to an Iraqi-run corrections system

e. (U) Detainee medical care and health management

f. (U) Detention facilities that meet required health, hygiene, and sanitation standards

g. (U) Court integration and docket management for criminal detainees

h. (U) Detainee legal processing

i. (U) Detainee databases and records, including integration with law enforcement and court databases

2. (U) Many of the findings and recommendations of MG Ryder's team are beyond the scope of this investigation. However, several important findings are clearly relevant to this inquiry and are summarized below (emphasis is added in certain areas):

A. (U) **Detainee Management (including movement, segregation, and accountability)**

1. (U) There is a wide variance in standards and approaches at the various detention facilities. Several Division/Brigade collection points and US monitored Iraqi prisons had flawed or insufficiently detailed use of force and other standing operating procedures or policies (e.g. weapons in the facility, improper restraint techniques, detainee management, etc.) though there were no military police units purposely applying inappropriate confinement practices.

2. (U) Currently, due to lack of adequate Iraqi facilities, Iraqi criminals (generally Iraqi-on-Iraqi crimes) are detained with security internees (generally Iraqi-on-Coalition offenses) and EPWs in the same facilities, though segregated in different cells/compounds.

3. (U) The management of multiple disparate groups of detained people in a single location by members of the same unit invites confusion about handling, processing, and treatment, and typically facilitates the transfer of information between different categories of detainees.

4. (U) The 800th MP (I/R) units did not receive Internment/Resettlement (I/R) and corrections specific training during their mobilization period. Corrections training is only on the METL of two MP (I/R) Confinement Battalions throughout the Army, one currently serving in Afghanistan, and elements of the other are at Camp Arifjan, Kuwait. MP units supporting JTF-GTMO received ten days of training in detention facility operations, to include two days of unarmed self-defense, training in interpersonal communication skills, forced cell moves, and correctional officer safety.

B. (U) **Means of Command and Control of the Detention and Corrections System**

1. (U) The 800th MP Brigade was originally task organized with eight MP(I/R) Battalions consisting of both MP Guard and Combat Support companies. Due to force rotation plans, the 800th redeployed two Battalion HHCs in December 2003, the 115th MP Battalion and the 324th MP Battalion. In December 2003, the 400th MP Battalion was relieved of its mission and redeployed in January 2004. The 724th MP Battalion redeployed on 11 February 2004 and the remainder is scheduled to redeploy in March and April 2004. They are the 310th MP Battalion, 320th MP Battalion, 530th MP Battalion, and 744th MP Battalion. The units that remain are generally understrength, as Reserve Component units do not have an individual personnel replacement system to mitigate medical losses or the departure of individual Soldiers that have reached 24 months of Federal active duty in a five-year period.

2. (U) The 800th MP Brigade (I/R) is currently a CFLCC asset, TACON to CJTF-7 to conduct Internment/Resettlement (I/R) operations in Iraq. All detention operations are conducted in the CJTF-7 AO; Camps Ganci, Vigilant, Bucca, TSP Whitford, and a separate High Value Detention (HVD) site.

3. (U) The 800th MP Brigade has experienced challenges adapting its task organizational structure, training, and equipment resources from a unit designed to conduct standard EPW operations in the COMMZ (Kuwait). Further, the doctrinally trained MP Soldier-to-detainee population ratio and facility layout templates are predicated on a compliant, self-disciplining EPW population, and not criminals or high-risk security internees.

4. (U) EPWs and Civilian Internees should receive the full protections of the Geneva Conventions, unless the denial of these protections is due to specifically articulated military necessity (e.g., no visitation to preclude the direction of insurgency operations).

5. (U) AR 190-8, Enemy Prisoners of War, Retained Personnel, Civilian Internees, and other Detainees, FM 3-19.40, Military Police Internment and Resettlement Operations, and FM 34-52, Intelligence Interrogations, require military police to provide an area for intelligence collection efforts within EPW facilities. Military Police, though adept at passive collection of intelligence within a facility, do not participate in Military Intelligence supervised interrogation sessions. Recent intelligence collection in support of Operation Enduring Freedom posited a template whereby military police actively set favorable conditions for subsequent interviews. Such actions generally run counter to the smooth operation of a detention facility, attempting to maintain its population in a compliant and docile state. **The 800th MP Brigade has not been directed to change its facility procedures to set the conditions for MI interrogations, nor participate in those interrogations.**

6. MG Ryder's Report also made the following, inter alia, near-term and mid-term recommendations regarding the command and control of detainees:

a. (U) Align the release process for security internees with DoD Policy. The process of screening security internees should include intelligence findings, interrogation results, and current threat assessment.

b. (U) Determine the scope of intelligence collection that will occur at Camp Vigilant. Refurbish the Northeast Compound to separate the screening operation from the Iraqi run Baghdad Central Correctional Facility. **Establish procedures that define the role of military police Soldiers securing the compound, clearly separating the actions of the guards from those of the military intelligence personnel.**

c. (U) **Consolidate all Security Internee Operations, except the MEK security mission, under a single Military Police Brigade Headquarters for OIF 2.**

d. (U) **Insist that all units identified to rotate into the Iraqi Theater of Operations (ITO) to conduct internment and confinement operations in support of OIF 2 be organic to CJTF-7.**

IO COMMENTS REGARDING MG RYDER'S REPORT

1. (U) The objective of MG Ryder's Team was to observe detention and prison operations, identify potential systemic and human rights issues, and provide near-term, mid-term, and long-term recommendations to improve CJTF-7 operations and transition of the Iraqi prison system from US military control/oversight to the Coalition Provisional Authority and eventually to the Iraqi Government. The Findings and Recommendations of MG Ryder's Team are thorough and precise and should be implemented immediately.

2. (U) **Unfortunately, many of the systemic problems that surfaced during MG Ryder's Team's assessment are the very same issues that are the subject of this investigation. In fact, many of the abuses suffered by detainees occurred during, or near to, the time of that assessment.** As will be pointed out in detail in subsequent portions of this report, I disagree with the conclusion of MG Ryder's Team in one critical aspect, that being its conclusion that the 800th MP Brigade had not been [t]asked to change its facility procedures to set the conditions for MI interviews. **While clearly the 800th MP Brigade and its commanders were not tasked to set conditions for detainees for subsequent MI interrogations, it is obvious from a review of comprehensive CID interviews of suspects and witnesses that this was done at lower levels.**

3. (U) I concur fully with MG Ryder's conclusion regarding the effect of AR 190-8. Military Police, though adept at passive collection of intelligence within a facility, should not participate in Military Intelligence supervised interrogation sessions. Moreover, Military Police should not be involved with setting "favorable conditions" for subsequent interviews. These actions, as will be outlined in this investigation, clearly run counter to the smooth operation of a detention facility.

PRELIMINARY INVESTIGATIVE ACTIONS

1. (U) Following our review of MG Ryder's Report and MG Miller's Report, my investigation team immediately began an in-depth review of all available documents regarding the 800th MP Brigade....

2. (U) In addition to military police and legal officers from the CFLCC PMO and SJA Offices we also obtained the services of two individuals who are experts in military police detention practices and training....

3. (U) In addition to MG Ryder's and MG Miller's Reports, the team reviewed numerous reference materials including the 12 October 2003 CJTF-7 Interrogation and Counter-Resistance Policy, the AR 15-6 Investigation on Riot and Shootings at Abu Ghraib on 24 November 2003, the 205th MI Brigade's Interrogation Rules of Engagement (IROE), facility staff logs/journals and numerous records of AR 15-6 investigations and Serious Incident Reports (SIRs) on detainee escapes/shootings and disciplinary matters from the 800th MP Brigade.

4. (U) On 2 February 2004, I took my team to Baghdad for a one-day inspection of the Abu Ghraib Prison (BCCF) and the High Value Detainee (HVD) Complex in order to become familiar with those facilities. We also met with COL Jerry Mocello, Commander, 3rd MP Criminal Investigation Group (CID), COL Dave Quantock, Commander, 16th MP Brigade, COL Dave Phillips, Commander, 89th MP Brigade, and COL Ed Sannwaldt, CJTF-7 Provost Marshal. On 7 February 2004, the team visited the Camp Bucca Detention Facility to familiarize itself with the facility and operating structure. In addition, on 6 and 7 February 2004, at Camp Doha, Kuwait, we conducted extensive training sessions on approved detention practices. We continued our preparation by reviewing the ongoing CID investigation and were briefed by the Special Agent in Charge, CW2 Paul Arthur. We refreshed ourselves on the applicable reference materials within each team member's area of expertise, and practiced investigative techniques. I met with the team on numerous occasions to finalize appropriate witness lists, review existing witness statements, arrange logistics, and collect potential evidence. We also coordinated with CJTF-7 to arrange witness attendance, force protection measures, and general logistics for the team's move to Baghdad on 8 February 2004. (ANNEXES 4 and 25)

5. (U) At the same time, due to the Transfer of Authority on 1 February 2004 between III Corps and V Corps, and the upcoming demobilization of the 800th MP Brigade Command, I directed that several critical witnesses who were preparing to leave the theater remain at Camp Arifjan, Kuwait until they could be interviewed (ANNEX 29). My team deployed to Baghdad on 8 February 2004 and conducted a series of interviews with a variety of witnesses (ANNEX 30). We returned to Camp Doha, Kuwait on 13 February 2004. On 14 and 15 February we interviewed a number of witnesses from the 800th MP Brigade. On 17 February we returned to Camp Bucca, Iraq to complete interviews of witnesses at that location. From 18 February thru 28 February we collected documents, compiled references, did follow-up interviews, and completed a detailed analysis of the volumes of materials accumulated throughout our investigation. On 29 February we finalized our executive summary and out-briefing slides. On 9 March we submitted the AR 15-6 written report with findings and recommendations to the CFLCC Deputy SJA, LTC Mark Johnson, for a legal sufficiency review. The out-brief to the appointing authority, LTG McKiernan, took place on 3 March 2004.

FINDINGS AND RECOMMENDATIONS
(PART ONE)

(U) **The investigation should inquire into all of the facts and circumstances surrounding recent allegations of detainee abuse, specifically, allegations of maltreatment at the Abu Ghraib Prison (Baghdad Central Confinement Facility).**

1. (U) The US Army Criminal Investigation Command (CID), led by COL Jerry Mocello, and a team of highly trained professional agents have done a superb job of investigating several complex and extremely disturbing incidents of detainee abuse at the Abu Ghraib Prison. They conducted over 50 interviews of witnesses, potential criminal suspects, and detainees. They also uncovered numerous photos and videos portraying in graphic detail detainee abuse by Military Police personnel on numerous occasions from October to December 2003. Several potential suspects rendered full and complete confessions regarding their personal involvement and

the involvement of fellow Soldiers in this abuse. Several potential suspects invoked their rights under Article 31 of the Uniform Code of Military Justice (UCMJ) and the 5th Amendment of the U.S. Constitution.

2. (U) In addition to a comprehensive and exhaustive review of all of these statements and documentary evidence, we also interviewed numerous officers, NCOs, and junior enlisted Soldiers in the 800th MP Brigade, as well as members of the 205th Military Intelligence Brigade working at the prison. We did not believe it was necessary to re-interview all the numerous witnesses who had previously provided comprehensive statements to CID, and I have adopted those statements for the purposes of this investigation.

REGARDING PART ONE OF THE INVESTIGATION, I MAKE THE FOLLOWING SPECIFIC FINDINGS OF FACT:

1. (U) That Forward Operating Base (FOB) Abu Ghraib (BCCF) provides security of both criminal and security detainees at the Baghdad Central Correctional Facility, facilitates the conducting of interrogations for CJTF-7, supports other CPA operations at the prison, and enhances the force protection/quality of life of Soldiers assigned in order to ensure the success of ongoing operations to secure a free Iraq.

2. (U) That the Commander, 205th Military Intelligence Brigade, was designated by CJTF-7 as the Commander of FOB Abu Ghraib (BCCF) effective 19 November 2003. That the 205th MI Brigade conducts operational and strategic interrogations for CJTF-7. That from 19 November 2003 until Transfer of Authority (TOA) on 6 February 2004, COL Thomas M. Pappas was the Commander of the 205th MI Brigade and the Commander of FOB Abu Ghraib (BCCF).

3. (U) That the 320th Military Police Battalion of the 800th MP Brigade is responsible for the Guard Force at Camp Ganci, Camp Vigilant, & Cellblock 1 of FOB Abu Ghraib (BCCF). That from February 2003 to until he was suspended from his duties on 17 January 2004, LTC Jerry Phillabaum served as the Battalion Commander of the 320th MP Battalion. That from December 2002 until he was suspended from his duties, on 17 January 2004, CPT Donald Reese served as the Company Commander of the 372nd MP Company, which was in charge of guarding detainees at FOB Abu Ghraib. I further find that both the 320th MP Battalion and the 372nd MP Company were located within the confines of FOB Abu Ghraib.

4. (U) That from July of 2003 to the present, BG Janis L. Karpinski was the Commander of the 800th MP Brigade. (Annex 45)

5. (S) That between October and December 2003, at the Abu Ghraib Confinement Facility (BCCF), numerous incidents of sadistic, blatant, and wanton criminal abuses were inflicted on several detainees. This systemic and illegal abuse of detainees was intentionally perpetrated by several members of the military police guard force (372nd Military Police Company, 320th Military Police Battalion, 800th MP Brigade), in Tier (section) 1-A of the Abu Ghraib Prison (BCCF). The allegations of abuse were substantiated by detailed witness statements and the discovery of extremely graphic photographic evidence. Due to the extremely sensitive nature of these photographs and videos, the ongoing CID investigation, and the potential for the criminal prosecution of several suspects, the photographic evidence is not included in the body of my investigation. The pictures and videos are available from

the Criminal Investigative Command and the CTJF-7 prosecution team. In addition to the aforementioned crimes, there were also abuses committed by members of the 325th MI Battalion, 205th MI Brigade, and Joint Interrogation and Debriefing Center (JIDC). Specifically, on 24 November 2003, SPC Luciana Spencer, 205th MI Brigade, sought to degrade a detainee by having him strip and returned to cell naked.

6. (S) I find that the intentional abuse of detainees by military police personnel included the following acts:

a. (S) Punching, slapping, and kicking detainees; jumping on their naked feet;

b. (S) Videotaping and photographing naked male and female detainees;

c. (S) Forcibly arranging detainees in various sexually explicit positions for photographing;

d. (S) Forcing detainees to remove their clothing and keeping them naked for several days at a time;

e. (S) Forcing naked male detainees to wear women's underwear;

f. (S) Forcing groups of male detainees to masturbate themselves while being photographed and videotaped;

g. (S) Arranging naked male detainees in a pile and then jumping on them;

h. (S) Positioning a naked detainee on a MRE Box, with a sandbag on his head, and attaching wires to his fingers, toes, and penis to simulate electric torture;

i. (S) Writing "I am a Rapest" [sic] on the leg of a detainee alleged to have forcibly raped a 15-year old fellow detainee, and then photographing him naked;

j. (S) Placing a dog chain or strap around a naked detainee's neck and having a female Soldier pose for a picture;

k. (S) A male MP guard having sex with a female detainee;

l. (S) Using military working dogs (without muzzles) to intimidate and frighten detainees, and in at least one case biting and severely injuring a detainee;

m. (S) Taking photographs of dead Iraqi detainees.

7. (U) These findings are amply supported by written confessions provided by several of the suspects, written statements provided by detainees, and witness statements. . . .

8. (U) In addition, several detainees also described the following acts of abuse, which under the circumstances, I find credible based on the clarity of their statements and supporting evidence provided by other witnesses:

a. (U) Breaking chemical lights and pouring the phosphoric liquid on detainees;

b. (U) Threatening detainees with a charged 9mm pistol;

c. (U) Pouring cold water on naked detainees;

d. (U) Beating detainees with a broom handle and a chair;

e. (U) Threatening male detainees with rape;

f. (U) Allowing a military police guard to stitch the wound of a detainee who was injured after being slammed against the wall in his cell;

g. (U) Sodomizing a detainee with a chemical light and perhaps a broom stick.

h. (U) Using military working dogs to frighten and intimidate detainees with threats of attack, and in one instance actually biting a detainee.

9. (U) I have carefully considered the statements provided by the following detainees, which under the circumstances I find credible based on the clarity of their statements and supporting evidence provided by other witnesses: . . .

10. (U) I find that contrary to the provision of AR 190-8, and the findings found in MG Ryder's Report, Military Intelligence (MI) interrogators and Other US Government Agency's (OGA) interrogators actively requested that MP guards set physical and mental conditions for favorable interrogation of witnesses. Contrary to the findings of MG Ryder's Report, I find that personnel assigned to the 372nd MP Company, 800th MP Brigade were directed to change facility procedures to "set the conditions" for MI interrogations. I find no direct evidence that MP personnel actually participated in those MI interrogations.

11. (U) I reach this finding based on the actual proven abuse that I find was inflicted on detainees and by the following witness statements.:

a. (U) **SPC Sabrina Harman, 372nd MP Company,** stated in her sworn statement regarding the incident where a detainee was placed on a box with wires attached to his fingers, toes, and penis, "that her job was to keep detainees awake." She stated that MI was talking to CPL Grainer. She stated: **"MI wanted to get them to talk. It is Grainer and Frederick's job to do things for MI and OGA to get these people to talk."**

b. (U) **SGT Javal S. Davis, 372nd MP Company,** stated in his sworn statement as follows: **"I witnessed prisoners in the MI hold section, wing 1A being made to do various things that I would question morally. In Wing 1A we were told that they had different rules and different SOP for treatment. I never saw a set of rules or SOP for that section just word of mouth. The Soldier in charge of 1A was Corporal Granier. He stated that the Agents and MI Soldiers would ask him to do things, but nothing was ever in writing he would complain (sic)."** When asked why the rules in 1A/1B were different than the rest of the wings, SGT Davis stated: **"The rest of the wings are regular prisoners and 1A/B are Military Intelligence (MI) holds."** When asked why he did not inform his chain of command about this abuse, SGT Davis stated: **"Because I assumed that if they were doing things out of the ordinary or outside the guidelines, someone would have said something. Also the wing belongs to MI and it appeared MI personnel approved of the abuse."** SGT Davis also stated that he had heard MI insinuate to the guards to abuse the inmates. When asked what MI said he stated: **"Loosen this guy up for us." ["]Make sure he has a bad night." "Make sure he gets the treatment."** He claimed these comments were made to CPL Granier and SSG Frederick. Finally, SGT Davis stated that (sic): **"the MI staffs to my understanding have been giving Granier compliments on the way he has been handling the MI holds. Example being statements like, Good job, they're breaking down real fast. They answer every question. They're giving out good information, finally, and Keep up the good work. Stuff like that."**

c. (U) **SPC Jason Kennel, 372nd MP Company,** was asked if he were present when any detainees were abused. He stated: **"I saw them nude, but MI would tell us to take away their mattresses, sheets, and clothes."** He could not recall who in MI had instructed him to do this, but commented that, "if they wanted me to do that they needed to give me paperwork." He was later informed that "we could not do anything to embarrass the prisoners."

d. (U) **Mr. Adel L. Nakhla,** a US civilian contract translator was questioned about several detainees accused of rape. He observed (sic): **"They (detainees) were** all naked, a bunch of people from MI, the MP were there that night and the inmates were ordered by SGT Granier and SGT Frederick ordered the guys while questioning them to admit what they did. They made them do strange exercises by sliding on their stomach, jump up and down, throw water on them and made them some wet, called them all kinds of names such as "gays" do they like to make love to guys, then they handcuffed their hands together and their legs with shackles and started to stack them on top of each other by insuring that the bottom guys penis will touch the guy on tops butt."

e. (U) **SPC Neil A Wallin, 109th Area Support Medical Battalion**, a medic testified that: "**Cell 1A was used to house high priority detainees and cell 1B was used to house the high risk or trouble making detainees. During my tour at the prison I observed that when the male detainees were first brought to the facility, some of them were made to wear female underwear, which I think was to somehow break them down.**"

12. (U) I find that prior to its deployment to Iraq for Operation Iraqi Freedom, the 320th MP Battalion and the 372nd MP Company had received no training in detention/internee operations. I also find that very little instruction or training was provided to MP personnel on the applicable rules of the Geneva Convention Relative to the Treatment of Prisoners of War, FM 27-10, AR 190-8, or FM 3-19.40. Moreover, I find that few, if any, copies of the Geneva Conventions were ever made available to MP personnel or detainees.

13. (U) Another obvious example of the Brigade Leadership not communicating with its Soldiers or ensuring their tactical proficiency concerns the incident of detainee abuse that occurred at Camp Bucca, Iraq, on May 12, 2003. Soldiers from the 223rd MP Company reported to the 800th MP Brigade Command at Camp Bucca, that four Military Police Soldiers from the 320th MP Battalion had abused a number of detainees during in[-]processing at Camp Bucca. An extensive CID investigation determined that four soldiers from the 320th MP Battalion had kicked and beaten these detainees following a transport mission from Talil Air Base.

14. (U) Formal charges under the UCMJ were preferred against these Soldiers and an Article-32 Investigation conducted by LTC Gentry. He recommended a general court martial for the four accused, which BG Karpinski supported. Despite this documented abuse, there is no evidence that BG Karpinski ever attempted to remind 800th MP Soldiers of the requirements of the Geneva Conventions regarding detainee treatment or took any steps to ensure that such abuse was not repeated. Nor is there any evidence that LTC(P) Phillabaum, the commander of the Soldiers involved in the Camp Bucca abuse incident, took any initiative to ensure his Soldiers were properly trained regarding detainee treatment.

RECOMMENDATIONS AS TO PART ONE OF THE INVESTIGATION:

1. (U) Immediately deploy to the Iraq Theater an integrated multi-discipline Mobile Training Team (MTT) comprised of subject matter experts in internment/resettlement operations, international and operational law, information technology, facility management, interrogation and intelligence gathering techniques, chaplains, Arab cultural awareness, and medical practices as it pertains to I/R activities. This team needs to oversee and conduct comprehensive training in all aspects of detainee and confinement operations.

2. (U) That all military police and military intelligence personnel involved in any aspect of detainee operations or interrogation operations in CJTF-7, and subordinate units, be immediately provided with training by an international/operational law attorney on the specific provisions of The Law of Land Warfare FM 27-10, specifically the Geneva Convention Relative to the Treatment of Prisoners of War, Enemy Prisoners of War, Retained Personnel, Civilian Internees, and Other Detainees, and AR 190-8.

3. (U) **That a single commander in CJTF-7 be responsible for overall detainee operations throughout the Iraq Theater of Operations.** I also recommend that the Provost Marshal General of the Army assign a minimum of two (2) subject matter experts, one officer and one NCO, to assist CJTF-7 in coordinating detainee operations.

4. (U) That detention facility commanders and interrogation facility commanders ensure that appropriate copies of the Geneva Convention Relative to the Treatment of Prisoners of War and notice of protections be made available in both English and the detainees' language and be prominently displayed in all detention facilities. Detainees with questions regarding their treatment should be given the full opportunity to read the Convention.

5. (U) That each detention facility commander and interrogation facility commander publish a complete and comprehensive set of Standing Operating Procedures (SOPs) regarding treatment of detainees, and that all personnel be required to read the SOPs and sign a document indicating that they have read and understand the SOPs.

6. (U) That in accordance with the recommendations of MG Ryder's Assessment Report, and my findings and recommendations in this investigation, all units in the Iraq Theater of Operations conducting internment/confinement/detainment operations in support of Operation Iraqi Freedom be OPCON for all purposes, to include action under the UCMJ, to CJTF-7.

7. (U) Appoint the C3, CJTF as the staff proponent for detainee operations in the Iraq Joint Operations Area (JOA). . . .

8. (U) That an inquiry UP AR 381-10, Procedure 15 be conducted to determine the extent of culpability of Military Intelligence personnel, assigned to the 205th MI Brigade and the Joint Interrogation and Debriefing Center (JIDC) regarding abuse of detainees at Abu Ghraib (BCCF).

9. (U) That it is critical that the proponent for detainee operations is assigned a dedicated Senior Judge Advocate, with specialized training and knowledge of international and operational law, to assist and advise on matters of detainee operations.

FINDINGS AND RECOMMENDATIONS
(PART THREE)

(U) **Investigate the training, standards, employment, command policies, internal procedures, and command climate in the 800th MP Brigade, as appropriate:**

. . . REGARDING PART THREE OF THE INVESTIGATION, I MAKE THE FOLLOWING SPECIFIC FINDINGS OF FACT:

1. (U) I find that BG Janis Karpinski took command of the 800th MP Brigade on 30 June 2003 from BG Paul Hill. BG Karpinski has remained in command since that

date. The 800th MP Brigade is comprised of eight MP battalions in the Iraqi TOR: 115th MP Battalion, 310th MP Battalion, 320th MP Battalion, 324th MP Battalion, 400th MP Battalion, 530th MP Battalion, 724th MP Battalion, and 744th MP Battalion.

2. (U) Prior to BG Karpinski taking command, members of the 800th MP Brigade believed they would be allowed to go home when all the detainees were released from the Camp Bucca Theater Internment Facility following the cessation of major ground combat on 1 May 2003. At one point, approximately 7,000 to 8,000 detainees were held at Camp Bucca. Through Article-5 Tribunals and a screening process, several thousand detainees were released. Many in the command believed they would go home when the detainees were released. In late May–early June 2003 the 800th MP Brigade was given a new mission to manage the Iraqi penal system and several detention centers. This new mission meant Soldiers would not redeploy to CONUS when anticipated. Morale suffered, and over the next few months there did not appear to have been any attempt by the Command to mitigate this morale problem.

3. (U) There is abundant evidence in the statements of numerous witnesses that soldiers throughout the 800th MP Brigade were not proficient in their basic MOS skills, particularly regarding internment/resettlement operations. Moreover, there is no evidence that the command, although aware of these deficiencies, attempted to correct them in any systemic manner other than ad hoc training by individuals with civilian corrections experience.

4. (U) I find that the 800th MP Brigade was not adequately trained for a mission that included operating a prison or penal institution at Abu Ghraib Prison Complex. As the Ryder Assessment found, I also concur that units of the 800th MP Brigade did not receive corrections-specific training during their mobilization period. MP units did not receive pinpoint assignments prior to mobilization and during the post mobilization training, and thus could not train for specific missions. The training that was accomplished at the mobilization sites were developed and implemented at the company level with little or no direction or supervision at the Battalion and Brigade levels, and consisted primarily of common tasks and law enforcement training. However, I found no evidence that the Command, although aware of this deficiency, ever requested specific corrections training from the Commandant of the Military Police School, the US Army Confinement Facility at Mannheim, Germany, the Provost Marshal General of the Army, or the US Army Disciplinary Barracks at Fort Leavenworth, Kansas.

5. (U) I find that without adequate training for a civilian internee detention mission, Brigade personnel relied heavily on individuals within the Brigade who had civilian corrections experience, including many who worked as prison guards or corrections officials in their civilian jobs. Almost every witness we interviewed had no familiarity with the provisions of AR 190-8 or FM 3-19.40. It does not appear that a Mission Essential Task List (METL) based on in-theater missions was ever developed nor was a training plan implemented throughout the Brigade.

6. (U) I also find, as did MG Ryder's Team, that the 800th MP Brigade as a whole, was understrength for the mission for which it was tasked. Army Doctrine dictates that an I/R Brigade can be organized with between 7 and 21 battalions, and that

the average battalion size element should be able to handle approximately 4000 detainees at a time. This investigation indicates that BG Karpinski and her staff did a poor job allocating resources throughout the Iraq JOA. Abu Ghraib (BCCF) normally housed between 6000 and 7000 detainees, yet it was operated by only one battalion. In contrast, the HVD Facility maintains only about 100 detainees, and is also run by an entire battalion.

7. (U) Reserve Component units do not have an individual replacement system to mitigate medical or other losses. Over time, the 800th MP Brigade clearly suffered from personnel shortages through release from active duty (REFRAD) actions, medical evacuation, and demobilization. In addition to being severely under-manned, the quality of life for Soldiers assigned to Abu Ghraib (BCCF) was extremely poor. There was no DFAC, PX, barbershop, or MWR facilities. There were numerous mortar attacks, random rifle and RPG attacks, and a serious threat to Soldiers and detainees in the facility. The prison complex was also severely over-crowded and the Brigade lacked adequate resources and personnel to resolve serious logistical problems. Finally, because of past associations and familiarity of Soldiers within the Brigade, it appears that friendship often took precedence over appropri-ate leader and subordinate relationships.

8. (U) With respect to the 800th MP Brigade mission at Abu Ghraib (BCCF), I find that there was clear friction and lack of effective communication between the Commander, 205th MI Brigade, who controlled FOB Abu Ghraib (BCCF) after 19 November 2003, and the Commander, 800th MP Brigade, who controlled detainee operations inside the FOB. There was no clear delineation of responsibility between commands, little coordination at the command level, and no integration of the two functions. Coordination occurred at the lowest possible levels with little oversight by commanders.

9. (U) I find that this ambiguous command relationship was exacerbated by a CJTF-7 Fragmentary Order (FRAGO) 1108 issued on 19 November 2003. Para-graph 3.C.8, Assignment of 205th MI Brigade Commander's Responsibilities for the Baghdad Central Confinement Facility, states as follows:

3.C.8. A. (U) 205 MI BRIGADE.

3.C.8. A. 1. (U) EFFECTIVE IMMEDIATELY COMMANDER 205 MI BRIGADE ASSUMES RESPONSIBILITY FOR THE BAGHDAD CON-FINEMENT FACILITY (BCCF) AND IS APPOINTED THE FOB COM-MANDER. UNITS CURRENTLY AT ABU GHRAIB (BCCF) ARE TACON TO 205 MI BRIGADE FOR "SECURITY OF DETAINEES AND FOB PROTECTION."

Although not supported by BG Karpinski, FRAGO 1108 made all of the MP units at Abu Ghraib TACON to the Commander, 205th MI Brigade. This effec-tively made an MI Officer, rather than an MP Officer, responsible for the MP units conducting detainee operations at that facility. This is not doctrinally sound due to the different missions and agendas assigned to each of these respective specialties.

10. (U) Joint Publication 0-2, Unified Action Armed Forces (UNAAF), 10 July 2001 defines Tactical Control (TACON) as the detailed direction and control of movements or maneuvers within the operational area necessary to accomplish assigned missions or tasks.

"TACON is the command authority over assigned or attached forces or commands or military capability made available for tasking that is limited to the detailed direction and control of movements or maneuvers within the operational area necessary to accomplish assigned missions or tasks. TACON is inherent in OPCON and may be delegated to and exercised by commanders at any echelon at or below the level of combatant commander."

11. (U) Based on all the facts and circumstances in this investigation, I find that there was little, if any, recognition of this TACON Order by the 800th MP Brigade or the 205th MI Brigade. Further, there was no evidence if the Commander, 205th MI Brigade clearly informed the Commander, 800th MP Brigade, and specifically the Commander, 320th MP Battalion assigned at Abu Ghraib (BCCF), on the specific requirements of this TACON relationship.

12. (U) It is clear from a comprehensive review of witness statements and personal interviews that the 320th MP Battalion and 800th MP Brigade continued to function as if they were responsible for the security, health and welfare, and overall security of detainees within Abu Ghraib (BCCF) prison. Both BG Karpinski and COL Pappas clearly behaved as if this were still the case.

13. (U) With respect to the 320th MP Battalion, I find that the Battalion Commander, LTC (P) Jerry Phillabaum, was an extremely ineffective commander and leader. Numerous witnesses confirm that the Battalion S-3, MAJ David W. DiNenna, basically ran the battalion on a day-to-day basis. At one point, BG Karpinski sent LTC (P) Phillabaum to Camp Arifjan, Kuwait for approximately two weeks, apparently to give him some relief from the pressure he was experiencing as the 320th Battalion Commander. This movement to Camp Arifjan immediately followed a briefing provided by LTC (P) Phillabaum to the CJTF-7 Commander, LTG Sanchez, near the end of October 2003. BG Karpinski placed LTC Ronald Chew, Commander of the 115th MP Battalion, in charge of the 320th MP Battalion for a period of approximately two weeks. LTC Chew was also in command of the 115th MP Battalion assigned to Camp Cropper, BIAP, Iraq. I could find no orders, either suspending or relieving LTC (P) Phillabaum from command, nor any orders placing LTC Chew in command of the 320th. In addition, there was no indication this removal and search for a replacement was communicated to the Commander CJTF-7, the Commander 377th TSC, or to Soldiers in the 320th MP Battalion. Temporarily removing one commander and replacing him with another serving Battalion Commander without an order and without notifying superior or subordinate commands is without precedent in my military career. LTC (P) Phillabaum was also reprimanded for lapses in accountability that resulted in several escapes. The 320th MP Battalion was stigmatized as a unit due to previous detainee abuse which occurred in May 2003 at the Bucca Theater Internment Facility (TIF), while under the command of LTC (P) Phillabaum. Despite his proven deficiencies as both a commander and leader, BG Karpinski allowed LTC (P) Phillabaum to remain in command of her most troubled battalion guarding, by far, the largest number of detainees in the 800th MP Brigade. LTC (P) Phillabaum was suspended from his duties by LTG Sanchez, CJTF-7 Commander on 17 January 2004.

14. (U) During the course of this investigation I conducted a lengthy interview with BG Karpinski that lasted over four hours, and is included verbatim in the

investigation Annexes. BG Karpinski was extremely emotional during much of her testimony. What I found particularly disturbing in her testimony was her complete unwillingness to either understand or accept that many of the problems inherent in the 800th MP Brigade were caused or exacerbated by poor leadership and the refusal of her command to both establish and enforce basic standards and principles among its soldiers.

15. (U) BG Karpinski alleged that she received no help from the Civil Affairs Command, specifically, no assistance from either BG John Kern or COL Tim Regan. She blames much of the abuse that occurred in Abu Ghraib (BCCF) on MI personnel and stated that MI personnel had given the MPs "ideas" that led to detainee abuse. In addition, she blamed the 372nd Company Platoon Sergeant, SFC Snider, the Company Commander, CPT Reese, and the First Sergeant, MSG Lipinski, for the abuse. She argued that problems in Abu Ghraib were the fault of COL Pappas and LTC Jordan because COL Pappas was in charge of FOB Abu Ghraib.

16. (U) BG Karpinski also implied during her testimony that the criminal abuses that occurred at Abu Ghraib (BCCF) might have been caused by the ultimate disposition of the detainee abuse cases that originally occurred at Camp Bucca in May 2003. She stated that **"about the same time those incidents were taking place out of Baghdad Central, the decisions were made to give the guilty people at Bucca plea bargains. So, the system communicated to the soldiers, the worst that's gonna happen is, you're gonna go home."** I think it important to point out that almost every witness testified that the serious criminal abuse of detainees at Abu Ghraib (BCCF) occurred in late October and early November 2003. The photographs and statements clearly support that the abuses occurred during this time period. The Bucca cases were set for trial in January 2004 and were not finally disposed of until 29 December 2003. There is entirely no evidence that the decision of numerous MP personnel to intentionally abuse detainees at Abu Ghraib (BCCF) was influenced in any respect by the Camp Bucca cases.

17. (U) Numerous witnesses stated that the 800th MP Brigade S-1, MAJ Hinzman and S-4, MAJ Green, were essentially dysfunctional, but that despite numerous complaints, these officers were not replaced. This had a detrimental effect on the Brigade Staff's effectiveness and morale. Moreover, the Brigade Command Judge Advocate, LTC James O'Hare, appears to lack initiative and was unwilling to accept responsibility for any of his actions. LTC Gary Maddocks, the Brigade XO did not properly supervise the Brigade staff by failing to lay out staff priorities, take overt corrective action when needed, and supervise their daily functions.

18. (U) In addition to poor morale and staff inefficiencies, I find that the 800th MP Brigade did not articulate or enforce clear and basic Soldier and Army standards. I specifically found these examples of unenforced standards:

a. There was no clear uniform standard for any MP Soldiers assigned detention duties. Despite the fact that hundreds of former Iraqi soldiers and officers were detainees, MP personnel were allowed to wear civilian clothes in the FOB after duty hours while carrying weapons.

b. Some Soldiers wrote poems and other sayings on their helmets and soft caps.

c. In addition, numerous officers and senior NCOs have been reprimanded/disciplined for misconduct during this period. . . .

d. (U) Saluting of officers was sporadic and not enforced. LTC Robert P. Walters, Jr., Commander of the 165th Military Intelligence Battalion (Tactical Exploitation), testified that the saluting policy was enforced by COL Pappas for all MI personnel, and that BG Karpinski approached COL Pappas to reverse the saluting policy back to a no-saluting policy as previously existed.

19. (U) I find that individual Soldiers within the 800th MP Brigade and the 320th Battalion stationed throughout Iraq had very little contact during their tour of duty with either LTC (P) Phillabaum or BG Karpinski. BG Karpinski claimed, during her testimony, that she paid regular visits to the various detention facilities where her Soldiers were stationed. However, the detailed calendar provided by her Aide-de-Camp, 1LT Mabry, does not support her contention. Moreover, numerous witnesses stated that they rarely saw BG Karpinski or LTC (P) Phillabaum.

20. (U) In addition I find that psychological factors, such as the difference in culture, the Soldiers' quality of life, the real presence of mortal danger over an extended time period, and the failure of commanders to recognize these pressures contributed to the perversive atmosphere that existed at Abu Ghraib (BCCF) Detention Facility and throughout the 800th MP Brigade.

21. As I have documented in other parts of this investigation, I find that there was no clear emphasis by BG Karpinski to ensure that the 800th MP Brigade Staff, Commanders, and Soldiers were trained to standard in detainee operations and proficiency or that serious accountability lapses that occurred over a significant period of time, particularly at Abu Ghraib (BCCF), were corrected. AR 15-6 Investigations regarding detainee escapes were not acted upon, followed up with corrective action, or disseminated to subordinate commanders or Soldiers. Brigade and unit SOPs for dealing with detainees if they existed at all, were not read or understood by MP Soldiers assigned the difficult mission of detainee operations. Following the abuse of several detainees at Camp Bucca in May 2003, I could find no evidence that BG Karpinski ever directed corrective training for her soldiers or ensured that MP Soldiers throughout Iraq clearly understood the requirements of the Geneva Conventions relating to the treatment of detainees.

22. On 17 January 2004 BG Karpinski was formally admonished in writing by LTG Sanchez regarding the serious deficiencies in her Brigade. LTG Sanchez found that the performance of the 800th MP Brigade had not met the standards set by the Army or by CJTF-7. He found that incidents in the preceding six months had occurred that reflected a lack of clear standards, proficiency and leadership within the Brigade. LTG Sanchez also cited the recent detainee abuse at Abu Ghraib (BCCF) as the most recent example of a poor leadership climate that "permeates the Brigade." I totally concur with LTG Sanchez' opinion regarding the performance of BG Karpinski and the 800th MP Brigade.

RECOMMENDATIONS AS TO PART THREE OF THE INVESTIGATION:

1. (U) That **BG Janis L. Karpinski, Commander, 800th MP Brigade** be Relieved from Command and given a General Officer Memorandum of Reprimand for the following acts which have been previously referred to in the aforementioned findings:

- Failing to ensure that MP Soldiers at theater-level detention facilities throughout Iraq had appropriate SOPs for dealing with detainees and that

Commanders and Soldiers had read, understood, and would adhere to these SOPs.

- Failing to ensure that MP Soldiers in the 800th MP Brigade knew, understood, and adhered to the protections afforded to detainees in the Geneva Convention Relative to the Treatment of Prisoners of War.
- Making material misrepresentations to the Investigation Team as to the frequency of her visits to her subordinate commands.
- Failing to obey an order from the CFLCC Commander, LTG McKiernan, regarding the withholding of disciplinary authority for Officer and Senior Noncommissioned Officer misconduct.
- Failing to take appropriate action regarding the ineffectiveness of a subordinate Commander, LTC (P) Jerry Phillabaum.
- Failing to take appropriate action regarding the ineffectiveness of numerous members of her Brigade Staff including her XO, S-1, S-3, and S-4.
- Failing to properly ensure the results and recommendations of the AARs and numerous 15-6 Investigation reports on escapes and shootings (over a period of several months) were properly disseminated to, and understood by, subordinate commanders.
- Failing to ensure and enforce basic Soldier standards throughout her command.
- Failing to establish a Brigade METL.
- Failing to establish basic proficiency in assigned tasks for Soldiers throughout the 800th MP Brigade.
- Failing to ensure that numerous and reported accountability lapses at detention facilities throughout Iraq were corrected.

2. (U) **That COL Thomas M. Pappas, Commander, 205th MI Brigade**, be given a General Officer Memorandum of Reprimand and Investigated UP Procedure 15, AR 381-10, US Army Intelligence Activities for the following acts which have been previously referred to in the aforementioned findings:

- Failing to ensure that Soldiers under his direct command were properly trained in and followed the IROE.
- Failing to ensure that Soldiers under his direct command knew, understood, and followed the protections afforded to detainees in the Geneva Convention Relative to the Treatment of Prisoners of War.
- Failing to properly supervise his soldiers working and "visiting" Tier 1 of the Hard-Site at Abu Ghraib (BCCF).

3. (U) That **LTC (P) Jerry L. Phillabaum, Commander, 320th MP Battalion**, be Relieved from Command, be given a General Officer Memorandum of Reprimand, and be removed from the Colonel/O-6 Promotion List for the following acts which have been previously referred to in the aforementioned findings:

- Failing to properly ensure the results, recommendations, and AARs from numerous reports on escapes and shootings over a period of several months were properly disseminated to, and understood by, subordinates.
- Failing to implement the appropriate recommendations from various 15-6 Investigations as specifically directed by BG Karpinski.

- Failing to ensure that Soldiers under his direct command were properly trained in Internment and Resettlement Operations.
- Failing to ensure that Soldiers under his direct command knew and understood the protections afforded to detainees in the Geneva Convention Relative to the Treatment of Prisoners of War.
- Failing to properly supervise his soldiers working and "visiting" Tier 1 of the Hard-Site at Abu Ghraib (BCCF).
- Failing to properly establish and enforce basic soldier standards, proficiency, and accountability.
- Failure to conduct an appropriate Mission Analysis and to task organize to accomplish his mission.

4. (U) **That LTC Steven L. Jordan, Former Director, Joint Interrogation and Debriefing Center and Liaison Officer to 205th Military Intelligence Brigade,** be relieved from duty and be given a General Officer Memorandum of Reprimand for the following acts which have been previously referred to in the aforementioned findings:

- Making material misrepresentations to the Investigating Team, including his leadership roll at Abu Ghraib (BCCF).
- Failing to ensure that Soldiers under his direct control were properly trained in and followed the IROE.
- Failing to ensure that Soldiers under his direct control knew, understood, and followed the protections afforded to detainees in the Geneva Convention Relative to the Treatment of Prisoners of War.
- Failing to properly supervise soldiers under his direct authority working and "visiting" Tier 1 of the Hard-Site at Abu Ghraib (BCCF).

5. (U) **That MAJ David W. DiNenna, Sr., S-3, 320th MP Battalion,** be Relieved from his position as the Battalion S-3 and be given a General Officer Memorandum of Reprimand for the following acts which have been previously referred to in the aforementioned findings:

- Received a GOMOR from LTG McKiernan, Commander CFLCC, on 25 May 2003, for dereliction of duty for failing to report a violation of CENTCOM General Order #1 by a subordinate Field Grade Officer and Senior Noncommissioned Officer, which he personally observed; GOMOR was returned to Soldier and not filed.
- Failing to take corrective action and implement recommendations from various 15-6 investigations even after receiving a GOMOR from BG Karpinski, Commander 800th MP Brigade, on 10 November 03, for failing to take corrective security measures as ordered; GOMOR was filed locally.
- Failing to take appropriate action and report an incident of detainee abuse, whereby he personally witnessed a Soldier throw a detainee from the back of a truck.

6. (U) **That CPT Donald J. Reese, Commander, 372nd MP Company,** be Relieved from Command and be given a General Officer Memorandum of

Reprimand for the following acts which have been previously referred to in the aforementioned findings:

- Failing to ensure that Soldiers under his direct command knew and understood the protections afforded to detainees in the Geneva Convention Relative to the Treatment of Prisoners of War.
- Failing to properly supervise his Soldiers working and "visiting" Tier 1 of the Hard-Site at Abu Ghraib (BCCF).
- Failing to properly establish and enforce basic soldier standards, proficiency, and accountability.
- Failing to ensure that Soldiers under his direct command were properly trained in Internment and Resettlement Operations.

7. (U) **That 1LT Lewis C. Raeder, Platoon Leader, 372nd MP Company**, be Relieved from his duties as Platoon Leader and be given a General Officer Memorandum of Reprimand for the following acts which have been previously referred to in the aforementioned findings:

- Failing to ensure that Soldiers under his direct command knew and understood the protections afforded to detainees in the Geneva Convention Relative to the Treatment of Prisoners of War.
- Failing to properly supervise his soldiers working and "visiting" Tier 1 of the Hard-Site at Abu Ghraib (BCCF).
- Failing to properly establish and enforce basic Soldier standards, proficiency, and accountability.
- Failing to ensure that Soldiers under his direct command were properly trained in Internment and Resettlement Operations.

8. (U) That SGM Marc Emerson, Operations SGM, 320th MP Battalion, be Relieved from his duties and given a General Officer Memorandum of Reprimand for the following acts which have been previously referred to in the aforementioned findings:

- Making a material misrepresentation to the Investigation Team stating that he had "never" been admonished or reprimanded by BG Karpinski, when in fact he had been admonished for failing to obey an order from BG Karpinski to "stay out of the towers" at the holding facility.
- Making a material misrepresentation to the Investigation Team stating that he had attended every shift change/guard-mount conducted at the 320th MP Battalion, and that he personally briefed his Soldiers on the proper treatment of detainees, when in fact numerous statements contradict this assertion.
- Failing to ensure that Soldiers in the 320th MP Battalion knew and understood the protections afforded to detainees in the Geneva Convention Relative to the Treatment of Prisoners of War.
- Failing to properly supervise his soldiers working and "visiting" Tier 1 of the Hard-Site at Abu Ghraib (BCCF).
- Failing to properly establish and enforce basic soldier standards, proficiency, and accountability.

- Failing to ensure that his Soldiers were properly trained in Internment and Resettlement Operations.

9. (U) That **1SG Brian G. Lipinski, First Sergeant, 372nd MP Company,** be Relieved from his duties as First Sergeant of the 372nd MP Company and given a General Officer Memorandum of Reprimand for the following acts which have been previously referred to in the aforementioned findings:

- Failing to ensure that Soldiers in the 372nd MP Company knew and understood the protections afforded to detainees in the Geneva Convention Relative to the Treatment of Prisoners of War.
- Failing to properly supervise his soldiers working and "visiting" Tier 1 of the Hard-Site at Abu Ghraib (BCCF).
- Failing to properly establish and enforce basic soldier standards, proficiency, and accountability.
- Failing to ensure that his Soldiers were properly trained in Internment and Resettlement Operations.

10. (U) That **SFC Shannon K. Snider, Platoon Sergeant, 372nd MP Company,** be Relieved from his duties, receive a General Officer Memorandum of Reprimand, and receive action under the Uniform Code of Military Justice for the following acts which have been previously referred to in the aforementioned findings:

- Failing to ensure that Soldiers in his platoon knew and understood the protections afforded to detainees in the Geneva Convention Relative to the Treatment of Prisoners of War.
- Failing to properly supervise his soldiers working and "visiting" Tier 1 of the Hard-Site at Abu Ghraib (BCCF).
- Failing to properly establish and enforce basic soldier standards, proficiency, and accountability.
- Failing to ensure that his Soldiers were properly trained in Internment and Resettlement Operations.
- Failing to report a Soldier, who under his direct control, abused detainees by stomping on their bare hands and feet in his presence.

11. (U) That **Mr. Steven Stephanowicz, Contract US Civilian Interrogator, CACI, 205th Military Intelligence Brigade,** be given an Official Reprimand to be placed in his employment file, termination of employment, and generation of a derogatory report to revoke his security clearance for the following acts which have been previously referred to in the aforementioned findings:

- Made a false statement to the investigation team regarding the locations of his interrogations, the activities during his interrogations, and his knowledge of abuses.
- Allowed and/or instructed MPs, who were not trained in interrogation techniques, to facilitate interrogations by "setting conditions" which were neither authorized and in accordance with applicable regulations/policy. He clearly knew his instructions equated to physical abuse.

12. (U) That **Mr. John Israel, Contract US Civilian Interpreter, CACI, 205th Military Intelligence Brigade**, be given an Official Reprimand to be placed in his employment file and have his security clearance reviewed by competent authority for the following acts or concerns which have been previously referred to in the aforementioned findings:

- Denied ever having seen interrogation processes in violation of the IROE, which is contrary to several witness statements.
- Did not have a security clearance.

13. (U) I find that there is sufficient credible information to warrant an Inquiry UP Procedure 15, AR 381-10, US Army Intelligence Activities, be conducted to determine the extent of culpability of MI personnel, assigned to the 205th MI Brigade and the Joint Interrogation and Debriefing Center (JIDC) at Abu Ghraib (BCCF). Specifically, I suspect that **COL Thomas M. Pappas, LTC Steve L. Jordan, Mr. Steven Stephanowicz**, and **Mr. John Israel** were either directly or indirectly responsible for the abuses at Abu Ghraib (BCCF) and strongly recommend immediate disciplinary action as described in the preceding paragraphs as well as the initiation of a Procedure 15 Inquiry to determine the full extent of their culpability.

OTHER FINDINGS/OBSERVATIONS

1. (U) Due to the nature and scope of this investigation, I acquired the assistance of Col (Dr.) Henry Nelson, a USAF Psychiatrist, to analyze the investigation materials from a psychological perspective. He determined that there was evidence that the horrific abuses suffered by the detainees at Abu Ghraib (BCCF) were wanton acts of select soldiers in an unsupervised and dangerous setting. There was a complex interplay of many psychological factors and command insufficiencies. . . .

2. (U) During the course of this investigation I conducted a lengthy interview with BG Karpinski that lasted over four hours, and is included verbatim in the investigation Annexes. BG Karpinski was extremely emotional during much of her testimony. What I found particularly disturbing in her testimony was her complete unwillingness to either understand or accept that many of the problems inherent in the 800th MP Brigade were caused or exacerbated by poor leadership and the refusal of her command to both establish and enforce basic standards and principles among its Soldiers.

3. (U) Throughout the investigation, we observed many individual Soldiers and some subordinate units under the 800th MP Brigade that overcame significant obstacles, persevered in extremely poor conditions, and upheld the Army Values. We discovered numerous examples of Soldiers and Sailors taking the initiative in the absence of leadership and accomplishing their assigned tasks. . . .

CONCLUSION

1. (U) Several US Army Soldiers have committed egregious acts and grave breaches of international law at Abu Ghraib/BCCF and Camp Bucca, Iraq. Furthermore, key senior leaders in both the 800th MP Brigade and the 205th MI Brigade failed to comply with established regulations, policies, and command directives in preventing detainee abuses at Abu Ghraib (BCCF) and at Camp Bucca during the period August 2003 to February 2004.

2. (U) Approval and implementation of the recommendations of this AR 15-6 Investigation and those highlighted in previous assessments are essential to establish the conditions with the resources and personnel required to prevent future occurrences of detainee abuse.

- **Source:** Antonio M. Taguba, "Article 15-6: Investigation of the 800th Military Police Brigade," Findlaw, http://news.findlaw.com/nytimes/docs/iraq/tagubarpt.html.
- **Analysis:** The Abu Ghraib prisoner abuse scandal seriously damaged U.S. legitimacy in Iraq and throughout the Arab world. The investigation into the incidents of physical and sexual abuse of prisoners found both individual wrongdoing and institutional failures. Perpetrators were tried and convicted, but the higher command was exonerated of deliberate criminality. The report did, however, identify the poor training and inadequate oversight of military police responsible for the prison.

    The report was criticized for letting senior leaders off too easily. Amid a deteriorating security situation, the high command pressured troops on the ground to get good intelligence so that the insurgents could be eliminated. Rounding up and interrogating suspects seemed the best way to get this information. Encouragement to soften up suspects given to guards by interrogators, combined with overcrowding and poor oversight of prison personnel, led inevitably to abuses.

GETTING IT RIGHT

As the insurgency progressed into its second and third years, more and more soldiers and analysts recognized the need for a new approach. This recognition led to better tactics, improved doctrine, and ultimately to an effective COIN strategy. These changes took a few years to implement. During those years many more Iraqi and American lives were lost redeeming a situation that had been created in no small measure by bad policy and poor preparation.

- **Document 68: Excerpt of Prepared Testimony of Kenneth Pollack, Brookings Institution**
- **When:** July 18, 2005
- **Where:** Washington, DC
- **Significance:** Pollack argued for a shift in U.S. strategy for combating the insurgency in Iraq.

Mr. Chairman and Senator Biden, thank you for allowing me to come before you to discuss the future of Iraq, and particularly our efforts to secure that country to make reconstruction possible. As you have both repeatedly reminded us, the reconstruction of Iraq is a vital interest of the United States, just as it is vital to the people of Iraq. As we all know, and have repeatedly had reinforced to us, security is absolutely critical to the broader reconstruction effort. Without security, reconstruction will fail. And until we have dealt with the pressing problems of security, it will be impossible for us to perceive, let alone solve, many of the other matters troubling Iraq. If we get security right, everything is possible, although nothing is guaranteed.

I have confined my remarks to the four options you have outlined. I will begin with your first option, and address each in turn. . . .

Mr. Chairman, I believe that after two years of trying to secure Iraq with our current strategy, it is becoming increasingly clear that we have the wrong strategy for the job. Our current approach probably was the appropriate strategy in the immediate aftermath of the fall of Baghdad, but the inadequate number of troops we brought to Iraq and a series of other mistakes rendered this approach largely infeasible. Today, our problems have metastasized, and I believe that we must fundamentally change our strategy to cope with the new challenges we face.

Our effort to secure Iraq faces two overarching and interlocking problems: a full-blown insurgency and a continuing state of semi-lawlessness. Both are equally important. Reconstruction will likely fail if either is unaddressed. I believe that current U.S. strategy in Iraq is misguided because it is not properly tailored to defeat the first problem and largely ignores the second.

Today, and since the fall of Baghdad, the United States has employed what I would call a "post-conflict stabilization" model of security operations. The key element of this strategy is providing simultaneous security for the entire country by concentrating Coalition forces on those areas of greatest unrest to try to quell the violence quickly and keep it from spreading. Had the United States brought sufficient ground forces to blanket the country immediately after the fall of Saddam's regime—as many warned—and had we not made a series of other mistakes, like failing to provide our troops with orders to maintain law and order, to impose martial law and prevent looting, I think this strategy might very well have succeeded.

However, our continued reliance on this approach is failing. To borrow a military term usually employed in a different realm of operations, today we are reinforcing failure. By continuing to concentrate our overstretched forces on the areas of greatest insurgent activity we are depriving most of Iraq's populated areas of desperately-needed security forces, and by emphasizing offensive search and sweep missions, we are making ever more enemies among Iraq's Sunni tribal population. In other words, we are failing to protect those Iraqis who most want reconstruction to succeed and we are further antagonizing the community that is most antipathetic to our goals.

This approach runs directly contrary to the principal lessons of counterinsurgent warfare.

In 1986, Dr. Andrew F. Krepinevich, then a major in the Army, published what is widely-regarded as the seminal work on American military performance in Vietnam, titled *The Army and Vietnam*. In this book, Krepinevich demonstrated that the Army high command—for reasons entirely of its own choosing—largely refused to employ a traditional counterinsurgency strategy against the Viet Cong and North Vietnamese Army forces. The Military Assistance Command-Vietnam (MACV) repeatedly shut down other efforts, by the Marines and by Army Special Forces, to employ a traditional counterinsurgency (COIN) strategy. Krepinevich further demonstrated that these stillborn COIN campaigns had all proven far more successful before they were terminated than MACV's cherished offensive operations.

Mr. Chairman, I do not know why it is that the United States has not yet adopted a traditional counterinsurgency strategy in Iraq. I suspect that it is for reasons far more mundane and far better-intentioned than MACV's rationale was in that earlier war, because I know General Abizaid to be a superb soldier and a wise commander. However, whatever the rationale, it is clear that the United States has so far failed to employ a traditional counterinsurgency strategy in Iraq, just as we did in Vietnam, and as a result we are failing in Iraq just as we failed in Vietnam.

Mr. Chairman, if you were to pick up a copy of Dr. Krepinevich's book, you would find, I think a great many chilling passages. Passages where Krepinevich explains how history has demonstrated that a guerrilla campaign can be defeated, and how the United States failed to employ such a strategy in Vietnam. These passages are unsettling precisely because they so closely echo our problems and mistakes in Iraq today. We are once again failing to use a true COIN strategy in Iraq, and committing too many of the very same errors we made in Vietnam.

The crux of a traditional counterinsurgency strategy is never to reinforce failure, but always to reinforce success. As Mao Zedong once wrote, the guerrilla is like a fish who swims in the sea of the people—thus, if you can deprive the guerrilla of support from the people, he will be as helpless as a fish out of water.

The goal of a true-COIN campaign is to deprive the guerrilla of that access. The COIN force begins by securing a base of operations by denying one portion of the country to the insurgency. This portion can be as big or as small as the COIN force can handle—the bigger the COIN force available, the larger the area. Within this area, the COIN force provides the people with security, in all senses of the word. In Iraq, this would mean security from insurgent attack as well as from ordinary (and organized) crime. In so doing, the COIN force creates a secure space in which political and economic life can flourish once again. Ideally, the COIN force would pour resources into this area to make it economically dynamic and take advantage of the security the COIN campaign has provided, both to cement popular support for the COIN campaign and to make it attractive to people living outside the secure area so that they will support the COIN campaign when it shifts to their region.

The increasing attractiveness of these safe areas also solve the intelligence problem that COIN forces inevitably face. Ultimately, there is no way that a COIN force can gather enough intelligence on insurgent forces through traditional means to exterminate them. Instead, as the British learned in Northern Ireland, the only way to gather adequate information on the insurgents is to convince the local populace to volunteer such information, which they will do only if they are enthusiastic supporters of the COIN campaign and feel largely safe from retaliation by the insurgents. When these conditions are met, the counterinsurgents enjoy a massive advantage in intelligence making the further eradication of the insurgents easy, and almost an afterthought.

In addition, the COIN forces use these "safe zones" to train indigenous forces who can assist them in subsequent security operations. Once this base of operations is truly secure and can be maintained by local indigenous forces, the COIN forces then spread their control to additional parts of the country, performing the same set of steps as they did in the original area. . . .

The key, as Krepinevich and every other expert on counterinsurgency operations observes, is to start by securing the population and providing them with material incentives, in the form of real security and a thriving economy, that will cause them to reject the insurgency and support the COIN campaign. This is why a COIN strategy is best understood as a strategy of reinforcing success; because the counterinsurgents concentrate their forces where their support is strongest, and where they therefore can do the most good.

Instead, the approach we are employing in Iraq—concentrating our forces in Iraq's western provinces where the insurgents are thickest and support for reconstruction weakest—means reinforcing failure. Such an approach has repeatedly resulted in failures in guerrilla warfare throughout history. Our efforts to "take the fight to the enemy" and mount offensive sweep operations designed to kill insurgents and eliminate their strongholds have failed to even dent the insurgency so far, and likely will continue to do so, as was the case in Vietnam and other lost guerrilla wars. . . .

Against a full-blown insurgency, such as we are facing in Iraq, offensive operations cannot succeed and are ultimately counterproductive. The guerrilla does not need to stand and fight but can run or melt back into the population and so avoid crippling losses. If the COIN forces do not remain and pacify the area for the long term, the guerrillas will be back within weeks, months, or maybe years, but they will be back nonetheless. Meanwhile, the concentration of forces on these sweep operations means a major diversion of effort away from securing the population. In Iraq, this has left the vast bulk of the population largely unprotected both against insurgent attacks and normal crime—organized and unorganized.

Moreover, the tactics of our offensive operations have contributed to the alienation of the Sunni tribal community, driving many otherwise agnostic Iraqis into the arms of the insurgents. Many American units continue to see the targets of their raids as enemies and treat them as such—invariably turning them and their neighbors into enemies regardless of their feelings beforehand. Often, the priority American formations place on force protection comes at the expense of the larger mission—the safety, psychological disposition, and dignity of Iraqis. Busting down doors, ordering families down on the floor, holding them down with the sole of a boot, searching women in the presence of men, waiving around weapons, ransacking rooms or whole houses, and confiscating weapons all come with a price. Because too much of the intelligence that the United States is relying on is poor, it is not a rare occurrence that houses raided turn out to be innocuous. In some cases, the wanted personnel may have been there at some point and fled, but in others no one in the house was guilty at all. Indeed, too often, U.S. forces are directed to raid a house or arrest a person by someone else who simply has a grudge against them and turns them in to the Americans as an insurgent to settle a personal score.

An example of both the potential of true counterinsurgency operations and the danger of refusing to employ them can be found in the experience of the Iraqi town of Fallujah. Until the fall of 2004, Fallujah was a major insurgent stronghold. The town was then taken by U.S. forces in a full-scale conventional assault in which, American commanders touted as major victories both the number of insurgents killed and the psychological gains of taking this stronghold from the enemy. However, within just a few months, the insurgents had reemerged with no noticeable impact on their operations or lethality. On the other hand, unlike many other towns in the Sunni triangle, a fair number of American and Iraqi forces remained in Fallujah after the assault, providing it with greater security than in most neighboring towns, but not as much as was the case immediately after the assault when large numbers of American ground troops were present. Likewise, the U.S. and the Iraqis did begin to pump resources into the city, and reached out to local shaykhs to try to form a new political process, and to give local residents an incentive to participate in the national political process. As a result, Fallujah has been a modest success story. However, because promised funds have not been forthcoming, because the Marines in Fallujah are spread thinly and the Iraqi forces are not indigenous (and are often Shi'ah), the insurgency has begun to make a come back in Fallujah.

Thus Fallujah demonstrates what a successful approach might look like, but only if it is handled properly. And unfortunately, Fallujah is more the exception than the rule. Elsewhere in Iraq, U.S. forces clear the areas without staying in force, without leaving behind indigenous security forces willing and able to secure the area, and so without leaving the kind of security environment that would make it possible to try to revive either the local economy or the local political process.

Southern Iraq and the persistent popularity of Muqtada as-Sadr (and other, similar figures) is another example of the problems created by our current security strategy. The predominantly Shi'i southeast of Iraq is overwhelmingly supportive of reconstruction, yet we find growing frustration with reconstruction, the United States, and the transitional Iraqi government throughout that community. Why? Because the people are still plagued by organized and random crime, which makes their economic life difficult, keeps unemployment high and incomes low, contributes to frequent power outages and gasoline shortages, and prevents the restoration of clean water and sanitation, among other problems. This frustration, allowed to fester over time, is driving Iraqis into the arms of the Muqtada as-Sadr's of Iraq, whose message is a simple one: the Americans are either unwilling or unable to provide you with the basic necessities of life, but we can. They employ the model that Hizballah and Hamas have used to such success, providing tangible, material benefits in return for support. This is exactly what Muqtada as-Sadr provides the residents of Sadr City and what other shaykhs, alims, and other would-be potentates provide other Iraqis in different parts of the country.

This is a disastrous course that could push Iraq into fragmentation and civil war. It is already convincing any number of groups (and not just the Kurds), that they should pursue autonomy from the central government, which is increasingly seen as out of touch, corrupt, and wholly focused on its own (irrelevant) squabbles over power.

Mr. Chairman, this analysis leads me to the conclusion that the United States must dramatically re-orient our strategy for securing Iraq. We must adopt a true counterinsurgency strategy, of the traditional "spreading oil stain" variety. We must simultaneously recognize that even if we do so, securing Iraq is going to take a very long time. In this respect, I was heartened to hear Secretary of Defense Rumsfeld acknowledge that success in Iraq would likely require over a decade. He is surely right, but he is only likely to be right if the United States adopts the right strategy to do so.

Painted in broad brush strokes, a true counterinsurgency strategy for Iraq would focus on securing enclaves (Kurdistan, much of southeastern Iraq, Baghdad, and a number of other major urban centers, along with the oilfields and some other vital economic facilities) while, initially, leaving much of the countryside to the insurgents. The Coalition would consolidate its security forces within those enclaves, thereby greatly improving the ratio of security personnel to civilians, and allowing a major effort to secure these enclaves to allow local economic and political development at a micro-level. The Coalition would likewise redirect its political efforts and economic resources solely into the secured enclaves—both to ensure that they prosper and because those would be the only areas where it would be worth investing in the short run. Such a strategy might therefore mean foregoing such things as national elections or rebuilding the entire power grid, because they might be impossible in a situation where the Coalition forces had abdicated control over large areas of the country.

The concentrated security focus should allow local economic and political developments to make meaningful progress, which in turn should turn around public opinion within the enclaves (making the Iraqis living in the enclaves more willing to support the reconstruction effort and, hopefully, making those Iraqis outside the enclaves more desirous of experiencing the same benefits).

Once these enclaves were secured, and as additional Iraqi security forces were trained or foreign forces brought in, they would be slowly expanded to include additional communities—hence the metaphor of the spreading oil stain. In every case, the Coalition would focus the same security, political, and economic resources on each new community brought into the pacified zone. If implemented properly, a true counterinsurgency approach can succeed in winning back the entire country. However, it means ceding control over swathes of it at first and taking some time before Iraq will be seen as a stable, unified, pluralist state. Nevertheless it may be the only option open to us if, as is the case at present, the U.S.-led coalition cannot control large parts of the country and cannot keep the peace in those areas where it does operate.

At a more tactical level, a true COIN campaign in Iraq would make securing the Iraqi people its highest priority. American forces in Iraq, unfortunately remain preoccupied with force protection and with tracking down the insurgents who are attacking them, and as a result they are providing little security to the Iraqi people. U.S. forces generally remain penned up in formidable cantonments. They are cut off from the populace and have little interaction with them. In the field, they come out to attend to logistical needs and to conduct raids against suspected insurgents. In the cities, they generally come out only to make infrequent patrols—which are virtually always conducted mounted in Bradley fighting vehicles or HMMWVs (the ubiquitous "Humvees" or "Hummers") at speeds of 30–50 kms per hour. Indeed, prior to the January elections, American forces did (temporarily) engage in foot patrols in cities like Mosul and the result was an immediate, but equally temporary, increase in morale and support for the U.S. presence.

It is a constant (and fully justified) complaint of Iraqis that the Americans have no presence and make no effort to stop street crime or the attacks on them by the insurgents. Many British officers (and some Americans too) argue that the United States should instead be employing the kind of foot patrols backed by helicopters and/or vehicles that the British Army learned to use in Northern Ireland, and that all NATO forces eventually employed in the Balkans. This is the only way that American forces can get out, reassure the Iraqi civilians, find out from them where the troublemakers are, and respond to their problems.

Adopting a true counterinsurgency strategy, coupled with its attendant tactics such as guarding population centers and key infrastructure, foot patrols, presence, and the eradication of crime and attacks on Iraqis would doubtless expose U.S. personnel to greater risks. However, they are absolutely necessary if reconstruction is to succeed in Iraq. There is no question that force protection must always be an issue of concern to any American commander, but it cannot be the determining principle of U.S. operations. American military forces are in Iraq because the reconstruction of that country is critical to the stability of the Persian Gulf and a vital interest of the United States. In their current mode of operations, our troops are neither safe nor are they accomplishing their most important mission. Consequently, executing that mission must become the highest concern of U.S. military commanders, and their current strategy—focusing on force protection and offensive operations against the insurgents—is misguided. If it does not change, the reconstruction may fail outright and all of the sacrifices of the American people and our service men and women will have been for nothing.

- **Source:** Kenneth Pollack, senior fellow and director of Saban Center for Middle East Policy, Brookings Institution, prepared testimony on Iraq security for Senate Foreign Relations Committee, July 18, 2005.

- **Analysis:** Recognizing the nature of a threat does not automatically lead to an effective strategy for countering it. After what analysts have referred to as a "wasted year" in Iraq, the United States and its coalition partners recognized that they faced a complex insurgency. However, U.S. forces lacked experience and training for such a conflict. They relied on conventional means, in particular superior firepower, to respond to the pervasive threat. This approach not only failed to defeat the insurgents, it alienated Iraqi civilians, who often suffered as a result of the heavy-handed tactics.

  Kenneth Pollack of the Brookings Institution argued that the United States must adopt a traditional counterinsurgency strategy. Troops should switch from continual sweeps to clear-and-hold operations. They should create enclaves out of which they could expand to gain control of the country area by area. This approach would also allow them to win the trust of local people and train and deploy Iraqi security forces.

- **Document 69: Excerpt of *National Strategy for Victory in Iraq***
- **When:** November 2005
- **Where:** Washington, DC
- **Significance:** The White House released a new plan for victory in Iraq.

Victory in Iraq is Defined in Stages

- **Short term**, Iraq is making steady progress in fighting terrorists, meeting political milestones, building democratic institutions, and standing up security forces.
- **Medium term**, Iraq is in the lead defeating terrorists and providing its own security, with a fully constitutional government in place, and on its way to achieving its economic potential.
- **Longer term**, Iraq is peaceful, united, stable, and secure, well integrated into the international community, and a full partner in the global war on terrorism. . . .

The Enemy Is Diffuse and Sophisticated

- The enemy is a combination of rejectionists, Saddamists, and terrorists affiliated with or inspired by Al Qaida. Distinct but integrated strategies are required to defeat each element.
- Each element shares a common short-term objective—to intimidate, terrorize, and tear down—but has separate and incompatible long-term goals.
- Exploiting these differences within the enemy is a key element of our strategy.

Our Strategy for Victory is Clear

We will help the Iraqi people build a new Iraq with a constitutional, representative government that respects civil rights and has security forces sufficient to maintain domestic order and keep Iraq from becoming a safe haven for terrorists.

To achieve this end, we are pursuing an integrated strategy along three broad tracks, which together incorporate the efforts of the Iraqi government, the Coalition, cooperative countries in the region, the international community, and the United Nations.

- *The Political Track* involves working to forge a broadly supported national compact for democratic governance by helping the Iraqi government:

  - *Isolate* enemy elements from those who can be won over to the political process by countering false propaganda and demonstrating to all Iraqis that they have a stake in a democratic Iraq;

- *Engage* those outside the political process and invite in those willing to turn away from violence through ever-expanding avenues of participation; and

- *Build* stable, pluralistic, and effective national institutions that can protect the interests of all Iraqis, and facilitate Iraq's full integration into the international community.

- *The Security Track* involves carrying out a campaign to defeat the terrorists and neutralize the insurgency, developing Iraqi security forces, and helping the Iraqi government:

  - *Clear* areas of enemy control by remaining on the offensive, killing and capturing enemy fighters and denying them safe-haven;

  - *Hold* areas freed from enemy influence by ensuring that they remain under the control of the Iraqi government with an adequate Iraqi security force presence; and

  - *Build* Iraqi Security Forces and the capacity of local institutions to deliver services, advance the rule of law, and nurture civil society.

- *The Economic Track* involves setting the foundation for a sound and self-sustaining economy by helping the Iraqi government:

  - *Restore* Iraq's infrastructure to meet increasing demand and the needs of a growing economy;

  - *Reform* Iraq's economy, which in the past has been shaped by war, dictatorship, and sanctions, so that it can be self-sustaining in the future; and

  - *Build* the capacity of Iraqi institutions to maintain infrastructure, rejoin the international economic community, and improve the general welfare of all Iraqis.

This Strategy is Integrated and its Elements are Mutually Reinforcing.

- **Source:** *National Strategy for Victory in Iraq* (Washington, DC: GPO, 2005), pp. 1–2.

- **Analysis:** Two and one-half years after the president declared "mission accomplished," the White House released its plan for defeating the complex insurgency that racked the country. The strategy contained all the right elements in an integrated and mutually reinforcing strategy. It called for increased security to create an environment in which economic and political development might occur. The plan also called for the Iraqis to assume increasing responsibility for all aspects of its implementation.

   Although the plan identified the correct approach to COIN, it required an additional element to be successful. The Iraqi government and people would have to accept and work to implement it. This element would take an additional year to accomplish. Only with the Anbar Awakening would the COIN effort improve significantly.

- **Document 70: Excerpt of Report to Congress on Status of Iraq**
- **When:** 2006
- **Where:** Washington, DC
- **Significance:** This report presented an optimistic view of progress in Iraq.

This report to Congress on measuring stability and security in Iraq is submitted pursuant to section 9010 of the Department of Defense Appropriations Act 2006, Public Law 109-148. This is the fourth in a series of reports on this subject and the second of these reports under Section 9010. The most recent report was submitted in February 2006.

The report is divided into two sections corresponding to the indicators and measures identified in Section 9010. The first section of the report, "Stability and Security in Iraq," describes trends and progress towards meeting goals for political stability, strengthening economic activity, and achieving a stable security environment in Iraq. The second section of the report, "Security Forces Training and Performance," describes progress in the training, development, and readiness of the Iraqi Security Forces, including the forces of the Ministry of Defense (MOD) and the police and paramilitary forces of the Ministry of Interior (MOI)....

Measures of Stability and Security and the National Strategy for Victory in Iraq

The President's National Strategy for Victory in Iraq focuses on helping the Iraqi people build a new Iraq with a constitutional and representative government that respects political and human rights and with sufficient security forces to maintain domestic order and keep Iraq from becoming a safe haven for terrorists. To this end, the United States is pursuing an integrated strategy along three broad tracks:

- **Political:** helping the Iraqi people forge a broadly supported compact for democratic government.
- **Economic:** assisting the Iraqi government in establishing the foundations for a sound economy with the capacity to deliver essential services.
- **Security:** developing the capacity of Iraqis to secure their country while carrying out a campaign to defeat the terrorists and neutralize the insurgency. Each of these tracks is integrated with the others; success in each is necessary for success along the other tracks. Security depends on a democratic political process, which in turn depends in part on economic opportunity. Economic progress depends on securing the Iraqi infrastructure against sabotage and attack and protecting the Iraqi people from terrorist attacks that undermine individual participation in economic development and the political process.

The National Strategy for Victory in Iraq uses measurable trends indicating progress along each of these tracks to indicate where programs are achieving success and where it is necessary to increase efforts or adjust implementation of the strategy.

The President's strategy also identifies eight strategic objectives, or pillars, of the integrated political, economic, and security strategy: defeat the terrorists and neutralize the insurgency; transition Iraq to security self-reliance; help Iraqis forge a national compact for democratic government; help Iraq build government capacity and provide essential services; help Iraq strengthen its economy; help Iraq strengthen the rule of law and promote civil rights; increase international support for Iraq; and strengthen public understanding of Coalition efforts and public isolation of the insurgents. Key indicators of progress since the last report include the following.

Political Progress. The Iraqi people met two critical milestones in their country's democratic advance. On April 22, 2006, the Council of Representatives (the Iraqi Parliament) elected senior members of the new government, including the President, two Deputy Presidents, the Speaker of the Council of Representatives, and the Speaker's two deputies. At the same time, Nuri al-Maliki was nominated as the new Prime Minister. Under the Constitution, the Prime Minister was given a month to form his cabinet. On May 20, 2006, the Prime Minister met his Constitutional deadline by naming and winning Council of Representatives approval for his cabinet, and Iraq's national unity government was sworn in the same day. With the exception of the Defense and Interior portfolios, cabinet positions were filled by consensus among Iraq's major political parties.

From the outset, Prime Minister al-Maliki sought to fill the Interior and Defense portfolios with competent individuals who were non-sectarian and not associated with any militias. Prime Minister al-Maliki continues to consider candidates for these two critical posts, and permanent ministers for Defense and Interior should be named soon. In the meantime, Prime Minister al-Maliki will be the acting Minister of Interior and Deputy Prime Minister Dr. Salam al-Zawba'i will be the acting Minister of Defense. . . .

Economic Activity. The Iraqi government continued to make progress implementing its economic agenda, despite numerous challenges. The delay in forming the new government led to a postponement of the first quarterly review under Iraq's Standby Arrangement with the International Monetary Fund and slowed some reform efforts. The Iraqi economy has demonstrated overall macroeconomic stability since the last report, the currency remains stable, and reserves are above targets. Iraq continues to reduce external debt on the basis of the Paris Club members' agreement in November 2004 and similar treatment from non-Paris Club creditors. Despite some variation due to acts of violence and technical issues, electrical production is at the same levels as reported in February 2006—about 6% higher than for the same period in 2005. The average oil production for the first four months of 2006 remained steady at an average of 1.9 million barrels per day (mbpd). This is still short of the Iraqi Ministry of Oil goal of 2.5 mbpd [million barrels per day].

Oil exports increased from an average of 1.2 mbpd early in the first quarter to 1.4 mbpd. More than 90% of government revenue comes from oil exports, and lower than desired export volumes have been somewhat offset by higher prices for Iraqi oil.

The Security Environment. Anti-Iraqi forces—extremists and terrorists—continue to fail in their campaign to derail the political process, to alienate the Iraqi people from democratic governance and security institutions, and to foment civil war. They attack Iraqi civilians, officials, and Security Forces with a goal of undermining the legitimately elected Government of Iraq and the democratic process. The February 22 bombing of the Golden Mosque of Samarra produced an upsurge in sectarian and militia violence but did not produce the civil war hoped for by its perpetrators. Iraqi government and religious leaders were united in condemning the attacks and in restraining sectarian unrest. The Iraqi Security Forces (ISF) also played a key role, operating effectively and with restraint. The performance of the ISF was critical to halting the spread of violence, keeping the perpetrators of the bombing from achieving their broader strategic goal. Although polls indicated that a majority of Iraqis were concerned that sectarian violence could spread to become civil war, the same polls indicated that perceptions of neighborhood safety remained relatively unchanged. This view reflects data that indicate that more than 80% of terrorist attacks were concentrated in just 4 of Iraq's 18 provinces. Twelve provinces, containing more than 50% of the population, experienced only 6% of all attacks.

Iraqi Security Forces. The Ministry of Defense (MOD) and the Ministry of Interior (MOI) Security Forces continue to increase in size and capability, and are increasingly taking over the lead combat responsibility from Coalition forces.

Training, equipping, and fielding of Security Forces personnel continue. As of May 15, 2006, 117,900 MOD personnel have been trained and equipped, including 116,500 in the Iraqi Army, Support Forces, and Special Operation Forces. This is 86% of MOD authorized force strength. The Iraqi Air Force now includes 600 trained and equipped personnel, which reflects 37% of authorized strength, and the Iraqi Navy is at 70% of authorized strength, with 800 trained and equipped personnel. Furthermore, 145,500 MOI personnel, including police, National Police, border forces, and other MOI personnel, have been trained and equipped, which reflects 77% of the MOI authorized end-strength. The MOD and the MOI are on track to complete initial training and equipping of 100% of their authorized end-strength by the end of December 2006, at which time the initial build-up will be completed and efforts will focus on replacing losses. The total number of Iraqi soldiers and police who have completed initial training and equipping is approximately 263,400, an increase of about 36,100 since the last report.

The number of Iraqi units able to take the lead in combat operations against the insurgency continues to increase. Iraqi planned, Iraqi-conducted, and most important, Iraqi-led missions continue throughout Iraq. As of May 15, 111 Iraqi Army, Special Operations, and Strategic Infrastructure Battalions are conducting counter-insurgency operations, 9% more than reported in February. This is 89% of the total number of battalions authorized. Seventy-one of these battalions are in the lead in military operations in their sectors, with the Coalition in a supporting role. All 28 authorized Iraqi National Police battalions are in the fight, with 2 in the lead.[1]

---

[1]The "National Police" refers to units formerly known as the Ministry of Interior National Special Police (e.g., National Police Commandos and Public Order Battalions) and not to the Iraqi Police Service ("beat cops"), which is a national police service.

More Iraqi units are assuming the security lead in their territory.

Fifty-seven Iraqi Army battalions and six National Police battalions now have the security lead in their territory. The ISF have the lead in 60% of Baghdad; for Iraq as a whole, the area for which the ISF have the lead has risen to 30,000 square miles, an increase of 20,000 from the February 2006 report. Two divisions, 16 brigades, and 63 battalions of the ISF now have the lead for security responsibility in their respective areas of operation. In addition, the MOD, MOI, or Ministry of Finance has assumed control and responsibility for 34 Forward Operating Bases from Coalition forces.

- **Source:** *Measuring Stability and Security in Iraq: Mandated Report to Congress* (Washington: GPO, 2006), pp. 1–4.
- **Analysis:** This report presented an optimistic assessment of progress toward stability in Iraq. It mustered an impressive array of statistics to measure effectiveness in all categories articulated in the *National Strategy* (**Document 69**). However, in discussing the security situation, the report ignored key factors. While violence was confined to four of Iraq's 18 provinces, these were the most populous ones. Mounting casualty figures contradicted the optimism of the report. In addition, many of the Iraqi security forces the report boasted were not capable of operating independently. Units also showed a definite ethnic bias. The conclusions of this report to Congress do not square with the conclusions of the Iraq Study Group (**Document 71**).

- **Document 71: Excerpt of *Report of the Iraq Study Group***
- **When:** December 6, 2006
- **Where:** Washington, DC
- **Significance:** The report presented an extremely negative view of the situation in Iraq.

The situation in Iraq is grave and deteriorating. There is no path that can guarantee success, but the prospects can be improved. In this report, we make a number of recommendations for actions to be taken in Iraq, the United States, and the region. Our most important recommendations call for new and enhanced diplomatic and political efforts in Iraq and the region, and a change in the primary mission of U.S. forces in Iraq that will enable the United States to begin to move its combat forces out of Iraq responsibly. We believe that these two recommendations are equally important and reinforce one another. If they are effectively implemented, and if the Iraqi government moves forward with national reconciliation, Iraqis will have an opportunity for a better future, terrorism will be dealt a blow, stability will be enhanced in an important part of the world, and America's credibility, interests, and values will be protected.

The challenges in Iraq are complex. Violence is increasing in scope and lethality. It is fed by a Sunni Arab insurgency, Shiite militias and death squads, al Qaeda, and widespread criminality. Sectarian conflict is the principal challenge to stability. The Iraqi people have a democratically elected government, yet it is not adequately advancing national reconciliation, providing basic security, or delivering essential services. Pessimism is pervasive. If the situation continues to deteriorate, the consequences could be severe. A slide toward chaos could trigger the collapse of Iraq's government and a humanitarian catastrophe. Neighboring countries could intervene. Sunni-Shia clashes could spread. Al Qaeda could win a propaganda victory and expand its base of operations. The global standing of the United States could be diminished. Americans could become more polarized.

During the past nine months we have considered a full range of approaches for moving forward. All have flaws. Our recommended course has shortcomings, but we firmly believe that it includes the best strategies and tactics to positively influence the outcome in Iraq and the region.

External Approach

The policies and actions of Iraq's neighbors greatly affect its stability and prosperity. No country in the region will benefit in the long term from a chaotic Iraq. Yet Iraq's neighbors are not doing enough to help Iraq achieve stability. Some are undercutting stability. The United States should immediately launch a new diplomatic offensive to build an international consensus for stability in Iraq and the region. This diplomatic effort should include every country that has an interest in avoiding a chaotic Iraq, including all of Iraq's neighbors. Iraq's neighbors and key states in and outside the region should form a support group to reinforce security and national reconciliation within Iraq, neither of which Iraq can achieve on its own.

Given the ability of Iran and Syria to influence events within Iraq and their interest in avoiding chaos in Iraq, the United States should try to engage them constructively. In seeking to influence the behavior of both countries, the United States has disincentives and incentives available. Iran should stem the flow of arms and training to Iraq, respect Iraq's sovereignty and territorial integrity, and use its influence over Iraqi Shia groups to encourage national reconciliation. The issue of Iran's nuclear programs should continue to be dealt with by the five permanent members of the United Nations Security Council plus Germany. Syria should control its border with Iraq to stem the flow of funding, insurgents, and terrorists in and out of Iraq.

The United States cannot achieve its goals in the Middle East unless it deals directly with the Arab-Israeli conflict and regional instability. There must be a renewed and sustained commitment by the United States to a comprehensive Arab-Israeli peace on all fronts: Lebanon, Syria, and President Bush's June 2002 commitment to a two-state solution for Israel and Palestine. This commitment must include direct talks with, by, and between Israel, Lebanon, Palestinians (those who accept Israel's right to exist), and Syria. As the United States develops its approach toward Iraq and the Middle East, the United States should provide additional political, economic, and military support for Afghanistan, including resources that might become available as combat forces are moved out of Iraq.

Internal Approach

The most important questions about Iraq's future are now the responsibility of Iraqis. The United States must adjust its role in Iraq to encourage the Iraqi people to take control of their own destiny. The Iraqi government should accelerate assuming responsibility for Iraqi security by increasing the number and quality of Iraqi Army brigades. While this process is under way, and to facilitate it, the United States should significantly increase the number of U.S. military personnel, including combat troops, imbedded in and supporting Iraqi Army units. As these actions proceed, U.S. combat forces could begin to move out of Iraq. The primary mission of U.S. forces in Iraq should evolve to one of supporting the Iraqi army, which would take over primary responsibility for combat operations. By the first quarter of 2008, subject to unexpected developments in the security situation on the ground, all combat brigades not necessary for force protection could be out of Iraq. At that time, U.S. combat forces in Iraq could be deployed only in units embedded with Iraqi forces, in rapid-reaction and special operations teams, and in training, equipping, advising, force protection, and search and rescue.

Intelligence and support efforts would continue. A vital mission of those rapid reaction and special operations forces would be to undertake strikes against al Qaeda in Iraq. It is clear that the Iraqi government will need assistance from the United States for some time to come, especially in carrying out security responsibilities. Yet the United States must make it clear to the Iraqi government that the United States could carry out its plans, including planned redeployments, even if the Iraqi government did not implement their planned changes. The United States must not make an open-ended commitment to keep large numbers of American troops deployed in Iraq. As redeployment proceeds, military leaders should emphasize training and education of forces that have returned to the United States in order to restore the force to full combat capability. As equipment returns to the United States, Congress should appropriate sufficient funds to restore the equipment over the next five years.

The United States should work closely with Iraq's leaders to support the achievement of specific objectives—or milestones—on national reconciliation, security, and governance. Miracles cannot be expected, but the people of Iraq have the right to expect action and progress. The Iraqi government needs to show its own citizens—and the citizens of the United States and other countries—that it deserves continued support. Prime Minister Nouri al-Maliki, in consultation with the United States, has put forward a set of milestones critical for Iraq. His list is a good start, but it must be expanded to include milestones that can strengthen the government and benefit the Iraqi people. President Bush and his national security team should remain in close and frequent contact with the Iraqi leadership to convey a clear message: there must be prompt action by the Iraqi government to make substantial progress toward the achievement of these milestones.

If the Iraqi government demonstrates political will and makes substantial progress toward the achievement of milestones on national reconciliation, security, and governance, the United States should make clear its willingness to continue training, assistance, and support for Iraq's security forces and to continue political, military, and economic support. If the Iraqi government does not make substantial progress toward the achievement of milestones on national reconciliation, security, and governance, the United States should reduce its political, military, or economic support for the Iraqi government.

Our report makes recommendations in several other areas. They include improvements to the Iraqi criminal justice system, the Iraqi oil sector, the U.S. reconstruction efforts in Iraq, the U.S. budget process, the training of U.S. government personnel, and U.S. intelligence capabilities.

Conclusion

It is the unanimous view of the Iraq Study Group that these recommendations offer a new way forward for the United States in Iraq and the region. They are comprehensive and need to be implemented in a coordinated fashion. They should not be separated or carried out in isolation. The dynamics of the region are as important to Iraq as events within Iraq. The challenges are daunting. There will be difficult days ahead. But by pursuing this new way forward, Iraq, the region, and the United States of America can emerge stronger.

- **Source:** James Baker III and Lee Hamilton, *Report of the Iraq Study Group*, available at http://www.uspoliticsguide.com/US-Politics-Directory/Iraq-Study-Group-Report.htm, accessed January 16, 2012.
- **Analysis:** The Baker-Hamilton report painted a grim picture of the situation in Iraq. It advocated a two-pronged strategy with an external and an internal component. The United States needed to engage Iraq's neighbors, especially Syria and Iran, who contributed to unrest within the country. The report also insisted that the Iraqis had to take greater responsibility for their own country. The time had come, the report argued, for U.S. forces to step back and let Iraqis take the lead. U.S. forces should act in a supporting role and then only if locals proved willing to take the initiative. The report was so pessimistic that many readers considered withdrawal from Iraq the best option.

- **Document 72: Excerpt of *Field Manual 3-24: Counterinsurgency***
- **When:** 2006
- **Where:** Washington, DC
- **Significance:** The new manual was the first major change in COIN doctrine since the Vietnam War.

1-159. COIN is an extremely complex form of warfare. At its core, COIN is a struggle for the population's support. The protection, welfare, and support of the people are vital to success. Gaining and maintaining that support is a formidable challenge. Achieving these aims requires synchronizing the efforts of many nonmilitary and HN agencies in a comprehensive approach.

1-160. Designing operations that achieve the desired end state requires counterinsurgents to understand the culture and the problems they face. Both insurgents and counterinsurgents are fighting for the support of the populace. However, insurgents are constrained by neither the law of war nor the bounds of human decency as Western nations understand them. In fact, some insurgents are willing to commit suicide and kill innocent civilians in carrying out their operations—and deem this a legitimate option. They also will do anything to preserve their greatest advantage, the ability to hide among the people. These amoral and often barbaric enemies survive by their wits, constantly adapting to the situation. Defeating them requires counterinsurgents to develop the ability to learn and adapt rapidly and continuously. This manual emphasizes this "Learn and Adapt" imperative as it discusses ways to gain and maintain the support of the people.

1-161. Popular support allows counterinsurgents to develop the intelligence necessary to identify and defeat insurgents. Designing and executing a comprehensive campaign to secure the populace and then gain its support requires carefully coordinating actions along several LLOs over time to produce success. One of these LLOs is developing HN security forces that can assume primary responsibility for combating the insurgency. COIN operations also place distinct burdens on leaders and logisticians. All of these aspects of COIN are described and analyzed in the chapters that follow.

Table 4-1 Successful and unsuccessful counterinsurgency operational practices

Successful Practices	Unsuccessful Practices
• Emphasize intelligence	• Overemphasize killing and capturing the enemy rather than securing and engaging the populace
• Focus on population, its needs and its security	
• Establish and expand secure areas	• Conduct large-scale operations as norm
• Isolate insurgents from the populace (population control)	• Concentrate military forces in large bases for protection
• Conduct effective, pervasive, and continuous information operations	• Focus special forces primarily on raiding
• Provide amnesty and rehabilitation for those willing to support the new government	• Place low priority on assigning quality advisors to host-nation forces
• Place host-nation police in the lead with military support as soon as the security situation permits	• Build and train host-nation security forces in the U.S. military's image
• Expand and diversify the host-nation police force	• Ignore peacetime government processes, including legal procedures
• Train military forces to conduct counterinsurgency operations	• Allow open borders, airspace, and coastlines.
• Embed quality advisors and special forces with host-nation forces	
• Deny sanctuary to insurgents	
• Encourage strong political and military cooperation and information sharing	
• Secure host-nation borders	
• Protect key infrastructure	

- **Source:** *FM 3-24: Counterinsurgency* (Washington, DC: Headquarters, Department of the Army, 2006), 1-28-29.
- **Analysis:** General David Petraeus oversaw the production of a new COIN manual based on extensive study of past campaigns and lessons learned in Iraq and Afghanistan. The manual emphasized using all elements of national power, known as the DIME (diplomatic, informational, military, and economic, later expanded to "DIME-FIL," adding "financial, intelligence, law enforcement"), to defeat insurgency. Emphasis should be on gaining the trust and support of local people through improving their quality of life, traditionally referred to as "winning hearts and minds." While military force would continue to play a role in COIN, its use would be limited and focused. The manual also advocated giving junior officers greater responsibility for making tactical decisions, what it described as "empowering the lowest level."

DID YOU KNOW?

General David Petraeus

David Petraeus (b. 1952) is a four-star U.S. Army general appointed to head the Central Intelligence Agency in 2011. Prior to heading the CIA he commanded the International Stabilization Force in Afghanistan, U.S. Central Command, and Multinational Forces Iraq. Petraeus, who holds a Ph.D. from Princeton University, emerged as an authority on counterinsurgency through his successful handling of the situation in Mosul when he commanded the 101st Airborne Division there in 2003 and 2004, which he wrote about in the *Washington Post* and the *Military Review*. As director of the Combined Arms Center at Fort Leavenworth, Petraeus oversaw the drafting of a new manual, *FM 3-24: Counterinsurgency* (2006), the first major revision of U.S. COIN doctrine since the Vietnam War.

- **Document 73: Excerpt of Presidential Address to American People**
- **When:** January 10, 2007
- **Where:** Washington, DC
- **Significance:** The president explained the "new way forward," which came to be called the "surge strategy."

To establish its authority, the Iraqi government plans to take responsibility for security in all of Iraq's provinces by November. To give every Iraqi citizen a stake in the country's economy, Iraq will pass legislation to share oil revenues among all Iraqis. To show that it is committed to delivering a better life, the Iraqi government will spend $10 billion of its own money on reconstruction and infrastructure projects that will create new jobs. To empower local leaders, Iraqis plan to hold provincial elections later this year. And to allow more Iraqis to re-enter their nation's political life, the government will reform de-Baathification laws, and establish a fair process for considering amendments to Iraq's constitution.

America will change our approach to help the Iraqi government as it works to meet these benchmarks. In keeping with the recommendations of the Iraq Study Group, we will increase the embedding of American advisers in Iraqi Army units, and partner a coalition brigade with every Iraqi Army division. We will help the

Iraqis build a larger and better-equipped army, and we will accelerate the training of Iraqi forces, which remains the essential U.S. security mission in Iraq. We will give our commanders and civilians greater flexibility to spend funds for economic assistance. We will double the number of provincial reconstruction teams. These teams bring together military and civilian experts to help local Iraqi communities pursue reconciliation, strengthen the moderates, and speed the transition to Iraqi self-reliance. And Secretary Rice will soon appoint a reconstruction coordinator in Baghdad to ensure better results for economic assistance being spent in Iraq.

As we make these changes, we will continue to pursue al Qaeda and foreign fighters. Al Qaeda is still active in Iraq. Its home base is Anbar Province. Al Qaeda has helped make Anbar the most violent area of Iraq outside the capital. A captured al Qaeda document describes the terrorists' plan to infiltrate and seize control of the province. This would bring al Qaeda closer to its goals of taking down Iraq's democracy, building a radical Islamic empire, and launching new attacks on the United States at home and abroad.

Our military forces in Anbar are killing and capturing al Qaeda leaders, and they are protecting the local population. Recently, local tribal leaders have begun to show their willingness to take on al Qaeda. And as a result, our commanders believe we have an opportunity to deal a serious blow to the terrorists. So I have given orders to increase American forces in Anbar Province by 4,000 troops. These troops will work with Iraqi and tribal forces to keep up the pressure on the terrorists. America's men and women in uniform took away al Qaeda's safe haven in Afghanistan—and we will not allow them to re-establish it in Iraq.

Succeeding in Iraq also requires defending its territorial integrity and stabilizing the region in the face of extremist challenges. This begins with addressing Iran and Syria. These two regimes are allowing terrorists and insurgents to use their territory to move in and out of Iraq. Iran is providing material support for attacks on American troops. We will disrupt the attacks on our forces. We'll interrupt the flow of support from Iran and Syria. And we will seek out and destroy the networks providing advanced weaponry and training to our enemies in Iraq.

We're also taking other steps to bolster the security of Iraq and protect American interests in the Middle East. I recently ordered the deployment of an additional carrier strike group to the region. We will expand intelligence-sharing and deploy Patriot air defense systems to reassure our friends and allies. We will work with the governments of Turkey and Iraq to help them resolve problems along their border. And we will work with others to prevent Iran from gaining nuclear weapons and dominating the region.

- **Source:** Presidential address to the nation, January 10, 2007, available at http://georgewbush-whitehouse.archives.gov/news/releases/2007/01/20070110-7.html, accessed June 21, 2011.

- **Analysis:** The administration accepted the recommendations of the Baker-Hamilton report. To implement its recommendations, the president ordered deployment of additional troops to Iraq. This "surge" would eventually total approximately 28,000 troops. The United

States would place greater emphasis on training and advising Iraqi troops, who were to accept increasing responsibility for internal security.

At the time, the surge strategy came under intense criticism. It appeared to be a case of doubling down on a bad bet, spending even more U.S. blood and treasure on what many deemed a lost cause. During the next year, the situation in Iraq did improve markedly, but debate continues as to whether this improvement owed more to the surge or to the Anbar Awakening, which occurred at about the same time.

- • **Document 74: Excerpt of "Anbar Awakening: The Tipping Point"**
- • **When:** March/April 2008
- • **Where:** Fort Leavenworth, Kansas
- • **Significance:** This article described the nature of the Anbar Awakening.

Convincing the local sheiks to join us and undertake another uprising was an immense challenge, but obtaining their support was the lynchpin of the second part of our strategy. We knew it would be pivotal when we arrived in Ramadi in June. The sheiks' memory of their first, failed attempt at establishing the Al Anbar People's Council (late 2005–early 2006) was the main obstacle to our plan in this regard. The Sunni tribal alliance was fragmented and weak compared to the growing Al-Qaeda forces that controlled Ramadi in those days.

At the same time, area tribal sheiks had no great love for U.S. forces or the Iraqi Army. Early in the insurgency, they had directly and indirectly supported former-regime nationalist insurgents against U.S. forces, and as a result they had temporarily established an alliance of convenience with AQIZ. Many tribal members were killed or captured combating coalition forces, which diminished the sheiks' ability to provide income for their tribes. These conditions in turn enabled AQIZ to recruit from those families in need of money. Another aggravating factor was that IA forces initially stationed in Anbar consisted largely of southern Iraqi Shi'ites. Ramadi area inhabitants regarded them as agents of the Sadr militia or Badr Corps, with a covert agenda to kill off Sunni tribes and enable a Shi'ite takeover of Anbar.

Nevertheless, the tribal leaders were still fed up with Al Qaeda's violence and frustrated by their own loss of prestige and influence in their traditional heartlands. The brigade staff believed that by offering convincing incentives, we could create a tribal alliance that could produce lasting security in Ramadi. To persuade the tribes to cooperate, we first needed to understand the human terrain in our AO, and that task fell to an outstanding and talented junior officer, Captain Travis Patriquin.

An Arabic-speaking former Special Forces Soldier and an infantry officer assigned as the Ready First's S-9/engagements officer, Patriquin coordinated brigade-level local meetings and discussions. He quickly gained the sheiks' confidence through his language and interpersonal skills and developed strong personal bonds with their families. He strengthened these bonds during meetings between the brigade commander or deputy commanding officer and the sheiks. Battalion and company commanders also worked on improving relations with the townspeople on a daily basis. Thus, the sheiks' growing trust of the brigade's officers led them to support our efforts to reinvigorate police recruiting.

- **Source:** Major Neil Smith and Colonel Sean MacFarland, "Anbar Awakening: The Tipping Point," *Military Review*, March/April 2008, available at http://www.army.mil/professionalWriting/volumes/volume6/april_2008/4_08_3_pf.html, accessed June 21, 2011.
- **Analysis:** The Anbar Awakening arose spontaneously as a grassroots effort by Iraqi sheiks to get rid of al-Qaeda in Iraq, whom they hated as much if not more than they did the United States. American officers saw in this effort an opportunity to engage the local population. Exploiting the ancient Arab proverb, "the enemy of my enemy is my friend," they cooperated with local leaders to rid their communities of the al-Qaeda threat. Stationing U.S. units in towns and villages built trust. Recruiting for the Iraqi police improved, and development could proceed. The Awakening eventually benefited the struggle against Iraqi insurgents as well as foreign terrorists.

- **Document 75: Excerpt of Testimony of General David Petraeus to Congress**
- **When:** September 10, 2007
- **Where:** Washington, DC
- **Significance:** The commander of CENTCOM reported on the success of the surge.

Mr. Chairmen, Ranking Members, Members of the Committees, thank you for the opportunity to provide my assessment of the security situation in Iraq and to discuss the recommendations I recently provided to my chain of command for the way forward. At the outset, I would like to note that this is my testimony. Although I have briefed my assessment and recommendations to my chain of command, I wrote this testimony myself. It has not been cleared by, nor shared with, anyone in the Pentagon, the White House, or Congress.

As a bottom line up front, the military objectives of the surge are, in large measure, being met. In recent months, in the face of tough enemies and the brutal summer heat of Iraq, Coalition and Iraqi Security Forces have achieved progress in the security arena. Though the improvements have been uneven across Iraq, the overall number of security incidents in Iraq has declined in 8 of the past 12 weeks, with the numbers of incidents in the last two weeks at the lowest levels seen since June 2006.

One reason for the decline in incidents is that Coalition and Iraqi forces have dealt significant blows to Al Qaeda-Iraq. Though Al Qaeda and its affiliates in Iraq remain dangerous, we have taken away a number of their sanctuaries and gained the initiative in many areas.

We have also disrupted Shia militia extremists, capturing the head and numerous other leaders of the Iranian-supported Special Groups, along with a senior Lebanese Hezbollah operative supporting Iran's activities in Iraq.

Coalition and Iraqi operations have helped reduce ethno-sectarian violence, as well, bringing down the number of ethno-sectarian deaths substantially in Baghdad and across Iraq since the height of the sectarian violence last December. The number of overall civilian deaths has also declined during this period, although the numbers in each area are still at troubling levels.

Iraqi Security Forces have also continued to grow and to shoulder more of the load, albeit slowly and amid continuing concerns about the sectarian tendencies of some elements in their ranks. In general, however, Iraqi elements have been standing and fighting and sustaining tough losses, and they have taken the lead in operations in many areas. Additionally, in what may be the most significant development of the past 8 months, the tribal rejection of Al Qaeda that started in Anbar Province and helped produce such significant change there has now spread to a number of other locations as well.

Based on all this and on the further progress we believe we can achieve over the next few months, I believe that we will be able to reduce our forces to the pre-surge level of brigade combat teams by next summer without jeopardizing the security gains that we have fought so hard to achieve.

Beyond that, while noting that the situation in Iraq remains complex, difficult, and sometimes downright frustrating, I also believe that it is possible to achieve our objectives in Iraq over time, though doing so will be neither quick nor easy.

- **Source:** General David Petraeus, "Report to Congress on the Situation in Iraq," September 10–11, 2007, available at http://www.defense.gov/pubs/pdfs/Petraeus-Testimony20070910.pdf, accessed June 21, 2011.
- **Analysis:** One year after the beginning of the Anbar Awakening and six months after deployment of surge forces was complete, General Petraeus reported that conditions in Iraq had improved dramatically and would continue to do so. U.S. casualties had declined along with the number of incidents. That trend would continue to the present. The general was perhaps a bit optimistic about the timetable for withdrawal, but by no more than a year.

- **Document 76: Excerpt of President Obama's Speech at Camp Lejeune**
- **When:** February 27, 2009

- **Where:** Camp Lejeune, North Carolina
- **Significance:** The newly elected president announced a timetable for withdrawal from Iraq.

Today, I can announce that our review is complete, and that the United States will pursue a new strategy to end the war in Iraq through a transition to full Iraqi responsibility.

This strategy is grounded in a clear and achievable goal shared by the Iraqi people and the American people: an Iraq that is sovereign, stable, and self-reliant. To achieve that goal, we will work to promote an Iraqi government that is just, representative, and accountable, and that provides neither support nor safe-haven to terrorists. We will help Iraq build new ties of trade and commerce with the world. And we will forge a partnership with the people and government of Iraq that contributes to the peace and security of the region.

What we will *not* do is let the pursuit of the perfect stand in the way of achievable goals. We cannot rid Iraq of all who oppose America or sympathize with our adversaries. We cannot police Iraq's streets until they are completely safe, nor stay until Iraq's union is perfected. We cannot sustain indefinitely a commitment that has put a strain on our military, and will cost the American people nearly a trillion dollars. America's men and women in uniform have fought block by block, province by province, year after year, to give the Iraqis this chance to choose a better future. Now, we must ask the Iraqi people to seize it. The first part of this strategy is therefore the responsible removal of our combat brigades from Iraq.

As a candidate for President, I made clear my support for a timeline of 16 months to carry out this drawdown, while pledging to consult closely with our military commanders upon taking office to ensure that we preserve the gains we've made and protect our troops. Those consultations are now complete, and I have chosen a timeline that will remove our combat brigades over the next 18 months. Let me say this as plainly as I can: by August 31, 2010, our combat mission in Iraq will end.

As we carry out this drawdown, my highest priority will be the safety and security of our troops and civilians in Iraq. We will proceed carefully, and I will consult closely with my military commanders on the ground and with the Iraqi government. There will surely be difficult periods and tactical adjustments. But our enemies should be left with no doubt: this plan gives our military the forces and the flexibility they need to support our Iraqi partners, and to succeed.

After we remove our combat brigades, our mission will change from combat to supporting the Iraqi government and its Security Forces as they take the absolute lead in securing their country. As I have long said, we will retain a transitional force to carry out three distinct functions: training, equipping, and advising Iraqi Security Forces as long as they remain non-sectarian; conducting targeted counter-terrorism missions; and protecting our ongoing civilian and military efforts within Iraq. Initially, this force will likely be made up of 35–50,000 U.S. troops.

Through this period of transition, we will carry out further redeployments. And under the Status of Forces Agreement with the Iraqi government, I intend to remove all U.S. troops from Iraq by the end of 2011. We will complete this transition to Iraqi responsibility, and we will bring our troops home with the honor that they have earned.

As we responsibly remove our combat brigades, we will pursue the second part of our strategy: sustained diplomacy on behalf of a more peaceful and prosperous Iraq. The drawdown of our military should send a clear signal that Iraq's future is now its own responsibility. The long-term success of the Iraqi nation will depend upon decisions made by Iraq's leaders and the fortitude of the Iraqi people. Iraq is a sovereign country with legitimate institutions; America cannot—and should not—take their place. However, a strong political, diplomatic, and civilian effort on our part can advance progress and help lay a foundation for lasting peace and security.

- **Source:** President Obama's speech to marines at Camp Lejeune, NC, February 27, 2009, available at http://www.whitehouse.gov/the_press_ office/Remarks-of-President-Barack-Obama-Responsibly-Ending-the-War-in-Iraq/, accessed June 21, 2011.

- **Analysis:** One month after taking office, President Barack Obama announced a timetable for withdrawal of troops from Iraq. He promised that combat troops would be withdrawn by the summer of 2010. The president acknowledged that while the security situation had improved, Iraq remained a fragile state in need of U.S. support for years to come. That support, however, would increasingly be in the form of support and advising as Iraqi forces took more and more responsibility for internal security.

    As promised, the president withdrew all but approximately 50,000 troops by the summer of 2010. While technically designated as non-combat forces, these remaining troops could of course engage in military operations as needed. During fiscal year 2011, the United States had approximately 42,800 troops in Iraq.[2] According to an agreement with the Iraqi government, remaining units were withdrawn by December 31, 2011.

CONCLUSION

Conventional militaries have great difficulty conducting COIN campaigns, largely because force plays a crucial but limited role in such conflicts. In the case of Iraq, several factors made COIN even more difficult. Failure to plan for the possibility of an insurgency left troops on the ground poorly prepared to deal with it. The reluctance of the administration to acknowledge that an insurgency was unfolding delayed development of an effective response. An engrained Army belief,

---

[2]Amy Belasco, *Troop Levels in the Afghan and Iraq Wars, FY2001-FY2012: Cost and Other Potential Issues* (Washington, DC: Congressional Research Service, 2009), p. 9.

held at least since the end of the Vietnam War, that COIN should be relegated to the special forces community, left regular soldiers untrained in and often willing to learn about unconventional conflict.

U.S. soldiers and Marines did adjust, but only after many missteps and much trial and error. A new COIN manual aided excellent junior officers and senior noncommissioned officers to develop effective tactics. The surge strategy combined with the Anbar Awakening recouped the situation. U.S. troops have been withdrawn, and the prognosis for a prosperous and democratic Iraq is cautiously optimistic.

5

THE ROUGH ROAD
TO DEMOCRACY

DID YOU KNOW?

Sunni

The Sunni are the majority branch of Islam that developed out of a mid-seventh-century split in Islam. Following the death of the Prophet Mohammed, a dispute arose over who would lead the community of the faithful. The majority of Muslims at the time believed that the next caliph should be a righteous leader chosen by the leaders of the community. The minority who came to be called Shi'a believed the next caliph should be a direct descendant of the Prophet. This political split soon developed into a theological one. Sunni Muslims, whose name derives from the Arab word *sunnah*, meaning "example," follow the Quran but also accept the authority of the *hadiths*, or "sayings of the Prophet." Although more than 80 percent of the world's Muslims are Sunni, they comprise only about 35 percent of the Iraq population. Despite their minority status, however, Sunni Arabs have been the governing elite of the country since its creation.

GOVERNING IRAQ

The United States never intended to govern Iraq. The invasion planners envisioned a situation in which Iraqi forces would return to their barracks and surrender as intact units, Iraqi civil servants would continue to run their departments, and normal government could be restored quickly. The chaos following the collapse of Saddam Hussein's regime demonstrated the folly of those optimistic expectations. The United States had to govern Iraq directly for a year. During that time it oversaw elections for a provisional government. That government in turn had to draft a constitution and hold elections to newly created offices.

Several factors complicated the arduous task of creating a democratic government in Iraq. Because the state had been ruled by a series of autocrats from its inception, people had little experience of democracy. Ethnic and sectarian divisions complicated matters as did the tribal, clan, and family networks that overlay them. The Sunni Arab minority resented loss of the privileged position it had enjoyed since the creation of modern Iraq. The Shi'a Arab majority felt that its time to rule had come. Years of persecution made it reluctant to cooperate with the Sunnis. Kurds in northern Iraq had enjoyed autonomy since the establishment of a no-fly zone over their territory following the 1991 Gulf War. Remembering intense persecution by Hussein, they did not wish to be ruled from Baghdad. To make matters worse, the Iraqi constitution had be written in the midst of an active insurgency.

INTERIM GOVERNMENT

The United States had never intended to administer, let alone govern, Iraq. Planners assumed that removing Hussein would produce a wave of relief and gratitude from the Iraqi people. Civil servants, especially police, fire, and emergency responders, would continue to do their jobs. After a brief transition, the coalition would be able to hand authority to a democratically elected Iraqi government.

The reality proved to be quite different than this optimistic vision. Iraqis were grateful to be liberated from the tyranny of Hussein. Ordinary government, however, collapsed, creating a power vacuum that U.S. forces could not fill. The administration had no choice but to form an interim government to run Iraq for the first year of the occupation.

- **Document 77: Excerpt of Coalition Provisional Authority Regulation Number 1**
- **When:** May 16, 2003
- **Where:** Baghdad
- **Significance:** The regulation created the Coalition Provisional Authority (CPA) as Iraq's interim government.

Pursuant to my authority as Administrator of the Coalition Provisional Authority (CPA), relevant U.N. Security Council resolutions, including Resolution 1483 (2003), and the laws and usages of war, I hereby promulgate the following:

Section 1

The Coalition Provisional Authority

1) The CPA shall exercise powers of government temporarily in order to provide for the effective administration of Iraq during the period of transitional administration, to restore conditions of security and stability, to create conditions in which the Iraqi people can freely determine their own political future, including by advancing efforts to restore and establish national and local institutions for representative governance and facilitating economic recovery and sustainable reconstruction and development.

2) The CPA is vested with all executive, legislative and judicial authority necessary to achieve its objectives, to be exercised under relevant U.N. Security Council resolutions, including Resolution 1483 (2003), and the laws and usages of war. This authority shall be exercised by the CPA Administrator.

3) As the Commander of Coalition Forces, the Commander of U.S. Central Command shall directly support the CPA by deterring hostilities; maintaining Iraq's territorial integrity and security; searching for, securing and destroying weapons of mass destruction; and assisting in carrying out Coalition policy generally.

> **DID YOU KNOW?**
>
> **Shi'a**
>
> The Shi'a are the minority branch of Islam arising from a seventh-century schism. *Shi'a* means "partisan of Ali," a reference to Ali, the fourth caliph, who believed that rulers of the Islamic community must be direct descendants of the Prophet Mohammed. Theological differences soon added to this leadership struggle. While Shi'a share with Sunni Muslims the core beliefs of Islam, they also hold to some tenets not accepted by the Sunni. For example, imams have far greater authority in Shi'a than they do in Sunni Islam. High-ranking clerics known as ayatollahs often exercise considerable political as well as religious power, which explains the importance of figures like Ayatollah Sistani in Iraq. Although they make up no more than 20 percent of the world Muslim population, Shi'a comprise more than 60 percent of the Iraqi population. Persecuted by Saddam Hussein, they believe their time to rule has come.

- **Source:** "Coalition Provisional Authority Regulation Number 1," May 16, 2003, available at http://www.iraqcoalition.org/regulations/20030516_CPAREG_1_The_Coalition_Provisional_Authority_.pdf, accessed June 18, 2008.
- **Analysis:** The Bush administration appointed L. Paul Bremer III as head of the interim government of Iraq. Bremer promulgated the resolution creating the CPA he had been chosen to run. He based his authority for doing so in part on UN Security Council Resolution

DID YOU KNOW?

Kurds

The Kurds are an Indo-European ethnolinguistic group of 30 million people whose territory includes parts of northeastern Syria, northern Iraq, southeastern Turkey, and northwestern Iran. France and Britain had an opportunity to create an independent Kurdistan when they dismembered the Ottoman Empire after the First World War but decided against this approach. By the time of the 1920 Cairo Conference, which drew the map of modern Iraq, the British knew that considerable oil reserves lay in the areas of Mosul and Kirkuk, so they decided to include them in the newly created country. Iraqi Kurds, who are Sunni Muslims but ethnically different from Iraqi Arabs, suffered intense persecution by Saddam Hussein. Following the 1990–1991 Gulf War, this persecution became so intense that the U.S.-led coalition created a no-fly zone over their territory to protect them. This history of persecution by Baghdad has led the Iraqi Kurds to insist upon maintaining the regional autonomy they have acquired.

1483, which called upon member nations to "to assist the people of Iraq in their efforts to reform their institutions."* He also cited the "laws and usages of war," a large body of documents and legal precedents that gave an occupation force authority over and responsibility for the people whose territory it controlled.

The regulation gave Bremer sweeping powers to govern. The CPA would be responsible for all executive, legislative, and judicial functions. The commander of coalition forces was to support the CPA. However, cooperation between the CPA and Multinational Forces Iraq was fraught with difficulty.

- **Document 78: Excerpt of Coalition Provisional Authority Regulation Number 6, Governing Council of Iraq**
- **When:** July 13, 2003
- **Where:** Baghdad
- **Significance:** The regulation took the first step toward a democratic Iraq by establishing a provisional Governing Council.

Pursuant to my authority as Administrator of the Coalition Provisional Authority (CPA), relevant U.N. Security Council resolutions, including Resolution 1483 (2003), and the laws and usages of war,

Recognizing that, as stated in paragraph 9 of Resolution 1483, the Security Council supports the formation of an Iraqi interim administration as a transitional administration run by Iraqis, until the people of Iraq establish an internationally recognized, representative government that assumes the responsibilities of the CPA,

Noting that on July 13, 2003, the Governing Council met and announced its formation as the principal body of the Iraqi interim administration referred to in paragraph 9 of Resolution 1483,

Affirming that the CPA and the Special Representative of the U.N. Secretary General have worked together and will continue to work together in a cooperative and consultative process to support the formation and operation of the Governing Council and welcomed the formation of the Governing Council on July 13, 2003,

---

*UN Security Council Resolution 1483, UN Document S/RES/1483 (2003), available at http://www.un.org/Docs/sc/unsc_resolutions03.html, accessed March 20, 2012.

Acknowledging that, consistent with Resolution 1483, the Governing Council has certain authorities and responsibilities as representatives of the Iraqi people, including ensuring that the Iraqi people's interests are represented in both the interim administration and in determining the means of establishing an internationally recognized, representative government,

Emphasizing that, consistent with Resolution 1483, the Governing Council and the CPA, each in coordination with the Special Representative of the U.N. Secretary General, undertake to work together in a cooperative and consultative process for the benefit of the Iraqi people, I hereby promulgate the following:

Section 1

Recognition of Governing Council

The CPA recognized the formation of the Governing Council as the principal body of the Iraqi interim administration, pending the establishment of an internationally recognized, representative government by the people of Iraq, consistent with Resolution 1483.

Section 2

Relationship between Governing Council and the CPA

1) In accordance with Resolution 1483, the Governing Council and the CPA shall consult and coordinate on all matters involving the temporary governance of Iraq, including the authorities of the Governing Council.

2) All officials of the CPA are hereby instructed promptly to respond to all requests for experts, technical assistance or other support requested by the Governing Council.

Section 3

Entry into Force

The Regulation shall enter into force on the date of signature.

- **Source:** "Coalition Provisional Authority Regulation Number 6: Governing Council of Iraq," http://www.iraqcoalition.org/regulations/20030713_CPAREG_6_Governing_Council_of_Iraq_.pdf, accessed June 18, 2008.
- **Analysis:** The Governing Council put an Iraqi face on the transitional government as UN Resolution 1483 mandated. As the regulation made clear, however, the council would be largely advisory. It would "consult and coordinate" with the CPA but would not have the authority to make decisions on its own. The degree of support it enjoyed among Iraqis, many of whom considered it a tool of the

occupation, is less clear. Creation of this body did not stem the rising tide of insurgency.

- **Document 79: Excerpt of Iraqi Transitional Law**
- **When:** March 8, 2004
- **Where:** Baghdad
- **Significance:** The Transitional Law established a government for Iraq until a new constitution could be written and approved.

PREAMBLE

The people of Iraq, striving to reclaim their freedom, which was usurped by the previous tyrannical regime, rejecting violence and coercion in all their forms, and particularly when used as instruments of governance, have determined that they shall hereafter remain a free people governed under the rule of law.

These people, affirming today their respect for international law, especially having been amongst the founders of the United Nations, working to reclaim their legitimate place among nations, have endeavored at the same time to preserve the unity of their homeland in a spirit of fraternity and solidarity in order to draw the features of the future new Iraq, and to establish the mechanisms aiming, amongst other aims, to erase the effects of racist and sectarian policies and practices.

This Law is now established to govern the affairs of Iraq during the transitional period until a duly elected government, operating under a permanent and legitimate constitution achieving full democracy, shall come into being.

CHAPTER ONE—FUNDAMENTAL PRINCIPLES

Article 1.

(A) This Law shall be called the "Law of Administration for the State of Iraq for the Transitional Period," and the phrase "this Law" wherever it appears in this legislation shall mean the "Law of Administration for the State of Iraq for the Transitional Period."

(B) Gender-specific language shall apply equally to male and female.

(C) The Preamble to this Law is an integral part of this Law.

Article 2.

(A) The term "transitional period" shall refer to the period beginning on 30 June 2004 and lasting until the formation of an elected Iraqi government pursuant to a permanent constitution as set forth in this Law, which in any case shall be no later than 31 December 2005, unless the provisions of Article 61 are applied.

(B) The transitional period shall consist of two phases.

(1) The first phase shall begin with the formation of a fully sovereign Iraqi Interim Government that takes power on 30 June 2004. This government shall be constituted in accordance with a process of extensive deliberations and consultations with cross-sections of the Iraqi people conducted by the Governing Council and the Coalition Provisional Authority and possibly in consultation with the United Nations. This government shall exercise authority in accordance with this Law, including the fundamental principles and rights specified herein, and with an annex that shall be agreed upon and issued before the beginning of the transitional period and that shall be an integral part of this Law.

(2) The second phase shall begin after the formation of the Iraqi Transitional Government, which will take place after elections for the National Assembly have been held as stipulated in this Law, provided that, if possible, these elections are not delayed beyond 31 December 2004, and, in any event, beyond 31 January 2005. This second phase shall end upon the formation of an Iraqi government pursuant to a permanent constitution . . .

CHAPTER THREE—THE IRAQI TRANSITIONAL GOVERNMENT

Article 24.

(A) The Iraqi Transitional Government, which is also referred to in this Law as the federal government, shall consist of the National Assembly; the Presidency Council; the Council of Ministers, including the Prime Minister; and the judicial authority.

(B) The three authorities, legislative, executive, and judicial, shall be separate and independent of one another.

(C) No official or employee of the Iraqi Transitional Government shall enjoy immunity for criminal acts committed while in office.

Article 25.

The Iraqi Transitional Government shall have exclusive competence in the following matters:

(A) Formulating foreign policy and diplomatic representation; negotiating, signing, and ratifying international treaties and agreements; formulating foreign economic and trade policy and sovereign debt policies;

(B) Formulating and executing national security policy, including creating and maintaining armed forces to secure, protect, and guarantee the security of the country's borders and to defend Iraq;

(C) Formulating fiscal policy, issuing currency, regulating customs, regulating commercial policy across regional and governorate boundaries in Iraq, drawing up the national budget of the State, formulating monetary policy, and establishing and administering a central bank;

(D) Regulating weights and measures and formulating a general policy on wages;

(E) Managing the natural resources of Iraq, which belongs to all the people of all the regions and governorates of Iraq, in consultation with the governments of the regions and the administrations of the governorates, and distributing the revenues resulting from their sale through the national budget in an equitable manner proportional to the distribution of population throughout the country, and with due regard for areas that were unjustly deprived of these revenues by the previous regime, for dealing with their situations in a positive way, for their needs, and for the degree of development of the different areas of the country;

(F) Regulating Iraqi citizenship, immigration, and asylum; and

(G) Regulating telecommunications policy.

- **Source:** *Law for the Administration for the State of Iraq*, March 8, 2004, available at http://www.au.af.mil/au/awc/awcgate/iraq/tal.htm, accessed January 16, 2012.

- **Analysis:** The CPA and the Governing Council reached agreement on the Transitional Law in November 2003. It was promulgated in March and came into effect in June. The law guaranteed Iraqis fundamental rights and basic freedoms. While it recognized Islam as the official religion of the state, the law guaranteed freedom of religion to all citizens. On the streets, however, persecution of Iraq's Christian minority was increasing.

  The law created an executive, legislative, and judicial branch. It called for the creation of a transitional government as soon as possible, including elections to the National Assembly no later than December 31, 2004. The interim government would be charged with drafting a constitution.

- **Document 80:** Excerpt of Government Accounting Office (GAO) report *Rebuilding Iraq*
- **When:** June 2004
- **Where:** Washington, DC
- **Significance:** The report provided a candid assessment of progress toward self-government.

Governance: Reforming and Rebuilding Iraq's Government

With U.S. and others' assistance, Iraqis have taken control of government institutions at the national and subnational levels. National ministries are providing some services to citizens as their facilities are being rebuilt, reforms are being introduced, and their staffs trained. According to the head of the now-dissolved CPA, all ministries were under Iraqi authority as of the transfer of power on June 28, 2004. However, the security situation hinders the ability of the ministries to provide needed services and maintain daily operations. To reform the rule of law, ongoing efforts have begun to establish a functioning independent judiciary, although courts are not at their pre-war capacity. As of June 2004, the CPA had completed a review of all Iraqi judges, took steps to reform Iraq's legal code, and issued orders to restore judicial independence. However, efforts to rebuild Iraq's judicial system and restore the rule of law face multiple challenges, including providing adequate security for judges and other court personnel, some of whom have been assassinated; ensuring the independence of the court system so that it operates without influence from the executive branch of the government; and providing adequate training for judges and attorneys. U.S. officials said that rehabilitating and reforming Iraq's judicial system will likely take years.

- **Source:** Government Accounting Office, *Rebuilding Iraq: Resource, Security, Governance, Essential Services, and Oversight Issues* (Washington, DC: GAO, 2004), p. 3.
- **Analysis:** The GAO report applauded progress made towards Iraqi self-government. At the same time it recognized that the security situation was hampering efforts to govern the country. The interim government lacked legitimacy. Many Iraqis considered it the tool of the occupying power. They were also far more concerned with their own reduced quality of life than they were with national politics.

- **Document 81: L. Paul Bremer III on the CPA**
- **When:** June 28, 2004
- **Where:** Baghdad
- **Significance:** Bremer expressed his appreciation to members of the CPA.

The Coalition Provisional Authority ceases to exist today. I would like to extend my personal thanks to everyone who works and has worked at the Coalition Provisional Authority, its predecessor, the Office of Refugee and Humanitarian Assistance, and to the fine men and women who have served in the coalition forces. Both groups have served with courage in the face of huge risks. Many have paid the ultimate price. We owe them a debt of gratitude, which no words can express.

Each of you has participated in a process unique in history. A coalition of the willing came together and toppled a tyrant. Then, civilian volunteers from around the world came to try not only to repair the ravages of war but to reconstruct a country devastated by over three decades of misrule.

You have contributed to replacing the tyranny of one man with a broadly representative government pledged to uphold the rights of all.

You have contributed to rebuilding Iraq and modernizing its economy.

You have contributed to making a better life for the citizens of this wonderful country.

These are noble undertakings for which I am deeply grateful.

I thank you for your sacrifice and your service and wish each of you the very best in the coming years.

- **Source:** *OPEC Bulletin* 35, no. 5 (2004): 53–55.
- **Analysis:** The head of the CPA spoke with understandable pride in his staff and engaged in a bit of political cheerleading. The interim authority had accomplished much, not least of which was the transition to Iraqi self-government. Its reconstruction record, however, left much to be desired as the carefully chosen, cautious phrase "you have contributed to" suggests. Bremer's triumphal remarks could not hide the deteriorating security situation or the fragility of Iraq's new government.

- **Document 82: Speech Given by Iyad Allawi, Prime Minister of Iraq**
- **When:** June 28, 2004
- **Where:** Baghdad
- **Significance:** The new prime minister celebrated transfer of sovereignty from the CPA to a new Iraqi government.

Dear free people, our dear Iraq has now hit a setback, but it is a very temporary setback, and we will rise up after that like mountains, standing up very firm. And we will protect all the people regardless of religion, colour or any other consideration, so every Iraqi will have the right to their unified, united Iraq where brotherhood and justice prevail. And national unity and tolerance and brotherly behaviour and a spirit of peace and prosperity will prevail.

Changing this to reality is a matter that will take our fullest consideration and dedication. This will be our agenda, and that will prevail over all of Iraq. The national unity, dear brothers, dear free brothers, is a sacred issue. And the pluralism of national origin, religion and others should be a factor of progression, not divisiveness.

It is time that we helped each other and co-operated, we must listen to other opinions, and we must live according to Islamic values and the message of our Prophet, when he said all Muslims are equal like the teeth of the comb.

Please let us not be afraid of those outlaws that are fighting Islam and Muslims, because God is with us. Those are the grandsons of the heretics of Islam; they were rejected by history. They are targeting our people, supported by some mercenaries of Saddam and his gang. Those transgressors, some of them have already gone to hell, and some others are waiting for their turn. This gang that dominated our people and formed a coalition with the enemies of Islam, they will end up in disgrace and failure.

And here I caution those Baathists who have not committed crimes in the past, I ask them to stay away from the mercenaries of Saddam. Those who pledge to continue in their crimes, I ask all of those Baathists to fight the enemies of the people and to inform the government of any suspicious activities they see.

The Iraqi people are asked to tackle those challenges by scrutinizing any suspicious activity and informing the government and the police. Those mercenaries that came to Iraq from different countries to attack the Iraqi people—God willing, and with the support of our people—we will be on the lookout for them, and we will chase them and bring them to justice to get their fair punishment.

The decision by your government to invoke and engage the United Nations and the international peace force is a major and positive step so that we can tackle all the issues of Iraq: regaining the peace on the internal front and to bring back the police force; and to form an army according to constitutional, national and ethical values; and promoting and developing the Ministry of Defence and merging the national militia into the army.

All of those armed forces will be the hand that strikes all those who will try to bring Iraq back to the old times. The army is the Iraqi army, not the Saddam army. They are our brothers and sons.

Those who have not been brought back into the army will be rehabilitated to go back to the civic sector or to retire as honoured people. Dear brethren who are set free now, the transformation from the dictatorship to the civil society and democracy, this is another major task of our government so that we have an Iraq—a federal Iraq, a united Iraq. This task is a hard task, a complex task.

The transformation of societies will not take place in weeks or days or months, but this transformation will take years that are full of hope and patience and tolerance. But we will be steadfast, moving forward toward peace and security, stability and democracy. These will be our steps, God willing. I will not just make promises, and I will not put you before a dark or bright picture.

I just want to put the facts before you so that we, all together, work with free will and with objectiveness so that we can take care of the futures of our people. Dear free brethren, Iraq will never be isolated like Saddam wanted it to be. It will not be outside of history. We have to slowly and steadily move forward with the principles that will preserve our people . . . and values that [inaudible] from the sovereignty and common interests and the balancing of those interests.

We have to be active and interact with what goes on in the world. Iraq, God willing, with its resources, both human and agricultural, tourism, oil and other resources, is in the centre of action in the world, not on the margin.

That's why we have to strengthen our relationship with the US and the EU and regional organizations like the Arab League and the Organization of the Islamic Conference, and others like OPEC and UNESCO, the IMF, the WTO and the OSCE (Organization for Security and Co-operation in Europe) and all the other organizations, like NATO and the south-east Asian organizations, so that we can serve the interests of Iraq and its people and help to reinforce security and stability.

That's why I extend the hand of peace to Iran and Turkey, and also the hand of brotherhood and love to Syria, Kuwait and Saudi Arabia, asking them to stand with us and help us to build brotherly relationships where common interests prevail. We are, after all, brothers. And we are here to protect the interests of our people.

And we have to work together to handle the problems of the area in a civilized manner and to harness our relationship in the interest of our people and the progress of our people and prosperity of our people and the security of the region.

And I use this opportunity to salute many other important countries like Jordan, the United Arab Emirates and Egypt, and salute the brotherly countries that sympathized with us, like Bahrain and Oman and Pakistan and our friend, President Musharraf, for their support of Iraq. And I also salute Bangladesh and India for their participating in the multinational forces.

Dear brothers, restoring life to the economic sector and fighting unemployment and building infrastructure like power, water, sewage, and offering health services and educational services, and building our reserves of hard currency, and dealing with the problems that have accumulated over the past decades, and rethinking our investment laws to protect national employment and the workforce, and promoting the private sector and relying on the resources of Iraq—all of those are factors that are necessary for our development.

Also, developing the workforce will be our agenda regarding the economic and financial situation. This is hard because Saddam's policies led to the loss of billions of dollars in the area of oil-for-food. And the money for salaries and wages, we are trying to work hard to reschedule or have the debt forgiven in our negotiations with the lending countries and the IMF and other entities.

In addition to that, our oil production is regressing, it is going back, because of the terrorists and their targeting of power and oil facilities. So this will take time, maybe a year or two, until we build a strong and healthy economy. But that shouldn't mean that we are going to live in poverty in the next few years. We will move forward, God willing, building and working gradually until we get to our goals.

Our government will work with a clear agenda that has priorities to tackle the serious matters first and put in place linchpins for progression on the economic infrastructure so that the returns to the Iraqi people will be quick, the financial returns will be good. And we will study privatization and consider ways to promote investment. And here I call on all the countries of the world to participate in supporting Iraq and rebuilding Iraq.

Dear brothers, the Cabinet has almost finished its agenda, and we will present it to you when it is ready within a few days. And in a few days, Iraq will radiate with stability and security. And we will work positively with the neighbours and the friends, and we will reciprocate by two steps for every step given to Iraq by others and will work toward the security and tranquility and peace of our people. I call on you to make efforts in being patient in that direction.

I salute our scholars and our religious authorities, Muslims, Christians, Shia and Sunni. At the forefront of that is Ayatollah Sistani. I call on all our sheikhs and tribal leaders and all the leaders of our political movements and our social organizations to keep their voices loud and clear, to let the word of right prevail, and to fight the terrorists and to encourage the rule of law and to allow our judicial entities to exercise their role in the society, the rule of law and allowing justice to be objective and neutral. Our safety evolves in the society, and we are working in that direction.

Dear free brethren, I warn the forces of terror once again, we will not forget who stood by us and who stood against us in this crisis. Here I arouse the efforts of people to defend the sacred places and the country. I call on all the heroes of the past, all the regions in Iraq and the sons of all Iraq, and I'll arouse their efforts to eradicate the foreign terrorists that are killing our people and destroying our country.

May God be with Iraq, and may God make it a great country, and may God make Iraq a factor of stability and security in the region, and we ask God to help us manage Iraq. And peace be upon all of you.

- **Source:** *OPEC Bulletin* 35, no. 5 (2004): 53–55.
- **Analysis:** Iraq's new prime minister struck a more cautious note than did the former head of the CPA. Allawi welcomed the transfer of sovereignty but noted in some detail the grave circumstances under which it was taking place. Iraq, he noted, remained a deeply divided and embattled country. He invited all Iraqis, no matter their religion or ethnicity, to join in the challenging work of putting the nation back on course. He also reached out to the international community and neighboring states to help in the task of reform and rebuilding. Finally, he vowed to defeat he insurgency and warned all Iraqis of the dire consequences of joining it.

CONSTITUTION

The United States wished to hand responsibility for governing Iraq over to the Iraqis as soon as possible. The first task the new Iraqi government faced was drafting a constitution. This proved to be a daunting task. Iraq was deeply divided along ethnic and religious lines. To be accepted by the majority of Iraqis the constitution would need to create a federal state with considerable authority devolved to regions and provinces. Decentralization would, however, make national government difficult.

- **Document 83: Excerpt of Iraqi Constitution: Preamble and Basic Rights**
- **When:** October 15, 2005
- **Where:** Baghdad
- **Significance:** The preamble and opening articles articulated the mandate for the constitution and the rights it guaranteed for Iraqis.

THE PREAMBLE
In the name of God, the most merciful, the most compassionate. We have honored the sons of Adam. We are the people of the land between two rivers, the homeland of the apostles and prophets, abode of the virtuous imams, pioneers of

civilization, crafters of writing and cradle of numeration. Upon our land the first law made by man was passed, the most ancient just pact for homelands policy was inscribed, and upon our soil, companions of the Prophet and saints prayed, philosophers and scientists theorized and writers and poets excelled. Acknowledging God's right over us, and in fulfillment of the call of our homeland and citizens, and in response to the call of our religious and national leaderships and the determination of our great (religious) authorities and of our leaders and reformers, and in the midst of an international support from our friends and those who love us, marched for the first time in our history toward the ballot boxes by the millions, men and women, young and old, on the 30th of January, 2005....

We the people of Iraq who have just risen from our stumble, and who are looking with confidence to the future through a republican, federal, democratic, pluralistic system, have resolved with the determination of our men, women, the elderly and youth, to respect the rules of law, to establish justice and equality to cast aside the politics of aggression, and to tend to the concerns of women and their rights, and to the elderly and their concerns, and to children and their affairs and to spread a culture of diversity and defusing terrorism. We the people of Iraq of all components and shades have taken upon ourselves to decide freely and with our choice to unite our future and to take lessons from yesterday for tomorrow, to draft, through the values and ideals of the heavenly messages and the findings of science and man's civilization, this lasting constitution. The adherence to this constitution preserves for Iraq its free union, its people, its land and its sovereignty.

SECTION ONE: FUNDAMENTAL PRINCIPLES

Article 1: *Amendment:* (The Republic of Iraq is a single, independent federal state with full sovereignty. Its system of government is republican, representative Parliamentary and democratic. This Constitution is the guarantor of its unity.) The Republic of Iraq is an independent sovereign state. Its system of government is republican, representative (Parliamentary), democratic and federal.

Article 2:

First: Islam is the official religion of the State and it is a fundamental source of legislation: A. No law that contradicts the established provisions of Islam may be established. B. No law that contradicts the principles of democracy may be established. C. No law that contradicts the rights and basic freedoms stipulated in this constitution may be established.

Second: This Constitution guarantees the Islamic identity of the majority of the Iraqi people and guarantees the full religious rights of all individuals to freedom of religious belief and practice such as Christians, Yazedis, and Mandi Sabeans.

Article 3: *Amendment:* (Iraq is a country of many nationalities, religions and sects and is a founding and active member of the Arab League and is committed to its covenant. Iraq is a part of the Islamic world.) Iraq is a country of many nationalities, religions and sects, and is a part of the Islamic world, is a founding and active member of the Arab League, and is committed to its covenant.

Article 4: First: The Arabic language and Kurdish language are the two official languages of Iraq. The right of Iraqis to educate their children in their mother tongue, such as Turkmen, Syriac and Armenian, in government educational institutions in accordance with educational guidelines, or in any other language in private educational institutions, is guaranteed. Second: The scope of the term official language and the means of applying the provisions of this Article shall be defined by law which shall include: A. Publication of the official gazette, in the two languages; B. Speech, conversation and expression in official settings, such as the Council of Representatives, the Council of Ministers, courts, and official conferences, in either of the two languages; C. Recognition and publication of the official documents and correspondences in the two languages; D. Opening schools that teach the two languages, in accordance with the educational guidelines; E. Use of both languages in any settings enjoined by the principle of equality such as bank notes, passports and stamps. *Amendment:* (Third: The federal institutions and agencies in the Kurdistan region shall use the Arabic and Kurdish languages.) Third: The federal institutions and agencies in the Kurdistan region shall use both languages. Fourth: The Turkmen language and Syriac language are two other official languages in the administrative units in which they represent density of population. Fifth: Each region or governorate may adopt any other local language as an additional official language if the majority of its population so decide in a general referendum.

Article 5: The law is sovereign. The people are the source of authorities and its legitimacy, which the people shall exercise in a direct general secret ballot and through their constitutional institutions.

Article 6: Transfer of authority shall be made peacefully through democratic means as stipulated in this Constitution.

Article 7: First: No entity or program, under any name, may adopt racism, terrorism, the calling of others infidels, ethnic cleansing, or incite, facilitate, glorify, promote, or justify thereto, especially the Saddamist Baath in Iraq and its symbols, regardless of the name that it adopts. This may not be part of the political pluralism in Iraq.

This will be organized by law. Second: The State shall undertake combating terrorism in all its forms, and shall work to protect its territories from being a base or pathway or field for terrorist activities. . . .

SECTION TWO: RIGHTS AND LIBERTIES

CHAPTER ONE: RIGHTS

FIRST: Civil and Political Rights

Article 14: Iraqis are equal before the law without discrimination based on gender, race, ethnicity, origin, color, religion, creed, belief or opinion, or economic and social status.

Article 15: Every individual has the right to enjoy life, security and liberty. Deprivation or restriction of these rights is prohibited except in accordance with the law and based on a decision issued by a competent judicial authority.

Article 16: Equal opportunities are guaranteed for all Iraqis. The state guarantees the taking of the necessary measures to achieve such equal opportunities.

Article 17: First: Every individual shall have the right to personal privacy, so long it does not contradict the rights of others and public morals. Second: The sanctity of homes is inviolable and homes may not be entered, searched, or put in danger, except by a judicial decision, and in accordance with the law.

Article 18: *Amendment:* (First: Iraqi nationality is the right of every Iraqi and shall be the basis of his citizenship.)

First: An Iraqi is any person born to an Iraqi father or mother. *Amendment:* (Second: An Iraqi is any person born to an Iraqi father or mother. This will regulated by law.)

Second: Iraqi nationality is the right of every Iraqi and shall be the basis of his citizenship.

Third: A. An Iraqi citizen by birth may not have his nationality withdrawn for any reason. Any person who had his nationality withdrawn shall have the right to reclaim it, and this will be stipulated by law.

B. The Iraqi nationality shall be withdrawn from the naturalized in the cases stipulated by law.

Fourth: An Iraqi may have multiple nationalities. Everyone who assumes a senior, security sovereign position must abandon any other acquired nationality. This will be organized by law.

Fifth: Iraqi citizenship shall not be granted for the purposes of the policy of settling people that cause an imbalance in the population composition of Iraq.

Sixth: A law shall regulate the provisions of nationality. The competent courts shall consider the suits resulting from it.

Article 19:

First: The judiciary is independent and no power is above the judiciary except the law.

Second: There is no crime or punishment except by a stipulation. The punishment shall only be for an act that the law considers a crime when perpetrated. A harsher sentence than the applicable sentence at the time of the offense may not be imposed.

Third: Litigation shall be a safeguarded and guaranteed right for all.

Fourth: The right to a defense shall be sacred and guaranteed in all phases of investigation and trial.

Fifth: The accused is innocent until proven guilty in a fair legal trial. The accused may not be tried on the same crime for a second time after acquittal unless new evidence is produced.

Sixth: Every person has the right to be treated with justice in judicial and administrative proceedings.

Seventh: The proceedings of a trial are public unless the court decides to make it secret.

Eighth: Punishment is personal.

Ninth: A law does not have a retroactive effect unless the law stipulates otherwise. This exclusion shall not include laws relating to taxes and fees.

Tenth: Criminal law does not have a retroactive effect, unless it is to the benefit of the accused.

Eleventh: The court shall delegate a lawyer at the expense of the state for an accused of a felony or misdemeanor who does not have a defense lawyer.

Twelfth: A. (Unlawful) detention is prohibited. B. Detention or arrest is prohibited in places not designed for it, pursuant to prison regulations covered by health and social care and subject to the scrutiny of the law.

Thirteenth: The preliminary investigative documents must be submitted to the competent judge in a period not to exceed 24 hours from the time of the arrest of the accused. It may be extended only once and for the same period.

Article 20: The citizens, men and women, have the right to participate in public affairs and to enjoy political rights including the right to vote, to elect and to nominate.

Article 21:

First: No Iraqi shall be surrendered to foreign entities and authorities.

Second: A law shall regulate the right of political asylum to Iraq. No political refugee shall be surrendered to a foreign entity or returned forcibly to the country from which he fled.

Third: No political asylum shall be granted to a person accused of committing international or terrorist crimes or any person who inflicted damage on Iraq.

SECOND: Economic, social and cultural liberties

Article 22:

First: Work is a right for all Iraqis so as to guarantee them a decent living.

Second: The law regulates the relationship between employees and employers on economic basis and with regard to the foundations of social justice.

Third: The State guarantees the right of forming and joining professional associations and unions. This will be organized by law.

Article 23:

First: Personal property is protected. The proprietor shall have the right to benefit from, exploit and utilize personal property within the limits of the law.

Second: No property may be taken away except for the purposes of public benefit in return for just compensation. This will be organized by law.

Third: A. Every Iraqi has the right to own property throughout Iraq. No others may possess immovable assets, except as exempted by law. B. Owning property for the purposes of population change shall be prohibited.

Article 24: The State guarantees freedom of movement of Iraqi manpower, goods and capitals between regions and governorates. This will be organized by law.

Article 25: The State guarantees the reform of the Iraqi economy in accordance with modern economic principles to insure the full investment of its resources, diversification of its sources and the encouragement and the development of the private sector.

Article 26: The state guarantees the encouragement of investments in the various sectors. This will be organized by law.

Article 27:

First: Public property is sacrosanct, and its protection is the duty of each citizen.

Second: The provisions related to the protection of State properties and its management and the conditions for its disposal and the limits under which none of these properties can be relinquished shall all be regulated by law.

Article 28:

First: No taxes or fines may be imposed, amended, exempted or pardoned from, except in accordance with law.

Second: Low wage earners shall be exempted from taxes in a manner that ensures the upholding of the minimum wage required for survival. This will be organized by law.

Article 29:

First: A. The family is the foundation of society; the State preserves its entity and its religious, moral and patriotic values. B. The State guarantees the protection of motherhood, childhood and old age and shall care for children and youth and provides them with the appropriate conditions to further their talents and abilities.

Second: Children have right over their parents in regard to upbringing, care and education. Parents shall have right over their children in regard to respect and care especially in times of need, disability and old age.

Third: Economic exploitation of children shall be completely prohibited. The State shall take the necessary measures to protect them.

Fourth: All forms of violence and abuse in the family, school and society shall be prohibited.

Article 30:

First: The state guarantee to the individual and the family—especially children and women—social and health security and the basic requirements for leading a free and dignified life. The state also ensures the above a suitable income and appropriate housing.

Second: The State guarantees the social and health security to Iraqis in cases of old age, sickness, employment disability, homelessness, orphanage or unemployment, and shall work to protect them from ignorance, fear and poverty. The State shall provide them housing and special programs of care and rehabilitation. This will be organized by law.

Article 31: First: Every citizen has the right to health care. The state takes care of public health and provide the means of prevention and treatment by building different types of hospitals and medical institutions. Second: Individuals and institutions may build hospitals or clinics or places for treatment with the supervision of the state and this shall be regulated by law.

Article 32: The State cares for the handicapped and those with special needs and ensure their rehabilitation in order to reintegrate them into society. This shall be regulated by law.

Article 33: First: Every individual has the right to live in a safe environment. Second: The State undertakes the protection and preservation of the environment and biological diversity.

Article 34:

First: Education is a fundamental factor in the progress of society and is a right guaranteed by the state. Primary education is mandatory and the state guarantees to eradicate illiteracy.

Second: Free education is a right for all Iraqis in all its stages.

Third: The State encourages scientific research for peaceful purposes that serve man and supports excellence, creativity, invention and the different aspects of ingenuity.

Fourth: Private and public education is guaranteed. This shall be regulated by law.

CHAPTER TWO: LIBERTIES

Article 35:

First: A. The liberty and dignity of man are safeguarded. B. No person may be kept in custody or interrogated except in the context of a judicial decision. C. All forms of psychological and physical torture and inhumane treatment shall be prohibited. Any confession coerced by force, threat, or torture shall not be relied on. The victim shall have the right to compensation in accordance with the law for material and moral damages incurred.

Second: The State guarantees the protection of the individual from intellectual, political and religious coercion.

Third: Compulsory service (unpaid labor), serfdom, slave trade (slavery), trafficking of women and children, and the sex trade is prohibited. *Amendment:* (Fourth: The State will promote cultural activities and institutions in a way that is appropriate with Iraq's civilizational history and culture. It will take care to depend on authentic Iraqi cultural trends.)

Article 36: The state guarantees in a way that does not violate public order and morality: A. Freedom of expression, through all means. B. Freedom of press, printing, advertisement, media and publication. C. Freedom of assembly and peaceful demonstration. This shall be regulated by law....

- **Source:** Excerpts from *Final Draft Iraqi Constitution*, available at http://portal.unesco.org/ci/en/files/20704/11332732681iraqi_constitution_en.pdf/iraqi_constitution_en.pdf, accessed June 23, 2011.

- **Analysis:** The Iraqi people ratified the constitution in a referendum held October 15, 2005. The results were 79 percent in favor, 21 percent opposed, based upon 63 percent voter turnout. It should come as no surprise that a people who had suffered years of oppression should write extensive personal freedoms and civil liberties into their constitution. The document recognized Islam as the official religion while guaranteeing freedom of belief and practice to citizens of all faiths. It also prohibited passing of any laws that contradict "the established principles of Islam."

  The constitution recognized the multiethnic character of Iraqi society. It recognized Arabic and Kurdish as official languages. It also allowed people to educate their children in whatever language they spoke. At the same time, the constitution committed the country to upholding the covenant of the Arab League, to which Iraq belongs.

  The Iraqi constitution guaranteed the broad range of personnel freedoms and civil liberties found in most democratic countries. Freedom of speech, the press, and assembly were, however, restricted by the caveat that exercising them does not "violate public order and morality." This caveat allowed the government considerable latitude in restricting expression. The Iraqi constitution went beyond guarantees of human rights and civil liberties. The social and economic rights section guaranteed health, welfare, and education benefits without providing specific details.

- **Document 84: Excerpt of Iraqi Constitution, Section 2, Chapter One: "The Legislative Power"**
- **When:** October 15, 2005
- **Where:** Baghdad
- **Significance:** The constitution created a parliamentary democracy.

CHAPTER ONE: THE LEGISLATIVE POWER:

Article 46: The federal legislative power shall consist of the Council of Representatives and the Federation Council.

FIRST: The Council of Representatives

Article 47: First: The Council of Representatives shall consist of a number of members, at a ratio of one representative per 100,000 Iraqi persons representing the entire Iraqi people. They shall be elected through a direct secret general ballot. The representation of all components of the people in it shall be upheld.

Second: A candidate to the Council of Representatives must be a fully eligible Iraqi. Third: A law shall regulate the requirements for the candidate, the voter and all that is connected with the elections.

Fourth: The elections law aims to achieve a percentage of women representation not less than one-quarter of the Council of Representatives members.

Fifth: The Council of Representatives shall promulgate a law dealing with the replacement of its members on resignation, dismissal or death.

Sixth: No member of the Council of Representatives shall be allowed to hold any other official position or work. . . .

SECOND: The Federation Council

Article 62: A legislative council shall be established named the "Federation Council" to include representatives from the regions and the governorates that are not organized in a region. A law, enacted by a two-third majority of the members of the Council of representatives, shall regulate the Federation Council formation, its membership conditions and its specializations and all that is connected with it.

- **Source:** Excerpts from *Final Draft Iraqi Constitution*, available at http://portal.unesco.org/ci/en/files/20704/11332732681iraqi_constitution_en.pdf/iraqi_constitution_en.pdf, accessed June 23, 2011.
- **Analysis:** The constitution made Iraq a parliamentary democracy. Members of the Council of Representatives are elected on a proportional basis with one seat per 100,000 people. This approach allows them to represent the country as whole rather than specific areas.

In the absence of two strong parties, however, it leads to fragmented politics such as occurs in Israel.

In deference to federalism, the constitution created a bicameral legislature. However, it made no specific provision for how the Federal Council representing regions and entities was to function. The Council of Representatives was charged with defining the membership and function of the Federal Council. At present Iraq functions as a unicameral legislature. The constitution also declared that a future election law would try to have at least 25 percent of representatives be women.

- **Document 85: Excerpt of Iraqi Constitution, Section 3, Chapter Two, "Executive Power"**
- **When:** October 15, 2005
- **Where:** Baghdad
- **Significance:** The constitution strictly limited executive authority.

Article 63: The Federal Executive Power shall consist of the President of the Republic and the Council of Ministers and shall exercise its powers in accordance with the constitution and the law.

FIRST: The President of the Republic

Article 64: The President of the Republic is the Head of the State and a symbol of the unity of the country and represents the sovereignty of the country. He safeguards the commitment to the Constitution and the preservation of Iraq's independence, sovereignty, unity, the security of its territories in accordance with the provisions of the Constitution. . . .

Article 66:

First: A law shall regulate the nomination to the post of the President of the Republic.

Second: A law shall regulate the nomination of one deputy or more for the President of the Republic.

Article 67:

First: The Council of Representatives shall elect, from among the nominees, the President of the Republic by a two-thirds majority of its members.

Second: If any of the candidates does not receive the required majority vote then the two candidates who received the highest number of votes shall compete and the one who receives the highest number of votes in the second election shall be declared as President.

Article 68: The President shall take the Constitutional Oath before the Council of Representatives in the form stipulated in Article 48 of the Constitution.

Article 69:

First: The President of the Republic's term in office shall be limited to four years and may be elected for a second time and no more.

Second: A. The term of the President of the Republic shall finish at the end of the Council of Representatives' term. B. The President of the Republic will continue to exercise his functions until the elections for the Council of Representatives is completed and until it meets. The new President shall then be elected within 30 days of its first meeting.

C. If the position of president of the republic is vacant, for whatever reason, a new president will be elected in order to fill the vacancy for the remaining period of that president's term.

Article 70: The President of the Republic shall assume the following powers:

A. To issue a special pardon on the recommendation of the Prime Minister, except for anything concerning private claim and for those who have been convicted of committing international crimes, terrorism, and financial and administrative corruption.

B. To ratify international treaties and agreements after the approval by the Council of Representatives. Such international treaties and agreements are considered ratified after 15 days from the date of receipt.

C. To ratify and issue the laws enacted by the Council of Representatives. Such laws are considered ratified after 15 days from the date of receipt.

D. To call the elected Council of Representatives to convene during a period not to exceed 15 days from the date of approval of the election results and in the other cases stipulated in the Constitution.

E. To award medals and decorations on the recommendation of the Prime Minister in accordance with the law.

F. To accredit Ambassadors.

G. To issue Presidential decrees.

H. Ratify death sentences issued by the competent courts.

I. Perform the duty of the Higher Command of the armed forces for ceremonial and honorary purposes.

J. Exercise any other presidential powers stipulated in this Constitution . . .

SECOND: Council of Ministers

Article 73: First: The President of the Republic shall name the nominee of the Council of Representatives bloc with the largest number to form the Cabinet within 15 days from the date of the election of the president of the republic.

Second: The Prime Minister-designate shall undertake the naming of the members of his Cabinet within a period not to exceed 30 days from the date of his designation.

Third: In case the Prime Minister-designate fails to form the cabinet during the period specified in clause "Second," the President of the Republic shall name a new nominee for the post of Prime Minister within fifteen days.

Fourth: The Prime Minister-designate shall present the names of his Cabinet members and the ministerial program to the Council of Representatives. He is deemed to have gained its confidence upon the approval, by an absolute majority of the Council of Representatives, of the individual Ministers and the ministerial program.

Fifth: The President of the Republic shall name another nominee to form the cabinet within 15 days in case the Cabinet did not gain the confidence.

Article 74:

First: The conditions for assuming the post of the Prime Minister shall be the same as those for the President of the Republic, provided that he is at least 35 years old and has a college degree or its equivalent.

Second: The conditions for assuming the post of Minister shall be the same as those for members of the Council of Representatives provided that he holds a college degree or its equivalent.

Article 75: The Prime Minister is the direct executive authority responsible for the general policy of the State and the commander in chief of the armed forces. He directs the Council of Ministers, and presides over its meetings and has the right to dismiss the Ministers on the consent of the Council of Representatives.

Article 76: The Prime Minister and members of the Cabinet shall take the Constitutional Oath before the Council of Representatives in the form stipulated in Article 48 of the Constitution.

Article 77: The Cabinet shall exercise the following powers:

First: Plan and execute the general policy and the general plans of the State and oversee the work of the ministries and departments not associated with a ministry.

Second: To propose bills.

Third: To issue rules, instructions and decisions for the purpose of implementing the law.

Fourth: To prepare the draft of the general budget, the closing account, and the development plans.

Fifth: To recommend to the Council of Representatives to approve the appointment of under secretaries, ambassadors, State senior officials, Chief of Staff of the Armed Forces and his assistants, Division Commanders or higher, Director of the National Intelligence Service, and heads of security institutions.

Sixth: To negotiate and sign international agreements and treaties or designate any person to do so.

Article 78:

First: The President of the Republic shall take up the office of the Prime Minister in the event the post becomes vacant for any reason whatsoever.

Second: The President must designate another nominee to form the cabinet within a period not to exceed 15 days in accordance with the provisions of Article 73 of this Constitution.

Article 79: A law shall regulate the salaries and allowances of the Prime Minister and Ministers, and anyone of their grade.

Article 80: The responsibility of the Prime Minister and the Ministers before the Council of Representatives is of a joint and personal nature.

Article 81:

First: A law shall regulate the work of the security institutions and the National Intelligence Service and shall define its duties and authorities. It shall operate in accordance with the principles of human rights and be subject to the oversight of the Council of Representatives.

Second: The National Intelligence Service shall be attached to the Cabinet.

Article 82: The Council of Ministers shall establish internal bylaws to organize the work therein. . . .

- **Source:** Excerpts from *Final Draft Iraqi Constitution*, available at http://portal.unesco.org/ci/en/files/20704/11332732681iraqi_constitution_en.pdf/iraqi_constitution_en.pdf, accessed June 23, 2011.
- **Analysis:** All parliamentary systems are based on the British model. The majority party or a coalition able to produce a majority in parliament chooses the prime minister and his or her cabinet (called the Council of Ministers in Iraq). The prime minister wields real executive power, running the executive branch and serving as commander-in-chief of the armed forces. In the United Kingdom, the queen is the head of state. Because most parliamentary democracies do not have a monarch, they elect a president to assume what have become largely ceremonial and perfunctory duties. Iraq's president is elected by the Council of Representatives. One unusual provision allows the president to serve as prime minister should that office become unexpectedly vacant.

- **Document 86: Excerpt of Iraqi Constitution, Section 3, Chapter Three: "Judicial Authority"**
- **When:** October 15, 2005
- **Where:** Baghdad
- **Significance:** The constitution created an independent judiciary.

Article 84: The Judicial authority is independent. The courts, in their various types and classes, shall assume this authority and issue decisions in accordance with the law.

Article 85: Judges are independent and there is no authority over them except that of the law. No authority shall have the right to interfere in the Judiciary and the affairs of Justice.

Article 86: The Federal Judicial Authority is comprised of the Higher Juridical Council, Supreme Federal Court, Federal Court of Cassation, Public Prosecution Department, Judiciary Oversight Commission and other federal courts that are regulated in accordance with the law.

- **Source:** Excerpts from *Final Draft Iraqi Constitution*, available at http://portal.unesco.org/ci/en/files/20704/11332732681iraqi_constitution_en.pdf/iraqi_constitution_en.pdf, accessed June 23, 2011.
- **Analysis:** Saddam Hussein had made extensive use of extrajudicial power, detaining people without charge or trial, making use of torture, and applying extrajudicial punishments, including murder of regime opponents. The framers of the Iraqi constitution were thus understandably anxious to create an independent judiciary. According to the new

constitution, judges were to be independent, under authority of the law alone.

- **Document 87: Excerpt of Iraqi Constitution, Section 4, "Federal Powers"**
- **When:** October 15, 2005
- **Where:** Baghdad
- **Significance:** This section defined the extent and limits of federal powers.

Article 109: The federal authorities shall preserve the unity, integrity, independence, and sovereignty of Iraq and its federal democratic system.

Article 110: The federal government shall have exclusive authorities in the following matters:

First: Formulating foreign policy and diplomatic representation; negotiating, signing, and ratifying international treaties and agreements; negotiating, signing, and ratifying debt policies and formulating foreign sovereign economic and trade policy.

Second: Formulating and executing national security policy, including establishing and managing armed forces to secure the protection and guarantee the security of Iraq's borders and to defend Iraq.

Third: Formulating fiscal and customs policy; issuing currency; regulating commercial policy across regional and governorate boundaries in Iraq; drawing up the national budget of the State; formulating monetary policy; and establishing and administering a central bank.

Fourth: Regulating standards, weights, and measures.

Fifth: Regulating issues of citizenship, naturalization, residency, and the right to apply for political asylum.

Sixth: Regulating the policies of broadcast frequencies and mail.

Seventh: Drawing up the general and investment budget bill.

Eighth: Planning policies relating to water sources from outside Iraq and guaranteeing the rate of water flow to Iraq and its just distribution inside Iraq in accordance with international laws and conventions.

Ninth: General population statistics and census.

- **Source:** Excerpts from *Final Draft Iraqi Constitution*, available at http://portal.unesco.org/ci/en/files/20704/11332732681iraqi_constitution_en.pdf/iraqi_constitution_en.pdf, accessed June 23, 2011.
- **Analysis:** Given their experience living under the tyranny of Saddam Hussein, Iraqis were understandably leery of creating a strong executive. The constitution limited federal power to national defense, foreign affairs, and various regulatory and oversight functions such as weights and measures, currency, and so forth. Without limited federal

powers and delegation of considerable authority to provinces and regions, most Iraqis would not have voted for the constitution.

- **Document 88: Excerpt of Iraqi Constitution, Section 5, "Regions and Governorates"**
- **When:** October 15, 2005
- **Where:** Baghdad
- **Significance:** The constitution delegated considerable power to regions and governorates.

Article 116: The federal system in the Republic of Iraq is made up of a decentralized capital, regions, and governorates, as well as local administrations.

Article 117:

First: This Constitution, upon coming into force, shall recognize the region of Kurdistan, along with its existing authorities, as a federal region.

Second: This Constitution shall affirm new regions established in accordance with its provisions.

Article 118: The Council of Representatives shall enact, in a period not to exceed six months from the date of its first session, a law that defines the executive procedures to form regions, by a simple majority of the members present.

Article 119: One or more governorates shall have the right to organize into a region based on a request to be voted on in a referendum submitted in one of the following two methods:

First: A request by one-third of the council members of each governorate intending to form a region.

Second: A request by one-tenth of the voters in each of the governorates intending to form a region.

Article 120: Each region shall adopt a constitution of its own that defines the structure of powers of the region, its authorities, and the mechanisms for exercising such authorities, provided that it does not contradict this Constitution.

Article 121:

First: The regional powers shall have the right to exercise executive, legislative, and judicial powers in accordance with this Constitution, except for those authorities stipulated in the exclusive authorities of the federal government.

Second: In case of a contradiction between regional and national legislation in respect to a matter outside the exclusive authorities of the federal government, the regional power shall have the right to amend the application of the national legislation within that region.

Third: Regions and governorates shall be allocated an equitable share of the national revenues sufficient to discharge their responsibilities and duties, but having regard to their resources, needs, and the percentage of their population.

Fourth: Offices for the regions and governorates shall be established in embassies and diplomatic missions, in order to follow cultural, social, and developmental affairs.

Fifth: The regional government shall be responsible for all the administrative requirements of the region, particularly the establishment and organization of the internal security forces for the region such as police, security forces, and guards of the region.

Chapter Two [Governorates that are not incorporated in a region]

Article 122:

First: The governorates shall be made up of a number of districts, sub-districts, and villages.

Second: Governorates that are not incorporated in a region shall be granted broad administrative and financial authorities to enable them to manage their affairs in accordance with the principle of decentralized administration, and this shall be regulated by law.

Third: The governor, who is elected by the Governorate Council, is deemed the highest executive official in the governorate to practice his powers authorized by the Council.

Fourth: A law shall regulate the election of the Governorate Council, the governor, and their powers.

Fifth: The Governorate Council shall not be subject to the control or supervision of any ministry or any institution not linked to a ministry. The Governorate Council shall have independent finances.

Article 123: Powers exercised by the federal government can be delegated to the governorates or vice versa, with the consent of both governments, and this shall be regulated by law.

- **Source:** Excerpts from *Final Draft Iraqi Constitution*, available at http://portal.unesco.org/ci/en/files/20704/11332732681iraqi_constitution_en.pdf/iraqi_constitution_en.pdf, accessed June 23, 2011.

- **Analysis:** At the height of the insurgency some analysts considered partition of Iraq not only likely but perhaps desirable. Only by adopting a federal system with considerable devolution of powers could the framers of the constitution accommodate the various power centers in the country. The constitution recognized existing semiautonomous regions and governorates (provinces) and allowed for the creation of new ones by referendum. Regions had the right to draft constitutions. All powers not specifically granted to the federal government devolve to the regions and governorates. As with any federal state, especially one that came to the brink of civil war, the challenge for Iraq is to forge a truly Iraqi identity that transcends regional, ethnic, and sectarian differences.

DID YOU KNOW?

Governorates of Iraq

Iraq is divided into 18 governorates (provinces). The Sunni insurgency was most intense in the Diyala and Anbar provinces but also fought in four other northern governorates. Shi'a militias were active in eight southern provinces and the remaining four provinces. The new Iraqi constitution gives considerable administrative authority to Iraqi governorates.

- **Document 89: Excerpt of Iraqi Election Law**
- **When:** July 7, 2005
- **Where:** Baghdad
- **Significance:** The law defined requirements for voting and holding office and established voting districts.

Article 11

At least one woman must be among the first three nominees on the list and at least two women must be among the first six nominees on the list and so on until the end of the list. . . .

Article 15

First: The House of Representatives shall be composed of 275 members, 230 seats shall be distributed to the electoral districts and 45 of them shall be distributed as compensatory seats.

Second: Each governorate is one electoral district in accordance with official borders and shall be allotted a number of seats proportional to the number of registered voters in the governorate in accordance with the elections of January 30, 2005 "based on the public distribution list".

Article 17

The compensatory seats shall be distributed as follows:

1- The total number of valid votes in Iraq shall be divided by the number of the seats in the House of Representatives, to obtain the "national average".

2- The total number of votes obtained by each entity shall be divided by the "national average" to determine the number of seats allotted to it.

3- Compensatory seats shall first be allocated to entities which did not obtain representation in the election districts, but that obtained at least the national average of votes.

4- The remaining seats shall be distributed to the entities that have been allocated seats in the electoral districts based on ratio of the number of its votes to the total votes.

- **Source:** Iraqi Election Law, July 7, 2005, available at http://www.lgp-iraq .org/publications/index.cfm?fuseaction=pubDetail&ID=256&catId=74, accessed June 24, 2011.
- **Analysis:** The election law of 2005 contained the usual provisions establishing voting requirements and conditions for holding office. It also contained unusual provisions based upon the peculiar circumstances of Iraq. Article 11 required women be near the top of candidate lists, thus guaranteeing that they would be allotted at least some seats in the Council of Representatives. The law also provided a formula for proportional distribution of seats and for assigning seats to

victorious candidates. To make certain that all groups receive representation, the law created 45 compensatory seats to be given to entities that do not win any district seats. This convoluted system makes sense in the fractured politics of Iraq.

Elections held in January 2005 under the previous election law were boycotted by many Sunnis who believed their votes were underrepresented. Although the July 2005 law attempted to address these concerns, it had to be amended in December 2009 so that elections could be held on March 7, 2010. The amendment addressed Sunni concerns about voting by Iraqis living abroad, disputed voter registration in Kirkuk, and having the UN mediate election disputes. It also added 50 seats to the Council of Representatives.

DID YOU KNOW?

Nouri al-Maliki

Nouri al-Maliki (b. 1950) is currently serving his second term as prime minister of Iraq, an office he has held since 2006. A Shi'a dissident during the reign of Saddam Hussein, al-Maliki fled the country in 1979 to escape a death sentence and returned following the U.S. invasion in 2003. He belongs to the Islamic Dawa Party, a member of the United Iraqi Alliance, which won the last two elections. Al-Maliki has had great difficulty forming governments amid Iraq's fractured politics. He has been accused of treading softly with Shi'a militias while cracking down on Sunni insurgents. He enjoys the support of the United States, although his relations with Washington have often been strained.

The 2010 parliamentary elections revealed the deeply divided nature of Iraqi politics. Nine parties won seats, with three coalitions getting the most votes. After months of wrangling, the coalitions formed a government with Nouri al-Maliki as prime minister. Although the improved security situation had made governing Iraq easier, the country had a long way to go before becoming a fully functioning democracy.

THE CHALLENGE OF GOVERNING

The complexity of the Iraq Constitution reflects the equally complex nature of Iraqi politics. The country's deep ethnic and religious divides, exacerbated by decades of Saddam Hussein's brutal regime and two years of insurgency and terrorism, would make governing Iraq challenging. No constitution could prevent politicians putting the well-being of their particular group above that of Iraq as a whole. Promoting national unity remains a challenge for any Iraqi government.

- **Document 90: President George W. Bush, Address to the American People on the Iraqi Elections**
- **When:** January 30, 2005
- **Where:** Washington, DC
- **Significance:** Iraq elected its first legislature under the new constitution.

Today the people of Iraq have spoken to the world, and the world is hearing the voice of freedom from the center of the Middle East.

In great numbers, and under great risk, Iraqis have shown their commitment to democracy. By participating in free elections, the Iraqi people have firmly rejected the anti-democratic ideology of the terrorists. They have refused to be intimidated by thugs and assassins. And they have demonstrated the kind of courage that is always the foundation of self-government.

Some Iraqis were killed while exercising their rights as citizens. We also mourn the American and British military personnel who lost their lives today. Their sacrifices were made in a vital cause of freedom, peace in a troubled region, and a more secure future for us all.

The Iraqi people, themselves, made this election a resounding success. Brave patriots stepped forward as candidates. Many citizens volunteered as poll workers. More than 100,000 Iraqi security force personnel guarded polling places and conducted operations against terrorist groups. One news account told of a voter who had lost a leg in a terror attack last year, and went to the polls today, despite threats of violence. He said, "I would have crawled here if I had to. I don't want terrorists to kill other Iraqis like they tried to kill me. Today I am voting for peace."

Across Iraq today, men and women have taken rightful control of their country's destiny, and they have chosen a future of freedom and peace. In this process, Iraqis have had many friends at their side. The European Union and the United Nations gave important assistance in the election process. The American military and our diplomats, working with our coalition partners, have been skilled and relentless, and their sacrifices have helped to bring Iraqis to this day. The people of the United States have been patient and resolute, even in difficult days.

The commitment to a free Iraq now goes forward. This historic election begins the process of drafting and ratifying a new constitution, which will be the basis of a fully democratic Iraqi government. Terrorists and insurgents will continue to wage their war against democracy, and we will support the Iraqi people in their fight against them. We will continue training Iraqi security forces so this rising democracy can eventually take responsibility for its own security.

There's more distance to travel on the road to democracy. Yet Iraqis are proving they're equal to the challenge. On behalf of the American people, I congratulate the people of Iraq on this great and historic achievement.

- **Source:** George W. Bush, "President Congratulates Iraqis on Election," http://georgewbush-whitehouse.archives.gov/news/releases/2005/01/20050130-2.html, accessed July 13, 2011.

- **Analysis:** The Iraqi elections were one of the few bright spots in a disappointing year characterized by violence and instability. Under such circumstances the claim that Iraqis had "taken control of their country's destiny" was clearly an exaggeration. The 100,000 Iraqi security forces guarding polling places was also a pitifully small percentage of the total number of troops and police needed to restore order. Nonetheless, the ability to hold an election at all under such trying circumstances was a sign of progress.

- **Document 91: Joint Statement by President George W. Bush and Prime Minister Nuri al-Maliki of Iraq**
- **When:** November 30, 2006
- **Where:** Amman, Jordan
- **Significance:** The two leaders expressed concern about security in Iraq.

We were pleased to continue our consultations on building security and stability in Iraq. We are grateful to His Majesty King Abdullah II of Jordan for hosting these meetings here in Amman.

Our discussions reviewed developments in Iraq, focusing on the security situation and our common concern about sectarian violence targeting innocent Iraqis. In this regard, the Prime Minister affirms the commitment of his government to advance efforts toward national reconciliation and the need for all Iraqis and political forces in Iraq to work against armed elements responsible for violence and intimidation. The Prime Minister also affirms his determination with help from the United States and the international community to improve the efficiency of government operations, particularly in confronting corruption and strengthening the rule of law.

We discussed the plague of terrorism in Iraq which is being fomented and fueled by Al Qaeda. The people of Iraq, like the people of the United States and the entire civilized world, must stand together to face this common threat. The Prime Minister affirmed that Iraq is a partner in the fight against Al Qaeda. We agreed that defeating Al Qaeda and the terrorists is vital to ensuring the success of Iraq's democracy.

We discussed the means by which the United States will enhance Iraq's capabilities to further isolate extremists and bring all who choose violence and terror to full justice under Iraqi law.

We agreed in particular to take all necessary measures to track down and bring to justice those responsible for the cowardly attacks last week in Sadr City. The Prime Minister has also pledged to bring to justice those responsible for crimes committed in the wake of this attack.

We discussed accelerating the transfer of security responsibilities to the Government of Iraq; our hopes for strengthening the future relationship between our two nations; and joint efforts to achieve greater cooperation from governments in the region and to counter those elements that are fueling the conflict.

We received an interim report from the high-level Joint Committee on Accelerating the Transferring of Security Responsibility, and encouraged the Committee to continue its good work. We agreed that reform of the Iraqi security ministries and agencies and addressing the issue of militias should be accelerated. The ultimate solution to stabilizing Iraq and reducing violence is true national reconciliation and capable and loyal Iraqi forces dedicated to protecting all the Iraqi people.

We are committed to continuing to build the partnership between our two countries as we work together to strengthen a stable, democratic, and unified Iraq.

- **Source:** "Joint Statement by President George W. Bush and Prime Minister Nuri al-Maliki of Iraq," GPO Access, http://www.gpo.gov/fdsys/pkg/WCPD-2006-12-04/html/WCPD-2006-12-04-Pg2112.htm.
- **Analysis:** In this statement the Iraqi prime minister and the U.S. president discussed the security situation in Iraq. Although they acknowledged the problem of sectarian conflict, they blamed most of the violence on al-Qaeda. Significantly, the statement does not mention "insurgency." Just weeks before release of the *Report of the Iraq Study Group*, it was politically still more convenient to blame Iraq's troubles on outsiders. The two leaders also identified training and equipping Iraqi security forces as a top priority.

- **Document 92: State Department Briefing on Iraqi Government Coalition Agreement**
- **Date:** November 12, 2010
- **Where:** Washington, DC
- **Significance:** After much bickering and tortuous negotiation, Iraq formed a government.

MODERATOR: Good afternoon and welcome to the Foreign Press Center. We are pleased to have with us Deputy Assistant Secretary Michael Corbin, who is going to speak about the formation of the new Iraqi Government. We'll open it—he'll make a couple of quick remarks and we'll open it up to questions. And we'll just go ahead and turn the time over to Deputy Assistant Secretary Corbin.

MR. CORBIN: Thank you very much, Matt. That was very kind. What I'd like to do today is give some brief remarks and then address your questions on what is an extremely significant development in Iraq, which is the formation of the government that occurred yesterday. And what I'd like to do is open it up to questions so I'll be very brief. But we're in a constantly evolving situation there. What I'd like to make very clear is what we saw yesterday in terms of the Council of Representatives session meeting with the three major leaders together in the front row of the Council of Representatives was, as President Obama said, another historic milestone in Iraq's forward progress.

This is extremely significant because for the last almost eight months, the Iraqis have been working to come up with an inclusive government that represents all the different ethnic and sectarian communities that have long histories, as you know very well, of enmity in Iraq. And what we saw yesterday was these communities and their leaders coming together and opening a session where a framework has been worked out. There will be challenges. This will be a continuing process. But those Iraqis who on March 7th of this year, 62 percent of the electorate, voted for the two largest coalitions, the coalitions that are most secular and most representative of the broad spectrum of Iraq's communities, the State of Law coalition led by Prime Minister Maliki and the Iraqiya coalition led by Iyad Allawi. Those two coalitions came together and yesterday formed a government with the help of the Kurds.

This is extremely significant because there were many other options that the Iraqis could have chosen. In 2006, violence was the option when neighborhoods had to defend themselves against the terrorists who struck at night, when militias were the order of the day. In today's Iraq, we see a political compromise as the path that all the political leaders are choosing.

And it's taken a while for them to get to this government, but what we've seen is an inclusive, representative government where the first official who was elected was the Sunni speaker, Osama al-Nujaifi, who is a prominent Sunni leader in the country and was one of the top three vote getters in the election, the other two being Prime Minister Maliki and Iyad Allawi. He was the first one elected in the COR. The COR then chose a president, and the president nominated Prime Minister Maliki. They now have 30 days to form a government, and as we saw, there will be challenges, there will be theatrics. This is a hard task for any parliamentary system. These are—this is a coalition government that brings together all the people in the tent. And there are issues that were addressed through a separate process led by head of the Kurdistan Regional Government President Massoud Barzani, where issues such as de-Baathification, the powers of the office of the prime minister, and other such significant issues for Iraq were addressed.

What we see is that Iraq has taken this step of politics and compromise on its way to being better placed to be a partner both with the region and with the international community, completely different from what Saddam Hussein did to Iraq, where Iraq was a source of violence, of terrorism, of starting wars in the region. Iraq, with this government, has the opportunity to address a partnership with the rest of the region based on trade, based on cooperative ties, based on rebuilding the Iraq that we saw in the '50s when Iraq was a leader in education, in health, in agriculture in the region.

Part of the discussions that led to this government included the formation of a National Council for Strategic Policies. This is significant because it represents efforts to address the needs of all the communities in a way that security decisions are not made by one community but are made in consultation with all the communities. We also see, as I mentioned, discussions of issues such as de-Baathfication. These are hard issues and there will continue to be challenges. But what we saw yesterday in the COR session represents another step forward as Iraqis choose politics rather than violence on their way to integrating into the region.

I think with that I'll open it up for questions, as I'm sure you have many.

MODERATOR: And please remember to wait for the microphone and also to say your name and your news organization. We'll start right here up in the front and we'll work our way back.

QUESTION: Thank you, Ambassador Corbin.

MR. CORBIN: You promoted me. (Laughter.) Deputy Assistant Secretary.

QUESTION: I think you deserve to be Secretary probably in the future. I just came fresh from the region and I may have many questions for you, so forgive me if I throw them all at you at once, since there's not many people here. And I hope I will not take too much time.

You describe it as a forming the government. I think a little bit optimistic if we want to be very precise, because the government—there's assignment now for the prime minister to form the government. And my question here would be: Is it going to take seven days, seven months, or more to form that government?

The other issue is the National Council for Strategic, is it going to be another government competing with the official government in a way, and how are they going to sort things out?

The last thing I would say, the statement by the State Department talking about the Strategic Framework Agreement to expand and cooperate under the Strategic Framework Agreement, is that agreement going to be confirmed, going to be expanded in the timeframe also going to be adjusted? Or it's going to be—remain the same as a basis for the cooperation between United States and new government in Iraq?

Thank you very much.

MR. CORBIN: Thank you. First of all, under when the prime minister will form his cabinet, as it's called in Iraq the Council of Ministers, the prime minister has 30 days from yesterday to form that cabinet. We believe that now there has been the progress of a deal to come up with a framework of the new government, that the prime minister has the ability to form this government. Of course, there will be challenges as we go forward, but the basic framework has been agreed to. And that is the critical issue.

When we look at 2006, there were—most of the Council of Ministers was able to be formed quickly and there were just a few ministers that weren't chosen until the end, but it was a very different time, and as I said, violence dominated rather than politics. We think that a lot of the political work has been done in this period so we will see and expect the constitution to be recognized as we go forward.

In terms of the National Council on Strategic Policies, this is extremely important in balancing the different communities and the different positions in a way that allows security decisions and national security decisions to be made by the representatives of all the communities in the governance rather than one community or one position. And there were intense negotiations on how this national security council would be formed—or National Council for Strategic Policies would be formed, and we believe it will be an effective way to address the key issues that Iraq faces as it moves forward.

Finally in terms of the Strategic Framework Agreement, this is a partnership that has already been launched. This is a partnership that already has committees that are working. This is a partnership that involves the traditional areas of cooperation, in trade, in economics. And with the interim government, we continue that cooperation. We welcome the formation of a new partner in the new government to work on the Strategic Framework Agreement, but we see broad support from Iraqis to expend and to continue the activities under that agreement. And that is what we intend to do as we transition to a more civilian-led rather than security-led relationship with Iraq. And that's what the Embassy and the other civilian agencies that are in Iraq are focused on now as we go forward.

MODERATOR: We'll go right here in the middle.

QUESTION: Jean (inaudible) Monitor. Mr. Corbin, you described this step as an historic step forward. However, Mr. Allawi has been described as a Saudi boy in more sense than one. Does this mean that Mr. Maliki and his newcomers into the government are going closer and closer towards Iran now that the Saudis have less power to play?

And also, among the tasks that you described this government needs to achieve, I did not hear anything about delivering the most important services that Iraqis are suffering from, which is electricity and of course security. And while we're on the security issue, how does the United States Administration view the task of this newly formed government, when it's finally formed that is, as far as accountability is concerned for the recent massacre at the church in Baghdad.

MR. CORBIN: Thank you very much. First of all, I would reiterate and emphasize that this was an Iraqi solution for the Iraqi elections. It wasn't mad in Tehran, it wasn't made in Ankara, it wasn't made in Riyadh. This was an Iraqi solution that was hammered out in Iraq. The Iraqis have chosen to move forward in a way that uses politics to settle their issues rather than violence.

And you raise a very good point in terms of the issues that are before the Iraqi leaders as they move forward. I didn't mention all of them. Of course, the Arab-Kurd issues are significant, the issues of displaced persons who have remained out of their houses, the issue of refugees who are outside of Iraq who need to come back—there are many issues that the new government needs to address.

But clearly, when the Iraqi electorate voted on March 7th, they were talking about services, about electricity, about security, about having a government that's responsive to the Iraqi people. And our belief is the only government that could be responsive to all the communities in Iraq is the type of inclusive government that the framework deal has brought about, and that this is the path forward in terms of responding to those—to the Iraqi electorate. Remember, the Council of Representatives—most of the members are new. They were elected to represent their constituents in the different provinces around Iraq. And combating corruption, providing services, providing resources are issues that all Iraqis want the new government to face.

On your last point, clearly security remains an issue. Clearly, as the President said, this was a solution for those who seek an inclusive and cooperative path forward for Iraq, not those terrorists who seek to divide and seek to re-ignite sectarian tension. The attack on Our Lady of Salvation Church the Sunday before last was a heinous, awful humanitarian tragedy, and the terrorists who did it have no goals other than to seek to attack vulnerable communities and stir up sectarian passions, which we do not think the Iraqi people will respond to.

We worked with the Iraqi security forces for many years to improve their capabilities. We've worked with the government on the incredibly important role of the minorities in the fabric of Iraqi society. And we will continue to do that with the new government just as we did with the old government. And we saw all the leaders condemning the attacks on the church, but also on religious pilgrims that happened the next day or the day after. We see the terrorists will continue to do everything possible to undermine a cooperative, inclusive solution, and that's where we stand with the Iraqi people as they resist these efforts to undermine an inclusive and cooperative process.

MODERATOR: We'll go right in the back in the red.

QUESTION: Thank you very much. Mohamed Wafa from Middle East Broadcasting Network. We saw yesterday the—two-thirds of the Iraqi bloc walking out of the parliament before electing Talabani. Now this—the unagreement—the disagreement among Iraqiya themselves, the Iraqiya bloc, might prolong the formation of the government or even endanger the formation of the government. My question is: Do you have any—does Washington talk with any Iraqiya bloc members to alleviate the differences? And if you do, with who?

My second question is about the security, the Council of Strategic Policies. You said there had been intensive discussions about the council and what will be. Do you know by now exactly what will be the powers of Iyad Allawi, what will be the policies he will conduct, how he is going to cooperate or conduct his job?

Thank you very much.

MR. CORBIN: On the first question, the National Council on Strategic Policy does need to be legislative and there was agreement on how to move forward. Yesterday's session of the COR was to focus on the first steps that the COR must take that the Council of Representatives must take under the constitution. There will be action on the issues that have been agreed by the parties as we go forward and that will be coming in conjunction with formation of the new government, which is a process that obviously will take—the prime minister has 30 days and that will be a complex process of negotiation. But whether it will lead to stalemate or how it balances powers, I think it's very clear that the National Council on Strategic Policies is an attempt by Iraqis to address the fear of different communities that one community or ethnic group not make decisions that affect all the communities or that are specifically targeting another community.

So this council will allow that—the National Council will include representatives from the different communities who will have a say in how decisions that affect the other communities on national security, on division of resources, on other issues are made. And this has been a subject of intense discussion by the Iraqis. But I'll leave the Iraqis to give you the details on that. On de-Baathification, besides the issue of certain individuals yesterday in the COR who have de-Baathification proceedings against them such as Saleh Mutlaq, there was a discussion of the whole accountability and justice commission, which, as you know, was never dealt with by the last Council of Representatives and how to move forward on that process. So there are specific discussions on the general process, not just on individuals. But again, I have to leave it to the Iraqis to talk about the agreements they've reached there. But just be assured that this was one of the subjects for discussion.

MODERATOR: Okay, we'll stay in the back.

QUESTION: Jim Lobe, Inter Press Service. I wondered, what is your understanding about possible Sadrist participation in the new government? And also, could you comment on—generally on Iranian influence, both in the process in Iraq at this point with specific reference to some remarks made by General Robert Cone apparently yesterday or the day before saying that actually Iran had—in some ways was exercising—has been exercising a positive influence at the moment? Those are my questions.

MR. CORBIN: On the role of the Sadrists, the Sadrists ran in the elections on March 7th and won seats in the Council of Representatives. They won almost 40 seats in the Council of Representatives. This is a party that wants to participate in the government. And according to the inclusive framework, we saw yesterday that the deputy speaker, who was elected in the COR, is from the Sadrist trend. We believe that all the parties in this inclusive government have a role to play, but that no one party should be able to veto the government or take it in a direction that reflects only the interest of one community. So we do see that all those people who the Iraqi people voted for in this inclusive government will have a role to play that has to be constructive and that does address the needs of the Iraqi people. As to Iranian influence in Iraq, as I said, this was a solution that was made by Iraqis for Iraqis. Iraqis are the first ones to say how they want to set their relations with their neighbors, be it Saudi Arabia, Jordan, Turkey, or Iran. What we support the Iraqis in is building constructive relations based on trade and cultural exchanges and the other elements of cooperative regional intercourse and dialogue. And that's what the Iraqis are seeking. So we support the Iraqis as they work to develop their relations and we believe they will be the ones who determine how other countries relate with them and whether it is constructive or negative as these countries go forward.

MODERATOR: Hold—please wait for the microphone.

QUESTION: Could you say what he—he was referring to (inaudible).

MR. CORBIN: I am afraid I haven't seen General Cone's remarks. I know General Cone very well. What I would say is that every country has the possibility of having constructive relations with Iraq or negative interactions with Iraq. And what we see in the formation of this new government in the decision of the COR, which will lead to the new government, is that the Iraqis are building a government that we believe will be a partner or be a potential partner for all the countries in the region in that it will represent all the communities in Iraq and it will speak in a moderate voice that chooses politics rather than violence and will be able to work with the region.

MODERATOR: Okay, now we're going to (inaudible) over here on the right.

QUESTION: Priscilla Huff with Feature Story News. My first question is—just went straight out of my head. Sorry about that. My second question is—oh, is: Are you confident in the compromise that has been made between the parties that this is solid or is there something that you're worried about? And my first question— now I've remembered what it is—is: What request—have the Iraqis come to the U.S. with specific requests with need of help informing their government or is U.S. influence pulled back and you're really just an embassy? How involved are you in the process of the formation?

MR. CORBIN: On the first question in terms of the compromises, what I would say is: This country has seen so much division, has seen so much violence in its history, it's—these compromises are each going to be very complex. What we see and what we have faith in is a process where compromise is the means to settle these. It doesn't mean that each individual issue, whether it be the status of minority communities, the future of displaced persons, the Arab-Kurd 140—Article 140 issues, each of these difficult compromises requires negotiation. What has been established by the framework that led to the seating of the Council of Representatives yesterday was a reliance on compromise to settle these issues. Each issue will require continued compromise by the players. But we've seen the Kurds compromise, the Sunnis compromise, and the Shia compromise in the process that led to the agreement on a framework for this—for the seating of the COR yesterday. As to the U.S. influence, we're supporting an Iraqi process with Massoud Barzani who brought the parties together, including in a summit in Erbil, including bringing leaders there, including Kurd leading discussions among the players on some very thorny issues. We see that we have a role to play to strengthen our cooperation and help Iraq be a better partner for the region, but also to address the needs of its people as the Iraqi people expressed in the election of March 7th.

MODERATOR: Anybody who hasn't answered—asked a question?

QUESTION: Thank you. Nico Pandi, JiJi Press, Japan. Going back to the Sadrist movement for a moment, you mentioned how they had 40 seats in the election. I was wondering if you could comment on—there have been reports that they're seeking a large stake in the new government including heads of key ministry positions like defense, security, interior. I know Ambassador Jeffrey has voiced his concerns about that kind of arrangement. I was wondering if you could just comment how concerned you are that al-Maliki would seek to almost repay the Sadrist movement for their support of him in becoming prime minister. Thank you.

MR. CORBIN: We see the government that's created that's an inclusive government that includes representative of all communities as being based on compromise. And no one community will be given the control or the ability to decide or bring down the government. That's what the National Council for Strategic Policy is about, but more importantly, that's what the process that led to the seating of the COR yesterday was all about. So I absolutely—Ambassador Jeffrey spoke about the concerns of any community that takes a specific role and the Sadrists have had a role in violence in recent Iraqi history that would lead some to concern. But our approach to this is that all—that no community should be able to bring down the Iraqi Government or hijack the Iraqi Government for its own interests.

MODERATOR: Okay. We'll come back up to the front.

QUESTION: Thank you very much. It was a follow-up. I didn't take my time for the follow-up. How confident are you that in 30 days the cabinet going to be formed? And if not, what could happen then? The other thing is it seems to me the strategic—the National Council of Strategic Policies, you keep repeating the issue of inclusion—inclusiveness. Well, isn't the cabinet going to be inclusive also, as you suggested, so why you have to have another body? We don't know yet whether this is an executive branch body or a legislative body—it's not legislative—or advisory body.

In the final analysis, maybe Maliki will look at this—at Allawi and this council as an advisory council like the national security advisor for a president. Because if this body going to be another body like as minister of interior and minister of defense, so whose authority is this council going to be responding and responsive to the ministry of defense and ministry—on security matters, or to whom? So I think it's a vague situation as far as I'm concerned, and I think this issue probably going to be an issue to carry its weight into not allowing the cabinet to be formed in the timely manner as you suggested.

One last question, forgive me for giving it. It's outside Iraq, but it's a burning question since I came from Lebanon. Former President Bush admitted that he insisted on Olmert to prolong the war on Lebanon in 2006. What do you think this kind of statement and admission by the President going to affect the people there and the United States interests in the region?

MR. CORBIN: On your first question in terms of when the cabinet will be formed, where we are now is we're congratulating the Iraqis on a session of the Council of Representatives which was difficult but which was successful in making some significant historic position—deciding positions according to a framework. Of course, there will be negotiations for the cabinet, but it's too early to say now what the issues will be that may or may not prevent Prime Minister Maliki from making a choice of a cabinet.

I will say the Iraqi people have waited a long time for the formation of this government. They will be the ones who are pushing for this government to be formed quickly. They are disillusioned in some ways and frustrated that it's taken this long, and they will seek to see this government formed quickly. And the U.S. will do whatever possible to facilitate that for—because we see the importance of a strong and stable Iraq.

In terms of the National Council for Security Policies, we had a cabinet. We had a cabinet that was divided in 2006, although there was largely boycotts. We had a cabinet, a council of ministers, that had representatives of the different communities. It didn't work in terms of making decisions. The prime minister's office made more and more decisions. That's why the communities called for other means of checks and balances. And the National Council for Strategic Policies is a way of focusing not on the 30 different portfolios that make up a council of ministers, but on those specific issues that will need decisions.

And this is not an advisory body. This was negotiated in intense negotiations in terms of playing the role of meeting the needs of the different communities who don't want to—who do not want to see any one individual or community consolidate power in his own hands or in their community's hands, whether it be the person holding the president's office, the person holding the prime minister's office, or the person holding the speaker of the council of representatives. So there are specifics.

But I'll make very clear, as the Iraqis came up with this initiative, they will give you the specifics on how the National Council of Strategic Policies is going to work. But it was an important element in the forming of an agreement that led to the framework deal.

Thank you.

QUESTION: (Off-mike.)

MODERATOR: Hold—wait for the microphone.

QUESTION: How this council can enforce its policies, its suggestions, whatever it is—

MR. CORBIN: Well—

QUESTION: It's going to be in the government, in the cabinet? And they have the same people who are in the council they have representative in the cabinet.

So what we are doing here is—that have the power to enforce separately from the cabinet or the ministry in the cabinet their strategic plans or suggestions? They don't have—would they have military and security power attached to the national council?

MR. CORBIN: I think you're getting to the range of questions that talk about—that need to look at the agreement that was reached. But as someone mentioned, this needs to be legislated, and it is planned to be legislated so that the power is made clear. There will be a balance between the Council of Representatives, between the prime minister, between the president, and between the National Council of Security Policies and the Council of Ministers so that there will be an effective way of dealing with the very—the contentious issues that face the country as it goes forward.

But our point from yesterday is that the Iraqis have chosen to choose compromise and politics rather than violence as the way forward. Each issue, as I mentioned in an answer to another question, each issue will require different compromises, will face different setbacks, will face different challenges. But as long as the Iraqis are signed up to the process of addressing their real grievances and concerns, we see this as a positive step forward.

I think there was a follow-up.

QUESTION: (Off-mike.)

MR. CORBIN: Oh, and on—and that one is easy for me to answer because I'm not going to address Lebanon and the issues with Lebanon here.

QUESTION: Lebanon is like Iraq, you know.

MODERATOR: We'll do our final question.

MR. CORBIN: Yeah, the follow-up question that we had.

QUESTION: My follow-up question was on the Our Lady of Salvation incident. No one in his right mind would obviously justify taking churchgoers as hostages, but the responsibility, the onus, per se, is really on the Maliki government when they tried to launch a rescue operation that went, unfortunately, southwards at a tremendous human cost to the churchgoers per se.

Now, at the same time, the Maliki government was also held responsible by the leaks and WikiLeaks for conducting operations of the sort against its own people. How confident is the U.S. Administration that this new government with the same old faces will be held accountable for this type of human massacre, if you will, and taken in the general context of preventing the exodus of what's been coined as exodus of the Christians from the Orient, where this unfortunately plays right into that game? How confident is the U.S. or how much influence can the U.S. Administration play?

In addition to that, what is the Administration's current policy on capital punishment in Iraq?

MR. CORBIN: On the issue of minorities in Iraq, we are absolutely focused on not allowing the terrorists and extremists to drive anyone from Iraq. The conditions of these vulnerable communities have been one of our top priorities as we've worked to train the Iraqi security forces who have put elements in place to protect these communities.

Now, of course, the terrorists continue to target them because it's very hard to protect these communities or churches and places—and mosques are also attacked and places of worship. This is something that the U.S. and the international community will continue to work with the Iraqi Government on improving their abilities. We don't know what happened in the church. It was a heinous massacre that was launched by people who the only way to deal with these people is to not have any support for this type of terrorist activity that targets the future of Iraq.

The best way, we believe, to address that is having a government that is inclusive and responsive. As you said, we will hold this government accountable as we've tried to hold previous governments, but we will now have an inclusive government that we will hold responsible for any activities that occur in its territory, as the government has made clear that it wants to do.

And I absolutely will not make any link to anything that suggests that the Iraqi Government was responsible in any way for the attack on the minorities. What we see is that the Iraqi Government condemned the attack, that the Iraqi security forces have improved in their abilities, but they still need more work. And that's where we will continue to partner with the Iraqis as we go forward.

And I think with that, thank you very, very much for this opportunity. And I'm sure there will be more questions as we go forward, but it is a historic moment for Iraq. Thank you.

MODERATOR: Thank you.

- **Source:** U.S. State Department briefing on Iraqi coalition agreement, November 12, 2010, available at http://fpc.state.gov/150849.htm, accessed July 14, 2011.

- **Analysis:** The difficulty of producing a working government in Iraq illustrates the challenge of governing the country. Iraqis had gone to the polls for the second time under their new constitution on March 7, 2011. As expected, no party gained a majority, so any government would have to be a coalition. It took eight months for the political parties to reach an agreement on how to divide government offices. Meanwhile, the previous government continued to operate.

  While assistant secretary of state for Near Eastern affairs Michael Corbin sounded an optimistic note, he faced difficult questions following his prepared statement. One reporter noted that the agreement established a framework for forming a coalition but left many cabinet posts to be filled. This situation would persist well into 2011.

- **Document 93: U.S. Department of State Statement on Violence against Christians**

- **When:** December 31, 2010
- **Where:** Washington, DC
- **Significance:** The United States condemned attacks upon Christians in Iraq.

We condemn the violence against Christians carried out overnight by terrorists in Iraq. President Talabani, Prime Minister Maliki, and virtually every political bloc and major religious leader in Iraq have denounced attacks on Christians and stressed the centrality of Christians in the fabric of Iraqi society. We commend the Government of Iraq for increasing its security measures to protect Christian communities since the October 31 suicide bombing attack at Our Lady of Salvation Church.

We call on the Government of Iraq to redouble its efforts to protect Christians and apprehend the terrorists who are behind these acts.

- **Source:** Mark C. Toner, acting Department of State spokesperson, statement on attacks upon Christians in Iraq, December 31, 2010, available at http://www.state.gov/r/pa/prs/ps/2010/12/153812.htm, accessed July 14, 2011.
- **Analysis:** The year 2010 ended on a bad note with increased attacks on Iraqi Christians. These attacks followed the bombing of Our Lady of Salvation Church at the end of October in which 58 people were killed and more than 70 others injured. Christians had been the unheralded victims of sectarian violence whose primary adversaries were Iraqi Shi'a and Sunni Muslims. The U.S. and Iraqi governments condemned these attacks, and the Iraqi government acknowledged the important place Christians had in Iraq. Although traditional Islam respects Christians as "People of the Book," recipients of God's revelation and descendants of Abraham, radical Islamists attacked them.

U.S. WITHDRAWAL

Getting into Iraq had proven much easier than getting out. The surge strategy combined with the Anbar Awakening had improved the security situation, and more Iraqi police and military units were being trained and equipped each month. Both the U.S. public and the new president, Barack Obama, wanted to bring U.S. troops home. The White House did not, however, wish to see the fragile state revert to the chaos it had so recently escaped. A gradual withdrawal of U.S. forces as circumstances permitted seemed the best way to prevent such an eventuality.

- **Document 94:** Excerpt of "Agreement between the United States of America and the Republic of Iraq on the Withdrawal of United

States Forces from Iraq and the Organization of Their Activities during Their Temporary Presence in Iraq"

- **When:** November 17, 2008
- **Where:** Baghdad
- **Significance:** The agreement established a timetable for withdrawal of U.S. forces from Iraq.

Preamble

The United States of America and the Republic of Iraq, referred to hereafter as "the Parties":

Recognizing the importance of: strengthening their joint security, contributing to world peace and stability, combating terrorism in Iraq, and cooperating in the security and defense spheres, thereby deterring aggression and threats against the sovereignty, security, and territorial integrity of Iraq and against its democratic, federal, and constitutional system;

Affirming that such cooperation is based on full respect for the sovereignty of each of them in accordance with the purposes and principles of the United Nations Charter;

Out of a desire to reach a common understanding that strengthens cooperation between them;

Without prejudice to Iraqi sovereignty over its territory, waters, and airspace; and

Pursuant to joint undertakings as two sovereign, independent, and coequal countries;

Have agreed to the following:

Article 1

Scope and Purpose

This Agreement shall determine the principal provisions and requirements that regulate the temporary presence, activities, and withdrawal of the United States Forces from Iraq. . . .

Article 3

Laws

1. While conducting military operations pursuant to this Agreement, it is the duty of members of the United States Forces and of the civilian component to respect Iraqi laws, customs, traditions, and conventions and to refrain from any activities that are inconsistent with the letter and spirit of this Agreement. It is the duty of the United States to take all necessary measures for this purpose. . . .

Article 4

Missions

1. The Government of Iraq requests the temporary assistance of the United States Forces for the purposes of supporting Iraq in its efforts to maintain security and stability in Iraq, including cooperation in the conduct of operations against al-Qaeda and other terrorist groups, outlaw groups, and remnants of the former regime.

2. All such military operations that are carried out pursuant to this Agreement shall be conducted with the agreement of the Government of Iraq. Such operations

shall be fully coordinated with Iraqi authorities. The coordination of all such military operations shall be overseen by a Joint Military Operations Coordination Committee (JMOCC) to be established pursuant to this Agreement. Issues regarding proposed military operations that cannot be resolved by the JMOCC shall be forwarded to the Joint Ministerial Committee.

3. All such operations shall be conducted with full respect for the Iraqi Constitution and the laws of Iraq. Execution of such operations shall not infringe upon the sovereignty of Iraq and its national interests, as defined by the Government of Iraq. It is the duty of the United States Forces to respect the laws, customs, and traditions of Iraq and applicable international law.

4. The Parties shall continue their efforts to cooperate to strengthen Iraq's security capabilities including, as may be mutually agreed, on training, equipping, supporting, supplying, and establishing and upgrading logistical systems, including transportation, housing, and supplies for Iraqi Security Forces.

5. The Parties retain the right to legitimate self defense within Iraq, as defined in applicable international law.

Article 5

Property Ownership

1. Iraq owns all buildings, non-relocatable structures, and assemblies connected to the soil that exist on agreed facilities and areas, including those that are used, constructed, altered, or improved by the United States Forces.

2. Upon their withdrawal, the United States Forces shall return to the Government of Iraq all the facilities and areas provided for the use of the combat forces of the United States, based on two lists. The first list of agreed facilities and areas shall take effect upon the entry into force of the Agreement. The second list shall take effect no later than June 30, 2009, the date for the withdrawal of combat forces from the cities, villages, and localities. The Government of Iraq may agree to allow the United States Forces the use of some necessary facilities for the purposes of this Agreement on withdrawal. . . .

5. Upon the discovery of any historical or cultural site or finding any strategic resource in agreed facilities and areas, all works of construction, upgrading, or modification shall cease immediately and the Iraqi representatives at the Joint Committee shall be notified to determine appropriate steps in that regard.

6. The United States shall return agreed facilities and areas and any non-relocatable structures and assemblies on them that it had built, installed, or established during the term of this Agreement, according to mechanisms and priorities set forth by the Joint Committee. Such facilities and areas shall be handed over to the Government of Iraq free of any debts and financial burdens.

7. The United States Forces shall return to the Government of Iraq the agreed facilities and areas that have heritage, moral, and political significance and any non-relocatable structures and assemblies on them that it had built, installed, or established, according to mechanisms, priorities, and a time period as mutually agreed by the Joint Committee, free of any debts or financial burdens.

8. The United States Forces shall return the agreed facilities and areas to the Government of Iraq upon the expiration or termination of this Agreement, or

earlier as mutually agreed by the Parties, or when such facilities are no longer required as determined by the JMOCC, free of any debts or financial burdens.

9. The United States Forces and United States contractors shall retain title to all equipment, materials, supplies, relocatable structures, and other movable property that was legitimately imported into or legitimately acquired within the territory of Iraq in connection with this Agreement.

Article 6

Use of Agreed Facilities and Areas

1. With full respect for the sovereignty of Iraq, and as part of exchanging views between the Parties pursuant to this Agreement, Iraq grants access and use of agreed facilities and areas to the United States Forces, United States contractors, United States contractor employees, and other individuals or entities as agreed upon by the Parties.

2. In accordance with this Agreement, Iraq authorizes the United States Forces to exercise within the agreed facilities and areas all rights and powers that may be necessary to establish, use, maintain, and secure such agreed facilities and areas. The Parties shall coordinate and cooperate regarding exercising these rights and powers in the agreed facilities and areas of joint use.

3. The United States Forces shall assume control of entry to agreed facilities and areas that have been provided for its exclusive use. The Parties shall coordinate the control of entry into agreed facilities and areas for joint use and in accordance with mechanisms set forth by the JMOCC. The Parties shall coordinate guard duties in areas adjacent to agreed facilities and areas through the JMOCC. . . .

Article 9

Movement of Vehicles, Vessels, and Aircraft

1. With full respect for the relevant rules of land and maritime safety and movement, vessels and vehicles operated by or at the time exclusively for the United States Forces may enter, exit, and move within the territory of Iraq for the purposes of implementing this Agreement. The JMOCC shall develop appropriate procedures and rules to facilitate and regulate the movement of vehicles.

2. With full respect for relevant rules of safety in aviation and air navigation, United States Government aircraft and civil aircraft that are at the time operating exclusively under a contract with the United States Department of Defense are authorized to over-fly, conduct airborne refueling exclusively for the purposes of implementing this Agreement over, and land and take off within, the territory of Iraq for the purposes of implementing this Agreement. The Iraqi authorities shall grant the aforementioned aircraft permission every year to land in and take off from Iraqi territory exclusively for the purposes of implementing this Agreement. United States Government aircraft and civil aircraft that are at the time operating exclusively under a contract with the United States Department of Defense, vessels, and vehicles shall not have any party boarding them without the consent of the authorities of the United States Forces. The Joint Sub-Committee concerned with this matter shall take appropriate action to facilitate the regulation of such traffic.

3. Surveillance and control over Iraqi airspace shall transfer to Iraqi authority immediately upon entry into force of this Agreement.

4. Iraq may request from the United States Forces temporary support for the Iraqi authorities in the mission of surveillance and control of Iraqi air space.

5. United States Government aircraft and civil aircraft that are at the time operating exclusively under contract to the United States Department of Defense shall not be subject to payment of any taxes, duties, fees, or similar charges, including overflight or navigation fees, landing, and parking fees at government airfields. Vehicles and vessels owned or operated by or at the time exclusively for the United States Forces shall not be subject to payment of any taxes, duties, fees, or similar charges, including for vessels at government ports. Such vehicles, vessels, and aircraft shall be free from registration requirements within Iraq.

6. The United States Forces shall pay fees for services requested and received.

. . .

Article 12

Jurisdiction

Recognizing Iraq's sovereign right to determine and enforce the rules of criminal and civil law in its territory, in light of Iraq's request for temporary assistance from the United States Forces set forth in Article 4, and consistent with the duty of the members of the United States Forces and the civilian component to respect Iraqi laws, customs, traditions, and conventions, the Parties have agreed as follows:

Iraq shall have the primary right to exercise jurisdiction over members of the United States Forces and of the civilian component for the grave premeditated felonies enumerated pursuant to paragraph 8, when such crimes are committed outside agreed facilities and areas and outside duty status.

Iraq shall have the primary right to exercise jurisdiction over United States contractors and United States contractor employees.

The United States shall have the primary right to exercise jurisdiction over members of the United States Forces and of the civilian component for matters arising inside agreed facilities and areas; during duty status outside agreed facilities and areas; and in circumstances not covered by paragraph 1.

At the request of either Party, the Parties shall assist each other in the investigation of incidents and the collection and exchange of evidence to ensure the due course of justice.

Members of the United States Forces and of the civilian component arrested or detained by Iraqi authorities shall be notified immediately to United States Forces authorities and handed over to them within 24 hours from the time of detention or arrest. Where Iraq exercises jurisdiction pursuant to paragraph 1 of this Article, custody of an accused member of the United States Forces or of the civilian component shall reside with United States Forces authorities. United States Forces authorities shall make such accused persons available to the Iraqi authorities for purposes of investigation and trial.

The authorities of either Party may request the authorities of the other Party to waive its primary right to jurisdiction in a particular case. The Government of Iraq agrees to exercise jurisdiction under paragraph 1 above, only after it has determined and notifies the United States in writing within 21 days of the discovery of an alleged offense, that it is of particular importance that such jurisdiction be exercised.

7. Where the United States exercises jurisdiction pursuant to paragraph 3 of this Article, members of the United States Forces and of the civilian component shall be entitled to due process standards and protections pursuant to the Constitution and laws of the United States. Where the offense arising under paragraph 3 of this Article may involve a victim who is not a member of the United States Forces or of the civilian component, the Parties shall establish procedures through the Joint Committee to keep such persons informed as appropriate of: the status of the investigation of the crime; the bringing of charges against a suspected offender; the scheduling of court proceedings and the results of plea negotiations; opportunity to be heard at public sentencing proceedings, and to confer with the attorney for the prosecution in the case; and, assistance with filing a claim under Article 21 of this Agreement. As mutually agreed by the Parties, United States Forces authorities shall seek to hold the trials of such cases inside Iraq. If the trial of such cases is to be conducted in the United States, efforts will be undertaken to facilitate the personal attendance of the victim at the trial.

8. Where Iraq exercises jurisdiction pursuant to paragraph 1 of this Article, members of the United States Forces and of the civilian component shall be entitled to due process standards and protections consistent with those available under United States and Iraqi law. The Joint Committee shall establish procedures and mechanisms for implementing this Article, including an enumeration of the grave premeditated felonies that are subject to paragraph 1 and procedures that meet such due process standards and protections. Any exercise of jurisdiction pursuant to paragraph 1 of this Article may proceed only in accordance with these procedures and mechanisms.

9. Pursuant to paragraphs 1 and 3 of this Article, United States Forces authorities shall certify whether an alleged offense arose during duty status. In those cases where Iraqi authorities believe the circumstances require a review of this determination, the Parties shall consult immediately through the Joint Committee, and United States Forces authorities shall take full account of the facts and circumstances and any information Iraqi authorities may present bearing on the determination by United States Forces authorities.

10. The Parties shall review the provisions of this Article every 6 months including by considering any proposed amendments to this Article taking into account the security situation in Iraq, the extent to which the United States Forces in Iraq are engaged in military operations, the growth and development of the Iraqi judicial system, and changes in United States and Iraqi law.

Article 13

Carrying Weapons and Apparel

Members of the United States Forces and of the civilian component may possess and carry weapons that are owned by the United States while in Iraq according to the authority granted to them under orders and according to their requirements and duties.

Members of the United States Forces may also wear uniforms during duty in Iraq. . . .

Article 24

Withdrawal of the United States Forces from Iraq

Recognizing the performance and increasing capacity of the Iraqi Security Forces, the assumption of full security responsibility by those Forces, and based upon the strong relationship between the Parties, an agreement on the following has been reached:

1. All the United States Forces shall withdraw from all Iraqi territory no later than December 31, 2011.

2. All United States combat forces shall withdraw from Iraqi cities, villages, and localities no later than the time at which Iraqi Security Forces assume full responsibility for security in an Iraqi province, provided that such withdrawal is completed no later than June 30, 2009.

3. United States combat forces withdrawn pursuant to paragraph 2 above shall be stationed in the agreed facilities and areas outside cities, villages, and localities to be designated by the JMOCC before the date established in paragraph 2 above.

4. The United States recognizes the sovereign right of the Government of Iraq to request the departure of the United States Forces from Iraq at any time. The Government of Iraq recognizes the sovereign right of the United States to withdraw the United States Forces from Iraq at any time.

5. The Parties agree to establish mechanisms and arrangements to reduce the number of the United States Forces during the periods of time that have been determined, and they shall agree on the locations where the United States Forces will be present.

Article 25

Measures to Terminate the Application of Chapter VII to Iraq

Acknowledging the right of the Government of Iraq not to request renewal of the Chapter VII authorization for and mandate of the multinational forces contained in United Nations Security Council Resolution 1790 (2007) that ends on December 31, 2008;

Taking note of the letters to the UN Security Council from the Prime Minister of Iraq and the Secretary of State of the United States dated December 7 and December 10, 2007, respectively, which are annexed to Resolution 1790;

Taking note of section 3 of the Declaration of Principles for a Long-Term Relationship of Cooperation and Friendship, signed by the President of the United States and the Prime Minister of Iraq on November 26, 2007, which memorialized Iraq's call for extension of the above-mentioned mandate for a final period, to end not later than December 31, 2008:

Recognizing also the dramatic and positive developments in Iraq, and noting that the situation in Iraq is fundamentally different than that which existed when the UN Security Council adopted Resolution 661 in 1990, and in particular that the threat to international peace and security posed by the Government of Iraq no longer exists, the Parties affirm in this regard that with the termination on December 31, 2008 of the Chapter VII mandate and authorization for the multinational force contained in Resolution 1790, Iraq should return to the legal and international standing that it enjoyed prior to the adoption of UN Security Council Resolution 661 (1990), and that the United States shall use its best efforts to help Iraq take the steps necessary to achieve this by December 31, 2008.

Article 26

Iraqi Assets

1. To enable Iraq to continue to develop its national economy through the rehabilitation of its economic infrastructure, as well as providing necessary essential services to the Iraqi people, and to continue to safeguard Iraq's revenues from oil and gas and other Iraqi resources and its financial and economic assets located abroad, including the Development Fund for Iraq, the United States shall ensure maximum efforts to:

a. Support Iraq to obtain forgiveness of international debt resulting from the policies of the former regime.

b. Support Iraq to achieve a comprehensive and final resolution of outstanding reparation claims inherited from the previous regime, including compensation requirements imposed by the UN Security Council on Iraq.

2. Recognizing and understanding Iraq's concern with claims based on actions perpetrated by the former regime, the President of the United States has exercised his authority to protect from United States judicial process the Development Fund for Iraq and certain other property in which Iraq has an interest. The United States shall remain fully and actively engaged with the Government of Iraq with respect to continuation of such protections and with respect to such claims.

3. Consistent with a letter from the President of the United States to be sent to the Prime Minister of Iraq, the United States remains committed to assist Iraq in connection with its request that the UN Security Council extend the protections and other arrangements established in Resolution 1483 (2003) and Resolution 1546 (2003) for petroleum, petroleum products, and natural gas originating in Iraq, proceeds and obligations from sale thereof, and the Development Fund for Iraq.

Article 27

Deterrence of Security Threats

In order to strengthen security and stability in Iraq and to contribute to the maintenance of international peace and stability, the Parties shall work actively to strengthen the political and military capabilities of the Republic of Iraq to deter threats against its sovereignty, political independence, territorial integrity, and its constitutional federal democratic system. To that end, the Parties agree as follows:

In the event of any external or internal threat or aggression against Iraq that would violate its sovereignty, political independence, or territorial integrity, waters, airspace, its democratic system or its elected institutions, and upon request by the Government of Iraq, the Parties shall immediately initiate strategic deliberations and, as may be mutually agreed, the United States shall take appropriate measures, including diplomatic, economic, or military measures, or any other measure, to deter such a threat.

The Parties agree to continue close cooperation in strengthening and maintaining military and security institutions and democratic political institutions in Iraq, including, as may be mutually agreed, cooperation in training, equipping, and arming the Iraqi Security Forces, in order to combat domestic and international terrorism and outlaw groups, upon request by the Government of Iraq.

Iraqi land, sea, and air shall not be used as a launching or transit point for attacks against other countries.

Article 28

The Green Zone

Upon entry into force of this Agreement the Government of Iraq shall have full responsibility for the Green Zone. The Government of Iraq may request from the United States Forces limited and temporary support for the Iraqi authorities in the mission of security for the Green Zone. Upon such request, relevant Iraqi authorities shall work jointly with the United States Forces authorities on security for the Green Zone during the period determined by the Government of Iraq.

Article 29

Implementing Mechanisms

Whenever the need arises, the Parties shall establish appropriate mechanisms for implementation of Articles of this Agreement, including those that do not contain specific implementation mechanisms.

Article 30

The Period for which the Agreement is Effective

1. This Agreement shall be effective for a period of three years, unless terminated sooner by either Party pursuant to paragraph 3 of this Article.

- **Source:** "Agreement between the United States of America and the Republic of Iraq on the Withdrawal of United States Forces from Iraq and the Organization of Their Activities during Their Temporary Presence in Iraq," available at http://en.wikisource.org/wiki/Status_of_Forces_Agreement,_2008, accessed March 20, 2012.

- **Analysis:** Support for continued deployment of a large U.S. contingent in Iraq was waning. The Iraqi people wished to regain control of their country while the U.S. public had grown tired of the cost in blood and treasure of remaining. Neither Washington nor Baghdad, however, wished to see Iraq revert to the level of violence that had marked the years 2003 through 2007. A gradual draw-down of U.S. forces leading to a withdrawal date of December 31, 2011, seemed the best solution. The remainder of the document was similar to the status of forces agreements the Pentagon enters into with any country in which its troops are stationed.

- **Document 95: Presidential Address on the End of Combat Operations in Iraq**
- **When:** August 31, 2010
- **Where:** Washington, DC
- **Significance:** The president declared a formal end to the combat mission in Iraq.

Good evening. Tonight, I'd like to talk to you about the end of our combat mission in Iraq, the ongoing security challenges we face, and the need to rebuild our nation here at home.

I know this historic moment comes at a time of great uncertainty for many Americans. We've now been through nearly a decade of war. We've endured a long and painful recession. And sometimes in the midst of these storms, the future that we're trying to build for our nation—a future of lasting peace and long-term prosperity—may seem beyond our reach.

But this milestone should serve as a reminder to all Americans that the future is ours to shape if we move forward with confidence and commitment. It should also serve as a message to the world that the United States of America intends to sustain and strengthen our leadership in this young century.

From this desk, seven and a half years ago, President Bush announced the beginning of military operations in Iraq. Much has changed since that night. A war to disarm a state became a fight against an insurgency. Terrorism and sectarian warfare threatened to tear Iraq apart. Thousands of Americans gave their lives; tens of thousands have been wounded. Our relations abroad were strained. Our unity at home was tested.

These are the rough waters encountered during the course of one of America's longest wars. Yet there has been one constant amidst these shifting tides. At every turn, America's men and women in uniform have served with courage and resolve. As Commander-in-Chief, I am incredibly proud of their service. And like all Americans, I'm awed by their sacrifice, and by the sacrifices of their families.

The Americans who have served in Iraq completed every mission they were given. They defeated a regime that had terrorized its people. Together with Iraqis and coalition partners who made huge sacrifices of their own, our troops fought block by block to help Iraq seize the chance for a better future. They shifted tactics to protect the Iraqi people, trained Iraqi Security Forces, and took out terrorist leaders. Because of our troops and civilians—and because of the resilience of the Iraqi people—Iraq has the opportunity to embrace a new destiny, even though many challenges remain.

So tonight, I am announcing that the American combat mission in Iraq has ended. Operation Iraqi Freedom is over, and the Iraqi people now have lead responsibility for the security of their country.

This was my pledge to the American people as a candidate for this office. Last February, I announced a plan that would bring our combat brigades out of Iraq, while redoubling our efforts to strengthen Iraq's Security Forces and support its government and people.

That's what we've done. We've removed nearly 100,000 U.S. troops from Iraq. We've closed or transferred to the Iraqis hundreds of bases. And we have moved millions of pieces of equipment out of Iraq.

This completes a transition to Iraqi responsibility for their own security. U.S. troops pulled out of Iraq's cities last summer, and Iraqi forces have moved into the lead with considerable skill and commitment to their fellow citizens. Even as Iraq continues to suffer terrorist attacks, security incidents have been near the lowest on record since the war began. And Iraqi forces have taken the fight to al Qaeda, removing much of its leadership in Iraqi-led operations.

This year also saw Iraq hold credible elections that drew a strong turnout. A caretaker administration is in place as Iraqis form a government based on the results of that election. Tonight, I encourage Iraq's leaders to move forward with a sense of urgency to form an inclusive government that is just, representative, and accountable to the Iraqi people. And when that government is in place, there should be no doubt: The Iraqi people will have a strong partner in the United States. Our combat mission is ending, but our commitment to Iraq's future is not.

Going forward, a transitional force of U.S. troops will remain in Iraq with a different mission: advising and assisting Iraq's Security Forces, supporting Iraqi troops in targeted counterterrorism missions, and protecting our civilians. Consistent with our agreement with the Iraqi government, all U.S. troops will leave by the end of next year. As our military draws down, our dedicated civilians—diplomats, aid workers, and advisors—are moving into the lead to support Iraq as it strengthens its government, resolves political disputes, resettles those displaced by war, and builds ties with the region and the world. That's a message that Vice President Biden is delivering to the Iraqi people through his visit there today.

This new approach reflects our long-term partnership with Iraq—one based upon mutual interest and mutual respect. Of course, violence will not end with our combat mission. Extremists will continue to set off bombs, attack Iraqi civilians and try to spark sectarian strife. But ultimately, these terrorists will fail to achieve their goals. Iraqis are a proud people. They have rejected sectarian war, and they have no interest in endless destruction. They understand that, in the end, only Iraqis can resolve their differences and police their streets. Only Iraqis can build a democracy within their borders. What America can do, and will do, is provide support for the Iraqi people as both a friend and a partner.

Ending this war is not only in Iraq's interest—it's in our own. The United States has paid a huge price to put the future of Iraq in the hands of its people. We have sent our young men and women to make enormous sacrifices in Iraq, and spent vast resources abroad at a time of tight budgets at home. We've persevered because of a belief we share with the Iraqi people—a belief that out of the ashes of war, a new beginning could be born in this cradle of civilization. Through this remarkable chapter in the history of the United States and Iraq, we have met our responsibility. Now, it's time to turn the page.

As we do, I'm mindful that the Iraq war has been a contentious issue at home. Here, too, it's time to turn the page. This afternoon, I spoke to former President George W. Bush. It's well known that he and I disagreed about the war from its outset. Yet no one can doubt President Bush's support for our troops, or his love of country and commitment to our security. As I've said, there were patriots who supported this war, and patriots who opposed it. And all of us are united in appreciation for our servicemen and women, and our hopes for Iraqis' future.

The greatness of our democracy is grounded in our ability to move beyond our differences, and to learn from our experience as we confront the many challenges ahead. And no challenge is more essential to our security than our fight against al Qaeda.

Americans across the political spectrum supported the use of force against those who attacked us on 9/11. Now, as we approach our 10th year of combat in Afghanistan, there are those who are understandably asking tough questions about our mission there. But we must never lose sight of what's at stake. As we speak, al Qaeda continues to plot against us, and its leadership remains anchored in the border regions of Afghanistan and Pakistan. We will disrupt, dismantle and defeat al Qaeda, while preventing Afghanistan from again serving as a base for terrorists. And because of our drawdown in Iraq, we are now able to apply the resources necessary to go on offense. In fact, over the last 19 months, nearly a dozen al Qaeda leaders—and hundreds of al Qaeda's extremist allies—have been killed or captured around the world.

Within Afghanistan, I've ordered the deployment of additional troops who—under the command of General David Petraeus—are fighting to break the Taliban's momentum. As with the surge in Iraq, these forces will be in place for a limited time to provide space for the Afghans to build their capacity and secure their own future. But, as was the case in Iraq, we can't do for Afghans what they must ultimately do for themselves. That's why we're training Afghan Security Forces and supporting a political resolution to Afghanistan's problems. And next August, we will begin a transition to Afghan responsibility. The pace of our troop reductions will be determined by conditions on the ground, and our support for Afghanistan will endure. But make no mistake: This transition will begin—because open-ended war serves neither our interests nor the Afghan people's.

Indeed, one of the lessons of our effort in Iraq is that American influence around the world is not a function of military force alone. We must use all elements of our power—including our diplomacy, our economic strength, and the power of America's example—to secure our interests and stand by our allies. And we must project a vision of the future that's based not just on our fears, but also on our hopes—a vision that recognizes the real dangers that exist around the world, but also the limitless possibilities of our time.

Today, old adversaries are at peace, and emerging democracies are potential partners. New markets for our goods stretch from Asia to the Americas. A new push for peace in the Middle East will begin here tomorrow. Billions of young people want to move beyond the shackles of poverty and conflict. As the leader of the free world, America will do more than just defeat on the battlefield those who offer hatred and destruction—we will also lead among those who are willing to work together to expand freedom and opportunity for all people.

Now, that effort must begin within our own borders. Throughout our history, America has been willing to bear the burden of promoting liberty and human dignity overseas, understanding its links to our own liberty and security. But we have also understood that our nation's strength and influence abroad must be firmly anchored in our prosperity at home. And the bedrock of that prosperity must be a growing middle class.

Unfortunately, over the last decade, we've not done what's necessary to shore up the foundations of our own prosperity. We spent a trillion dollars at war, often financed by borrowing from overseas. This, in turn, has short-changed investments in our own people, and contributed to record deficits. For too long, we have put off tough decisions on everything from our manufacturing base to our energy policy to education reform. As a result, too many middle-class families find themselves working harder for less, while our nation's long-term competitiveness is put at risk.

And so at this moment, as we wind down the war in Iraq, we must tackle those challenges at home with as much energy, and grit, and sense of common purpose as our men and women in uniform who have served abroad. They have met every test that they faced. Now, it's our turn. Now, it's our responsibility to honor them by coming together, all of us, and working to secure the dream that so many generations have fought for—the dream that a better life awaits anyone who is willing to work for it and reach for it.

Our most urgent task is to restore our economy, and put the millions of Americans who have lost their jobs back to work. To strengthen our middle class, we must give all our children the education they deserve, and all our workers the skills that they need to compete in a global economy. We must jumpstart industries that create jobs, and end our dependence on foreign oil. We must unleash the innovation that allows new products to roll off our assembly lines, and nurture the ideas that spring from our entrepreneurs. This will be difficult. But in the days to come, it must be our central mission as a people, and my central responsibility as President.

Part of that responsibility is making sure that we honor our commitments to those who have served our country with such valor. As long as I am President, we will maintain the finest fighting force that the world has ever known, and we will do whatever it takes to serve our veterans as well as they have served us. This is a sacred trust. That's why we've already made one of the largest increases in funding for veterans in decades. We're treating the signature wounds of today's wars—post-traumatic stress disorder and traumatic brain injury—while providing the health care and benefits that all of our veterans have earned. And we're funding a Post-9/11 GI Bill that helps our veterans and their families pursue the dream of a college education. Just as the GI Bill helped those who fought World War II—including my grandfather—become the backbone of our middle class, so today's servicemen and women must have the chance to apply their gifts to expand the American economy. Because part of ending a war responsibly is standing by those who have fought it.

Two weeks ago, America's final combat brigade in Iraq—the Army's Fourth Stryker Brigade—journeyed home in the pre-dawn darkness. Thousands of soldiers and hundreds of vehicles made the trip from Baghdad, the last of them passing into Kuwait in the early morning hours. Over seven years before, American troops and coalition partners had fought their way across similar highways, but this time no shots were fired. It was just a convoy of brave Americans, making their way home.

Of course, the soldiers left much behind. Some were teenagers when the war began. Many have served multiple tours of duty, far from families who bore a heroic burden of their own, enduring the absence of a husband's embrace or a mother's kiss. Most painfully, since the war began, 55 members of the Fourth Stryker Brigade made the ultimate sacrifice—part of over 4,400 Americans who have given their lives in Iraq. As one staff sergeant said, "I know that to my brothers in arms who fought and died, this day would probably mean a lot."

Those Americans gave their lives for the values that have lived in the hearts of our people for over two centuries. Along with nearly 1.5 million Americans who have served in Iraq, they fought in a faraway place for people they never knew. They stared into the darkest of human creations—war—and helped the Iraqi people seek the light of peace.

In an age without surrender ceremonies, we must earn victory through the success of our partners and the strength of our own nation. Every American who serves joins an unbroken line of heroes that stretches from Lexington to Gettysburg; from Iwo Jima to Inchon; from Khe Sanh to Kandahar—Americans who have fought to see that the lives of our children are better than our own. Our troops are the steel in our ship of state. And though our nation may be travelling through rough waters, they give us confidence that our course is true, and that beyond the pre-dawn darkness, better days lie ahead.

Thank you. May God bless you. And may God bless the United States of America, and all who serve her.

- **Source:** Barack Obama, "Remarks by the President in Address to the Nation on the End of Combat Operations in Iraq," August 31, 2010, available at http://www.whitehouse.gov/the-press-office/2010/08/31/remarks-president-address-nation-end-combat-operations-iraq, accessed July 13, 2011.

- **Analysis:** In a formal address from the Oval Office, President Obama told the American people that the Iraq War was over. The last combat units, he announced, had already withdrawn. The remaining troops did of course have combat capability, but their mission was to support the Iraqi security forces. The president assured the Iraqi government that support would be provided until Iraq could manage without it.

  The president provided several reasons for his decision to end Operation Iraqi Freedom. The mission had accomplished its goal of liberating and securing Iraq. The United States had done as much as it could to stabilize and rebuild the country. Iraqis must step up to do the rest. Ending the war also fulfilled a campaign promise. Finally, Obama announced the need to devote more resources and attention to domestic matters, especially the weak economy.

- **Document 96: Department of Defense Teleconference Briefing from Iraq**
- **When:** November 8, 2010
- **Where:** Washington, DC, and Baghdad
- **Significance:** Lt. General Robert Cone reports on the assistance mission in Iraq.

I'd like to welcome to the Pentagon briefing room Lieutenant General Bob Cone, the deputy commanding general for Operations with U.S. Forces-Iraq. He is also the commanding general for III Corps and Fort Hood.

Lieutenant General Cone assumed his duties as deputy commander for operations in Iraq in March of this year. This is the first time he has joined us in this format. He will be speaking to us today from Al Faw Palace in Baghdad to provide an update on current operations and the new mission profile under Operation New Dawn.

General, with that, I'll send it to you for any opening remarks you'd like to make, and then we'll take questions.

GEN. CONE: Thanks very much. I'll keep my remarks very brief.

And first of all, let me thank those that are here today for coming out and asking questions. Really appreciate your participation in this conference.

Let me begin by saying that although the role for U.S. troops in direct combat operations here in Iraq ended on the 1st of September, the United States commitment to Iraq and its people has not ended. Our work continues every day under Operation New Dawn, with three primary mission sets. And those are advise, train and assist the Iraqi security forces; to continue to conduct partnered counterterrorism operations, to support the government of Iraq, U.S. embassy and U.S. agencies in improving Iraqi civil capacity; and of course, inherent in all of these missions is a level of force protection for all U.S. forces and civilians as they go about their duties.

As the deputy commanding general for operations, I am focused on several subtasks within this mission set. First, strengthen the Iraqi security forces to help continue to build their capacity for providing security in Iraq. This includes a wide array of tasks associated with advising Iraqi tactical units in the conduct of combat operations across Iraq. However, equally important is the emphasis that we have placed in helping the Iraqi security force develop complex systems, such as intelligence and logistics functions, that will be essential to their future success.

I would also add that we are focused on working with the Iraqis to ensure they are both a learning and adaptive organization with the practices necessary to professionally grow and improve in the future.

The second part of my job is keeping pressure on the extremist networks in close partnership with the Iraqi security forces. In this area, I can also cite significant progress on the part of the Iraqi special operation forces community. The capability to conduct counterterrorist operations is essential to maintain the security environment over the long haul here in Iraq.

Let me be clear: The nearly 650,000 Iraqi security forces are fully responsible for maintaining the security environment in Iraq today. We are supporting them in their efforts and are proud of how far they've come to date. Despite several recent high-profile attacks, Iraqi security forces have created an environment where violence is 20 percent below the 2009 average. It should also be noted that September and October of 2010 have been two of the lowest months on record for violence since 2003.

Sadly, Iraq still has extremists that attack innocent Iraqi civilians to try and stay relevant. But Iraq and the Iraqi people have rejected extremist ideology and sectarianism. We still have work to do here. And the just under 50,000 brave men and women I have the pleasure of working with are focused and committed to ensuring that Iraq becomes a sovereign, stable and self-reliant country.

With that, I'll be happy to take your questions.

COL. LAPAN: Viola.

Q: General Cone, this is Viola Gienger from Bloomberg News.

How do you see the Iraqi security forces' expertise currently, and how it is evolving on some of the capabilities that you provide to protect the U.S. civilians working in Iraq right now, and that will have to be turned over to someone else in December— after December 2011, such as counter-IED capabilities and so forth? What are some of the key areas that you feel that they may be able to take on? What kind of expertise do they have in those areas?

GEN. CONE: Yeah, the Iraqi security forces are a capable COIN force, and it's focused on counterinsurgency and internal security. And as a result of their efforts, we've seen attacks at a—at a level right now of 14 to 15 attacks per day across the nation.

They have work to do in a number of specialty-type capabilities that they'll continue to need work on. They have an emerging explosive ordnance detachment capability. They have some emerging forensic capabilities. They have some route-clearance capabilities. And all of these things are on glide path in the next 14 months as we continue to work with them and assist them, but they are emerging and carrying on.

I'd say, to your question, we will always have a requirement to provide some level of security for Americans that are in this country for the foreseeable future.

And I think it's important to understand that—you know, the proposals that we're talking about post-2011, I think, have provisions for security—personal-security detachments, et cetera, as we transition responsibility to the embassy.

So, good progress, a lot of work to do, and I think a good plan ahead.

COL. LAPAN: Kevin?

Q: General Cone, this is Kevin Baron from Stars and Stripes. The political stalemate there has gone on so much longer than anyone has—had expected. It has to have some sort of effect on your mission, particularly with training your counterparts in the Iraqi forces. Where does that stand now for you guys? Are you at a level of any kind of frustration? Are you completely immune? I can't imagine you are. What— how is this affecting your job?

GEN. CONE: Well, I think—I view it as a real opportunity. The Iraqis that we work with on a day-to-day basis, particularly some at the higher levels, you know, we're not certain they're going to keep their jobs. Guys like the minister of defense, minister of interior traditionally have turned over.

But I think what's been inspiring for us is how hard the Iraqis have worked in this environment, and, again, not for a single individual or for a particular party in power. They have done it based on an emerging understanding of the role of military forces in a democracy, an emerging democracy, and under constitutional law. And many of them will point out to you that what they've done in the last eight months is really about the Iraqi people and the constitution.

And I think if you look at some of the polls that show the acceptance of the Iraqi security forces by the Iraqi people, I think they recognize the fact that a lot of these

Iraqi policemen and soldiers, frankly, have carried on in this—in this post-election time frame and performed some of their best work.

A lot of people speculated, you know, in the March time frame, well, what happens if there's not a government? How will this work? I will tell you, it has really caused the Iraqis to do some self-examination in some ways and step up, particularly in the senior leader ranks. And I—so I think it's been a positive development overall. I think they've had some modicum of success.

You know, certainly attacks like we saw on the 31st of October and the 2nd of November are upsetting to them. But the fact of the matter is overall the security situation has been maintained. And the big difference of course is, you know, a year ago it was the U.S. assisting them or actually out in the streets with them. And this year, they've actually done better, and it's largely been exclusively through their efforts with us in an advisory role.

Q: General, Charley Keyes from CNN. You spoke several times about the lessening of violence. But you just mentioned those attacks last week, those coordinated attacks.

Could you just speak in a little more detail how you react to them, what impact they have on the overall security atmosphere, and what you see as their purpose?

GEN. CONE: Right. First off, I'm in a sort of a learning and teaching mode at this point. And so I think, as I talked about the Iraqis being learning and adaptive, one of the things I'd give them credit for is they ran a national after-action review on Saturday at the Ministry of Defense, and did a very logical and rational assessment of the attacks. And they were quite critical of their own performance, I think, in a healthy way in terms of improving for the future.

So I think, again, they work tirelessly.

And I can tell you that in terms of them being on alert for an extended period of time, and them, frankly, looking hard at how they're doing checkpoint operations, whether they're getting intelligence to the right places that they need to get it to. And, again, our job is to coach and teach and support them as they work through that analysis.

So I think, first off, there's a very healthy analysis. We assess, I think—it's no secret, I think, al Qaeda has taken credit for both the Christian church bombing and the attacks on 2 November. And again, we've analyzed that as part of the al Qaeda campaign.

Of course, we had been really since about the 25th of August without a—you know, a significant attack. And then we saw these attacks, again, targeted against the Christian community. And I'd point out that the grand ayatollah, Sistani, has condemned that, as have other Sunni leaders in the country. And again, I think the Iraqis are working through very hard the protection of minorities, both ethnic and religious minorities in the country. They recognize their responsibility. And I think they're upping the ante, as we continue.

As you know, there are a series of meetings going on today, and they are on high alert. They've taken everybody back from leave. And they're at 100 percent and focusing right now on improving security, and on critical areas and nodes.

COL. LAPAN: Joe.

Q: General, this is Joe Tabet with Al Hurra. Are you noticing, sir, any potential interference from other funded groups from the neighbors like Iran, for example?

GEN. CONE: Well, you know, there is a history of some influence here from Iran. And, again, you know, this is a very complex region. Iraq has to develop, you know, positive relationships with its neighbors. And I think that's very important that Iraq moves on in that direction.

We see all sorts of Iranian influence, some of it positive, in fact, and, in fact, we believe some of it negative, although it's very difficult to attribute that to the Iranian government or in fact does some of this lethal aid come across from other sources within Iran.

I think you would say that probably in the last couple months, in this period of government formation, I think that we think that the Iranian influence has diminished somewhat. And I think overall, that's probably appropriate for where we are, at least on the violence side, at this point in the formation of the government and in the current delicate political situation that we're in.

Q: (Off mike.) Regarding al Qaeda activities in Iraq, do you know if al Qaeda in Iraq appears to have become increasingly disconnected from al Qaeda in Pakistan, al Qaeda leadership in Pakistan?

GEN. CONE: There are—there is a belief that since the major attacks that took place in April, al Qaeda has been under significant duress, or at least the leadership of al Qaeda in Iraq, and has struggled to reconstitute at least its high-end authorities and linkage back to al Qaeda senior leadership, although I would argue, you know, they clearly are still effective, as evidenced by the attack we saw on the 2nd of November.

Again, this is sort of a different form of lower-level cellular formation, and there have been, we believe, some interim leaders that in fact have been—have been named. But the level of connectivity between those leaders and al Qaeda senior leadership is uncertain at this point.

Q: General, hi. It's Andrew Tilghman with Military Times. I'm wondering if you could give me any insight as to what the deployment schedules might look like heading into next year. I think that General Odierno had said something about the possibility of a six-month deployment schedule. As you look into 2011, do you see any changes on that timeline?

GEN. CONE: No, I think the Army has a plan in terms of sustaining the 50,000, and then obviously, when we reach the point when we will begin the final drawdown, some of the units that are coming in. But I think as we have analyzed it, what we're telling all units is to plan on a 12-month rotation over here. And I think that's prudent. You know, there may be some puts and takes as we go along the way, but in fact I think what the soldiers are being told by their Army leadership right now is pretty much on tap.

The 50,000 force has worked out well for us. You know, we've been in that set now for a couple of months. We did an assessment across the board to make sure that we had everything that we needed or we had things that we didn't need and in fact have managed, underneath the 50,000 number, some minor—minor changes, probably less than a thousand in terms of adjustments of little things like aviation or MPs or civil capacity teams, and then identifying some excesses and sending them back. But by and large, the current brigade rotation of one-year sets will continue.

Q: General, hi. It's David Cloud with the L.A. Times. I want to explore the glide path you talked about over the next 14 months. I'm curious whether the Iraqis that you deal with speak to you about a desire to have U.S. forces at some low level continue in Iraq after next—after a year from December. Obviously, that question has kind of been in abeyance for a while because of the political turmoil there. But it's not completely out of the question. I would assume that there would be some follow-on agreement that would allow some continuing small-level U.S. presence.

What do the Iraqis you deal with say about their desire to see that?

GEN. CONE: Yeah, if I were to—if they were to say that to me, what I would do is take it as an opportunity, as a learning point about the fact that they're soldiers and that their job—they should leave political decisions to politicians. And the reality is that what I tell them to do is make sure that you give your best military advice when you are asked, in regard to what capabilities, what are needed, et cetera; not, certainly, trying to bias the situation in any way. But I think it's very important that they learn what the role of the soldier is or the military leader is in terms of providing advice as time goes on.

And again, that will be a political decision and it will be, I presume, you know, at some point between the Iraqi government and the U.S. government. And it will be based on higher-level objectives. But right now we have a security agreement that says we will be out of here by the 1st of January 2012.

And I think what's been really interesting is—from my perspective is the credibility that we get by making an agreement with another nation and then honoring it and self-enforcing. I run a committee that basically tracks down violations of the security agreement. And in my time here, a little over eight months, we have not had a single incident. I mean, we've had, you know, accusations of, you know, violations of the security agreement. When they're investigated, what we find is there are none.

So we hold this meeting and basically say, has the United States—literally, the Iraqis kept a step forward, and say, "Have the—has the United States violated a security agreement?" And they say no. And then we move on to other issues. But I think that's very important in building credibility in this part of the world, the fact that we said we'd be at 50,000, and the fact that, barring a political change, we will be at zero on the first of January, 2012.

Q: Leaving aside the politics, though, which I understand, in your military judgment, will the Iraqis need continuing partnership and assistance after 2011 to fulfill the security requirements they face?

GEN. CONE: We have a comprehensive plan right now to work with the Iraqis. And that's why—I will tell you frankly we are very busy right now working with the Iraqis. Really when you focus on, sort of—there are 19 major capabilities that we work on with them, and then identifying the conditions that need to be established by the time we leave. We're working. We have a plan where we can leave here on— as scheduled. There are things that someone might like to do or think could be done better. But again, I think those things will come into the political negotiation.

Q: Okay. General, Larry Shaughnessy from CNN. I wanted to ask you about your other role as head of III Corps and Fort Hood. After the Article 32 hearing for Major Hasan is done and the other pre-trial matters are taken care of, a commander's going to have to decide if there's a recommendation for a court martial, to either go ahead with it or not. And then there might well be a recommendation for a death penalty.

Will you be involved in that in any way, as the commander of III Corps?

GEN. CONE: I won't from here.

And again, it depends on the timing of all this that plays out. And in fact, when I left, I signed over legal responsibility as a general court martial convening authority to my deputy when I departed the country.

So I've been over here. It will depend on how far this all progresses, and it will depend on other legal considerations that will be assessed at that time. But again, right now I am removed from the Fort Hood case, and I have—I have legal authority here over a like number of soldiers. So again, we'll deal with that, I think, in the future.

Q: There was a legal fight over whether or not you should be deposed in this—in the Hasan case. Did you ever sit for a deposition in the case?

GEN. CONE: I did not. I was in the process of deploying as that came down. And again, I think certainly given the technology we have today, you know, we could have done it from here, but to my knowledge there was never any request to be deposed since I've been here in Iraq.

So, again, you know, these are all, you know, important legal processes that we follow the procedures exactly to the law to make sure that this is—this case is fairly tried.

COL. LAPAN: Okay, General, it looks like you've exhausted the Pentagon Press Corps of questions, so I'll send it back to you for closing remarks.

GEN. CONE: Yeah, I—again, I'd just like to thank everybody again. You know, Veterans Day is coming up, and that's really important for, I think, for so many who've served this country and serve as an inspiration to everyone. And again, they're in our thoughts and prayers here in Iraq.

Here, we are—continue to grow capabilities and capacity for the security forces of Iraq, and again, things continue to move all the trends in a positive direction.

I'm—again, I'm proud of the work that our service members are doing in Iraq. And I can tell you that each and every one of them is making a difference.

Again, thanks for coming to the press conference, and I appreciate the opportunity to speak to you today. Thank you very much.

COL. LAPAN: General, thanks again for your time.

- **Source:** Department of Defense briefing, Operation New Dawn, November 8, 2010, available at http://www.defense.gov/transcripts/transcript.aspx?transcriptid=4713, accessed July 14, 2011.

- **Analysis:** The end of combat operations in Iraq did not mean the end of operations. The United States kept approximately 50,000 troops in country as part of Operation New Dawn, the successor to Operation Iraqi Freedom. The new mission was to "advise, train, and assist" Iraqi forces. Assisting Iraqi forces meant accompanying them into combat without taking the lead, so U.S. soldiers would still be in harm's way. General Cone's candid admission that 14 to 15 terrorist or insurgent incidents occurred in Iraq each day indicated that although conditions had improved, much remained to be done.

- **Document 97: Excerpt of NBC Interview with Defense Secretary Leon Panetta**
- **When:** July 11, 2011
- **Where:** Baghdad
- **Significance:** The new secretary of defense discussed the security situation in Iraq and the planned withdrawal of U.S. forces.

MR. MIKLASZEWSKI: Thanks for joining us, Mr. Secretary. Just today, three or four rockets landed in the Green Zone. Fifteen American soldiers were killed last month. I mean, it sounds like the war is back on. What's going on?

SEC. PANETTA: Well, there's some concerns, obviously. We did lose an awful lot of troops last month, and we're continuing to see attacks. And a lot of this that we think can be tracked to Iran and their supplying of weapons to insurgents here who are conducting these kinds of attacks. That raises a lot of concerns.

So my view is that, bottom line, it's they have the responsibility and the authority to ensure they do everything necessary to protect the troops—and that leaves us, if I ask the Iraqis, as a partner in this, to go after those who are attacking troops, that we want to be partners with them in that effort and conduct those kinds of operations. But we have a responsibility to defend our soldiers, and that's exactly what I'm going to do.

MR. MIKLASZEWSKI: Mr. Secretary, I talked to soldiers this morning who told me, they're coming after us again. But yet, they feel like their hands are somewhat tied because they don't feel the Iraqis have actually done enough, and in fact, are not willing to do enough, according to some soldiers. So what can the U.S. do if that's going to be the case? How are you going to protect those soldiers?

SEC. PANETTA: Well, you know, the point I have to make to the leadership here is that this is not just about protecting our soldiers; it's about protecting your country. And when these kinds of attacks are happening, it weakens Iraq.

And if you allow this kind of violence to go on, then it sends a signal to the world that you haven't developed the kind of security that needs to be done. So they have a responsibility. They have to respond to these attacks, as well. And that's the message that we're sending them. And it's also the responsibility that they're going to have to take on if they're going to be able to have a country that they can secure and defend.

MR. MIKLASZEWSKI: Now, the U.S. troops have the authority to defend themselves, but does that include unilateral action, if necessary? That is, can the U.S. respond unilaterally against that threat?

SEC. PANETTA: Well, you know, I don't want to go into the particulars of what steps we would take in order to do that, but what I'll tell you is I do have the authority and the responsibility to defend U.S. soldiers. And if necessary, we will take what actions are necessary to do that.

MR. MIKLASZEWSKI: Iran has been thumbing its nose at the U.S. for years on any number of fronts. You know that very well. So what possibly could the U.S. to do to prevent Iran from shipping those highly lethal weapons to Iran?

SEC. PANETTA: You know, I think—I think it's very important to let them know that, you know, we do not appreciate their support for terrorism, here or any-place else in the world. And they've been in engaging in basically not only equip-ping terrorists but supporting them.

And you know, that's not just a responsibility that we have; I think it's a respon-sibility that the world has to send the signal to Iran that we're not going to tolerate that—they can't just go around supporting terrorism in the world. The world is going to respond to that kind of behavior. If they want to be a member of the family of nations, they've got to act like it.

MR. MIKLASZEWSKI: The Iraqis have to make a decision sometime soon on whether they want additional U.S. troops to stay here in the country after the dead-line for withdrawal at the end of this year. You said this morning, "Damn it, make a decision." I mean, that's pretty tough talk, no?

SEC. PANETTA: Well, I think the time has come to make a decision. You know, obviously, there's been a lot of sacrifices made by U.S. men and women here and there have been a lot of casualties, but I think we've also put this country on the right path towards the future.

They are, in fact, able to secure and defend themselves and they are governed, at this time. But if this is going to continue—continue on the right path—then I think that partnership has to continue. And one of the keys to that is making the tough decisions that you have to make when you govern a country. If they want our sup-port in the future, then they've got to ask for it.

MR. MIKLASZEWSKI: And one of those tough decisions for President Obama was, do we keep additional forces here? Is the U.S. leaning to doing that to help the Iraqis in terms of security and training?

SEC. PANETTA: Well, right now, we are on track to withdraw our forces—pursuant to the agreement—to withdraw our forces by the end of this year. That's the track we're on, and we're going to begin that process in August. And we will fol-low that. If they do make a request, then obviously, the president—has indicated we will consider it. But the longer this goes on, the more difficult it is to consider it because, frankly we'd be on the way out. . . .

- **Source:** NBC interview with Leon Panetta, July 11, 2011, available at http://www.defense.gov/transcripts/transcript.aspx?transcriptid=4851, accessed July 14, 2011.
- **Analysis:** The new secretary of defense, Leon Panetta, toured Iraq and Afghanistan in July 2011. The NBC interview in Baghdad focused on the security situation in Iraq. An increase in violence during the spring and summer of 2011, including the deaths of several U.S. service

personnel, called into question the planned withdrawal of the remaining U.S. forces from Iraq by the end of the year. Panetta insisted Washington would observe the terms of the withdrawal agreement unless the al-Malaki government requested a change in this arrangement. He stressed that the time had come for the Iraqi prime minister to make a decision on the matter.

CONCLUSION

Iraq today is a democratic country in which all citizens can vote and run for office. In the years since the invasion it has gone from being a failed state to being a fragile one. Deep divisions within Iraqi society preclude creating a strong central government and call into question exactly what the Iraqi national identity truly is. Since the withdrawal of U.S. forces at the end of 2011, Iraq has continued to face violence but has not descended into civil war or faced a revived insurgency.

RESOURCES

WEBSITES

All departments of the U.S. government, the government of Iraq, and the United Nations have websites with documents and other materials relevant to the Iraq War. Many of these sites contain searchable archives of documents.

Defense Department: http://www.defense.gov
   This site contains current press releases, news items, and press briefings on Iraq as well as an archive of past ones.

Government Printing Office: www.gpo.gov/fdsys/
   This site is the way to access a wide range of U.S. government documents, including the Congressional Record.

Iraq Body Count: http://www.iraqbodycount.org/
   This site tallies Iraq War casualties, civilian and military, based upon a variety of sources.

Iraq Government: http://www.cabinet.iq/default.aspx
   The Iraqi cabinet maintains an English language version of its website with information on legislation and other activities of the central government.

Rand Corporation: http://www.rand.org/
   The Rand Corporation is a research institution that produces reports and studies on security topics, including Iraq.

State Department: http://www.state.gov/
   The website contains up-to-date information on the department's activities, country profiles, news releases, and an archive of materials such as press briefings and statements from the past.

Strategic Studies Institute, U.S. Army War College: http://www.strategicstudies institute.army.mil/

The Strategic Studies Institute is a government think tank that produces and commissions from independent scholars studies of current and past strategic and security policy issues.

United Nations: http://www.un.org/en/

The UN website contains current information on the activities of the organization and an archive of past documents.

UN Monitoring, Verification and Inspection Commission: http://www.unmovic.org/

The site contains documents and information about the work of the commission charged with monitoring Iraqi weapons programs to ensure that Saddam Hussein did not acquire WMD.

BLOGS

Blogs have become quite popular in the last decade. The Iraq War spawned hundreds of sites. They contain a wealth of up-to-the-minute information on conditions, events, and so forth, provided by U.S. soldiers in the field. However, because there are no filters or quality controls on the Internet, anyone can put up a website and make any sort of claim to experience. Even if the blog is legitimate, the person who runs it has no ability to verify the veracity of the posts sent to him. Assessing the quality or even the validity of the information on a blog is quite difficult. Blogs run by reputable news outlets are presumably more reliable, but even they cannot always verify that what sounds persuasive is in fact accurate. Readers must weigh what they read online against information garnered from reading and research.

Army of Dude: http://armyofdude.blogspot.com/

At War: Notes from the Frontlines: http://atwar.blogs.nytimes.com/

Baghdad Burning: http://riverbendblog.blogspot.com/

A Family in Baghdad: http://afamilyinbaghdad.blogspot.com/ (chronicles the experience of an Iraqi family)

Hello Iraq: http://devildog6771.wordpress.com/

Kaboom: A Soldier's War Diary: http://kaboomwarjournalarchive.blogspot.com/ 2010/01/another-long-overdue-update.html

Mudville Gazette: http://www.mudvillegazette.com/

My War: http://cbftw.blogspot.com/

A Soldier's Perspective: http://militarygear.com/asp/

BIBLIOGRAPHY

Official Publications

Baker, James A. III, and Lee H. Hamilton, et.al. *Report of the Iraq Study Group*. New York: Vintage Books, 2006.

FM 3-24 *Counterinsurgency*. Washington, DC: Headquarters, Department of the Army, 2006.

Books

Bremer, L. Paul, with Malcolm McConnell. *My Year in Iraq: The Struggle to Build a Future of Hope*. New York: Simon and Schuster, 2006.

Cordesman, Anthony. *The Iraq War: Strategy, Tactics, and Military Lessons*. Westport, CT: Praeger, 2003.

Engel, Richard. *A Fist in the Hornet's Nest: On the Ground in Baghdad Before, During and After the War*. New York: Hyperion, 2004.

Franks, Tommy, with Malcolm McConnell. *American Soldier*. New York: Reagan Books, 2004.

Galbraith, Peter W. *The End of Iraq: How American Incompetence Created a War without End*. New York: Simon and Schuster, 2006.

Gordon, Michael R., and Bernard E. Trainor. *Cobra II: The Inside Story of the Invasion and Occupation of Iraq*. New York: Vintage Books, 2006.

Gordon, Michael R., and Bernard E. Trainor. *The End Game: The Hidden History of America's Struggle to Build Democracy in Iraq*. New York: Pantheon, 2012.

Hendrickson, David C., and Robert W. Tucker. *Revisions in Need of Revising: What Went Wrong in the Iraq War*. Carlisle Barracks, PA: Strategic Studies Institute, U.S. Army War College, 2005.

Lansford, Tim. *9/11 and the Wars in Afghanistan and Iraq: A Chronology and Reference Guide*. Santa Barbara, CA: ABC-CLIO, 2011.

Marr, Phoebe. *The Modern History of Iraq*. Boulder, CO: Westview Press, 2011.

Mockaitis, Thomas R. *The "New" Terrorism: Myths and Reality*. Westport, CT: Praeger, 2007.

Packer, George. *The Assassins' Gate: America in Iraq*. New York: Farrar, Straus and Giroux, 2005.

Phillips, Kate, Shane Lauth, and Erin Schenck. *U.S. Military Operations in Iraq: Planning, Combat, and Occupation*. W. Andrew Terrill, ed. Carlisle Barracks, PA: Strategic Studies Institute, U.S. Army War College, 2006.

Polk, William. *Understanding Iraq*. New York: Harper Collins, 2005.

Ricks, Thomas. *Fiasco: The American Military Adventure in Iraq*. New York: Penguin, 2006.

Ricks, Thomas. *The Gamble: General David Petraeus and the American Military Adventure in Iraq, 2006–2008*. New York: Penguin, 2009.

Silverman, Michael. *Awakening Victory: How Iraqi Tribes and American Troops Reclaimed Al Anbar and Defeated Al Qaeda in Iraq*. Havertown, PA: Casemate, 2011.

West, Bing. *No True Glory: A Frontline Account of the Battle for Fallujah*. New York: Bantam, 2005.

Wood, Trish. *What Was Asked of Us: An Oral History of the Iraq War by the Soldiers Who Fought It*. New York: Little Brown and Company, 2006.

Woodward, Bob. *State of Denial*. New York: Simon and Schuster, 2006.

Articles

Doe, John. "Mismanaging Iraq." *National Interest* 78 (Winter 2004/2005).

Filkins, Dexter, and John Burns. "Deep in a US Desert, Practicing to Face the Iraqi Insurgency." *New York Times*, May 1, 2006, A1.

Garamone, Jim. "Training the Iraqi Security Forces, Tough, but Worth it." American Forces Press Services, January 10, 2005, http://www.defenselink.mil/news/newsarticle.aspx?id=24406.

Al Jandaly, Bassma, and Tanya Goudsouzian. "US Provoked Insurgency In Iraq—Former UN Official." *Gulf News*, February 16, 2004.

Klein, Naomi. "You Break It, You Pay for It." *Nation* 280, no. 2 (January 10, 2005).

Krane, Jim. "US Faces Complex Insurgency in Iraq." *Duluth News Tribune*, October 4, 2004.

Langewiesche, William. "Letter from Baghdad." *Atlantic Monthly*, January/February 2005.

Robinson, Linda. "The Battle for Baghdad." *US News and World Report* 141, no. 8 (September 4, 2006).

Sepp, Kalev I. "Best Practices in COIN." *Military Review* 85, no. 3 (May-June 2005).

"When Deadly Force Bumps into Hearts and Minds." *Economist* 374, no. 8407 (January 1, 2005).

INDEX

ABOUT THE AUTHOR

THOMAS R. MOCKAITIS is professor of history at DePaul University. He earned his BA from Allegheny College and his MA and PhD from the University of Wisconsin–Madison. Dr. Mockaitis has written several books and numerous articles on counterinsurgency, terrorism, and peace operations, including *The "New" Terrorism: Myths and Reality* (Praeger, 2007) and *Iraq and the Challenge of Counterinsurgency* (Praeger, 2008). He team-teaches counterterrorism courses for the Center for Civil-Military Relations at the Naval Post-Graduate School and is a frequent media commentator.